CONNECTICUT
BIRDS

CONNECTICUT BIRDS

Joseph D. Zeranski

Thomas R. Baptist

With a Contribution by
George A. Clark, Jr.

Illustrations by
Sheila McMahon

University Press of New England
Hanover and London

University Press of New England
Brandeis University
Brown University
Clark University
University of Connecticut
Dartmouth College
University of New Hampshire
University of Rhode Island
Tufts University
University of Vermont
Wesleyan University

© 1990 by Joseph D. Zeranski and Thomas R. Baptist

Printed in the United States of America

Library of Congress Cataloging in Publication Data

Zeranski, Joseph.
    Connecticut birds / Joseph D. Zeranski and Thomas R. Baptist ;
illustrations by Sheila McMahon.
        p.   cm.
    Includes bibliographical references.
    ISBN 0–87451–513–0
    1. Birds—Connecticut.   I. Baptist, Thomas R.   II. Title.
QL684.C8Z47   1990
598.29746—dc20   89–24941
                                                              CIP

5 4 3 2 1

To the memory of my mother,
Dorothy Cakavell Zeranski,
who, having patiently tolerated my endeavors,
would have derived much pleasure from this book.

— J. Z.

To my son Michael,
with the hope that this book contributes to mankind's
greater appreciation and respect for the natural environment.

— T. B.

Contents

Foreword

The environments we occupy are slowly but continuously changing, so it is difficult to assess the significance of population changes in bird numbers. This new book on Connecticut birds provides valuable clues to the status of today's avifauna. We are, unfortunately, reportedly involved in an era that will see mass extinctions comparable to those that depopulated the Earth at various times in the past. Earlier extinctions probably resulted from a collision with some wandering asteroid; this time the extinctions are being induced by humankind's takeover of the planet for our own teeming millions. If this process continues, therefore, this may be the last time we will be able to compile an annotated list at all comparable to those that picture Connecticut's birdlife of the last century or so. Instead of merely hoping this will not turn out to be true, we need to assess the impending threats and try to change the circumstances that are generating them.

The only detailed avifaunal report we have direct comparison to is that of Sage, Bishop, and Bliss, *The Birds of Connecticut*, a 1913 publication of the State Geological and Natural History Survey. For residents of southwestern Connecticut, reports on the birds of the New York City region afford even more detailed comparison because that region has been more intensively studied than most. Books by Ludlow Griscom (1923), Allan D. Cruickshank (1942), and John Bull (1964) have been principal references in the interim.

Fortunately, Connecticut has benefited from attracting several notable ornithologists as residents. Mabel Osgood Wright of Fairfield was one of the founders of the Audubon movement. Ernest Thompson Seton of Cos Cob taught a whole generation about woodcraft and wildlife. S. Dillon Ripley of Litchfield was director of the Department of Birds at Yale University's Peabody Museum before becoming secretary of the Smithsonian Institution and an authority on the birds of Southeast Asia. Roger Tory Peterson of Old Lyme has been the world's foremost popularizer of birds for a generation, thanks to his 1934 *Field Guide to the Birds* and a succession of revisions.

Interest in birds and birding has grown to the point that in 1984 a Connecticut Ornithological Association was organized. It then took over publication of the quarterly *The Connecticut Warbler,* first produced in 1981 by the Connecticut Audubon Society.

In the last decade also, there has been much talk of a book to revise our knowledge of Connecticut birdlife. A number of others undertook to provide us with such a book, but only Joseph Zeranski and Thomas Baptist have had the energy and the commitment to accomplish the task. We owe them our thanks, and we should see this new book as a reminder of how rich our birdlife still is and how important it is to do what must be done to preserve it so that future generations of our own kind may know how marvelous Nature's diversity is.

ROLAND C. CLEMENT

Acknowledgments

This book is, in reality, a cooperative effort. Hundreds of people have, over the years, contributed greatly to the body of knowledge pertaining to the avifauna of Connecticut. We found the previous work of five individuals especially outstanding. Rev. James Linsley authored the first statewide assessment of the state's birds in 1843 and thus provided valuable information that served as a basis of comparison for today's avian status. C. Hart Merriam, later to become chief of the Bureau of Biological Survey of the U.S. Department of Agriculture, wrote a comprehensive evaluation of Connecticut's birds in 1877 at the age of 22. John Sage, Louis Bishop, and Walter Bliss coauthored a complete review of the state's birds in 1913, which provided information used extensively in this work.

Several others have published accounts of portions of the state. Herbert Job, the first State Ornithologist, wrote about the birds of Litchfield County in 1908. Aaron Bagg and Samuel Eliot completed their monumental work on birds of the Connecticut River valley in 1937, including hundreds of accounts of records from the Connecticut portion of the valley. Aretas Saunders, one of the most skilled field ornithologists ever active in Connecticut, published many articles and reports on the state's birds from about 1907 to 1960, focusing primarily on Fairfield County. Locke Mackenzie wrote about the birds of Guilford in 1961. John Bull included in his *Birds of the New York City Area* and *Birds of New York State* many references to Connecticut, as did Allan Cruickshank and Edward Forbush. Jerauld Manter wrote about the birds in the vicinity of Storrs in 1975. All of these works contributed greatly to our compilation.

Many individuals contributed their personal records over the years, and some served as editors of major regional journals, newsletters, and publications covering Connecticut. Not the least of these were Robert Arbib, Roland Clement, Paul Desjardins, Robert Dewire, Davis Finch, Paul Howes, Stan Quickmire, Donald Shipley, and William Smith.

Some of the currently active birders who have provided thousands of hours in the field are Tom Burke, Tony Bledsoe, Robert Craig, Neil Currie, Buzz Devine, Frank Gallo, Jay Hand, Charles Hills, Gordon Lowry, Frank Mantlik, Noble Proctor, Dave Rosgen, Ray Schwartz, Fred and David Sibley, Mark Szantyr, Clay Taylor, and Chris Wood. We realize that this list is incomplete, for scores of others have contributed records we have included in our book. The expertise of the many amateur and professional field ornithologists active in Connecticut has contributed to the relatively recent understanding that a bird need not necessarily be killed to confirm its identity and existence, and for this the authors extend on behalf of all birds their gratitude and appreciation.

We thank those who offered their hospitality and who lent to us numerous reference materials, all of which aided our research: Ted Gilman of the Audubon Center of Greenwich; Nick Shoumatoff of the Trailside Museum in Pound Ridge, New York; Jack Clark and Frank Lawlor of the Bruce Museum in Greenwich; Tony Lauro, who generously made available the Proceedings of the Linnaean Society of New York; and Eleanor Stickney of the Peabody Museum at Yale University. Among other helpful contributions from Mrs. Stickney, the material compiled in the late 1960s by Frances and Barbara Sibley and lent by Mrs. Stickney was greatly appreciated.

Several individuals figured prominently in the completion of the book. Grace Baptist provided invaluable assistance in the use of the computer and word-processing programs. Paul Merola, Dale May, and Ken Metzler of the Connecticut Department of Environmental Protection provided valuable information about many species that the department is studying. Lauren Brown, Dick English, and Milan Bull reviewed portions of the manuscript and provided information that contributed to its completeness. Paul Desjardins and Frank Mantlik reviewed the entire manuscript and provided additional information and refinements. Tom Burke, editor of the *Mianus Field Notes,* gave moral support. Gus Daniels and Julio de la Torre, noted for their technical and editorial experience, contributed helpful comments on the layout and format of the book and greatly improved the clarity of the manuscript. Fred Purnell spent many hours with the authors working out the complexities of organizing the work and gave much support and humor when the authors' enthusiasm was waning. Sheila McMahon provided excellent artwork for the final product.

There are four individuals who deserve our most heartfelt thanks and appreciation, for without their input the book would surely not have been completed. Dennis Varza spent long hours assisting in the preliminary research of journals and newsletters, and his work contributed greatly to the completeness of the book. Louis Bevier and Paul Lehman critically reviewed the entire manuscript several times, commented on format and style, pointed out deficiencies, recommended changes, and gave essential advice and guidance. Finally, the authors owe their greatest debt of gratitude to George A. Clark, Jr., Connecticut State Ornithologist, who read the manuscript several times, offered many valuable criticisms, served as the final arbitor of many disputed issues, constantly gave encouragement and guidance, and instilled much motivation in his two former students.

October 1989   J. D. Z.
                                                                  T. R. B.

Introduction

The most recent detailed book on Connecticut birds, *Birds of Connecticut* by Sage, Bishop, and Bliss, was published in 1913—more than 75 years ago. Roger Tory Peterson once wrote: "A regional publication, embracing any one region, should be brought up to date every twenty or twenty-five years; there should be a new book for each generation of birdwatchers." A current book on Connecticut's birds has been sorely missed by professional and amateur ornithologists and the general public.

The purpose of this book is to provide a current summary of knowledge on the occurrence of birds in Connecticut. The book describes the present status of each species known in the state, together with a summary of historic changes in abundance and distribution.

This book is intended to benefit not only those who watch or study birds but also the birds themselves. We live in a world undergoing rapid technological and social changes, and natural habitats are often destroyed without an understanding of the ecological consequences of their destruction. If society is to preserve for the future as much as possible of our heritage of plants and animals, it is important that land-use decisions and actions be made on an informed basis.

We hope that this book will serve as a useful basis and stimulus for study, analysis, and evaluation of the state's birds. Although there is a vast quantity of information available about Connecticut's birds, the lack of a single summarizing source has been a serious handicap. With information on Connecticut's birds growing proportionately faster as decades pass, the task of synthesis becomes ever more challenging. At the same time, there is much to be learned about Connecticut birdlife, and future discoveries will gain their significance in the light of previous ones. We hope that readers will find much of interest in the following pages.

What we do know about changes in Connecticut's birdlife can be best understood in terms of the changing natural environment. Thus, following a brief historical overview of bird study in Connecticut, we begin our coverage of Connecticut's birds with a review of the distinctive features of the present environment and climate of the state. We then describe prehistoric and historic changes that have been influential and provide an extended survey and discussion of the status of each bird species.

Historical Notes on Connecticut Ornithology

Although no comprehensive review of the history of bird study in Connecticut has yet been prepared, a number of the important individuals and events can be identified. This section updates a previous brief survey (Clark 1986), which may be consulted for additional references.

Birds are difficult to approach—in comparison with many other kinds of animals—consequently, before 1900 most of the prominent ornithological studies involved the shooting of birds. Although records for the 1700s are sketchy, it is known that an Englishman, Ashton Blackburne, collected birds in Connecticut, including specimens of the Labrador Duck and Clapper Rail (Wystrach, 1975a,b). In 1808, Alexander Wilson (1766–1813), while traveling through Connecticut, obtained the first specimen of the Connecticut Warbler, previously unknown to science. Before about 1830 methods for preserving specimens from insect attack were generally ineffective, but following the introduction of the use of arsenic as a preservative, it became possible to amass and maintain permanent collections. In Connecticut the major period of shooting and preservation of specimens lasted from about 1845 to 1925. Although virtually all of these early collectors studies birds only as a hobby, many of them were skilled taxidermists and highly knowledgeable about Connecticut birds.

The Reverend James H. Linsley (1787–1843) published the first checklist of Connecticut birds in 1843. He included not only species known to occur but also ones anticipated. In 1877 C. Hart Merriam (1855–1942) provided the second checklist. A landmark publication was the third checklist of Connecticut birds, by Sage, Bishop, and Bliss, in 1913. John H. Sage (1847–1925), a banker from Portland, accumulated a lifetime collection of more than 5,000 specimens; he was also prominent on the national ornithological scene and served for 31 years as an officer of the American Ornithologists' Union (AOU). Louis Bishop (1865–1950) was a physician who practiced in New Haven, where a specially constructed small museum in his backyard housed his specimens.

Professor O. C. Marsh (1831–1899) of Yale was a leading investigator of fossil birds and dinosaurs. Although Marsh apparently did little directly concerned with Connecticut birds, George Bird Grinnell (1849–1938), who was for a time an assistant to Marsh, was an important collector of Connecticut birds. Numerous other collectors contributed to knowledge of Connecticut birds through the latter half of the 1800s and into the early 1900s (Sage et al.).

Sage and Grinnell were quite aware of sharp declines in the populations of numerous species then being subjected to unregulated hunting and, around the turn of the century, slaughter for the millinery trade. The extirpation of the Passenger Pigeon from Connecticut, followed by its complete demise, was symptomatic of more general trends. Both Sage and Grinnell strongly backed the Audubon movement, a great awakening of public interest in the late 1800s and early 1900s that eventually resulted in major legislation for the protection of birds. Not all legislative initiatives were successful; for example, repeated efforts to require cat licensing in Connecticut, went down to defeat in the legislature. It would be difficult to overstate the importance of the Audubon movement. Had it not occurred, our avifauna today would be greatly impoverished.

The turn of the century roughly marks the transition from the study of birds predominantly through collecting to the study of the living bird. An outstanding leader in the Audubon movement was Mabel Osgood Wright (1859–1934), who was prominent in the founding of the Connecticut Audubon Society in 1898 and in the subsequent growth of that organization. About this time colleges in the United States began to present courses in ornithology, and at the Connecticut Agricultural College (now the University of Connecticut) in Storrs an ornithology course was offered as early as 1900–1901. The growing popular interest in birds at that time led to new organizations, such as the New Haven Bird Club in 1907 and the Hartford Bird Study Club in 1909. The first organized bird-banding in North America was sponsored by the New Haven Bird Club in 1907.

Among the prominent figures in the Audubon movement was the Reverend Herbert K. Job (1864–1933), a popular lecturer, motion picture photographer, and writer, who gave up a ministry in Kent to become the State Ornithologist at Connecticut Agricultural College. In 1914 he began to direct the Department of Applied Ornithology of the National Association of Audubon Societies, forerunner of the present National Audubon Society. This department was located in Amston, Connecticut, on a large tract owned by industrialist Charles M. Ams, who simultaneously encouraged a program of game bird rearing and nature education while promoting nearby summerhoming development. However, neither effort was destined for long-term success; Ams' automobile manufacturing firm failed in 1917, and the Audubon center was no longer publicized after 1926.

With the Audubon movement came an increasing willingness to accept reports of birds based on sightings without collected specimens. By 1908, *The Auk,* the scientific journal of the AOU, was willing to publish a sight record of a Pileated Woodpecker seen by John Hutchins while driving near Litchfield. Use of a car in bird-finding was then still an innovative technique. During the 20th century a growing number of field observers, whom we now call "birders," have contributed ever more sight reports, providing, at present, a more comprehensive body of information on distribution of Connecticut birds than at any time in the past. Among the pioneers in field observation both in Connecticut and nationally was Aretas A. Saunders (1884–1970), who, among his many contributions, developed a system for illustrating birds' songs before the advent of tape recorders and sound spectrograph machines.

The most famous of all ornithologists of Connecticut, or indeed of the globe, is Roger Tory Peterson, who through his exemplary series of field guides, other writings, paintings, photography, and lectures has contributed more than anyone else to the current worldwide interest, both popular and scientific, in birds. Current efforts at bird conservation worldwide stem in large measure from the interest he has aroused.

Conservation efforts in the 20th century have moved away from the concerns of the first two decades to more recent problems with pollutants and habitat destruction. Particularly dramatic were the declines in certain diurnal birds of prey, such as the Osprey, from the 1940s into the 1970s. The national banning of most chlorinated hydrocarbon pesticides has led to a partial recovery of these raptorial populations. The causal relationships between pesticide use and population declines were much more difficult to unravel than were the causes of declines of populations resulting from direct slaughter around the turn of the century. Human influences on bird populations can now be more subtle than a century ago, and bird conservation must now include a scientifically sophisticated vigilance.

Starting in the 1930s, a series of ornithologists at the Yale Peabody Museum in New Haven made that institution a leading center for bird study. Among the ornithologists formerly on the staff there were Stanley C. Ball, S. Dillon Ripley, Phillip S. Humphrey, N. Phillip Ashmole, Charles G. Sibley, and Jon E. Ahlquist. Since the mid-1960s the University of Connecticut, the recently formed Connecticut State Museum of Natural History at Storrs (Clark 1984), and other institutions in the state have added ornithologists to their staffs and have become centers for ornithological studies. The state is also home to a large and increasing number of keen amateur ornithologists, many of whom have outstanding knowledge of birds. In recent decades the Connecticut Audubon Society and the National Audubon Society have continued major efforts in environmental education and guiding legislative action. The Nature Conservancy and numerous local land trusts have been active in preserving important natural areas in the state, and the state Department of Environmental Protection has been increasingly active in promoting the interests of non-game species in the state in addition to the continued efforts in behalf of game birds.

Observing migratory hawks along the coast and from inland ridges has become ever more popular (Welch), coordinated through a series of organizations including the Connecticut Audubon Council and Hawk Migration Association of North America. The Connecticut Ornithological Association (COA), founded in 1984, has become the central organization for bird study in the state. In 1984, the COA assumed responsibility for publication of a statewide journal of Connecticut ornithology, *The Connecticut Warbler*, begun under Connecticut Audubon Society sponsorship in 1981. The *Warbler* has become the major periodical reporting observations of Connecticut birds. In 1985 the COA formed the Connecticut Rare Records Committee, which reviews and evaluates unusual reports for the adequacy of documentation and publishes periodic summaries in the *Warbler*. In a major effort, sponsored by the National Audubon Society, hundreds of volunteers sought breeding birds throughout the state in the Connecticut Breeding Bird Atlas Project of 1982–1986. Another project sponsored by the National Audubon Society for many decades has been the Christmas Bird Count, the major source for information on bird populations wintering in the state. Nature centers and numerous local clubs have also provided important regional programs. Despite so much interest in birds, it remains surprisingly easy to ask significant questions about Connecticut birds that no one can yet answer. As ornithologists attempt in the future to answer such questions, the present work will be a major source to aid their efforts.

GEORGE A. CLARK, JR.

Description of Connecticut

ECOLOGY AND GEOGRAPHY

It is customary in a publication such as this to describe briefly the physical features of the area under study. In addition, because of the authors' interest in historic changes in bird populations and distribution, an overview of ecological changes in the state has been provided. Ongoing ecological changes indicate that further alterations and changes in bird populations can be expected. Thoughtful and careful observers of birds can detect and gain insights into environmental changes—in effect using birds as a "litmus test" to measure the quality of the natural systems supporting all life.

Recent predictions about the effects of acid rain, ozone depletion, the greenhouse effect, and the dramatic destruction of the world's rain forests are startling. The environment may be on the verge of suffering drastic and possibly catastrophic change, affecting both people and birds. The documentation of population changes in birds may prove crucial to the evaluation and understanding of unfolding ecological changes.

The principal ecological changes include (1) a gradual long-term movement northward of plants and animals since the retreat of the last glacier; (2) the reduction of the forest and wildlife since European settlement; (3) the creation of extensive farmland, peaking in about 1860; (4) the development of manufacturing and urbanization (accompanied by the concentration of pollution and intensive consumption of natural resources); (5) the return of a modified oak forest and other species of plants and animals that were reduced or extirpated from the state, and (6) the growth of a new "suburban" habitat.

Connecticut is 5,009 square miles (3,205,760 acres) in area and is situated in the southwestern corner of New England. The state is bounded on the east by Rhode Island, on the north by Massachusetts, on the west by New York, and on the south by Long Island Sound. Connecticut has 253 miles of shoreline on Long Island Sound, about 8,400 miles of rivers and streams, and approximately 6,000 lakes and ponds.

Topography of Connecticut

Connecticut is characterized by eastern and western highlands with peak elevations just over 2,000 feet above sea level, a large north-south central valley, and a fairly flat coastal region. The land has been subject to numerous glaciations and is dominated in most areas by rocky outcroppings, numerous wetlands and watercourses, small valleys, and generally shallow soils containing numerous stones and cobbles.

A few of the geographic features in the northeast hills are spectacular. One such feature consists of a group of narrow ridges, collectively called the Bolton Ridge, which has its southern terminus in Portland, Connecticut, and extends north into Maine. This feature separates the northeast hills from the Connecticut River valley. The large central portion of the northeast hills has been referred to as the Windham Hills and consists mostly of till-covered rolling hills. Unique in the state is Mohegan Ridge, running parallel to the coast from Stonington to Lyme, the only significant east-west formation in the state. These hills are composed of granite rather than the schist and gneiss found nearby (Bell).

The northwest hills are divided into fairly distinct northern and southern elements, separated by "Cameron's Line," stretching from Canton southwest to Ridgefield. The topography of the southern portion consists mostly of rolling hills and river valleys. In contrast, the northern section is characterized by high ridges, hills, and plateaus separated by large and often deep valleys. The northwest hills are extensions of the Taconic Mountains and Hudson Highlands of New York, as well as of the Berkshires of Massachusetts, which continue north as part of Vermont's Green Mountains. The Taconic Plateau is located in the extreme northwest corner of Connecticut and averages about 1,800 feet above sea level. Here is the highest spot in the state, Mt. Frissell in Salisbury, at 2,380 feet (Bell).

Rivers and Valleys of Connecticut

Connecticut has a multitude of rivers and streams, all of which drain directly or indirectly into Long Island Sound. The largest watercourse

TOPOGRAPHY
(above mean sea level)

1500 + ft.

1000 - 1499 ft.

500 - 999 ft.

0 - 499 ft.

0   5   10   15
miles

N

Topography of Connecticut

3

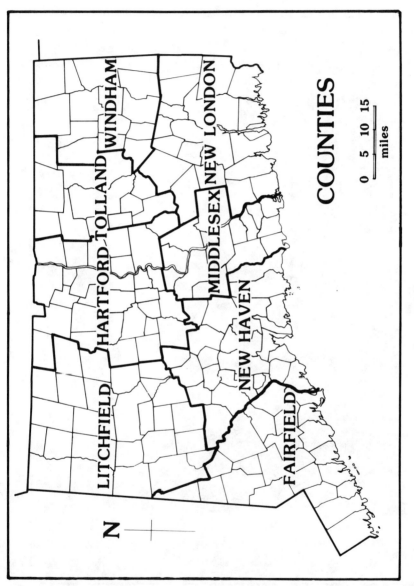

COUNTIES

0 5 10 15
miles

N

LITCHFIELD

HARTFORD

TOLLAND

WINDHAM

MIDDLESEX

NEW LONDON

NEW HAVEN

FAIRFIELD

Counties of Connecticut

4

TOWNS & CITIES

0 5 10 15
miles

N

Towns and cities of Connecticut

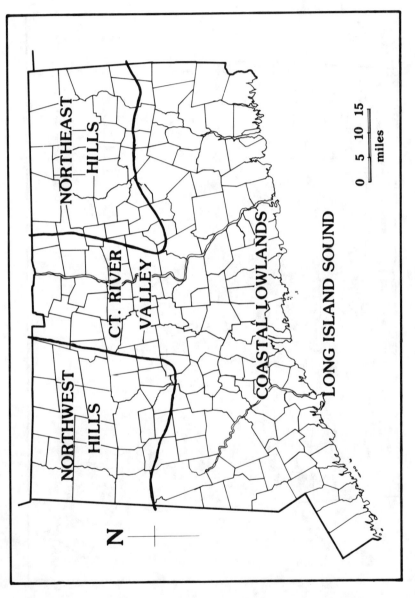

NORTHEAST HILLS

NORTHWEST HILLS

CT. RIVER VALLEY

COASTAL LOWLANDS

LONG ISLAND SOUND

N

0 5 10 15
miles

Avifaunal regions of Connecticut

in the state is the Connecticut River. Flowing out of northern New England, this river travels south through a flat lowland plain. The Connecticut River valley is greatest in width just north of Hartford, where the flat plain is 20 miles across. South of Middletown, the river turns southeast and follows a narrow valley to the coast.

The soils of the Connecticut River valley, atypical for New England, are red-brown in color because of the underlying sedimentary rock. For nearly 10,000 years, annual floods have left layers of silt and clay contributing to the fertility of the valley.

The Connecticut River is subject to tidal flows north to Windsor Locks, and it drops only 40 feet in elevation from the Massachusetts state line to Long Island Sound. Normally a slow moving and graceful river, spring melting of ice and snow can cause floods along the floodplain. The major instate tributary to the Connecticut River is the Farmington River, whose watershed contains many northwestern and central Connecticut towns. At the mouth of the Connecticut River are extensive saltwater marshes that provide a haven for wildlife. Of the 120,000 gallons of fresh water entering the Sound from all sources every second, about 70% comes from the Connecticut River (LIS).

In the eastern portion of the state the major river is the Thames. This deep river is tidal north to Norwich, where it branches into the Shetucket River, and eastward the Quinebaug River. Much of eastern Connecticut north of the coastal region is in the watershed of the Thames River.

The major drainage system of western Connecticut is the Housatonic River and its principal tributary, the Naugatuck River. North of Cameron's Line, many of the river valleys are narrow and deep-cut among high elevations. This fast-moving river drops about 648 feet from the Massachusetts border to the Sound, although south of Cameron's Line the flow is relatively slow.

Soils of Connecticut

After the glaciers retreated some 12,000 years ago, much of the state was left without significant soil deposits. Over time, many areas of exposed rock were subject to decomposition caused by weathering, erosion, and plant growth. The resulting soil now covers much of the rock and consists of varying amounts of sand, silt, and clay. A few areas of the state were left with thick deposits of dense compacted soil after the glaciers retreated. A thin layer of dark topsoil, rarely more than 8 inches thick, covers many areas of the state. This soil is chiefly composed of organic matter left from decaying plant material. The topsoil is thinnest at higher elevations and where the soil is exposed to weathering and erosion, and thickest in low-lying areas. Most soils in Connecticut are acidic, but some areas in the western portions of the state are alkaline.

Coast of Connecticut

Connecticut's coastal plain is not a true plain (normally composed chiefly of sedimentary deposits) but is more a coastal "slope." On average, the coastal lowlands extend inland about 12 miles and rise in elevation about 50 feet per mile. Most of the state's coastal region is composed of exposed bedrock and shallow soils (less than 3 feet thick) except at the mouths of the major rivers where fairly large deposits of sediment have accumulated over the centuries. Not far offshore are many islands, shoals, and rock outcroppings.

The intertidal areas along the shore are composed mostly of glacial drift, rocky ledges, artificial fill and bulkheads, a few sandy beaches, mudflats, and about 15,000 acres of salt marsh. The tidal range in Long Island Sound increases from east to west and varies from 2.3 feet at Noank to 7.5 feet at Greenwich (LIS).

Long Island Sound

Long Island Sound covers about 1,600 square miles of which about 700 square miles are in Connecticut waters. The Sound is approximately 110 miles long, reaches 25 miles in width, and averages about 65 feet deep. Its greatest depth is about 300 feet near the eastern end.

Long Island Sound is a large estuary with fresh water entering all along the coast. The surface salinity at the Race (between Fishers Island and Orient Point) is over 30 parts per thousand, decreasing westward to less than 20 parts per thousand at Fairfield. Salinity is lowest in early May and greatest in early November. The circulation of water within the Sound is complex. Apparently, the heavier saline water sinks and moves generally in an westward direction. The lighter fresh water stays closer to the surface and moves generally in an eastward direction. Silt deposited by rivers and human activities strongly influences the nature of the floor of the Sound. The water in Long Island Sound is rich in nutrients (often to an excessive degree) and supports a wide variety of plants and animals. Apparently, a problem of eutrophication and hypoxia has developed in recent years, leaving little or no oxygen in the western portions of the Sound during the summer months (LIS).

Woodlands of Connecticut

The landscape along much of the coast and inland along the Connecticut River valley consists mostly of urban and suburban sprawl, yet many areas of the state remain covered by woodlands. Although there is no substantial variation of tree species from one part of the state to another, most authorities on the state's forests have recognized several different forest classifications (Bromley; Braun; Jorgensen; Egler and Niering 1947, 1966, 1967).

Much of Connecticut's forest was called an oak-chestnut forest when chestnut trees were a predominant part of the forest. Since the demise of the chestnut, terms such as "oak-hickory" or "sprout hardwood" have been used to describe the forest cover (Braun; Jorgensen). Today, the dominant tree species in Connecticut include white, red and black oak. Widespread trees include red maple, pignut and shagbark hickory, and black birch. Mountain laurel is a common and widespread understory shrub in forested areas.

Some tree species favor areas with a certain soil moisture, acidity, and slope. Dry exposed sites along hilltops are typically inhabited by scarlet, white, black, and chestnut oaks, with an understory of huckleberry and lowbush blueberry. Midslope areas with moderate soil moisture seem to favor pignut hickory, black birch, white pine (in the northern portions of the state), and red oak, with an understory of mountain laurel, maple-leafed viburnam, hop hornbeam, and flowering dogwood. On wet sites (including lower slopes) red maple, tuliptree, white ash, and mockernut hickories are common. Shrubs associated with these trees are hornbeam, highbush blueberry, spicebush, and sweet pepperbush.

Wooded swamps (with year-round saturated soils) contain red maple, black ash, yellow birch, and several species of willows. River floodplains often support numbers of black and weeping willow, American sycamore, American elm, and silver maple.

The Northern hardwood forest typical of northern New England is at its southern limits in Connecticut in the northwest hills and portions of the northeast hills. This forest contains white pine, white and yellow birch, red oak, sugar maple, eastern hemlock, and American beech. Although the latter two species are present in southern portions of the state, they are largely restricted there to narrow, moist ravines. Most oaks and hickories are absent in the northern hardwood forest (Dowhan and Craig; Jorgensen).

In dry sandy soils, chiefly along the coast and the Connecticut River valley, remnants of a pitch pine forest exist in a few locations. This forest was formerly extensive. Also, there are isolated areas along the coast where pin oak, post oak, and westward, sweetgum and black walnut grow.

Avifaunal Regions of Connecticut

Dowhan and Craig describe in detail a series of "eco-regions" used to identify the ecology of the state. Since Connecticut is a relatively small geographical area with little difference in bird distribution and abundance from one end of the state to the other, the eco-regions set forth by Dowhan and Craig are too detailed and complex for use in this book. However, a simplification of Dowhan and Craig's eco-regions can depict general patterns of bird distribution that fit most species of birds found in the state. The following general areas seem appropriate:

• Long Island Sound
• Coastal lowlands
• Northwest Hills
• Northeast Hills
• Connecticut River valley

These general areas facilitate the description of distribution of many species that otherwise would be difficult to explain, but they are not appropriate in all cases. For example, Acadian Flycatcher has a disjunct nesting distribution in the state and occurs in wet deciduous woods in some areas and in hemlock ravines in other areas. Its range is not well described by or confined to the eco-regions listed above. Also, some species, such as Blue Jay, House Wren, and Song Sparrow, are ubiquitous in the state and occur in virtually all areas.

Long Island Sound hosts many bird species and a large number of individuals that winter, migrate, and summer on its waters. The inter-tidal zone, including that of offshore islands, is a crucial feeding and resting area for shorebirds, waders, and waterfowl. In recent decades, gulls, terns, herons, and a few species of shorebirds have reestablished nesting populations along the shores of Long Island Sound.

The coastal lowlands extend from the shoreline inland to about 750 feet above sea level. This eco-region is composed of a variety of habitats, including urban cities and towns, coastal and inland wetlands, moist forests, agricultural fields, and dry upland hilltops. Although many species occurring in this eco-region can also be found in other parts of the state, some—like Tufted Titmouse, Northern Mockingbird, and European Starling—are at their greatest abundance here. Migrating hawks are commonly observed flying over the coastal lowlands, sometimes in large numbers. Coastal thickets attract concentrations of migrating passerines. The moderate weather along the coast supports many "half-hardy" species in the early winter months, and some occasionally survive the winter.

In the northwest and northeast hills certain areas support species that typically nest north of Connecticut. Species such as Red-breasted Nuthatch, Hermit Thrush, Blackburnian Warbler, Yellow-rumped Warbler, Dark-eyed Junco, and White-throated Sparrow regularly nest in these areas. Some of these species appear to be expanding their nesting distribution in the state, possibly the result of an increase in the available nesting habitat caused by the maturation of the forest.

The Connecticut River valley exhibits certain characteristics that separate it from other eco-regions. The valley still contains large areas of grassy plains (most is floodplain land tilled by humans), and the weather of the valley more closely resembles that of the coast than of interior uplands and hills. The valley is an important migration corridor used by many passerines, ducks, and geese. In early winter many half-hardy species linger in the valley.

CLIMATE

New England's weather is well known for its vagaries. The weather often differs from day to day, and the same season in successive years may vary noticeably. In cooler months the prevalent movement of air masses is from the west or northwest; in the summer months most movement is out of the south or southwest. Connecticut's climate is characterized by distinct seasonal temperature changes that produce distinct winters and summers, and precipitation is evenly distributed throughout the year.

Along the coast to about 10 miles inland, the climate is influenced by Long Island Sound, whose water temperature lags behind the temperature of the interior land surface. The Sound's water temperature is the warmest in late August and early September (68°–72°F), and is the coldest in January, ranging from 32° to 41°F (Thomson et al.). The coastal area is cooled by summer sea breezes and warmed in winter by the more temperate waters of Long Island Sound.

Not surprisingly, winter is most severe in the northern portions of the state and mildest along the coast. The total number of days with temperatures staying below 32°F averages 15 to 20 along the coast,

20 to 40 in most of the interior, and almost 70 in the northwest hills. On average, temperatures are lowest during the third week of January, that month normally being the coldest; the average high temperature in January is 36°F, and the average low is 18°F. The number of days with temperatures below 0°F average 1 to 2 days along the coast, 2 to 5 days throughout most of the inland areas, and 2 to 9 days in the northwest hills. The official all-time low temperature was −37°F at Norfolk in 1943 (Brumbach).

The average last frost along the coast occurs about April 15, in the northeast hills about May 15, and in the northwest hills about May 20. In March and April average monthly mean temperatures increase about 11°F. Normally, the first period of consecutive days with temperatures greater than 43°F occurs in the northwest and northeast about April 12–13, along the coast about April 3–4, and earliest in the Connecticut Valley, on April 2. In May the prevailing wind is from the south or southwest. In spring and summer the north-south temperature differential averages 6 degrees F (Brumbach).

Summer's average frost-free period is 190 days along the coast, declining to about 150 days in northwest and northeast hills. The prevailing southwesterly winds average 7.5 mph in summer and early fall. July is the warmest month, with an average high temperaure of 83°F and an average low of 60°F; the warmest period is normally during the third week of that month. Temperatures greater than 100°F occur about once every 10 years along the coast and about twice a decade in the interior valleys. The all-time high temperature (measured at ground level) was 104°F at Norwalk in 1948 and at Cornwall in 1949, and a rooftop temperature of 105°F was recorded at Waterbury in 1926 (Brumbach).

During the fall the first frost normally occurs in the northwest hills about September 25; in the northeast hills, about September 30; and along the coast, about October 25. The decrease in average mean temperature per month during October, November, and December is about 11 degrees. Northwest winds predominate from November through April, averaging about 9.5 mph (Brumbach).

Precipitation is quite consistent from month to month, with August and September amounts augmented by occasional heavy rains from hurricanes and tropical storms. Each month averages about 4 inches of precipitation, except for October and February, which average 3.25 inches and 3.5 inches, respectively. Statewide, the average annual precipitation ranges from 44 to 50 inches, with up to 56 inches in west-central portions of the state. Yearly precipitation extremes are 78.5 inches in 1955 and only 23.6 inches in 1964 (Brumbach; Ludlum).

Snowfalls are apt to occur from mid-November to mid-April in the northwest hills and from late December to mid-March elsewhere in the state. Annual snowfall averages about 30 inches along the coast, approximately 60 inches over most of the interior portions, and more than 100 inches in at least two northwest locations. The all-time high annual snowfall occurred at Norfolk 177 inches during the winter of 1955–1956; and the lowest, 7.3 inches, occurred at New Haven in 1918–1919 (Brumbach; Ludlum).

A Summary
of the Natural
and Cultural History
of Connecticut

Because birds are affected by environmental conditions such as temperature, precipitation, nesting habitat, and food supply, a general description of Connecticut's natural and cultural history may provide insights into factors that have affected bird distribution and populations in prehistoric and historic times.

PREHISTORIC PERIOD

Within the last 2 million years, at least four separate glaciations have affected Connecticut. Each of these shaped and molded the land, carved valleys, and formed lakes and rivers. These glaciations were separated by relatively brief periods of warmer temperatures, during which the ice cover retreated northward and the glaciated areas once more became covered by vegetation (Jorgensen).

The most recent glaciation reached New England 40,000 years ago, when the advancing glaciers extended south into northwestern Vermont and northern Maine. Tundra and probably permafrost were present, especially near the glacier. Spruce and pine trees occurred in limited numbers. A variety of large mammals inhabited the area, including mastodons, mammoths, caribou, moose, two bison species, three species of woodland muskox, two shrub ox species, giant beaver, two capybara genera, and at least one species of saber-toothed cat (Parker).

The last glacier reached its maximum southern limit about 18,000 years ago (Parker). The glacier covered all of Connecticut and had a thickness of 6,000 to 7,000 feet at its' center and about 1,500 feet at its edge. This massive weight compressed the land mass substantially (Bell; LIS). The scouring action of the glacier as it passed over the land removed about 60 feet of surface material and deposited much of it to create Long Island, New York.

When the glacier finally retreated northward, it left a band of deposits (recessional moraines) near Connecticut's present shore. The deposits formed what are now the Captain's islands in Greenwich, the Norwalk islands, the Bridgeport and New Haven outwash deltas, Faulkner's Island in Guilford, and the Madison and Old Saybrook moraines (LIS).

The glacier retreated relatively rapidly, and by 14,000 years ago the state was essentially free of it, although large isolated blocks of ice, often covered with glacial debris, remained for centuries (Parker). The glacial Lake Hitchcock covered the Connecticut River valley north of Rocky Hill for 150 miles and lasted for 4,000 to 5,000 years until its earthen dam collapsed (LIS; Bell). The landscape consisted of scattered boulders of many sizes, large deposits of glacial till and outwash material, glacial ponds, and extensive areas of exposed bedrock.

Approximately 12,000 years ago the land was largely covered by sedges, grasses, mosses, lycopodium (ground pines), ferns, and small patches of woody vegetation. A thousand years later, spruce was extensive, probably indicating that the climate was cool and moist, and some birch and pine were present. By 10,000 years ago a mixed coniferous forest was developing in southwestern New England. Alder, birches, poplar, oak, ash, and fir were also present. White and gray birches were increasing; yellow birch and hemlock appeared somewhat later (Parker; Jorgensen).

The first people arrived about 10,000 years ago. It is widely thought that these visitors were roaming game hunters who used seasonal camps and were responsible for the extinction of a variety of large mammalian herbivores and other animals, totaling perhaps 32 genera, although changes in the climate or habitat also may have contributed to their demise (Parker).

Around 9,000 years ago spruce and lesser amounts of fir and larch were declining rapidly while oaks and hemlocks were expanding in distribution. Jack pine was at its peak. White pine, red maple, sugar maple, and American chestnut appeared. In southern New England deer, moose, fox, lynx, wolverine, and turkey were present. A period of rising temperatures began about then (Parker).

The climate continued to warm from 8,000 to 3,000 years ago. During this period native Americans successfully hunted animals and gathered a variety of nuts, berries, and seeds. Hemlock and pine reached their greatest numbers and subsequently declined (Jorgensen). Beech trees peaked in number between 4,000 and 5,000 years ago, and hickories and chestnuts increased.

From about 3,500 to 1,500 years ago several relatively short periods of cooling occurred. These fluctuations apparently had little effect on the overall composition of the forest, which changed little up to the historic period. The dominant tree species were American chestnut, red oak, white oak and black oak. The wildlife present also changed little during this period. In the last 14,000 years the average temperature may have increased 5° to 8° F overall (Jorgensen; Parker).

The size and number of native American villages gradually increased, partly because of the introduction and use of ceramics, the use of year-round villages, and the introduction of maize about 1,000 years ago (Parker; Merk).

Long Island Sound underwent major changes during the postglacial period. Eighteen thousand years ago the sea level was 250 feet lower than at present, and the coast was far to the southeast (Bell). As the glacier melted, water entered the ocean and raised the sea level. Large ridges formed an extensive freshwater lake where Long Island Sound is now located. About 8,000 years ago rising sea water flooded over the ridges and created the Sound.

The sea level continued to rise. From 8,000 to 3,500 years ago it rose about 1 mm annually and thereafter approximately 0.85 mm annually to about 1900. At present it is rising about 3 mm each year.

HISTORIC PERIOD

About 1600, just before the first significant influx of European settlers, much of the state was covered by an open, parklike forest interspersed with occasional treeless expanses, particularly along the coast and the major river valleys (Cronon; Russell 1982). The Indians periodically burned the forest understory, and this retarded fire-sensitive species such as sugar maple, yellow and black birch, juniper, beech, and hemlock—species that thereby were largely restricted to wetlands. Fire-tolerant species such as oak, chestnut and hickory predominated. These species also were typically mast-producing. The drier uplands, containing well-spaced and large-crowned trees, were largely covered by native grasses, often Little Bluestem, perennials, blackberries, raspberries, and snowberries (Cronon; Russell 1980). Scattered fires produced a variety of habitats, ranging from freshly burned fields and overgrown thickets to young sapling woods and mature forests. These areas were punctuated by marshes, meadows, wetland thickets, and wooded swamps (Cronon).

The semisedentary Indians were concentrated along the Connecticut River and the coast and were apparently largely absent from the northwestern portion of the state (Guillette). Even before the English settlement the native population was greatly reduced by a series of epidemics inadvertently introduced by European traders, perhaps in 1616–1619, certainly during the 1620s, when whole villages were wiped out, and again in 1633–1635, when a smallpox epidemic reduced some villages by 95% (Cronon; Russell 1980). This produced a short-lived reduction of human pressures on plants and animals, resulting in overgrown fields and a temporary resurgence of certain animal species (Cronon). Among the bird populations most affected were those of large species and those found in concentrations, such as colonial nesting birds (Cronon).

European Settlement and the Reduction of the Forest

In 1634 European settlers first arrived in numbers, settling in the fertile Connecticut River valley. Within 5 years, there were several nearby settlements, and in a decade towns were established along the western coast (Bell; Merk; Russell 1982). By the late 1670s the Connecticut River valley, the entire coast, and the Thames River valley were settled. By 1713 most of the state was divided into townships, and in the 1730s the remaining areas were sold to speculators (Merk). These last areas were hilly and less fertile than the lowlands but nevertheless had been converted to farmland by 1776 (Bell).

Preferred settlement sites were open grassy, or at least brushy, clearings, usually created by fires or periodic flooding, and they were frequently situated on abandoned Indian planting fields and high ground near marshes and navigable waterways (Barrows; Cronon; Russell 1980, 1982). The settlers used nearby natural resources more thoroughly than had the Indians, who moved their villages seasonally to places where food was plentiful (Cronon).

As the settlers arrived, new stresses were placed on the forest. Beavers, highly valued for their fur, were substantially reduced in the 1600s. The elimination of beavers and their dams resulted in the reduction of interconnected ponds and marshes (Barrow; Cronon). Man-made dams were constructed to create millponds, which more effectively interrupted the flow of water but were biologically less productive than beaver ponds. Cattle, horses, semiferal pigs, and eventually sheep were released to roam the woods, first for subsistence farming and later for commercial benefit. These animals roamed the woods in far greater concentrations than did the former native grazers (Cronon; Russell 1982) and impaired the forest's ability to reestablish itself. Under this intense pastoralism native grasses and perennials suffered while many new species, including clover and timothy, were introduced and prospered (Cronon). In the 1640s European honeybees spread throughout the countryside ahead of the advancing settlers, enabling many English plants to spread (Russell 1982, p. 32). Shortly after settlement, bounties were placed on crows and blackbirds (Russell 1982; Cronon).

The forest was cut, often the most mature trees first, to satisfy local and trade needs. Trees were girdled and forests burned to create farmland. For firewood alone the average family in New England used an estimated 30 to 40 cords of wood annually, which consumed about an acre of woodland each year. Despite efforts to conserve trees much of the valuable forest initially grew on commonland (owned by the community in common) and thus was consumed rapidly. Toward the end of the 18th century wood had become scarce, especially near the larger communities (Cronon).

During the colonial period hunting and trapping was pervasive, and game animals were reduced to a fraction of their former numbers. Many game species, such as deer and turkey, were virtually eliminated from southern New England by the end of the 1700s. Wolves, bears, foxes, and wildcats were viewed as threats to game and farm animals and were valued for their pelts; thus, they were extensively trapped (Cronon; Parker; Russell 1982). With the reduction of predators, small animals such as squirrels and passenger pigeons apparently increased (Parker).

Eventually, the forest was reduced to small, isolated remnants, often situated on land considered unfit for most farming uses. Near the beginning of the 19th century, during a 240-mile journey from Boston to New York, less than 10% of the distance was through woodlands, and that consisted of 50 or 60 separate parcels (Cronon). A forest is not merely a collection of trees but a complex of interrelating plants, animals, and microorganisms, and its decimation during the settlement period caused the decline of many native species.

Farming

As towns were settled, the "wilderness" was replaced by a mosaic of pastures, orchards, woodlots, and planting fields of many different sizes. The process of turning forest to tilled land changed the soil itself: without the annual deposit of leaves, the soil lost a major source of organic nutrients. The annual harvesting of crops depleted the supply of available plant nutrients in the soil. Within several years of settlement many areas experienced a loss of soil fertility, especially those areas in the northern hilly portions of the state (Cronon; Merk; Russell 1982). The natural diversity of plants in the forest was replaced by large areas of homogeneous and domesticated crops, which soon attracted concentrations of certain insects.

The treeless land was subjected to soil desiccation caused by direct sunlight and wind on the bare soils (Jorgensen). Without leaf litter, ground vegetation, and tree canopies, the soil's ability to absorb water was reduced, runoff increased, and soil erosion was extensive. Brooks and streams dried more often in summer, and flooding caused by the increase in hard-packed soils occurred with greater frequency. The erosion of soils increased the sedimentation of wetlands and waterbodies (Cronon). Ponds and swamps were subject to increased levels of sediment and silt, and many wetlands were purposely drained to create additional farmland.

If the three southern New England states contained at least 60,000 people in about 1600, and considering Connecticut's size, shoreline, and river valleys, then Connecticut may possibly have had about 20,000 residents (Russell 1980). The native American population dramatically declined from 1700 to 1730 while the number of settlers increased more than 350%. In the following 26 years the number of settlers grew from 38,000 to over 130,000 (Van Dusen 1975, 1961). In spite of the increase in population Massachusetts residents were still settling in the northwestern portion of Connecticut as late as 1740 (Destler). In 1790 the state contained approximately 238,000 people, and by 1830 it had grown to 298,000 (Russell 1980; 1982).

During the 1750s most people lived on small family farms or in small villages (Trecker). These labor-intensive farms needed much effort to produce a meager yield and became smaller each generation as heirs were given parcels to farm themselves. Also during the 1750s, there was a general change in agricultural emphasis from cultivation to livestock and meat production (Van Dusen 1975). By the latter half of the 1700s the state produced export surpluses for many farm products (Destler).

Trade was facilitated by the expansion and improvement of roads, especially during the Revolutionary War. By 1774 Connecticut's last frontier—Litchfield County—was largely settled (Van Dusen 1961., p. 106).

After the Revolutionary War the cost of farming increased, and the availability of inexpensive land in northern New England and to the west in New York and Pennsylvania led to a steady emigration of residents (Anderson; Merk; Russell 1982; Trecker; Van Dusen 1961). After the War of 1812 "Ohio Fever" struck, and many more Nutmeggers left for the west. In 1843 Connecticut's pioneer naturalist, James Linsley, produced his list of the birds of Connecticut.

During the first half of the 1800s the amount of acreage devoted to farming was at its greatest, peaking in the early 1860s, during the Civil War. At that time about 75% of the land was "improved" or modified for farming (Bell; Russell 1982). Then many of the native animals inhabiting woodlands were at their lowest numbers; some had been extirpated altogether. But the transformation of the land had positive effects on wildlife that favored fields, meadows, and marshes. Several smaller mammal species, including woodchucks, which favored grasslands and brushy areas, became widespread. Among birds many sparrow species maintained high numbers, as did Bobwhite, Upland Sandpiper, Bobolink, Eastern Meadowlark, Eastern Bluebird, and Brown-headed Cowbird. Rails were apparently more frequent in inland marshes and wetlands than they are today.

Agriculture after 1870 generally decreased—the value of crops declined, and the amount of cleared lands dropped steadily (Russell 1982). But some areas with good soils successfully produced specialized produce such as dairy products, tobacco, potatoes, and summer fruits and vegetables (Van Dusen 1961). Farmlands continued to decrease in this century, and by 1945 only 50% of the land was used for agricultural purposes, further declining to only 14% in 1985 (Bell).

The English had subdued the "wilderness" by introducing European technology, plants, and animals—a support system that enabled the settlers to survive and prosper in a new environment. The European system of land use enabled the land to support more people than it had in the precontact period and thereby imposed drastic changes in the environment of southern New England.

Manufacturing

Most pre–American Revolution manufacturing was done in homes and small shops, often by families on a part-time basis. Goods were largely produced for local consumption (Van Dusen 1975; Walsh). Many artisans, such as furniture makers, coopers, shipbuilders, carpenters, and tanners, directly utilized raw wood. Saw and gristmills were found along most streams of any substantial length. In response to the British blockades throughout the Revolutionary War, native craftsmen attempted to replace British products with those locally produced (Van Dusen 1961).

One industry that caused significant environmental impacts was iron making. After a rich deposit of limonite (iron ore) was discovered at Salisbury in the mid-1730s, this industry grew and had become important by the time of the Revolutionary War (Walsh). In 1800 about 50 forges were operating in the northwestern portion of the state, and by 1840 Connecticut was the fourth-largest producer of iron and steel in the country (Kuslan). Vast amounts of charcoal, made from partially burned deciduous trees, were required to operate the forges, and the forests of northwestern Connecticut were severely depleted for this purpose (Bell; Russell 1982).

Other noteworthy industries of the late 1700s that placed substantial demands on the forests were shipbuilding and brass and glass manufacturing (Walsh; Van Dusen 1975; Jorgensen).

After the Revolutionary War, the number of mill towns increased along rivers with power-generating waterfalls. At one time there were 203 mill towns in the state (Bell). As industry increased, so did the nature and amount of pollution in the rivers and lakes. Sewage generated from settled areas and discharges into rivers from mills and shops contributed to the degradation of water quality.

An important ingredient in land use changes was advancements in transportation. Roadways were steadily improved, turnpikes were established, and at least one viable canal was built. In the 1840s steamships were replacing sailing ships on the major rivers and the Sound. But the greatest contribution to a modern transportation system was the railroad. In the 1840s and 1850s railways spread across the state, first to carry farm produce from the interior to navigable waters and later to transport industrial goods (Anderson). Track length increased from 102 miles in 1840 to 601 miles in 1860 (Van Dusen 1961).

Coal-fired steam engines were increasingly used, replacing less reliable and limited waterpower and increasing the amount of air pollution. In 1870 steam far exceeded water as a source of power (Anderson). Industry was relocating to and expanding in larger towns along transportation routes, primarily in the major river valleys and along the coast

(Anderson; Bell). By the mid-1800s New Haven, Norwich, Bridgeport, Hartford, and Danbury had become important factory towns. Major products were metals (brass, iron, silver, and gold), firearms, textiles, clocks, and silver goods. The demands placed on the state by the Civil War provided a strong impetus for the growth of industry and manufacturing (Van Dusen 1961).

By 1870 90,000 workers were employed in manufacturing. One third of these were in textiles; at that time one seventh of the country's mechanics and machinists worked in Connecticut (Anderson). Between 1880, when it was the sixth-largest state in number of manufacturing companies, and 1910 the state became an important industrial center. During this period of transition, when much of the state remained open land, C. Hart Merriam authored his compilation of Connecticut birds in 1877.

Urbanization

Urbanized areas enlarged as a result of the growth of industry. In 1890 there were 123,000 rural residents and 623,000 residents of urban areas. By 1910 the number of rural residents had decreased and that of city residents had risen to 1 million (Anderson). Particularly illustrative of the growth of industry and urbanization was Bridgeport, which grew from 30,000 to about 150,000 people between 1880 and 1920 (Anderson). From 1880 to 1890, 76 rural farming towns lost residents while the state as a whole grew by 17%, almost totally in urban areas (Bell).

These enlarged cities had a striking effect on the environment (Dowhan and Craig). New types of machinery, capable of transforming land to unprecedented degrees, were put to use. Large permanent reservoirs were constructed along watercourses to provide public drinking water. New harbors were dredged, and existing ones were enlarged. Numerous jetties, seawalls, and breakwaters were built. Hills and steep grades were leveled. Inland wetlands, river floodplains, and coastal marshes were filled to provide sites for manufacturing and workers' housing. Elaborate new road systems were constructed. Sewage systems were designed and built to carry waste to watercourses, bays, and harbors. Most urban streams and harbors were severely polluted by sewage and industrial wastes. The need arose for public dumps for solid waste and garbage, and they usually were sited in wetlands. Coal was used to power factories and was widely used domestically for heating; polluted air became an accepted aspect of urban life.

The environment was not solely shaped by the creation of an urban infrastructure but also by the needs and customs of the state's residents. Wild game, traditionally a staple of the American diet, was furnished to the growing urban population by professional hunters, who combed the countryside for wildlife, particularly waterfowl and shorebirds. In addition to the popular American hobby of hunting, members of some ethnic groups regularly trapped and netted small birds for food. Falconry was apparently never very popular, but it nevertheless took a toll on raptors. Egg collecting was a widespread hobby, and eggs were widely traded among oologists (Dowhan and Craig). Wild birds were frequently caught and kept as pets, and stuffed birds, usually passerines, were considered tasteful decorations for Victorian parlors. Feathers were widely used as ornaments on women's hats and finery. Feather collecting created havoc for herons and terns and eliminated many nesting colonies along the coast.

Return of the Forest

With the exception of specialized crops, agriculture steadily declined in the last half of the 19th century and in the 20th century as improved transportation brought cheaper western and southern farm products to eastern markets. Abandoned agricultural lands were invaded by annual weeds (often of European origin), grasses, herbs, and vines and then by eastern red cedar, white pine (in northern areas), and juniper. On dry hillsides abandoned fields were overgrown with Little Bluestem, thickets of woody brush, and short-lived "pioneer" trees such as gray birch, aspen, sassafras, cherry, and black locust (Jorgensen). This second-growth forest spread during the last half of the 1800s. However, it was not a duplicate of the earlier colonial forest—it was missing a number of key components. Native Americans and their hunting, collecting, and land use practices were no longer an influence, and many game species such as bear, deer, turkey, and large predators had been virtually extirpated.

The widespread practice of creating ground fires to control underbrush was gradually reduced as agriculture declined and concerns about protecting forested areas grew. Without fire the distribution of trees in the forest was significantly altered (Niering). The local weather changes that occurred when the forest was abruptly cut were slowly reversed with its regrowth. Many of the forests were left uncut as cheaper lumber became available from outside the state and coal (and later oil) reduced the need for firewood. The reduction of ground fires and grazing facilitated the growth of woodlands with relatively thick understory vegetation. Fire-intolerant tree species comprised a significant portion of the new forest, and fire-tolerant species such as oaks and hickories were forced to compete without the advantage of fire.

More recent changes have altered the composition of the forest even further. In the 1910s and 1920s the chestnut blight was introduced from China. It swept through the state and eliminated one of the most important tree species, American chestnut. In the early colonial period this species dominated the state's forests (Dowhan and Craig). Introduced plants, notably trees such as black locust, catalpa, Norway spruce, and black maple, became naturalized. Gypsy moths were introduced from Europe and contributed to the mortality of their favored food trees—particularly oaks. Dutch elm disease, another introduced plague, substantially reduced the numbers of American elms. By midcentury Asian bittersweet invaded the forest edge. These and other changes contributed to the new forest community. As the woods increased, treeless areas decreased. Former sedge meadows and cattail marshes grew into red maple swamps. Both dry grasslands and wet meadows became much less numerous, and the fauna that favored these habitats steadily declined.

Conservation Awareness

In the middle of the 19th century the concept of environmental protection was virtually nonexistent. By 1890 concern about the environment was limited to an enlightened minority and was not given any regard by most people. Attitudes toward the conservation of natural resources began to shift by the early 1900s as appreciation of nature's complexity grew.

Responding to the destruction of natural resources (especially wildlife) was an emerging middle class that was better educated and more affluent, with time and energy to contribute to community interests. Aesthetic, humanitarian, and romantic, as well as practical, considerations that favored conservation began to replace the older, more exploitive approach to nature based on traditional rural values.

Out of these new attitudes about nature developed a conservation movement. Against great odds, conservationists challenged traditional values and advocated and initiated legislation to protect natural resources. Some of the leaders of this movement were "sportsmen" and hunters who held nature in high regard and who discouraged exploitation for profit (Reiger). Nature sanctuaries were created, such as Bird-

craft Museum at Fairfield in 1914, the first privately owned bird sanctuary in the country. Natural parks, state forests, nature centers, conservation organizations, and a host of periodicals and books also were
created or produced. Nesting boxes and feeding stations became popular.

State parks were developed (beginning in 1913) to provide for a
growing desire for refuge from urban harshness. Smaller municipal parks,
usually designed for passive use, more built as islands of greenery for
urban workers. Laws were enacted at all government levels to curtail
some of the most blatant forms of pollution and to protect wildlife
and other natural resources from overuse and loss. In 1916 federal restrictions were placed on market hunting and in the 1930s on general
hunting and trapping. Non-game birds were defined and protected, as
were severely impacted game species; open and closed hunting seasons
were established (the destructive spring hunts were abolished); daily
and seasonal limits were imposed; and regular reevaluation of a species'
abundance became an accepted wildlife-management tool. Some species
recovered quickly, others more slowly, and some have never recovered
from the devastation caused by gunners, plume hunters, and habitat
destruction. In 1951 hawks and owls (long persecuted by many who
believed them to be a threat to livestock and wildlife) were protected
by the state. After decades of supporting relatively few "game" species
of animals, in the 1980s the state finally began to attend to non-game
species by establishing a special department to begin management of
certain species—notably terns and Piping Plovers. Despite the increase of
environmental awareness, Connecticut has only just recently legislated
measures to define and protect certain endangered species.

Following extensive education and lobbying efforts, wetlands, both
inland and coastal, were given a degree of protection in the early
1970s (although there is current concern about the effectiveness of this
protection). Stronger air- and water-pollution control measures were
established during the same period. Pesticides came under greater scrutiny; DDT induced catastrophic declines in some raptors and was banned
by legislation after much dispute. The United States remains the largest
manufacturer of DDT today and exports large quantities to other coun-
tries.

Not all changes are caused by humans. Weather certainly influences
plant and animal populations. An example of what weather can do
occurred in 1816, the "year without a summer," when summertime
snows and frosts had a severe impact on the state's vegetation and
animals. Tropical storms and hurricanes are well known for bringing

pelagic and southern birds into the Sound. More than 40 recorded hurricanes have reached New England (Ludlum), the most severe occurring in 1635, 1683, 1815, 1821, and 1938 (Bell). An accelerated rise in sea level may jeopardize coastal habitats and the animals that depend on them (Bell).

New Suburban Environments

By the 1940s the older, industrially based cities reached their greatest period of wealth, population, and influence relative to surrounding areas. After World War II manufacturing was declining or leaving the state. Postwar prosperity led to the development of the suburbs. Initially, vacant lots around the cities were used for residential subdivisions. As open land in the cities became scarce, new developments were built on farmlands farther away from the older commercial centers. As this mobile population settled farther into the countryside, undeveloped land became scarce, and intensive human uses reached previously quiet rural areas. Recreational activities such as golf, swimming, and boating consumed more open land, beaches, and other shorefront sites.

This new suburban environment was characterized by a park-like, orderly appearance, with assemblages of plants designed to look attractive. Very limited before 1950, this new habitat dominated large portions of the state by 1980. The labor-intensive flower beds of pre-World War II were being replaced by plantings requiring less maintenance. A wide variety of plants was brought together that had little natural relationship to each other or to the state's native environment. An assortment of newly developed power tools, earth-moving equipment, and sophisticated chemicals was introduced to shape and manage the environment. Although creating the impression of a "natural," rather lush environment, this new habitat was inhospitable for many native animal species; although some, such as robins, squirrels, raccoons, skunks, and oppossums have prospered. Cardinals, mockingbirds, and titmice have found this new habitat suitable for their needs and have extended their ranges into the state from the south. The subdivision of natural habitats by human development has had profound effects on the distribution of birds (Askins, Philbrick, and Sugena).

The major environmental changes affecting bird populations during this century include (1) the decline of agriculture and the resulting decrease in farmland and increase in the amount of forested land; (2) the increase of the human population and the related spread of residential developments, roads, pollution, and other impacts on the environment; and (3) the increase of public awareness of the importance of environmental protection and related efforts to improve environmental quality.

Species Accounts

EXPLANATION

The first definite list of the birds of the state was written by Rev. James H. Linsley of Stratford and published in 1843. Linsley recorded 302 species, but of these Dr. C. Hart Merriam concluded that only 239 species had been reported with satisfactory evidence. Thirty-four years later, in 1877, Dr. Merriam prepared a complete list, containing 291 species, and of these several have not been recorded since in Connecticut. Thirty-four years after Merriam, *Birds of Connecticut* by Sage, Bishop, and Bliss was published in 1913 and listed 334 species. The list presented here includes 380 species, of which 13 are hypothetical and 4 are extinct or extirpated.

During the compilation of data for this publication a thorough search was conducted for accounts and records of birds in Connecticut. Information reviewed included (1) specimens in collections at the University of Connecticut, Yale Peabody Museum, Birdcraft Museum, and several other institutions; (2) the published literature, consisting mostly of books and periodicals and in a few cases unpublished personal journals; and (3) the authors' own field experience covering collectively more than 45 years.

Full status on the following list of Connecticut birds has been given to those species completely verified by collection of a specimen or by a photograph that has been examined by at least one authority. There are a number of species reported in Connecticut whose existence in the state is not supported by specimen or photographic evidence. Such species are termed "hypothetical" if (1) the species was satisfactorily identified by at least three sufficiently qualified observers, or (2) the species has been adequately documented in the historical literature, or (3) suspicion exists among authorities that the individual (otherwise capable of occurring here naturally) was not a "wild" bird but was an escapee from captivity or was assisted in its arrival in the state by human interference.

This approach to assembling a state list differs somewhat from that used by authors of other state lists, both in Connecticut and elsewhere.

Any one approach to the problem of evaluating sight records is not necessarily better than another. However, some authorities have accepted one-person sight records as sole evidence for placing a species on a state's list. There are inherent difficulties in identifying rare species, particularly those that are exceptionally difficult to identify even in ideal field conditions, and a single observer's judgment and identification may be less critical and less accurate than when three or more observers are involved. The authors believe that in consideration of the potential problems associated with uncorroborated, single-person sightings, the prudent course is to not accept such sightings as sole evidence for granting full or hypothetical status on the state list.

Those species that do not meet the criteria for inclusion as a full or hypothetical species are listed in Appendix A. The accounts listed in Appendix A are provided to inform the readers of the extent of published reports and to make such uncorroborated sightings available for reevaluation should new documentation come to light. Examination of additional documentation could result in the future elevation of some of these accounts from the Appendix to the main text.

The scientific and vernacular names used and the sequence of species follow those of the American Ornithologists' Union's *Checklist of North American Birds* (sixth edition, 1983 including 37th Supplement, 1989). Records and other information contained in this book are through December 1988. Each species account may consist of up to five sections: Status, Records, Comments, Subspecies, and Historical Notes.

1. **Status.** This section describes the current population and distribution of each species. We have modified the descriptive criteria set forth by John Bull in *Birds of the New York Area* (1964), which is based on a system proposed by Robert Arbib (AFN 11:63). These descriptive criteria are as follows:

Very abundant—over 1,000 individuals per day

Abundant—201 to 1,000 individuals per day

Very common—51 to 200 individuals per day

Common—21 to 50 individuals per day

Fairly common—7 to 20 individuals per day

Uncommon—1 to 6 individuals per day

Rare—1 to 6 individuals per season

Very rare—over 12 records but very infrequent

Casual—7 to 12 records

Accidental—1 to 6 records

Other terms used are as follows:

Resident: A species that can be found year-round in appropriate habitat.

Migrant: A species that is found in the state on its way to and/or from its breeding areas.

Visitor: A species that appears in the state for purposes other than breeding or migration.

Vagrant: A species for which Connecticut is well outside of its normal migration route, breeding range, and winter range.

Local: A species known to inhabit a specific and limited area or that is very scattered in its distribution.

Regional: The area encompassing Massachusetts, Rhode Island, Connecticut, New York, and New Jersey.

Regular: Reported annually.

Irregular: Not reported annually.

Straggler: An individual of a species that fails to depart from the state in the season or time period normal for that species and lingers into the following season (e.g., Eastern Phoebe in December, Greater Scaup in summer).

Each account begins with a description of abundance and the timing of fall and spring migration, then winter status, and then nesting status. In defining periods of time, months have been divided into three sections: early (the first 10 days), mid (the middle 10 days), and late (the last 10 days). The stated migration period is the time when the majority of the birds pass through the state. Occasionally, the term "midwinter" is used. This is the period between the first week of January and the last week in February. Similarly, "midsummer" signifies the period between the first week in July and the last week in August. Uneven statewide distribution is noted, as are localized nestings. References to Long Island Sound apply only to that part within Connecticut.

The authors have affixed the following significance to the differences between the terms "record" and "report": a *record* has been relatively well based and authenticated and has survived the scrutiny of reviewing authorities. A *report* is normally used when only one person has passed judgment on a sighting, such as the original observer. Of course, there is no fixed dividing line between the two terms, and certainly most reports are probably correct and accurate.

For those species listed as "accidental" or "casual," all known corroborated and published records are listed. Also, all known records that support a seasonal or regional status of three or fewer occurrences are listed (e.g., winter records of Broad-winged Hawk, spring records of Connecticut Warbler, inland records of King Eider). Usually, data for each record consist of the date, the location (by town), the observer(s), and the source of the information.

At the end of the status section of the majority of the species accounts, up to three "extreme" arrival and departure dates are listed. For those species summering in Connecticut or north of the state, the earliest spring arrival and latest fall departure are given. For those species that winter in Connecticut or south of the state, the earliest fall arrival and latest spring departure are given. For migrants that do not summer and winter in Connecticut, the earliest arrival and departure for both spring and fall migration are given. The listed dates were culled from published sources, and some unusual dates were excluded if there was significant question as to their accuracy and reliability. Several questionable dates have been included and are appropriately queried in the text. In some instances accurate arrival or departure dates are very difficult to determine because of the number of "off-season" records. For example, spring departure dates for Common Loon are not listed because of the number of summering, nonbreeding stragglers that have occurred over the years, which make nearly impossible the separation of truly late departures from summer stragglers.

The status given for each species is valid in most field situations, but certainly not all. For example, a less experienced observer may have difficulty in finding the numbers of a particular species that the text indicates should be present. And some species are highly variable or irregular in occurrence, appearing numerous in some years but absent in others. Some species are very conspicuous, whereas others are shy and secretive. Some birds appear in flocks, with large numbers present in one area but with virtually none present nearby. Furthermore, future changes in populations will undoubtedly modify the status of at least some of the species.

2. **Records.** This section lists the documentation found in the literature of rarer species, particularly those that are accidental or casual.

3. **Comments.** This section normally contains the authors' remarks concerning unusual reports, ancillary information, large concentrations, and other matters of interest.

4. **Subspecies.** In this section details are provided for those subspecies identifiable in the field or otherwise of some special interest.

5. **Historical Notes.** The purpose of this section is to describe the historical changes in status of each species. Whenever possible,

the first records and first nestings are stated. The works of in-state observers as well as nearby ornithologists were consulted. The historical accounts should enable the reader to appreciate the dynamic nature of most avian populations. Bird numbers are not static, as any observer of more than 10 years can signify. Almost invariably, earlier authors failed to define their descriptive terms precisely. In spite of this, the information contained in their works is still very useful in that the stated relative frequencies of occurrence over time may reflect actual changes in population.

ABBREVIATIONS

ad.	adult
AFN	*Audubon Field Notes*
AMNH	American Museum of Natural History
AmB	*American Birds*
AOU	American Ornithologists' Union
BcM	Birdcraft Museum
bd.	banded
BL	*Birdlore*
BM	Bruce Museum
BMAS	*Bulletin of Massachusetts Audubon Society*
BNEBL	*Bulletin of New England Birdlife*
BNOC	*Bulletin of the Nuttall Ornithological Club*
BSR	Biological Survey records
COAR	Connecticut Ornithological Association records
CW	*Connecticut Warbler*
et al.	and others
et multi al.	and many others
f.	female
fide	according to
HAS	Hartford Audubon Society records
imm.	immature
LIS	*Long Island Sound: An Atlas of Natural Resources*
m.	male
MFCYM	Mid Fairfield County Youth Museum
MFN	*Mianus Field Notes*
NHBCN	*New Haven Bird Club Newsletter*
NYBBA	*Atlas of Breeding Birds in New York State*
obs.	observer

OO	*The Oologist*
pers. comm.	personal communication
pers. obs.	personal observation
ph.	photograph
PLSNY	*Proceedings of the Linnaean Society of New York*
RNEB	*Record of New England Birds*
SCCC	Summary of Connecticut Christmas Counts
SCSU	Southern Connecticut State University
SMNC	Stamford Museum and Nature Center
sp. or spec.	specimen
unpub.	unpublished
UCM	University of Connecticut Museum
WB	*Wilson's Bulletin*
WMF	White Memorial Foundation checklist
YPM	Yale Peabody Museum

$$\text{oo } \text{oo oo } \text{oo}$$

Species List

LOONS (FAMILY GAVIIDAE)

Red-throated Loon (*Gavia stellata*)

STATUS: a fairly common migrant on Long Island Sound in April and from mid-October into December; very rare inland. Numbers vary during migration from year to year. In winter it is rare on the western Sound, uncommon to common eastward. It is accidental inland in winter: one was reported in the Lakeville–Sharon area on December 16, 1979 (AmB 34:404). It is a casual summer visitor from late May to early October and has been observed in full breeding plumage several times (A. Saunders, *Auk* 53:226; pers. obs.).

Earliest fall arrival: Sept. 7, 1975, 1952; Sept. 14, 1941; Sept. 18, 1966.
Latest spring departure: June 24, 1984; June 14, 1976; June 6, 1975.

COMMENTS: On October 26, 1969, 173 birds were counted between Milford and Guilford (NHBCN 7:3). Connecticut Christmas Bird Count data suggest a decline in winter numbers on Long Island Sound has occurred since about 1975 (SCCC).

Common Loon (*Gavia immer*)

STATUS: a fairly common migrant in coastal waters from late March to mid-May and from September through mid-November; uncommon to fairly common inland, usually overhead and on larger lakes and rivers. Usually rare in winter on western Long Island Sound, gradually increasing eastward to fairly common. Nonbreeding stragglers are rare from June through August, usually along the coast but infrequently inland on the larger lakes.

Earliest fall arrival: Aug. 20, 1972; Aug. 25, 1986; Aug. 28, 1966.
Latest spring departure: difficult to determine because of the number of reports of summering birds.

HISTORICAL NOTES: The extent of nesting of this species in Connecticut from the time of settlement to the mid-1800s is unknown. Arbib
(1963) suggested that "undoubtedly, the loon was far more widespread
as a breeding bird in pre-Columbian and early colonial days." Declines
in the late 1800s were attributed to hunting and the recreational use
of lakes (NYBBA). Merriam (1877) said that "it has been known to
breed on a pond at East Hampton," and Job (1922) reported it nesting
at Winchester in the early 1880s. Also, it nested on Lake Saltonstall
on the East Haven/Branford border in 1878 and 1890 (Sage et al.). In
this century there are no corroborated records of nesting. Bergstrom
commented vaguely that a pair and young were observed at Colches-
ter in 1948 but provided no details. There are several unsupported
reports of nesting in the 1950s. A report of two nesting pairs in 1977
in Litchfield County (AmB 31:1110) lacks satisfactory corroboration.
Similarly, reports in 1978 and 1985 (AmB 39:885) lack any supporting
details. The recreational use of large lakes may inhibit expansion of the
nesting range of this species into southern New England.

GREBES (FAMILY PODICIPEDIDAE*)*

Pied-billed Grebe (*Podilymbus podiceps*)

STATUS: an uncommon migrant from early April to late May. In fall it
is fairly common on fresh and brackish waters from late September to
mid-November. In winter it is uncommon in coastal estuaries, depending on unfrozen waters and is always rare offshore. It is a rare nester
west of the Connecticut River; it has nested in the mid-1980s at Stratford and Newtown and is suspected of nesting at Sharon, Cornwall,
and North Haven.
  Earliest fall arrival: Aug. 15, 1977; Aug. 25, 1966; Sept. 2, 1984.
  Latest spring departure: May 30, 1983; May 27, 1950; May 25, 1986.

HISTORICAL NOTES: This shy species was apparently never common
as a nester in Connecticut. Reports of nesting declined in southern New
England after 1850 (Griscom), probably the result of the draining of
marshy ponds and hunting (Bent 1919). Merriam (1877) reported nesting without providing details, Sage et al. (1913) suggested Litchfield
County and the Wilton area as breeding locations, but Job (1922)
reported no nesting records in Litchfield County. It nested at Fairfield
from 1934 to 1939 (A. Saunders, *Auk* 67:253). Nesting was reported in
the Guilford area through the 1940s (Mackenzie), in Litchfield County
in the 1960s (WMF), at Woodbridge in 1969 (AmB 24:665), and possibly
at Mansfield in the early 1970s (Manter 1975).

Since the late 1940s it has been reported more frequently in midwinter and early spring than in prior years (Bergstrom; Bull 1964; Hill 1965). On October 29, 1967, an unusually large concentration was noted: 32 were counted at one location in New Haven (NHBC).

Horned Grebe (*Podiceps auritus*)

STATUS: a fairly common migrant on Long Island Sound in March and April and from late October through November. It is occasionally abundant on peak migration days in late March and mid-November. Inland it is a rare to uncommon migrant on lakes and large rivers. In winter it is usually uncommon along the coast but is sometimes more numerous. In summer nonbreeding stragglers are very rare on Long Island Sound.

Earliest fall arrival: Aug. 25, 1916; Sept. 6, 1938; Sept. 12, 1983.

Latest spring departure: June 19, 1982; June 4, 1929; June 3, 1973, 1978.

HISTORICAL NOTES: This hardy grebe was apparently numerous in the 1800s. In the 1870s Merriam said it was "common," and it was called "abundant" (Averill) and "plentiful" (Wright) during the 1890s. In 1908 Job noted that it was a "fairly common migrant" in Litchfield County.

Numbers decreased significantly in the early 1900s, probably the result of excessive shooting. Sage et al. (1913) reported it was "formerly a common fall migrant and winter" visitor and "much rarer in recent years," noting only six fall and two spring records from 1905 to 1909.

Horned Grebe

In the 1920s it was "very rare" (Howes). Its numbers increased after protection laws were adopted, and by the early 1940s it was "common" in winter on Long Island Sound (Cruickshank); by the early 1960s it was said to be "common" (Mackenzie) and even "abundant" (Bull 1964). A slight decline was noted in the mid-1970s and early 1980s, but it has subsequently increased.

Forbush (1925) suggested that Horned Grebe formerly nested in the state, but a review of ornithological literature pertaining to the state does not support such a suggestion. Sage et al. state: "Mr. Job believes a pair bred in Litchfield County in 1906," but Job merely stated in his *List of Birds Observed in Litchfield County* that "[i]n May 1906, I captured one in a brook, whence it was unable to fly out."

COMMENTS: An unusually large concentration was noted on March 4, 1956, when more than 900 were counted at New London (RNEB 12:3).

Red-necked Grebe (*Podiceps grisegena*)

STATUS: variable in numbers. It is a rare to uncommon coastal migrant from late March to early May and in November. On peak migration days in mid-April it may be locally fairly common. It is a rare and erratic winter visitor on Long Island Sound; in some years it may not be present at all. It is very rare inland at any time. Accidental in summer: one "in poor plumage, close to shore" was seen on August 6, 1938, in Saybrook by W. Remington (BNEBL 2:8); one was seen "about" September 10, 1939, at Saybrook by W. Remington (BNEBL 3:9); one was observed on July 14 and 30, 1947, at Westport by A. Saunders (RNEB 3:6); and one was seen by many from July 14 to October 4, 1986, at Greenwich (D. Bova et al., MFN 14:5).

Earliest fall arrival: Oct. 10, 1987; Oct. 14, 1987; Oct. 15, 1910 (spec.).
Latest spring departure: May 22, 1954; May 12, 1988; May 8, 1979.

HISTORICAL NOTES: A review of historical sources pertaining to Connecticut reveals no apparent change in status. The largest known concentration in the state occurred on December 31, 1955, when 21 were counted at Westport (AFN 10:82).

Eared Grebe (*Podiceps nigricollis*)

STATUS: a very rare Long Island Sound visitor; reported in the northeast United States from September through May, with most reports from January to April.

RECORDS: The first sighting on the Atlantic seaboard was January 9–16, 1938, on Long Island, New York (Bull 1964), and the first New England sight record was in Massachusetts on March 27, 1949 (Griscom, AFN 3:201). The first specimen record on the Atlantic seaboard was on February 25, 1950, in Massachusetts (AFN 4:193).

In Connecticut the first specimen record was on December 22, 1964, when a male was collected at Mt. Carmel (Hamden) by J. Grandy (YPM No. 77316). Apparently, the only other documented record is of one photographed at Westport, present from February 28 to March 2, 1988 (F. Mantlik, F. Purnell, et al., CW 8:63).

There are at least eight published sight reports of Eared Grebe in Connecticut. Only the following were observed by two or more observers: The first sight report in the state was on December 29, 1962, by P. Spofford et al. at Westport (AFN 18:102); D. Finch et al. observed one April 6–8, 1967, at East Haven (AFN 22:537, RNEB 23:4); one was seen on March 30, 1979, by D. Sibley et al. at Old Lyme (AmB 33:751); D. Sibley and R. Schwartz reported one at New Haven on January 6, 1987 (CW 7:36). Four single-person sight reports are not satisfactorily corroborated (AmB 25:554; MFCYM 1971:5; CW 3:31, 7:36).

Western Grebe (*Aechmophorus occidentalis*)

STATUS: an accidental Long Island Sound visitor, reported in the northeast United States from mid-October to early May.

RECORDS: The first documented record was one photographed at West Haven, present from late October to about December 16, 1978 (AmB 33:154, 263, 401). There are at least six published sight reports, but only four are sufficiently corroborated: one was observed on Dec. 29, 1951, at Norwalk by L. Moe and J. Young (AFN 6:60, 187); one was sighted on Jan. 2, 1955, at Westport by P. Spofford, B. Cook, et al. (AFN 9:84); one was seen on Dec. 27, 1964, at New London by W. Morgan et al. (AFN 19:117, 19(2) II); and one was observed on Dec. 15, 1973, at New Haven by F. Sibley et al. (AmB 28:219, 616). Two sight reports are not adequately corroborated (AFN 16:104, 20:132, 400).

COMMENTS: In the 1985 AOU Check-list Supplement, Western Grebe was split into two separate species: Western Grebe (*A. occidentalis,* formerly known as the "dark phase" Western Grebe) and Clark's Grebe (*A. clarkii*). Connecticut records of Western Grebe prior to 1978 cannot be assigned to species based on the published descriptions of those sightings.

SHEARWATERS, ETC. (FAMILY PROCELLARIIDAE)
Northern Fulmar (*Fulmarus glacialis*)

STATUS: an accidental pelagic visitor. It is a regular but scarce visitor in the offshore waters of southern New England (Harrison).

RECORDS: The only Connecticut record is of a female collected (AMNH No. 749120) off Branford on October 10, 1909, by A. H. Verrill (*Auk* 27:462), which Forbush (1925) reported as the "first really authentic record for Connecticut as well as for all New England."

Black-capped Petrel (*Pterodroma hasitata*)

STATUS: an accidental pelagic vagrant from the West Indies.

RECORDS: The oiled-soaked remains of an individual were found by J. Holman at Fairfield on October 7, 1938 (BcM No. B1244) shortly after the Great Hurricane of September 21. The specimen, originally identified as a Greater Shearwater (*Puffinus gravis*), was reidentified in 1951 by R. C. Murphy as a female Black-capped Petrel (*P. hasitata*) (*Auk* 69:459).

Cory's Shearwater (*Calonectris diomedea*)

STATUS: an accidental pelagic visitor. It nests on island colonies in the eastern Atlantic and Mediterranean and migrates to the western Atlantic, arriving in July and departing by mid-November.

RECORDS: One was found by Mrs. J. Danaker about 40 miles inland at Woodbury on August 10, 1976, following Hurricane Belle; it was photographed and released by D. Junkin (AmB 31:226). Another was found in a weakened condition on October 5, 1985, at Bridgeport and was photographed and released on October 9 (M. Bull et al., COAR). There are at least four published sight reports but none are sufficiently corroborated.

Greater Shearwater (*Puffinus gravis*)

STATUS: an accidental pelagic visitor to Long Island Sound. It nests on islands in the southern Atlantic and migrates north in the western Atlantic to Labrador and Greenland. It is a regular offshore visitor in southern New England from late May to late October.

RECORDS: There are two specimen records of Greater Shearwater from Connecticut, but only one is extant: the remains of a male were found on a Saybrook beach on July 7, 1973 (YPM No. 95275). Merriam

(1877) reported that a specimen was taken at Granby but did not provide any date; its current disposition is unknown.

An injured Greater Shearwater was captured on November 9, 1985, at Branford and photographed. It was released on November 19, 1985, but did not survive (S. Ramsby et al., CW 7:47). There are several sight reports of this species from Connecticut, but none is satisfactorily corroborated (e.g., RNEB 3:83, CW 6:20).

HISTORICAL NOTES: Linsley (1843a) said it was frequently seen "near our southeast corner" but "not often" on Long Island Sound. High numbers were reported off southeastern New England through the 1880s followed by a decline caused by persecution by fishermen and poor bait years; an increase was reported after 1949 (Hill).

Manx Shearwater (*Puffinus puffinus*)

STATUS: a hypothetical pelagic visitor to Long Island Sound. This species normally migrates north in the western Atlantic before heading to Europe to nest. Nonbreeding individuals linger off the New England coast from May to late September and occur in greater concentrations at the Grand Banks, Newfoundland, and at the mouth of the Bay of Fundy (Terres).

RECORDS: There is one sight report of this species in Connecticut: a single bird was observed May 17, 1980, at Greenwich by T. Burke, F. Purnell, J. Zeranski et al. (AmB 34:755).

HISTORICAL NOTES: Since 1960, a marked increase has occurred in waters off southern New England. The first nesting on the North American continent occurred at Penikese Island, Massachusetts, June 6, 1973 (AmB 28:115, 135). It has subsequently been discovered nesting in Newfoundland.

STORM PETRELS (FAMILY HYDROBATIDAE)

Wilson's Storm-Petrel (*Oceanites oceanicus*)

STATUS: a very rare visitor from late June to late August with most occurrences in August. It is most likely to appear after tropical storms and hurricanes.

Earliest summer arrival: June 20, 1909; June 21, 1942; June 30, 1916.
Latest summer departure: Aug. 27, 1933; Aug. 21, 1948; Aug. 19, 1965.

HISTORICAL NOTES: This species was apparently frequently encountered on Long Island Sound before 1920. Linsley (1843a) said that he had seen it "not only in our Sound, but even west of Stratford, and sitting quietly upon the water." Merriam (1877) said it was "not common; occurs off the coast in summer." Sage et al. listed several sight reports of flocks believed to be this species on Long Island Sound in 1909 and 1911. G. Verrill said it was "common" on the Sound in 1915 and was "occasionally" noted at Stony Creek (*Auk* 38:583). In 1917 W. Smith reported it as "fairly common . . . for some years," having found it "among the [Norwalk] islands at times," where he once observed 20 individuals in 2 hours (BL 10:89). The subsequent decline may be attributable to the degradation of water quality of the Sound.

Following Hurricane Belle in 1976, there were several reports of this species from inland areas at Mansfield and Enfield (AmB 31:226). With the exception of those inland sightings, nearly all other published reports are from the Sound.

White-faced Storm-Petrel (*Pelagodroma marina*)

STATUS: an accidental pelagic vagrant. The subspecies *P. m. hypoleuca* nests in the eastern Atlantic Ocean and apparently disperses westward in late summer and fall (Harrison).

RECORDS: One was found at Milford after Hurricane Belle on August 10, 1976, by R. Muller (AmB 31:2, 226; BcM No. B587). This occurrence is apparently the only mainland United States record (AmB 40:401).

Leach's Storm-Petrel (*Oceanodroma leucorhoa*)

STATUS: a very rare late summer and fall visitor. Most reports are from Long Island Sound after periods of sustained easterly winds and hurricanes; less frequent inland. Reported from August to early November, with most occurrences in September and October.

Earliest fall arrival: Aug. 10, 1976; Aug. 17, 1964; Sept. 17, 1903 (sp.).

Latest fall departure: Nov. 7, 1951 (sp.); Oct. 27, 1857 (sp.); Oct. 18, 1904.

HISTORICAL NOTES: This pelagic species has probably always been rare on Long Island Sound. Linsley (1843a) makes no specific reference to any records, but Merriam (1877) said that he had "twice seen it on the Sound in the vicinity of Faulkner's Island and near New Haven" and that it was "more frequently seen outside than in the Sound." Sage et al. (1913) said it was "rarely seen within the limits of this state." Its nesting range expanded south into Massachusetts in 1933 (*Auk* 50:426).

GANNETS, BOOBIES (FAMILY SULIDAE)

Northern Gannet (*Morus bassanus*)

STATUS: a very rare visitor on eastern Long Island Sound from mid-March through May and from early October into December; casual on the western Sound. Accidental in midwinter: an immature was observed on January 18, 1943, at New London (BNEBL 7:112).

COMMENTS: An unprecedented flight into Long Island Sound, probably caused by thick fog, occurred on November 28–30, 1985, when 236 were seen at New London; decreasing westward, where 40 were seen at Greenwich; a few lingered after December 1 (CW 6:17, 20).

HISTORICAL NOTES: This species has apparently increased off southern New England since 1900, and in recent decades its migration begins earlier and ends later than formerly (Griscom and Snyder). Hill (1965) said the "recent cycle of mild winters has increased the number of wintering birds" off Cape Cod. Despite these trends in deeper offshore waters, the species remains very rare on Long Island Sound.

PELICANS (FAMILY PELECANIDAE)

American White Pelican (*Pelecanus erythrorhynchos*)

STATUS: an accidental vagrant. In southern New England, this species has been reported in May and, more frequently, from July through November.

RECORDS: One was collected on October 15, 1928, at Branford by R. Hill (*Auk* 61:471). The specimen was at one time at Yale Peabody Museum (No. 13510) but was not located there by the authors. One was photographed on May 29, 1989, at Greenwich by L. Brinker et al. (pers. obs.). One sight report has been satisfactorily corroborated: two birds were seen on May 27, 1944, at South Windsor by Vibert et al. (HAS, BMAS 28:208).

Uncorroborated sightings include one at Milford on January 23, 1974; one at New Haven, October 1–2, 1978 (AmB 33:154); and one in late June 1987 at Bridgeport (CW 8:66).

HISTORICAL NOTES: This species was apparently a regular migrant in flocks in the early 1600s in the lower Hudson River valley (Forbush 1925).

Brown Pelican (*Pelecanus occidentalis*)

STATUS: an accidental vagrant on Long Island Sound. It has been reported regionally in May and June and, more frequently, from July through September. In the 1980s, this species has wandered northward into the Middle Atlantic states with increasing frequency.

RECORDS: One was caught alive by Levi Thrall on June 6, 1902, at Guilford (Sage et al.). A female was found at New Haven in June 1905 by R. Hill and is presently mounted at Yale Peabody Musuem (No. 13876). The remnants of one were found at Westport by D. and E. Maclay on March 12, 1977 (YPM skeleton No. 11509, AmB 31:972), which may be the remains of the bird reported at Darien shortly after Hurricane Belle in the fall of 1976. Although there are several published reports of sightings in the state by single observers, none is sufficiently corroborated (e.g., *Auk* 67:253).

CORMORANTS (FAMILY PHALACROCORACIDAE)

Great Cormorant (*Phalacrocorax carbo*)

STATUS: a fairly common winter visitor from late September to late April along the coast at jetties, breakwaters, and islands; accidental inland except along the Connecticut River, where it is rare. It is accidental in summer: an immature summered at Stamford Harbor in 1976 and 1977 (D. Bova et al., AmB 30:927, 32:138, MFN 4:7,8).
    Earliest fall arrival: Sept. 5, 1933 (spec.); Sept. 8, 1975; Sept. 10, 1987.
    Latest spring departure: May 28, 1986; May 26, 1982; May 21, 1977.

HISTORICAL NOTES: C. Townsend suggested that this large cormorant was "abundant" in early colonial New England (Bent 1922). It was reported by Linsley (1843a) at Stonington. In the 1870s, it was a "tolerably common winter visitant" (Merriam), but by the early 1900s it had decreased to "very rare fall migrant" (Sage et al.). In 1908 it was listed as "so rare as not normally found in New Haven" (Honeywill et al.). In the 1920s it was a "rare migrant and winter visitor" (Forbush 1925) and in 1922 C. Townsend believed it no longer nested in North America (Bent 1922), although it continued to winter south to New York. After 1930 numbers increased locally, and it was regular along coastal Long Island (Cruickshank). Bull (1964) noted that it was uncommon to locally very common on Long Island Sound in winter. A review of recent Christmas Bird Count data suggests that its numbers have stabilized since the early 1960s (SCCC) although its nesting range has expanded — reaching Maine by 1983 and Massachusetts in 1984 (AmB 38:984).

Double-crested Cormorant (*Phalacrocorax auritus*)

STATUS: a common to abundant coastal migrant from April to mid-May, and from late September to late October; occasionally very abundant in fall. It is rare to uncommon inland but occasionally occurs in large flocks. Rare in early winter except in estuaries of larger rivers, particularly the Mystic River, where it can be fairly common and may linger through the winter.

It is a common coastal visitor in summer but seldom nests. In recent years it has nested along the coast at Norwalk, Branford, Guilford, Madison, and Stonington. Also, it has nested since 1985 on inland lakes at northern Stamford and East Windsor. Nesting is suspected at New Hartford.

Earliest spring arrival: Mar. 27, 1985; Apr. 6, 1967; Apr. 7, 1966.

Latest fall departure: difficult to determine because of the number of winter reports.

HISTORICAL NOTES: During the colonial period, this species abandoned nesting colonies along the northeast coast in a losing confrontation with advancing civilization and was persecuted by people who considered it a competitor for coastal food fish (NYBBA). The East Coast population declined to a low point in the 1920s (Palmer 1962), but the decline and contraction of its nesting range was documented earlier. It was considered to be a rare migrant before the early 1900s by Linsley (1843a), Merriam (1877), and Sage et al. (1913), with only 13 reports from 1875 to 1908. Spring sightings in 1916 and 1917 were worthy enough to warrant publication (*Auk* 64:137).

It slowly increased from the 1930s to the mid-1940s: it nested at Penobscot Bay, Maine, just prior to 1922 (Bent 1922), south to Massachusetts in 1937 (Griscom and Snyder), and in northern New York in 1945 (*Auk* 64:137). Numbers stabilized during the next 20 years (AmB 38:984). In the early 1960s it was a "common to very abundant coastal migrant," "regular summer visitor" locally, and "local and rare in winter" (Bull 1964). It has increased since about 1970; the Massachusetts population doubled every 3 years from 1972 to 1984, and it nested at Fisher's Island, New York, in 1977 (AmB 38:985). The first reported nesting in this state was in 1979 at East White Rock in the Norwalk

Islands (C. Wood, AmB 33:845). In the 1980s it continued to increase in both summer and winter, and inland reports were "routine" (AmB 41:53).

FRIGATEBIRDS (FAMILY FREGATIDAE)

Magnificent Frigatebird (*Fregata magnificens*)

STATUS: an accidental vagrant from the West Indies and southern Florida. This species has been reported north to Newfoundland after tropical storms and hurricanes.

RECORDS: A female (current location of specimen unknown) was shot in the fall of 1859 at Guilford by Capt. O. Brooks (Merriam; Sage et al.). An immature was sighted at Greenwich on August 25, 1979, by A. and M. Ivanoff (MFN 7:6) and photographed at the Thimble Islands, Branford, on August 28, 1979 (AmB 34:139); what was probably the same bird was sighted near the Housatonic River on September 6, 1979 (C. Wood, AmB 34:139).

HERONS, BITTERNS (FAMILY ARDEIDAE)

American Bittern (*Botaurus lentiginosus*)

STATUS: a rare to uncommon migrant from early April to mid-May and from August to late October; a few linger through December. It is rare in midwinter along the coast, occurring chiefly at larger marshes. It is a rare and very local nester at large inland marshes.

HISTORICAL NOTES: Widespread draining and filling of marshes has contributed to a long-term nesting decline (Griscom and Snyder; Bagg and Eliot; Mackenzie; Manter). Merriam (1877) said it was "common in summer," but Sage et al. (1913) noted it was "rare" in that season. Mackenzie (1961) said it was "formerly a regular but uncommon resident in the fresh water ponds" and added that it "had not been seen since the fall of 1955." In the 1980s American Bitterns "continue to be reported in reduced numbers" (R. Forster, AmB 41:55). Craig (1978) suspected that chlorinated hydrocarbons were involved in its decline.

Least Bittern (*Ixobrychus exilis*)

STATUS: a rare migrant from late April to early May and from early August to late September. A rare nester in fresh and brackish marshes;

since 1982 it has nested at Stratford, Waterford, and Stonington and inland at Durham and South Windsor. Nesting is suspected but not corroborated at several other inland locations. It is accidental in early winter: a male was collected on December 16, 1940, at New Haven (YPM No. 224); one was flushed from a marsh at East Haven on December 7, 1981 (CW 2:24); and one was collected on November 4, 1932, at Hadlyme by A. Brockway (YPM No. 223).

Earliest spring arrival: Apr. 8, 1915; Apr. 18, 1919; Apr. 20, 1982.
Latest fall departure: Oct. 9, 1938; Sept. 26, 1924; Sept. 22, 1902.

HISTORICAL NOTES: This inconspicuous species has been adversely affected by the draining and filling of wetlands. Merriam (1877) said it "seems to be, at present, a pretty regular summer resident" and added that it was "particularly abundant throughout the state during the season of 1875." However, Sage et al. noted only eight reports from 1896 to 1910 and described it as "rather rare" in summer but formerly "common." Mackenzie (1961) called it "rare in Guilford." This species continues to be absent from most parts of the state.

Great Blue Heron (*Ardea herodias*)

STATUS: a fairly common migrant from late March to late May and from August to mid-November. It is a rare to uncommon coastal visitor in winter; less frequent during severe winters. Nonbreeding visitors are uncommon in summer.

Expanding its nesting range, it is a rare to uncommon nester in the northwest hills south to Sherman, Washington, and Thomaston and east to Burlington, New Hartford, and Hartland. It is similarly a local nester in the northeast hills west to Stafford, Tolland, and Coventry and south to Lebanon, Scotland, and Sterling. Also, it has recently nested at North Stonington. Nesting is suspected but unconfirmed at several other inland areas. In 1987, 25 nesting locations were noted, ranging in size from 1 to 55 nests (CW 8:68).

HISTORICAL NOTES: This conspicuous species was probably a common nester in the state during the early colonial period. However, it suffered from widespread hunting during the 1800s (NYBBA). Linsley (1843a) recorded it at Stratford but did not provide comment. Merriam (1877) vaguely stated that it was a summer resident and did not mention any specific nesting information. Sage et al. (1913) noted that it was a "very rare summer resident" and mentioned only one nest, which was found in 1900 at Winchester (Winsted). It was not reported in winter until 1910 (Smith), but winter reports increased after 1920 (Forbush 1925; Bagg and Eliot; Shipley; Bull 1964; Hill).

The Great Blue Heron was not known to nest again in the state until 1975, when nesting colonies were found in both Litchfield and Windham counties. Its nesting range became more widespread in eastern Connecticut during the 1980s.

COMMENTS: An unusually large migratory concentration was noted on August 16, 1959, when 58 were observed at a single location in South Windsor (RNEB 15:1).

Great Egret (*Casmerodius albus*)

STATUS: a fairly common coastal migrant and summer visitor from April to early November. It nests in small numbers on the coast at Greenwich, Norwalk, Branford, and Stonington. Inland, it is a rare to uncommon migrant and summer visitor on mudflats along ponds and lakes and at large marshes.

This species is accidental in winter: one was sighted on February 24, 1946, at Fairfield by F. Novak (Hills 1978); one was seen on January 14 and February 22, 1953, at Guilford (Mackenzie); one spent the winter of 1969–70 at Greenwich (P. Spofford, pers. comm.); and one was seen on January 3, 1976, at Milford (AmB 30:248).

Earliest spring arrival: Mar. 17, 1986; Mar. 19, 1976; Mar. 23, 1985.

Latest fall departure: Dec. 16, 1984; Dec. 15, 1979; Dec. 12, 1976.

HISTORICAL NOTES: The Great Egret was reported north to Canada in the 1600s (Forbush 1925). Excessive hunting to meet the demand for its plumes for use in women's apparel nearly caused its extinction. By the mid-1800s it was a "very rare" visitor in Connecticut (Merriam; Griscom and Snyder; Bull 1964), although at times it was locally very common (Mackenzie). At the turn of the century it continued to decrease: Sage et al. listed only 15 reports from 1876 to 1910.

With the protection laws in effect it increased as a coastal migrant after 1920 (Griscom; Bailey 1955; Griscom and Snyder; Smith; Hill) and has been reported annually since 1912 (*Auk* 35:341). In July 1919 "many hundreds of people had the pleasure of seeing" one at Waterbury (BL 21:360). By the early 1940s it was "regular" near Norwalk (Smith) and was reported more frequently in spring and summer after the great flight of 1948, when 150 were observed at Hartford (Smith; Mackenzie; HAS). By 1964 it was no less than a "common summer visitor" (Bull 1964).

The recovery of this impressive species was evidenced by nestings in New Jersey in 1928, New York in 1953, and Massachusetts in 1954 (WB 73:390). Nesting resumed in Connecticut at Sheffield Island, Norwalk by 1961 according to L. Bradley and P. Spofford (Bull 1964).

Snowy Egret (*Egretta thula*)

STATUS: a fairly common migrant and summer visitor in coastal marshes and mudflats from mid-April to early November; it is sometimes common during peak migration days in late August. It is usually a rare inland visitor but is occasionally uncommon on mudflats along lakes and rivers. It sometimes lingers into December on the coast. It nests very locally along the coast at Greenwich, Norwalk, Branford, and Stonington.

Earliest spring arrival: Mar. 2, 1975; Mar. 5, 1974; Mar. 20, 1982.
Latest fall departure: Dec. 26, 1977; Dec. 16, 1979; Nov. 30, 1982.

HISTORICAL NOTES: The Snowy Egret was "common" and nested here during the colonial period (Forbush 1925). A substantial decline caused by widespread shooting and clubbing by feather collectors resulted in virtual extirpation from Connecticut by the late 1800s. Linsley (1843a) saw it only once at Stratford. Merriam (1877) said it was a "rare accidental visitor from the south."

Aided by protective laws, the population slowly recovered. The first state record in 50 years was in August, 1931, at Darien (BL 33:405). It was a regular visitor at Long Island, New York by the early 1940s (Cruickshank), with a notable regional increase after an influx in 1948 (Griscom and Snyder; Bailey 1955; Mackenzie; Bull 1964). Increasing dramatically in Connecticut during the 1950s, the species was an "uncommon to common summer visitor" by the early 1960s (Bull 1964).

Nesting resumed in New York in 1949 (AFN 3:229), in Massachusetts in 1955 (Bergstrom), and in Connecticut at Sheffield Island, Norwalk, by 1961 (L. Bradley and P. Spofford, AFN 16:462).

COMMENTS: An unusually large concentration of 300 Snowy Egrets was observed on August 3, 1985, at Stratford (D. Varza, CW 6:19). Also noteworthy were 87 observed on a single mudflat in Greenwich on August 27, 1985 (pers. obs.).

Little Blue Heron (*Egretta caerulea*)

STATUS: an uncommon coastal visitor from May to mid-September; sometimes fairly common from August into early September, when immature birds wander north into the state. It is very rare inland. It nests sporadically along the coast at Greenwich, Norwalk, and Stonington.

Earliest spring arrival: Apr. 3, 1960; Apr. 6, 1964; Apr. 9, 1973.

Latest fall departure: Dec. 16, 1979; Nov. 30, 1965; Nov. 15, 1987.

HISTORICAL NOTES: This species was an "accidental" visitor to southern New England until about 1880 (Hill). From 1876 to 1910 there were no more than 12 reports statewide—mostly in August, with a maximum concentration of 10 birds (Sage et al.). An influx was noted in July 1929, when at least 77 were reported from five widely separated localities in the state (BL 31:340). After 1930 it was observed annually (Bergstrom).

Expanding northward, it first nested in New York in 1958 (WB 73:390) and in Connecticut at Sheffield Island, Norwalk, by 1971 (Hills 1978).

Tricolored Heron (*Egretta tricolor*)

STATUS: a rare but regular coastal visitor from mid-May to late September. It has not been confirmed inland. It nests sporadically at the Norwalk Islands.

Earliest spring arrival: Apr. 18, 1984; Apr. 19, 1964; Apr. 26, 1971.

Latest fall departure: Dec. 26, 1982; Dec. 16, 1978; Oct. 8, 1985.

HISTORICAL NOTES: This species has apparently always been rare in the state. It was not recorded by Linsley, Merriam, or Sage et al.

Griscom (1923) listed only one record in New York—of a specimen collected on Long Island in 1836. Cruickshank listed 14 reports in New York from 1925 to 1941, and an increase there from 1953 to 1963 corresponded to its increase as a nesting bird in New Jersey (Bull 1964). It first nested in New Jersey in 1948 and in New York in 1955 (WB 73:390).

In Connecticut it was first observed on June 14, 1947, at Westport by A. Saunders (*Auk* 65:312) and not again until 1962 at Norwalk (Bull 1964). One observed on July 2, 1967, at Milford was called the third state record (AFN 22:591). It was regular in the 1970s (AmB 25:831) and first nested in 1976 at Chimon Island, Norwalk (D. Berg, A. Sanborn, AmB 30:927).

Cattle Egret (*Bubulcus ibis*)

STATUS: a rare to locally uncommon coastal visitor from early May to late August; very rare inland. It sporadically nests on the Norwalk Islands. It is most apt to be found along the western coast.

Earliest spring arrival: Apr. 6, 1973; Apr. 13, 1962; Apr. 18, 1961.

Latest fall departure: Nov. 23, 1962; Nov. 11, 1984; Nov. 8, 1961 (spec.).

HISTORICAL NOTES: This species probably crossed from Africa to northern South America, presumably unassisted, around 1887 and was first seen in North America at Clewiston, Florida, in 1941 or 1942 (Terres). Expanding its range, the first North American nesting record was in 1953 in Florida (Terres). It was first reported in Massachusetts on April 23, 1952 (BMAS 37:139), and in New York May 17–27, 1954 (AFN 8:300).

In Connecticut the Cattle Egret was first reported April 20–May 12, 1957, at Glastonbury by O. Rhines, L. Whittles, et al. (AFN 11:328), and reports increased thereafter. In 1960 it was reported at Saybrook, South Windsor, Glastonbury, Cromwell, and Bloomfield (AFN 14:370). It was first reported at Guilford in 1961 (Mackenzie). A large influx occurred in the northeast United States in the spring of 1962, the first sighting of which was at Wilton on April 13 and at Stonington at about the same time; 30 were seen at Middletown (AFN 16:392). It first nested in Connecticut at the Norwalk Islands in 1971 (AmB 25:837). It was first reported in the Storrs area in 1972 (Manter 1975).

COMMENTS: An unusually large concentration of Cattle Egrets was noted when 40 were counted on July 25, 1983, at Milford (CW 3:41).

Green-backed Heron (*Butorides striatus*)

STATUS: a fairly common migrant from late April to mid-May, and from August to late October; it very rarely lingers through December. It is a widespread but uncommon breeder in trees and dense shrubs near fresh or brackish water throughout the state. It is accidental in midwinter: January 9, 1972, at East Haven (N. Proctor et al., AmB 26:582) and the remains of one were found on January 6, 1968, at East Haven (D. Finch, RNEB 24:1).

Earliest spring arrival: Mar. 9, 1984; Mar. 24, 1928, 1951; Mar. 26, 1983.

Latest fall departure: Dec. 28, 1969; Dec. 21, 1975; Dec. 16, 1978.

HISTORICAL NOTES: Probably numerous in the 1800s, the widespread draining and filling of marshes caused a gradual decline of its numbers after 1910 (Hill 1965). Before the 1930s it was a "common" local nester (Merriam; Sage et al.; Job; Howes; Bagg and Eliot 1937). By the 1970s it was an "uncommon" nester (Manter; Pink and Waterman 1980).

COMMENTS: A concentration of 50 birds counted on July 30, 1938, at a single location in Saybrook was noteworthy (S. Eliot, *Auk* 56:77).

Black-crowned Night-Heron (*Nycticorax nycticorax*)

STATUS: a fairly common coastal migrant from late March to early May and from August to late October; it is occasionally very common on peak migration days in mid-September. It regularly lingers in small numbers to late December along the coast and inland along the Connecticut River but is very rare in midwinter. Inland, it is fairly common in migration, principally along larger rivers, and is a rare and local nester. It nests in colonies along the coast on offshore islands and in secluded swamps.

Earliest spring arrival: Mar. 6, 1966; Mar. 8, 1973; Mar. 12, 1913.

Fall dates are difficult to determine because of the number of records of overwintering birds.

HISTORICAL NOTES: The Black-crowned Night-Heron has declined since 1900 and particularly after World War II (Sage et al.; Shipley; Manter; Hill 1965). The decline is mostly from the loss of nesting and feeding habitat. It nests more locally and in smaller colonies than

Black-crowned Night Heron

formerly (Bagg and Eliot; Hill 1965). The largest nesting colony, on Chimon Island, Norwalk, contained 1,044 birds in 1988 (CW 9:8).

Apparently, the first winter report in the state was in January 1915 (*Auk* 38:584), and winter reports increased during the 1950s (Bull 1964). However, New England Christmas Bird Counts reveal a steady decline in winter numbers from 1974 to at least 1983 (AmB 37:280).

Yellow-crowned Night-Heron (*Nyctanassa violacea*)

STATUS: a rare to uncommon coastal migrant and summer visitor from mid-April to early October; most apt to be found near its nesting sites. It is very rare in November and December. It is very rare inland. It is a rare nester along the coast in Norwalk, Fairfield, Bridgeport, and Milford and possibly along the Connecticut River at Essex.

Earliest spring arrival: Mar. 17, 1954; Mar. 22, 1955; Mar. 26, 1976.
Latest fall departure: Dec. 29, 1961; Dec. 25, 1987; Dec. 21, 1952.

HISTORICAL NOTES: This southern species was first found in Connecticut at Norwalk on April 21, 1922, by W. Smith (BL 25:393). Reports increased in the 1940s. The first nesting occurred at South Norwalk in 1953, when two nests were found by W. Smith and J. Malkin (AFN 7:299). In 1977 six to eight pairs nested on Shea Island, Norwalk (AmB 31:1111).

IBISES (FAMILY THRESKIORNITHIDAE)

White Ibis (*Eudocimus albus*)

STATUS: a casual visitor. It sporadically wanders north into Connecticut in May and somewhat more frequently in late summer, from mid-July to October after the nesting season.

HISTORICAL NOTES: This striking bird was first reported in New England at Milford, Connecticut, on May 23, 1875, by G. B. Grinnell (Sage et al. 1913). The next Connecticut report was at Litchfield in July 1961 (AFN 15:453). It is increasingly found in the northeast United States; there were five reports in Connecticut from 1970 to 1980, of which four were in the month of September (AmB 25:26, 33:30, 34:253, 34:755, 35:158).

Glossy Ibis (*Plegadis falcinellus*)

STATUS: a rare to uncommon coastal migrant and summer visitor from late April to mid-September. In summer it may be fairly common near its nesting areas; very rare inland. It is a sporadic nester at the coast in Norwalk and Stonington. It is very rare in early winter.

Earliest spring arrival: Apr. 9, 1971, 1983; Apr. 11, 1959; Apr. 12, 1928, 1988.

Latest fall departure: Nov. 29, 1985; Nov. 8, 1981; Nov. 6, 1987.

HISTORICAL NOTES: The Glossy Ibis was a regular visitor to Connecticut in the early 1800s. In about 1837 Linsley collected five specimens at Stratford. In 1850 a major influx occurred, and one was collected at Middletown (Sage et al. 1913). Apparently, it was not reported again until April 1928, when one was observed at South Windsor by C. Vibert et al. (Bagg and Eliot 1937). Regularly reported in New England from the mid-1940s, it was locally regular in Connecticut by the 1960s (Bull 1964). The first published nesting report in the state was in 1971, when three pairs were observed at Chimon Island, Norwalk (AmB 25:837).

STORKS (FAMILY CICONIIDAE)

Wood Stork (*Mycteria americana*)

STATUS: an accidental summer vagrant.

RECORDS: The first Connecticut record was an immature photographed at South Windsor June 30–July 6, 1949 (M. French et al., AFN 3:231). An "invasion" occurred in 1955 when two or three different immatures were reported July 8–28 at Bloomfield, July 16 at Portland, and in "mid-July" in Somers (L. Whittles et al., AFN 9:366). However, the account of these sightings published by HAS is different: one was seen at Ellington on July 13 by R. Arnold, and one was present at Bloomfield from July 20 to August 8, seen by many club members. Adding to the confusion, the dates published in RNEB (11:142) differ from the HAS account by including the July 16 sighting at Portland.

SWANS, GEESE, DUCKS (FAMILY ANATIDAE)

Fulvous Whistling-Duck (*Dendrocygna bicolor*)

STATUS: an accidental vagrant. There is one corroborated record: three birds were present May 16–29, 1987, at North Stonington (photographed, N. Weismuller et al., CW 7:45,53).

COMMENTS: Reports of sightings in 1970 at Fairfield and in 1974 at West Hartford are not satisfactorily corroborated.

Tundra Swan (*Cygnus columbianus*)

STATUS: a rare migrant from late October through December and from early March into April; occurs primarily along the coast and the Connecticut River valley. It is casual in midwinter. Accidental in summer: a young bird was observed June 3–5, 1927, at South Windsor by C. Vibert, G. Griswold et al. (HAS) and photographed by T. Burgess (Bagg and Eliot 1937).
   Earliest fall arrival: Oct. 19, 1986; Oct. 30, 1972; Nov. 1, 1973.
   Latest spring departure: Apr. 30, 1917; Apr. 6, 1984; Apr. 3, 1932.

HISTORICAL NOTES: Morton and other early chroniclers suggested that this species occurred in great numbers in migration and winter during the early 1600s (Forbush 1916). Subjected to widespread and intensive hunting, it was "very rare" by the 1800s. Linsley (1843a) recorded it only four times, and Merriam (1877) called it a "rare, almost accidental, visitor." Sightings have increased slightly in recent decades (Griscom and Snyder 1955; Hill 1965). This species has been reported annually since at least 1972, almost always individually or in small numbers, although 25 were present at Madison on November 25, 1978 (AmB 33:155), and *500* were reportedly observed migrating over Wilton on April 6, 1984 (CW 4:63).

Mute Swan (*Cygnus olor*)

STATUS: introduced. A fairly common resident along the coast, and it is locally very common in winter. Inland, it nests on lakes and large rivers but is rare in the northeast hills; it is uncommon in winter in the Connecticut River valley.

HISTORICAL NOTES: This Eurasian native was introduced on Long Island and in the lower Hudson River valley in the late 1880s (NYBBA). By 1921 one flock on the Hudson River contained 26 birds (*Auk* 39:100). Prior to World War I captive birds were kept for ornamental purposes at several Fairfield County estates (W. Finch, pers. comm.) It was first reported in the "wild" in 1936 at Bridgeport, and it was "very rare" at Stamford in 1939 (Hills 1978). In Berlin feral birds were reported before 1935 (Bagg and Eliot 1937). In the 1940s it was a local resident and apparently nested in coastal Fairfield County. In the 1950s it was reported as a "visitor" at eastern New Haven County (Mackenzie) and has since become a widespread nester along the coast. It was first reported in South Windsor in 1955 (HAS) and in the northeast hills in 1962 (Manter 1975). It attempted to nest in New Haven in 1969 (NHBCN 7:2) and succeeded there in 1970; a sighting in South Windsor that same year was termed "rare" (AFN 24:583). In the 1980s its nesting range expanded inland, and nesting was reported north to Salisbury in 1986 (CW 7:10).

Greater White-fronted Goose (*Anser albifrons*)

STATUS: a very rare vagrant from mid-October to early April. As with other unusual waterfowl, the origin of any particular individual is difficult to determine. This species is known to be kept in captivity, and several sightings in the state were of individuals known to have escaped from aviaries or game farms.

HISTORICAL NOTES: Forbush (1916) stated that the White-fronted Goose was formerly an "uncommon" spring and fall migrant, which decreased in numbers from 1845 to 1880 and was thereafter (to at least 1912) an East Coast straggler. The first Connecticut report was of an immature taken off Guilford in 1940 by J. Dolin, but the specimen was not preserved. This was followed by three birds, a male and two females, taken on November 5, 1943, at Westbrook by E. Mulliken (*Auk* 62:309).

SUBSPECIES: The Greenland race *(A. a. flavirostris)* has been documented here several times by photograph and specimen evidence. It can be separated from other races by its yellow-orange rather than pink bill and darker plumage with heavier barring. The race breeding in Canada, *A. a. frontalis,* has occurred on the East Coast (Bull 1974). Additional field work is needed to resolve the question of which subspecies is most apt to be found in Connecticut.

Snow Goose (*Chen caerulescens*)

STATUS: an uncommon migrant from late March into early May and from October to mid-December; it is sometimes abundant during peak migration days in April and November, when large flocks pass overhead. It is usually more frequent in fall. In winter it is rare to uncommon along the coast and very rare inland; casual in summer from June to mid-September.
Earliest fall arrival: Aug. 21, 1967; Sept. 19, 1980; Sept. 24, 1983.
Latest spring departure: June 4, 1986; May 24, 1976; May 17, 1980.

HISTORICAL NOTES: This species was an abundant migrant during the colonial period, when it may have wintered regularly. However, it was "very rare" by the mid-1800s, probably the result of overhunting (Forbush 1925; Bagg and Eliot; Griscom and Snyder; Hill 1965). Sage et al. reported three records from 1876 to 1910. In the 1920s it was "rare" or "casual" (Griscom; Forbush 1925), although some were reported at Glastonbury in 1921 after an absence of many years (*Auk* 40:273). In 1922 a few were found at Portland, East Windsor, and Glastonbury (*Auk* 39:251). It was reported at Greenwich in 1926 after an absence of 20 years (*Auk* 43:363). In the 1930s it was reported regularly as a migrant on Long Island, New York (Cruickshank 1942).

Increasing rapidly after hunting laws were implemented, it was an "abundant" migrant and "rare to uncommon in midwinter" at Long Island, New York, by the 1960s (Bull 1964). Reports increased into the 1970s.

COMMENTS: This species often migrates in large flocks at heights of 2,000 to 3,000 feet, occasionally to 10,000 feet and frequently at night, and thus is often difficult to observe. In fall its migration route is centered along the Connecticut River valley (AmB 27:749, 28:113). It is less frequent in the eastern portions of the state.

In late May, 1968, Mrs. C. Chapin of Old Saybrook discovered a pair of Snow Geese nesting on an island in the estuary of the Connecticut River between Lyme and Old Saybrook. Roger Tory Peterson viewed the nest on June 3, and photographs were taken; none of the eggs hatched, and the adults were not observed after June 23 (BMAS 8:2). This unusual event is difficult to explain as Connecticut is hundreds of miles south of the nearest known nesting area of the species.

SUBSPECIES: The most eastern of the subspecies is the "Greater" Snow Goose (*C. c. atlantica*). Perhaps 95% or more of the Snow Geese sighted in Connecticut are of this race (Bellrose 1976). During the 1970s, only 800 to 1,200 "Lesser" Snow Geese (*C. c. caerulescens*) wintered annually along the East Coast (Bellrose). The blue phase of the "Lesser" Snow Goose (formerly considered a distinct species) is a rare migrant in Connecticut.

Brant (*Branta bernicla*)

STATUS: an uncommon migrant from late March to late May and from mid-October to late November, occasionally into December. It is occasionally abundant on peak migrations days in late April and early November when large flocks pass over the state. In winter it is rare to occasionally very common at the coast; not reported inland. Nonbreeding stragglers are very rare in summer, from mid-June to late September.

Earliest fall arrival: Oct. 5, 1983; Oct. 9, 1978; Oct. 11, 1965.

Latest spring departure: June 16, 1954, 1977; June 13, 1974; June 11, 1950.

HISTORICAL NOTES: Forbush (1916) stated it was one of the most "abundant" of all waterfowl before 1840. Linsley (1843a) said, referring to Stratford, "the brant is common here in winter." However, the southern New England population was reduced by 90% by 1850 (Forbush 1916). In the late 1800s, it was a "common" or "tolerably common" migrant and occasional in winter (Merriam; Wright 1897). Sage et al. listed only five reports from 1893 to 1903 and noted it was a "rare straggler on the Sound in fall and winter."

Beginning in 1931, the destruction of eel grass *(Zostera marina),* the Brants' principal winter food, by a parasite caused a drastic reduction in numbers of Brant. There was speculation that inadequate diet and loss of vigor caused delays in spring migrations during the late 1930s (Cruickshank; Griscom and Snyder; Bull 1964). Brant recovered slightly in the late 1940s and reached pre-1931 numbers by 1953 in New York (Bull). It has since increased during migration and in winter.

COMMENTS: Like the Snow Goose, this species frequently migrates in large flocks at great heights, often at night. Its principal migration route is west of Connecticut from the middle Atlantic coast inland to St. James Bay. A secondary route is from Long Island along the New England coast to the St. Lawrence River estuary (Erskin). A notable example of the latter migration route occurred on December 20, 1981, when 4,188 were observed high above Long Island Sound heading southwest (F. Purnell et al., MFN 9:9).

Barnacle Goose (*Branta leucopsis*)

STATUS: a hypothetical vagrant. This species has been reported in eastern North America from Baffin Island and Labrador to North Carolina; a casual visitor along Atlantic coast from late October to late March.

R. Naylor et al. reported one with a "Richardson's" Canada Goose *(B. canadensis hutchinsii)* and two hybrid juveniles at Southbury from November 22, 1984 to January 10, 1985, in a large flock of Canada Geese (photographed, CW 5:16–18). Other sightings of this species include one in spring and fall 1987 at Preston (CW 8:38), one at Westport in December 1969 (AFN 23:160, 459), and one at Madison on January 29, 1941 (HAS).

COMMENTS: This species is commonly held in captivity in the United States by aviculturalists and zoos; many are known to have escaped and are believed to now migrate with Canada Geese or wander on their own. Therefore, the natural occurrence of the species in Connecticut is open to question. However, recent records from northeastern Canada and reports from the 19th century indicate that some vagrants may reach North America; thus, it is possible that some wild birds might occur in New England (M. Szantyr, CW 5:16).

The circumstances surrounding the Southbury sighting are such that there is a possibility that the Barnacle Goose was wild. This record is unusual enough to warrant publication for future reference and reevaluation.

HISTORICAL NOTES: Linsley (1843a) made reference to an occurrence of this species at Stonington but provided no details.

Canada Goose (*Branta canadensis*)

STATUS: a common to very abundant migrant from March to May and from early September to December. It is fairly common to abundant at the coast in winter and often common inland except during winters with extensive snow cover and ice when it is rare. It is a common and widespread nester throughout the state on the coast and on the shores of ponds, lakes, and streams.

COMMENTS: Concentrations occasionally exceeding 500 birds may occur in winter, particularly at urban parks and golf courses, where the manipulated short-grass habitat is relished by this species. The feeding of these birds by people contributes to their tameness (Converse; Conover and Chasko).

HISTORICAL NOTES: In the early 1600s flocks up to 3,000 birds were occasionally present in midwinter (Forbush 1916). It was "enormously abundant" during the colonial period, principally as a migrant (Hill 1965). It decreased to a "common" migrant, with few birds wintering, by the 1870s (Merriam 1877). Sage et al. (1913) reported only four winter records from 1876 to 1909. In the winter of 1915–1916 W. Smith found 200 in Greenwich (*Auk* 39:462). By the mid-1920s it increased and was a "common to abundant" migrant and "uncommon" in winter in southern New England (Forbush 1925; Howes 1928). The decline and subsequent increase recorded during this period is largely attributable to overhunting in the 1700s and 1800s, followed by protection in 1908. The wintering numbers of Canada Geese have increased significantly from the early 1960s through the 1980s.

In the late 1930s feral birds were reported in the New York City area as year-round residents (Cruickshank 1942). Nine birds in late May 1932 at Fairfield were unusual enough to warrant publication (A. Saunders, *Auk* 53:226). A nonmigratory population was "abundant" at the southwest Connecticut coast by the early 1960s (Bull 1964), and a year-round flock was noted along the "southwestern coast of Connecticut" in 1966 (AFN 20:404). It expanded into the interior highlands, where it has nested since the mid-1950s and was "common" in winter since 1965 (Pink and Waterman 1980). It first nested in Newtown in 1971 (AmB 25:838), and it nested in the Storrs area by the early 1970s (Manter 1975). Expansion was supplemented by Department of Environmental Protection releases and management of breeding habitats.

SUBSPECIES: Most authorities recognize 11 subspecies of Canada Goose (Bellrose 1976). The North Atlantic race *(B. c. canadensis)* is the most common of the wild birds wintering in southern New England. The Mid-Atlantic race *(B. c. interior)* migrates over western Connecticut and principally winters on the Delmarva Peninsula. "Richardson's" Canada Goose *(B. c. hutchinsii)* is occasionally reported in Connecticut (spec., November 12, 1961, Fairfield, plus several sight records). The nonmigratory population largely, if not completely, consists of the introduced "Giant" race, *B. c. maxima*. Bull (1964) mentions that the "Lesser" Canada Goose *(B. c. parvipes)* has been sighted in the New York area in winter but has not been verified by a specimen.

Wood Duck (*Aix sponsa*)

STATUS: an uncommon inland migrant from early March to early May and from late September to November; it is occasionally common in fall. Very rare on Long Island Sound. It usually nests in tree cavities in mature woodlands near fresh water and in man-made nestboxes placed in inland marshes and ponds. In midwinter it is accidental inland (January 9, 1880, Norwich, Bagg and Eliot 1937; winter of 1977–1978, Mansfield, AmB 32:321) and is very rare near the coast.

COMMENTS: An unusually large concentration of 155 birds was reported at South Windsor on September 1, 1970 (AmB 25:34). A waterfowl feeding station at north Stamford attracted large numbers of wintering Wood Ducks during the 1980s; 83 were noted on December 18, 1983.

Wood Duck

HISTORICAL NOTES: Forbush (1916) wrote: "Years ago, [it was the] most abundant of all waterfowl." It was "abundant" or "common" into the 1850s (Cruickshank; Griscom and Snyder 1955). It was "tolerably common" in the 1870s (Merriam 1877) but suffered from overhunting and was "rare" (Cruickshank; Sage et al. 1913) or "scarce" (Job 1922) by about 1910. Hunting pressures compelled the United States and Canada to declare in 1918 a closed hunting season, which continued through 1941 (Kortwright). This species remained generally "very rare" to about 1925 (Howes; Smith; Shipley; Forbush 1925; Bailey 1955).

Protection from hunting, release of captive-reared birds, and the placement of nest boxes contributed to an increase in its population in the 1930s (Bagg and Eliot; Bailey 1955). Some biologists believe that an increase in beavers contributed to its recovery; Wood Ducks are known to favor woodlands bordering beaver ponds as sites for nesting (Ermer). Also, the aging of the state's forests provided additional natural nesting cavities. E. Mulliken (1938) said it was an "abundant breeder and summer resident" and added that it had "increased greatly in recent years." By the early 1960s it was an occasionally very common migrant, local breeder, and a rare winter visitor (Bull 1964).

Green-winged Teal (*Anas crecca*)

STATUS: an uncommon migrant from late March to early May and from late August to December on fresh and brackish ponds and marshes; it is sometimes very common on peak migration days. Individuals occasionally linger through December; it is rare in midwinter. Very rare in summer; since 1980, nesting has been suspected but unproved at Milford and Stratford.

Earliest fall arrival: Aug. 2, 1978; Aug. 12, 1966; Aug. 14, 1975.

Latest spring departure: June 6, 1974; May 31, 1987; May 29, 1973.

HISTORICAL NOTES: This species was a "plentiful" or "common" migrant to about 1850 (Merriam; Bagg and Eliot; Cruickshank 1942; Bull 1964; Hill 1965) and "at times, abundant" (Forbush 1916). Greatly reduced by hunting by the early 1900s, it was called "rare" (Bagg and Eliot; Smith; Cruickshank 1942), "uncommon" (Job 1922), and a "tolerably common" migrant (Sage et al. 1913). Only one winter record was listed by Sage et al. (1913). In 1938 E. Mulliken said it was a "common migrant."

Increasing slowly after hunting laws were implemented, this species became a "common" migrant by the 1940s (Smith; Bagg and Eliot; Cruickshank; Hill 1965). Bull (1964) noted a decline in New York from about 1950 through 1962, but its population has subsequently stabilized; Reynolds (1985) found "no evidence of a decline in survival or recruitment." Two possible nesting pairs were found along the lower Connecticut River in June 1974 (AmB 29:131).

SUBSPECIES: The Eurasian form, "Eurasian Green-winged Teal" *(A. c. crecca),* formerly considered a separate species, is a casual winter visitor to Connecticut.

American Black Duck (*Anas rubripes*)

STATUS: a common migrant throughout the state from early March to late April and from September through December. In winter it is fairly common to abundant at the coast but is generally uncommon inland. It is an uncommon nester in various settings throughout the state, including freshwater and tidal marshes and along ponds, streams, and rivers.

HISTORICAL NOTES: Long prized by duck hunters throughout the northeast, this species decreased from "abundant" or "very abundant" in the 1860s (Merriam; Bagg and Eliot 1937) to "common or uncommon" in migration and "rare" in summer by 1913 (Forbush 1916; Sage et al.

1913). Hunting restrictions imposed in 1908 contributed to an increase after 1915 (Bagg and Eliot 1937). Inland in the 1930s, it was "very common" in migration, "common" in summer, and "local" in winter (Bagg and Eliot 1937). Mulliken (1938) said it was an "abundant breeder" statewide. Bull (1964) noted it was an abundant winter visitor at the coast and a fairly common to locally common nester. It has decreased in recent years, probably the result of habitat loss, hybridization with mallards, overhunting, ingestion of lead shot, acid rain effects on food supply, or a combination thereof (NYBBA).

Mallard (*Anas platyrhynchos*)

STATUS: a common resident in salt- and freshwater marshes, ponds, and streams. It is a common to abundant migrant from March to late April and from late September to mid-November. Inland, its numbers vary in winter, but it is often fairly common.

COMMENTS: Releases of captive birds have established a nonmigratory population that is "semidomesticated." These local birds are augmented in late fall and winter by the truly wild population that nests far north and west of Connecticut.

HISTORICAL NOTES: In the 1860s this species was a "very rare" visitor from the west (Hill 1965) and was not known to nest in Connecticut. From the 1870s to about 1890, Wright (1897), Sage et al. (1913), and Howes (1928) called it a "rare" fall migrant. It was first reported in the northeast hills in 1892 (Manter 1975). Shortly after 1900 many were pen-raised and released; by then it was an "uncommon" fall migrant and occasional in winter (Sage et al.; Bagg and Eliot 1937). By 1908 it was regular in fall and spring in Litchfield County (Job 1922). It was believed to have nested in the "wild" at Fairfield in 1921 (Hills 1978). Increasing both as a nester and winter visitor, it was occasionally locally "common" by the mid-1920s (Forbush 1925) and continued to increase in the 1930s (Bull 1964). By 1937 Bagg and Eliot called it "uncommon" to "fairly common" in migration, occasional as a nester and uncommon in winter. By 1938 successful "restocking" had occurred at several locations in the state (Mulliken 1938). Cruickshank (1942) reported that 100 migrants a day could be seen in nearby New York. By the early 1960s it was a resident, reflecting a rapid increase, and also was common to locally abundant in late fall and winter (Bull 1964).

This species frequently hybridizes with American Black Ducks, and hybrids are fairly common in the state.

Northern Pintail (*Anas acuta*)

STATUS: an uncommon to fairly common migrant in March and April and from late September to mid-November. It is rare to uncommon in winter along the coast at marshes and shallow ponds and at brackish ponds and estuaries. Nonbreeding stragglers are very rare in summer.

Earliest fall arrival: Aug. 17, 1966; Aug. 20, 1972; Aug. 25, 1986.

Latest spring departure: May 23, 1959; May 17 1939 1954; May 14, 1950.

HISTORICAL NOTES: In southern New England the Northern Pintail was an "abundant" migrant into the mid-1850s but suffered from hunting and was "rare" by the early 1900s (Bagg and Eliot; Hill 1965). Merriam (1877) provided few reports but noted that it was a "rather common" migrant at the mouth of the Connecticut River. It was described by Sage et al. (1913) as formerly a "rare" fall straggler, increasing after 1903 and occasionally wintering. Fall birds were noted in 1913 and 1919 (*Auk* 38:582). It has increased markedly since the 1920s after hunting laws were implemented (Cruickshank; Griscom and Snyder; Bull 1964). A. Saunders reported 38 in Fairfield on November 3, 1938 (Hills 1978). E. Mulliken (1938) said it was a "locally common migrant," particularly along the lower Connecticut and Housatonic rivers.

Blue-winged Teal (*Anas discors*)

STATUS: an uncommon migrant from late March to mid-May and from mid-August to late October; it is occasionally very common during peak migration days in early October. It is very rare in December. Accidental in midwinter: four were seen on February 22, 1956, at Old Lyme (RNEB 12:3); seven on January 2, 1965 (P. Spofford, West Haven, AFN 20:134); one on January 1, 1983, at Groton (CW 3:23); one on January 21, 1984, at Westport (CW 4:36); and one wintered in 1977–1978 at Manchester (R. Craig, AmB 32:321). Reports of nesting in the 1980s in large inland marshes at Durham, South Windsor, and Litchfield lack documentation; additional fieldwork is needed to determine the nesting status of this species in the state.

Earliest spring arrival: Mar. 10, 1974; Mar. 11, 1976; Mar. 13, 1982.

Latest spring departure: May 24, 1980; May 22, 1954; May 21, 1976.

Earliest fall arrival: July 18, 1977; July 24, 1960; July 28, 1980.

Latest fall departure: Dec. 29, 1985; Dec. 19, 1982; Nov. 17, 1955.

HISTORICAL NOTES: Forbush (1916) noted that the Blue-winged Teal was once one of the most numerous ducks in New England, even more abundant than the Green-winged Teal. It was an "abundant" New England migrant and nester to about 1850 (Forbush 1916; Bagg and Eliot; Hill 1965). Hunting pressures and the loss of many inland marshes certainly contributed to its decline: in the 1870s it was a "common" fall migrant (Merriam 1877) but was "rare" by 1910 (Griscom and Snyder 1955). An increase in the migrant population was noted in the 1920s, probably the result of hunting restrictions (Forbush 1925). In 1938 E. Mulliken said it was a "less common [migrant] in Connecticut than in recent years."

There are few documented nesting reports of Blue-winged Teal in Connecticut in this century. It may have nested at South Windsor in 1931; C. Vibert confirmed it there in 1934 (*Auk* 51:512). It "apparently nested" on the Mianus River near Stamford in 1935 (BL 37:464). It was called a "local summer resident" in the Hartford area in 1964 (HAS). It remains a sporadic and very rare nester in the state.

Northern Shoveler (*Anas clypeata*)

STATUS: a rare migrant from mid-March to late May and from early September to mid-November, chiefly along the coast; very rare inland. In winter it is usually rare at the coast and very rare inland. Occasionally, nonbreeding individuals are reported in summer.

HISTORICAL NOTES: Forbush (1916) noted the Northern Shoveler was "probably much more numerous in New England in the early days of settlement." Apparently, a decline in its population began after 1860 (Forbush 1916). Merriam (1877) called it a "rare" migrant, although G. B. Grinnell said it was "not particularly rare" in October. In 1908, Job (1922) said it was "formerly a common duck . . . now rare." Sage et al. (1913) listed only seven records from 1854 to 1894. It was "very rare" from 1890 to the early 1920s (Howes; Bagg and Eliot; Griscom and Snyder; Cruickshank 1942), with a single bird collected in October of 1916 (*Auk* 38:582). It increased somewhat thereafter (Forbush 1925; Griscom and Snyder; Bull 1964).

Gadwall (*Anas strepera*)

STATUS: an uncommon migrant from late March to mid-May and from mid-August to mid-November, primarily at the coast; it is occasionally common during peak migration days in fall. In winter it is usually rare to uncommon on the western coast but is fairly common east of Guilford, favoring brackish water and estuaries; very rare inland in winter. It is a rare to locally uncommon nester along the coast.

HISTORICAL NOTES: In August 1842 Linsley reported "flocks" of this species during migration at Stratford. Forbush (1916) wrote that it was "not uncommon" to 1850, and Merriam (1877) considered it "not a common" migrant in the 1870s. Sage et al. (1913) mentions only three records from 1883 to 1912, and Job (1922) said that by 1900 it was "one of the rarest ducks." In the 1920s Forbush (1925) considered it "rare" in migration and "casual" in winter. Slightly increasing by 1930 (Bagg and Eliot; Griscom and Snyder; Hill 1965), it was more apparent through the 1940s and very noticeable thereafter (Cruickshank; Bull 1964).

It first nested in New York in 1947 (Bull). The first nesting in Connecticut was noted in 1972, when D. Finch reported "now breeds commonly at Barn Island in Stonington" (AmB 26:834), although possibly nesting pairs were reported as early as 1931 (Bagg and Eliot 1937) and at Stratford in 1972 (AmB 26:838). In 1974 it was noted that "southern New England's recently established Gadwalls continue to increase" (AmB 28:113).

Eurasian Wigeon (*Anas penelope*)

STATUS: a rare coastal visitor from Europe, chiefly in winter but occasionally during migration; most apt to be seen from late October to April among flocks of American Wigeon. Accidental inland: one was at Cheshire on November 2, 1958 (French, AFN 13:14); one was at Oxford on December 14, 1974 (H. Crandall and K. Mitchell, AmB 29:240); one was observed at South Windsor March 3–28, 1985, and another there on March 23, 1986 (P. Desjardins, pers. comm.). Accidental in summer: one was seen at Greenwich on June 24, 1931, by R. Burdsall (Shipley 1931).

Earliest fall arrival: Oct. 1, 1952; Oct. 12, 1938; Oct. 17, 1971.

Latest spring departure: May 8, 1988; Apr. 10, 1971; Apr. 7, 1931.

HISTORICAL NOTES: Regionally, it was an "accidental" visitor before 1900 but was numerous from the 1930s to 1953 (Bull 1964); less frequent since 1953. The first Connecticut record was on January 2, 1920, at Westbrook (E. Tullock, *Auk* 38:583), and the second was on January 3, 1931, at Greenwich (R. T. Peterson, BL 33:127).

American Wigeon (*Anas americana*)

STATUS: a fairly common migrant from early March to early May and from early September through December; it is occasionally abundant during peak migration days in November and early December, particularly along the coast. In winter it is uncommon to abundant in coastal ponds and estuaries; variable but usually uncommon inland.

Earliest fall arrival: Aug. 8, 1984; Aug. 9, 1975; Aug. 12, 1927.

Latest spring departure: May 20, 1973; May 19, 1946, 1975; May 18, 1981.

HISTORICAL NOTES: Apparently numerous before 1800, this handsome species decreased rapidly after 1870 (Griscom and Snyder 1955). Merriam (1877) noted that it was "not particularly rare during migrations" and that it "may winter." Forbush (1916) called it one of the "rarest" southern New England dabbling ducks at the turn of the century. Job (1922) mentioned it was a "scarce migrant" and Sage et al. (1913) said it was "rare" in winter. It was rare enough to compel L. Bishop to publish reports of it in November 1913 and October 1915 (*Auk* 38:582). It increased locally in winter from the early 1920s (Forbush 1925; Bagg and Eliot; Shipley; Cruickshank 1942); in 1927 a flock of about 3,000 birds wintered in Niantic Bay (YPM records). Noticeable growth as a migrant and winter visitor has occurred since 1948 (Griscom and Snyder; Bull 1964; Hill 1965).

This species is currently expanding its nesting range southeastward from Canada. It first nested in western Pennsylvania in 1936 and in western New York in 1954. It nested on Long Island in 1961 and in the lower Hudson River valley in 1974 (NYBBA).

Canvasback (*Aythya valisineria*)

STATUS: a fairly common coastal migrant from March to late April and from late October to early December; it can be locally abundant in late March and mid-November. In winter it is usually uncommon but may be locally abundant in brackish waters and estuaries. Inland it is rare to uncommon in migration. Nonbreeding stragglers are casual in summer from mid-May to October.

Earliest fall arrival: Oct. 14, 1988; Oct. 15, 1943, 1972; Oct. 17, 1982.

Latest spring departure: May 15, 1980; May 9, 1976; May 8, 1975.

HISTORICAL NOTES: The Canvasback was probably a scarce migrant in the early 1800s. Linsley (1843a) listed only two reports of this species. It was a "rare" fall migrant and "straggler" in the late 1800s (Merriam; Averill; Forbush 1916). Sage et al. (1913) called it a "very rare accidental winter visitor" and listed seven records in 35 years.

It slowly increased regionally after 1908 (Griscom and Snyder; Forbush 1916; Bagg and Eliot; Hill 1965) with records noted in the state in 1912, 1914, and 1917 (*Auk* 38:582). By the 1920s it remained "rarer" than Redhead in the New York City area (Griscom). It was unreported in the Stamford area by Howes (1928) but increased in the 1930s and was somewhat stabilized by about 1940 (Hill; Griscom and Snyder; Bellrose 1976). In the early 1960s it was a "common to locally very abundant visitant" along the western coast (Bull) but was "unaccountably rare" in the Guilford area although found in "large rafts" further east (Mackenzie). In 1978 P. Vickery wrote that "there seems little question that Canvasbacks have increased their numbers in southern New England" (AmB 33:155).

Redhead (*Aythya americana*)

STATUS: a rare to occasionally uncommon coastal migrant from March to mid-April and from late October through December. Inland it is a rare migrant. In winter it is rare on western Long Island Sound, increasing to uncommon eastward; rare inland.

Earliest fall arrival: Oct. 10, 1976; Oct. 13, 1945; Oct. 14, 1967, 1983.
Latest spring departure: May 7, 1922; May 6, 1927; Apr. 20, 1972.

HISTORICAL NOTES: This species was "very abundant" in southern New England during the early colonial period (Bailey 1955). However, it was "rare" in the 1870s in Connecticut (Merriam 1877) and "very rare" just before 1900 (Sage et al. 1913). An increase was noted during the first two decades of the 1900s (Sage et al.; Howes 1928), but its numbers fluctuated thereafter. It was not numerous in the 1930s (Cruickshank 1942). Mulliken (1938) said "in recent years [it] decreased from a more or less common migrant in the lower Connecticut River . . . now considered rare." As a migrant, it may have decreased during this century (Griscom and Snyder 1955), although wintering birds have increased locally in southeastern New England since about 1949 (Hill 1965). Apparently, it increased in the 1970s as an inland migrant (Pink and Waterman 1980).

COMMENTS: An unusually large concentration occurred on February 26, 1949, when A. Saunders counted 42 on an Easton lake (Hills 1978).

Ring-necked Duck (*Aythya collaris*)

STATUS: a fairly common inland migrant from early March to mid-April and from late October to early December, particularly on large rivers and lakes; it is sometimes abundant on peak migration days in early November. Rare on brackish and salt water. In winter its numbers vary depending on the amount of ice on ponds, lakes, and large rivers;

it is usually uncommon to fairly common. It is casual in summer from mid-May to October.

Earliest fall arrival: Sept. 24, 1966; Sept. 27, 1982; Oct. 1, 1983.

Latest spring departure: May 23, 1984; May 15, 1943, 1988; May 4, 1940.

HISTORICAL NOTES: This species may have been numerous in the colonial period (Forbush 1916), but it was a "very rare" migrant in the 1800s (Griscom and Snyder; Hill 1965). Sage et al. (1913) said it was "accidental" and listed six records from 1883 to 1898. It was "not ordinarily to be found" in the New Haven area (Honeywill et al. 1908). Two females collected on October 29, 1919, were worthy of publication (*Auk* 38:582). In the mid-1920s it was "not so rare as Gadwall or the Shoveller" but "occurs less often than European Widgeon" (Forbush 1925). It was not a regular spring migrant in the state until 1930 (*Auk* 56:134). Steadily increasing since the early 1930s (Shipley; Bagg and Eliot; Cruickshank; Griscom and Snyder; Bailey 1955; Bull 1964; Manter; Pink and Waterman 1980), it began wintering in the state in the early 1960s.

COMMENTS: A large concentration of this species was recorded on October 25, 1979, when 625 were counted on Laurel Reservoir in Stamford (MFN 7:9).

Tufted Duck (*Aythya fuligula*)

STATUS: a hypothetical vagrant from Eurasia, casual in New England in winter and spring.

RECORDS: There are three reports of this species in the state but none accompanied by photographic or specimen evidence. One was seen on November 11, 1956, at Niantic (G. T. Austin et al., WB 81:332); a male was seen from January 11 to February 7, 1971 at New London and Groton (G. Bissell, J. Slater, et al., AmB 25:548); and one was seen on November 8, 1975, at Lakeville (Salisbury) by W. R. Peterson (AmB 30:30).

COMMENTS: A male that exhibited the plumage characteristics of a hybrid Scaup species-X Tufted Duck was present at West Haven from January 20 to February 20, 1984 (AmB 38:293, CW 4:36, pers. obs.). The origin of individuals appearing in New England is difficult to determine; this species is a popular aviary resident.

Greater Scaup (*Aythya marila*)

STATUS: a common coastal migrant from March to mid-May and from early October through December; frequently found in offshore congregations of greater than 250 individuals, sometimes larger. Inland it is rare to occasionally uncommon during migration. In winter it is fairly common to locally abundant at the coast but irregular and rare inland. Nonbreeding individuals occasionally linger in summer along the coast.

Earliest fall arrival: Aug. 17, 1966; Sept. 5, 1886; Sept. 15, 1984.

Latest spring departure: June 17, 1979, 1974; June 4, 1982.

HISTORICAL NOTES: The wintering population of this well-known diving duck declined 50% to 90% from 1880 to 1908 in southern New England (Forbush 1916), when flocks of up to 1,000 birds still occurred on Long Island Sound. It was a "common visitor to the larger lakes" in Litchfield in 1908 (Job 1922) and a "common" winter visitor at the coast (Sage et al., 1913). It increased markedly prior to the early 1930s (Bagg and Eliot; Hill 1965). E. Mulliken (1938) called it "the most abundant of all the ducks in Connecticut." In January 1948 the U.S. Fish and Wildlife Service counted 51,000 scaup statewide by aerial survey. In late December 1957 more than 16,000 were counted off Westport (AFN 12:264), and Bull (1964) called it a "very abundant" winter visitor. Other high counts include 8,000 at New Haven Harbor in March 1971. Recent data suggest that a significant decline in winter numbers has occurred since about 1960, particularly along the western Sound (SCCC).

Lesser Scaup (*Aythya affinis*)

STATUS: an uncommon to locally fairly common migrant from early March to mid-April and from late October to early December; usually rare to uncommon inland. Variable in winter; usually rare but occasionally fairly common. Accidental in summer: one was seen from July 1 through September 1917 at South Windsor (HAS); another was there on July 18, 1931 (Bagg and Eliot 1937); and one thought to be oiled was observed at West Haven on July 16 through August 19, 1967 (RNEB 23:7).

Earliest fall arrival: Sept. 27, 1975; Oct. 2, 1986; Oct. 4, 1971.

Latest spring departure: May 10, 1926; May 7, 1934; May 4, 1935.

COMMENTS: It prefers freshwater ponds and lakes but is frequently sighted on brackish and salt water, especially in winter. Both species of scaup may occur together on inland lakes and at the coast. Confusion with Greater Scaup has resulted in an incomplete understanding of its actual numbers; it may be more common than generally thought.

HISTORICAL NOTES: Merriam (1877) called this species a "common winter resident." It declined 25% to 50% in Massachusetts by the early 1900s (Forbush 1916). In the late 1920s it was variously called "tolerably common," "not uncommon," and "uncommon" (Forbush 1925; Sage et al. 1913; Howes 1928); it sharply decreased thereafter (Griscom and Snyder; Bagg and Eliot; Cruickshank 1942). In the 1980s further declines have been noted (SCCC).

Common Eider (*Somateria mollissima*)

STATUS: a very rare winter visitor from mid-October to occasionally as late as April on Long Island Sound east of Guilford; casual on the western Sound. There are no corroborated inland reports.

Earliest fall arrival: Sept. 18, 1988; Sept. 19, 1986; Sept. 30, 1971.

Latest spring departure: May 29, 1887 (spec.); Apr. 28, 1968; Apr. 14, 1954.

HISTORICAL NOTES: Presumably abundant in the North Atlantic before 1850, it nested south to Boston in early 1880s (Forbush 1916). This northern species was probably never abundant in historic times on Long Island Sound: Sage et al. (1913) listed five records from before 1843 to 1909 in Connecticut. Griscom and Snyder (1955) noted a decline of winter numbers in Massachusetts during the early part of this century, followed by an increase after 1940. Bull (1964) reported "it has increased greatly since 1942" along eastern Long Island and was more abundant than King Eider in New York by the 1960s. On December 27, 1955, 20 were counted in the New London area (AFN 10:81).

SUBSPECIES: Both the American race *(S. m. dresseri)* and the northern race *(S. m. borealis)* have been found in Connecticut *(Auk* 47:93). Occurrences of the northern race in the state have been very infrequent. It is not readily separable in the field.

King Eider (*Somateria spectabilis*)

STATUS: a rare winter visitor and migrant on Long Island Sound from late November to mid-May. Casual in summer: there are at least seven records of individuals lingering on the Sound from June through August. Accidental inland: one was collected at Portland on November 17, 1886 (Sage et al. 1913), and one was seen at South Windsor January 20–22, 1919 (HAS; Bagg and Eliot 1937).

Earliest fall arrival: Oct. 22, 1890 (spec.); Nov. 11, 1893 (spec.); Nov. 17, 1886 (spec.).

Latest spring departure: May 30, 1978 (spec.); May 26, 1934; May 22, 1949.

HISTORICAL NOTES: Forbush (1925) said it was formerly "not rare in migration in Connecticut." Sage et al. (1913) list 12 records from

1876 to 1910. Griscom and Snyder (1955) stated it was "rarer before 1936." Bull (1964) noted it was reported "occasionally on Long Island Sound, although rare at the west end," and added that its numbers have remained stable in recent decades.

COMMENTS: In late April and May, King Eiders occasionally accompany migrating flocks of White-winged Scoters flying west over Long Island Sound (MFN 10:4, 11:3, 12:3).

Labrador Duck (*Camptorhynchus labradorius*)

STATUS: extinct; formerly occurred in winter on the Atlantic coast south to Long Island and possibly New Jersey (Bent 1925).

COMMENTS: This species was once present on Long Island Sound. Linsley (1843a) collected a specimen at Stratford; its present disposition is not known. Also, a specimen was sent "from Connecticut to Mrs. Blackburn in England" (T. Pennant, 1785, *Arctic Zoology*, 2:559). The whereabouts of this specimen is also unknown. Merriam (1877) described this species as "a very rare winter visitor"—probably referring only to Linsley's record.

Harlequin Duck (*Histrionicus histrionicus*)

STATUS: a very rare winter visitor and migrant on Long Island Sound. Although this species is regionally reported from October to May, most Connecticut reports are in November and December. It is accidental inland: one was seen at Winsted (Winchester) in October 1901 or 1902 by W. Parsons (Job 1922); and a male and female were seen on Bantam Lake in Litchfield on November 12, 1958, by Mrs. S. Lincoln and G. Loery (COAR). Accidental in summer: an oiled bird was present from August 6 to September 7, 1967, at West Haven (RNEB 23:8).
  Earliest fall arrival: Nov. 4, 1986; Nov. 7, 1967; Nov. 12, 1958.
  Latest spring departure: June 6, 1983; June 2, 1957; May 15, 1965.

HISTORICAL NOTES: Before 1840 this handsome duck was "common" in New England and summered as far south as Maine but was "rare" thereafter (Forbush 1916). There are at least 20 published sightings in Connecticut waters from 1900 to 1989.

Oldsquaw (*Clangula hyemalis*)

STATUS: a common coastal migrant from March to early April and from late October to December; it is sometimes abundant during peak

Oldsquaw

migration days in late March and late November. It is very rare inland. It is usually very common in winter on Long Island Sound. Very rare in summer. Nonbreeding individuals sometimes linger along the coast.

Earliest fall arrival: Sept. 23, 1984; Oct. 14, 1905; Oct. 15, 1890.

Latest spring departure: June 22, 1971; June 14, 1973; May 30, 1954.

HISTORICAL NOTES: This long-tailed diver was found in immense flocks during the early 1800s (Forbush 1916). Merriam (1877) noted it was "common" in winter and "particularly abundant during the migrations." Merriam also reported that in November "hundreds of thousands can be seen on the Sound, covering the water as far as the eye can reach in every direction, and almost deafening one by their constant . . . cackle," adding that it was "by far the most abundant duck found along our coast." During the late 1800s it was locally "common" (Averill, Wright 1897) and declined noticeably from 1880 to after 1910 (Forbush 1916). Yet it remained "abundant in winter" and was most numerous on the eastern portion of the Sound (Sage et al. 1913).

In the 1920s it was an "abundant migrant, common winter resident" (Forbush 1925) and "formerly fairly common, now rare" on the western Sound (Griscom). Griscom and Snyder (1955) noted that since the 1920s numbers of Oldsquaw have not matched those of pre-1900.

E. Mulliken (1938) said it was a "common" migrant and winter visitor. By the early 1960s it had become a "common to occasionally very abundant winter visitant on Long Island Sound" (Bull 1964). Waterfowl surveys conducted by the Connecticut Department of Environmental Protection show a decrease in midwinter numbers of Oldsquaw in the 1980s.

Black Scoter *(Melanitta nigra)*

STATUS: the least numerous of the scoters, this species is a rare to uncommon coastal migrant and winter visitor from October to mid-April; it can be fairly common in the eastern portions of the Sound during peak migration days in late October and late March. It is very rare inland on large lakes. Accidental in summer: one was seen on August 19, 1986, at West Haven (CW 7:23), three were observed on June 10, 1982, at New Hartford (P. Desjardins, pers. comm.), and one was observed on June 12, 1953, at Guilford (Mackenzie 1961).

Earliest fall arrival: Sept. 21, 1957; Oct. 1, 1967; Oct. 2, 1893.

Latest spring departure: May 25, 1954; May 17, 1950; Apr. 30, 1950.

HISTORICAL NOTES: Forbush (1916) said that Black Scoters declined more before 1890 than the other scoters. In the 1870s it was a "tolerably common" winter resident (Merriam 1877) but was "uncommon" by the 1890s (Averill 1892). Sage et al. (1913) called it a "rare fall migrant" and mentioned only 11 reports from 1879 to 1909, 10 of which were in October and 1 in April. In the 1920s it was "uncommon in Connecticut in migration" (Forbush 1925) but unreported on western Long Island Sound (Griscom; Howes 1928). On October 22, 1933, a late night fog caused the grounding of more than 300 birds at Norfolk, and many died (*Auk* 51:228). Mulliken (1938) said it was "not common" on Long Island Sound. Offshore of Massachusetts its numbers remained stable from 1935 to 1960 (Hill 1965). Cruickshank (1942) noted that Black Scoters were much less common on western Long Island Sound than on the eastern portion in the 1940s. In the early 1960s it was "common to locally abundant migrant and winter visitor on . . . Long Island Sound" (Bull 1964), less frequently encountered since.

Surf Scoter *(Melanitta perspicillata)*

STATUS: an uncommon migrant and winter visitor on Long Island Sound from October to late April; it can be common during peak migration days in November and March. It is generally more numerous on the eastern portions of the Sound. It is a very rare inland migrant. Nonbreeding stragglers are very rare in summer on Long Island Sound.

Earliest fall arrival: Sept. 17, 1966; Sept. 18, 1891; Sept. 21, 1957.
Latest spring departure: May 27, 1972; May 25, 1954; May 20, 1966.

HISTORICAL NOTES: Forbush (1916) said it was formerly the most numerous of the scoters, "although the White-wing is a close second." Merriam (1877), Averill (1892), and Sage et al. (1913) all noted it was a "common winter resident" on Long Island Sound. In about 1915 the winter population (centered off Rhode Island and Massachusetts) collapsed to 10 to 20% of its former numbers (Forbush 1925; Hill 1965). Its population apparently stabilized in the 1920s and 1930s: Mulliken (1938) said it was "abundant" and Cruickshank (1942) said it was "a very common winter visitant on . . . all but the extreme western end of Long Island Sound." Griscom and Snyder (1955) said it remained "much less" numerous than the White-winged Scoter. In the 1960s it was a "common to very abundant migrant and winter visitor on . . . Long Island Sound, particularly at the eastern end" (Bull 1964).

White-winged Scoter (*Melanitta fusca*)

STATUS: a fairly common migrant on Long Island Sound from mid-April to early May and from mid-October to late November; it is occasionally abundant on peak migration days in late October, November, and early May. It is generally common in winter but is uncommon on western Long Island Sound. In summer nonbreeding stragglers are rare along the coast. Inland it occurs regularly in migration but is rarely detected because of nocturnal flights.

Earliest fall arrival: Sept. 12, 1942; Sept. 13, 1959, 1964; Sept. 18, 1966.

Latest spring departure: June 2, 1950; June 1, 1936; May 30, 1954.

COMMENTS: During fall migration there is an eastward movement along Long Island Sound. In spring migrating flocks move westward along the coast and head inland in the early evening if favorable southerly winds are present.

HISTORICAL NOTES: This species has fluctuated in numbers during the past two centuries. Forbush (1916) described a 50% decline in numbers from 1840 to 1890, although Merriam (1877) noted it was "extremely abundant in migration" with "some remaining throughout the winter." Averill (1892) and Sage et al. (1913) called it a "common winter resident" in the 1890s and early 1900s. Forbush (1925) noted it was "common to abundant" in maritime New England. However, Griscom (1923) called it "rare" on western Long Island Sound. Howes

(1928) said it was "very common" in the Stamford area, as did Shipley (1931). Hill (1965) said the White-winged Scoter population remained stable from about 1940 to 1965. CruickshanK (1942) said it was "fairly common" on the western Sound and "common eastward." About 12,000 were counted on December 22, 1946, at Fairfield (Hills 1978), and on October 24, 1953, 20,000 were counted at Clinton (RNEB 9:224). Bull (1964) noted it was "very abundant" in migration and during winter on the Sound.

A study of Connecticut Christmas Bird Count data and a review of the Connecticut Department of Environmental Protection aerial surveys reveals that a significant decline in winter numbers has occurred, beginning in about 1964 and continuing through the 1980s.

Common Goldeneye (*Bucephala clangula*)

STATUS: a common migrant and winter visitor on Long Island Sound from early November to mid-April; it is sometimes abundant on peak migration days in early December and mid-March. In winter it is fairly common to very common on the coast. Inland it is sometimes common on large lakes during migration and winter. In summer nonbreeding stragglers are rare on the Sound.

Earliest fall arrival: Oct. 17, 1954; Oct. 23, 1977; Oct. 24, 1976.

Latest spring departure: June 10, 1955; June 6, 1964; June 4, 1966.

HISTORICAL NOTES: The wintering population of this species declined from about 1850 to 1900 (Hill 1965); it was "tolerably common" or "uncommon" on Long Island Sound in winter after 1900 (Sage et al., 1913; Howes 1928). Mulliken (1938) said it was "abundant" on the Sound and inland on large rivers and lakes. Increasing, it became a "common to very abundant winter visitor on Long Island Sound and adjacent bays" by the early 1960s (Bull 1964).

Barrow's Goldeneye (*Bucephala islandica*)

STATUS: a very rare winter visitor on Long Island Sound from mid-November to late March. Most sightings are in larger estuaries, where freshwater rivers meet Long Island Sound. It has not been reported west of Westport. It is accidental inland: a drake with an unidentified female was reported at South Windsor on November 19, 1939, by M. Hoffman et al. (*Auk* 57:244), and a drake was reported about 7 miles inland at Woodbridge March 25–27, 1976, by N. Proctor et al. (AmB 30:691).

Earliest fall arrival: Nov. 14, 1867; Nov. 19, 1939; Nov. 28, 1987.
Latest spring departure: Mar. 27, 1926, 1976; Mar. 23, 1985; Mar. 21, 1937, 1974.

HISTORICAL NOTES: Linsley did not mention this species. Merriam (1877) called it "a rare winter visitant" and reported that a male was purchased by John H. Sage on November 14, 1867, "from a man who said it was killed on the Sound." Sage et al. (1913) listed the Merriam account and added that two males were taken at Lake Saltonstall, East Haven, on December 25, 1883, but "unfortunately were not preserved." On March 21, 1937, A. Saunders reported a pair at Fairfield (Bagg and Eliot). S. Broker (*The status of Barrow's Goldeneye in Connecticut,* CW 4:56–62) lists 18 reports from 1939 to 1984.

Bufflehead (*Bucephala albeola*)

STATUS: a common migrant and winter visitor on lakes, rivers, and coastal embayments form mid-October to May; it is occasionally abundant during peak migration days in November and April. Nonbreeding stragglers sometimes linger in summer through August.
Earliest fall arrival: Sept. 12, 1898; Sept. 27, 1941; Sept. 29, 1880 (spec.).
Latest spring departure: June 10, 1954; June 2, 1957; May 25, 1974.

HISTORICAL NOTES: The wintering population of this species declined after 1875 (Forbush 1916). It was a "common winter resident" in the 1870s and 1890s (Merriam; Averill 1892). Sage et al. (1913) reported it was "formerly an abundant winter resident . . . now not more than tolerably common." In the winter of 1916–1917 small flocks were noted that were joined by migrants in the spring (*Auk* 35:340). In the early 1920s it was "rare on the Sound" (Griscom; Cruickshank 1942); increasing in the mid-1920s (Bellrose 1976), it became "common" in the late 1920s (Howes 1928). Growing steadily from the early 1930s, it became "uncommon, but regular" by the early 1940s (Cruickshank 1942; Griscom and Snyder; Hill; Bellrose 1976). It was a "locally common to abundant winter visitant" on the western Sound in the early 1960s (Bull 1964). According to the Connecticut Department of Environmental Protection aerial surveys, its numbers in winter have remained stable in the 1970s and 1980s.

Bagg and Eliot (1937) speculated that it formerly nested in the northeastern United States.

Hooded Merganser (*Lophodytes cucullatus*)

STATUS: an uncommon migrant on larger ponds, lakes, and brackish waters from mid-October to early December and from mid-March to late April; it may be fairly common in early November and late March. In winter it is generally uncommon on the coast, less frequent inland. It is a rare to locally uncommon nester in freshwater swamps and marshes in the northwest hills and along the Connecticut River.

Earliest fall arrival: Sept. 1, 1975; Sept. 4, 1966; Sept. 16, 1978.
Latest spring departure: June 30, 1981; June 14, 1957; June 13, 1937.

HISTORICAL NOTES: Until 1900 the combination of fewer nesting trees and unrestricted hunting accounted for the scarcity of this colorful species throughout its range (Palmer 1976). In the 1870s it was "not common" in winter in Connecticut (Merriam 1877) but decreased to "rare" in the 1890s (Averill 1892). By the early 1900s it was a "rare and irregular" migrant (Sage et. al. 1913). Griscom (1923) reported an increase in the New York City area from about 1919, where it was "very rare." In Connecticut it was an "uncommon migrant and rare in winter" in the 1920s (Forbush 1925). It increased steadily through the 1940s (Cruickshank 1942) into the 1950s (Bailey 1955; Griscom and Snyder 1955). By the 1960s it was "locally common to very common" in winter and during migration (Bull 1964).

It reportedly nested at Winsted (Winchester) in about 1893 (Job 1922), and a female with six young was found at Farmington on June 13, 1937 (*Auk* 55:123). It was believed to have nested in 1957 at Falls Village (Canaan), when "actions indicated that young were in the vicinity" (AFN 11:391). Definite nesting was reported in 1963 at Litchfield (AFN 17:450), and possible nesting was noted at Litchfield in 1966 (AFN 20:555). Nesting was confirmed at New Fairfield in 1968 (L. Pierson, pers. comm.). Nesting has subsequently been reported annually in summer in the northwest hills and on the Connecticut River.

Common Merganser (*Mergus merganser*)

STATUS: a fairly common migrant and winter visitor on large rivers, especially the Connecticut River, and lakes from mid-November to late April; it is sometimes very common on peak migration days in late March and from late November to early December. In winter its numbers may vary, depending on the amount of ice on lakes and rivers. It is rare on salt water. A rare nester in the northern Farmington River watershed.

Earliest fall arrival: Sept. 24, 1961; Oct. 9, 1951, 1965; Oct. 21, 1973.
Latest spring departure: May 28, 1953; May 25, 1949; May 18, 1955.

HISTORICAL NOTES: The status of this large diving duck before the mid-1800s is unknown. Forbush (1916) noted a decrease in its numbers during the late 1800s. Sage et al. (1913) said it was "tolerably common" from December through February, but to April in Litchfield County and the Connecticut River, possibly indicating that birds attempted to nest at those locations. In 1938 E. Mulliken said it was "abundant" in migration and winter. In Massachusetts, Hill (1965) noted a gradual increase in winter since 1935. Bull (1964) suggested that it lingered later in the spring than it did prior to 1900.

Apparently, it first nested in Connecticut in 1962 at Barkhamsted Reservoir (M. Kittredge, AFN 16:462). In the 1980s breeding has been confirmed there several times; nesting in New Milford and Kent is suspected but uncorroborated.

Red-breasted Merganser (*Mergus serrator*)

STATUS: a common coastal migrant and winter visitor from mid-October to mid-May; it is occasionally abundant on peak migration days in March and late November. Inland it is rare except on the lower Connecticut River, where it may be uncommon north to Haddam.

This species is not known to nest in Connecticut. In summer non-breeding stragglers are rare but regular on Long Island Sound. However, Bull (1974) reported nesting at seven sites on Long Island, including Fisher's Island, in 1933 and 1968; nesting was also confirmed on Long Island in the early 1980s (NYBBA).

Earliest fall arrival: Sept. 13, 1935; Sept. 28, 1971; Sept. 29, 1974.
Latest spring departure: June 27, 1971; June 26, 1972; June 21, 1947.

HISTORICAL NOTES: Merriam (1877) noted that this fish-eating species was a "common migrant" and "plentiful in fall." It was a "common winter visitor" in the 1890s (Averill 1892). Sage et al. (1913) called it a "rather common winter resident," and Forbush (1916) reported a decline of up to 50% in Massachusetts from 1885 to 1908. Griscom (1923) reported it was "common to abundant" in migration and winter on eastern Long Island Sound, and Howes (1928) said it was "not common" in winter at the western end. By the early 1940s it was "abundant" in migration and "common" in winter in the New York City area (Cruickshank 1942). Bull (1964) suggested a slight decrease occurred during the 1940s and 1950s. Hill (1965) perhaps correctly speculated that it was irregularly cyclic in numbers for most of this century. Aerial surveys conducted by the Connecticut Department of Environmental Protection in the 1970s and 1980s indicate its numbers have remained stable.

Ruddy Duck (*Oxyura jamaicensis*)

STATUS: an uncommon migrant and winter visitor on coastal ponds and estuaries and, to a lesser degree, on inland lakes and ponds from early October to May; it can be fairly common at favored locations. Fall migration peaks in early to mid-November. It it normally less numerous in spring. Nonbreeding stragglers are very rare in summer.

Earliest fall arrival: Aug. 10, 1919; Aug. 27, 1982; Aug. 29, 1965.

Latest spring departure: June 17, 1975; June 5, 1893; May 24, 1952.

HISTORICAL NOTES: In Massachusetts, it was "common to abundant" before 1885 but declined thereafter (Forbush 1916 , Griscom and Snyder 1955). In Connecticut, Merriam (1877) noted it was "not rare during migrations" and added that it was "rather common at the mouth of the Connecticut River." It was "rare to uncommon" in the 1890s (Averill 1892). However, Sage et al. (1913) said it was "formerly a fairly common fall migrant on the Sound and larger lakes; now rare. Very rare in the spring." They reported only eight records from 1896 to 1910. By about 1910 Massachusetts had experienced a 60% decline in numbers (Griscom and Snyder 1955), but a gradual increase was reported thereafter. In the 1920s Griscom (1923) called it "very rare," and Forbush (1925) noted that it was "formerly a common migrant . . . now rather rare and irregular." Bull (1964) said it had "increased considerably" in the New York City area since the mid-1940s. An unusually large concentration was noted in the winter of 1953–1954 at Saybrook, when 850 were counted (AFN 8:240). By the early 1960s it was a "common to locally abundant fall migrant and winter visitor" (Bull 1964).

The nesting range of this species is chiefly in the Canadian prairies and north-central United States, but it sporadically nests in the eastern states. The first Long Island nesting record was in 1955, and it has nested there regularly since. It first nested in New Jersey in 1958 but has not nested in Connecticut.

VULTURES (FAMILY CATHARTIDAE*)*

Black Vulture (*Coragyps atratus*)

STATUS: a very rare visitor from the south but increasing. It has been reported at least 28 times in the state; most sightings are between early July and early December. It is casual from January to mid-May, although spring records have become more numerous in the 1980s. Nearly all reports are of single birds.

Turkey Vulture (*Cathartes aura*)

STATUS: an uncommon to fairly common migrant from early April to early May and from late September to mid-November; it is sometimes very common at hawk-watch locations on peak migration days in October. It nests locally inland but not in coastal areas. In winter it is rare in most locations but has increased in the 1980s and is locally uncommon. In all seasons it is most frequent away from the coast.

HISTORICAL NOTES: Turkey Vultures were recorded during the 1600s in New England (Josselyn 1672). A review of Linsley (1843a, b), Merriam (1877), and Sage et al. (1913) reveals that it was more frequent in the 1820s than in the following 100 years. It was a "rare visitor from the south" in the 1870s (Merriam 1877) and was generally considered a straggler into the early 1900s (Griscom and Snyder 1955). Sage et al. listed 12 Connecticut records from 1874 to 1910. L. Bishop saw his first in the state in 1913 (*Auk* 38:582). A bird shot in 1927 was called the 19th state record (*Auk* 44:419).

Expanding its range northward, the first modern nesting in New York occurred in 1925 (Bull 1974) and in Connecticut at the Sherman–New Fairfield area in 1930 (PLSNY No. 43–44, BL 33:257). It increased in the following 10 years (Bagg and Eliot; Griscom and Snyder; Bull 1964) and became a regular visitor in parts of Litchfield County (A. Bagg, *Auk* 68:315). It probably nested in Redding in the early 1940s (*Auk* 68:315). It nested east to New Haven County in 1947, to New London County in 1954 (Mackenzie 1961), and north to Mansfield in 1965 (Manter 1975). It has since become a widespread but local nester in rural areas throughout the state.

The first winter record was on February 26, 1931, at Kensington (Berlin) (BL 33:192). The next record was of a roost of about 30 birds in the winter of 1947–1948 in Kent (*Auk* 70:491) and then in 1949–1950 at the Easton, Weston, and Redding area (*Auk* 68:322). Twenty-one birds were found in North Guilford in January 1962 (AFN 18:341). By the early 1960s it was a fairly common migrant in lower Fairfield County (Bull 1964). Subsequently, it has become more widespread and frequent in all seasons. A winter roost of about 35 birds was found at Voluntown in 1986 (AmB 41:56, 41:254).

OSPREYS *(*FAMILY **PANDIONIDAE***)*

Osprey (*Pandion haliaetus*)

STATUS: an uncommon migrant in April and fairly common from early September to mid-October; it is sometimes very common at coastal hawk-watch locations on peak migration days in late September and early October. Although the majority pass through the state in October, a few infrequently linger through November. In migration it is most frequent along the coast and in the hillier portions of the state west of the Connecticut River. Its nesting range is expanding westward, and it breeds locally along the coast from the Pawcatuck River west to Guilford.

Earliest spring arrival: Mar. 17, 1935, 1985; Mar. 19, 1960, 1964; Mar. 20, 1971.

Latest fall departure: Jan. 3, 1954, 1982; Dec. 30, 1963; Dec. 27, 1953.

COMMENTS: A review of the published literature reveals that there are at least 10 December and January reports of this species—there is even one from mid-February. Specimen or photographic evidence is

Osprey

needed to confirm the presence of this species in Connecticut during the winter months.

HISTORICAL NOTES: In the early 1800s this fish-eating raptor presumably nested throughout the region along Long Island Sound and along larger rivers and lakes. In the late 1870s Merriam (1877) noted it nested "abundantly" along the coast, particularly east of the Connecticut River. It no longer nested at Stamford and Fairfield after the 1890s, as coastal development eliminated significant habitats (Wright; Howes 1928), but it remained a "fairly common summer resident" at New Haven in 1908 (Honeywill et al. 1908). Job (1922) said that in 1908 it was a "usually rather scarce migrant, but quite common along rivers, especially the Housatonic" and added that a pair reportedly nested "a number of years ago" in Litchfield County. Bent (1937) reported a decline during the first few decades of this century, adding that nesting was limited to the area near the mouth of the Connecticut River.

By 1935 the Long Island, New York, population was less than half of what it was prior to 1882 (Hoehn, CW 2:49). In 1938 more than 200 nests were counted along the lower Connecticut River (*Auk* 81:173). By the late 1940s a decline was observed that became more pronounced in the 1950s (Bull 1964; Hill 1965; Poole and Spitzer 1983). Human use of chlorinated hydrocarbons, including DDT, caused eggshells to break during incubation, and nesting failures caused a 31% annual reduction in breeding birds (*Auk* 81:173). In 1960 the nesting population was reduced to 71 pairs, and in 1963 to 24 pairs (*Auk* 81:173). By 1970 nesting Ospreys were nearly extirpated from Connecticut; only eight active nests remained, representing less than 10% of the population present in 1938 (Poole and Spitzer 1983), and in 1974 only one active pair remained (AmB 34:236).

The banning of DDT in 1972, the erection of nesting platforms, and a program to transfer eggs from Chesapeake Bay to Connecticut resulted in an increase in nesting success (Hoehn, CW 2:49; Poole and Spitzer 1983). In the late 1970s migrants were observed more frequently and in greater numbers. From 1980 nesting success increased 8–10% annually, which, if continued, would bring the nesting population to 60–70% of the pre-DDT numbers by the year 2000 (Poole and Spitzer). By 1982 its nesting range extended from the Connecticut River east to the state line on the Pawcatuck River (Hoehn, CW 2:49). In 1987, 74 young fledged from 35 nests, and in 1988, 95 young fledged from 54 nests (*Connecticut Environment* 16:16).

HAWKS, EAGLES, KITES (FAMILY ACCIPITRIDAE)

American Swallow-tailed Kite (*Elanoides forficatus*)

STATUS: a casual wanderer; reported regionally from late April to early October, with most reports in May and early June. In the southeastern United States it nests north to Georgia and South Carolina but has decreased throughout its range in recent years (Terres 1980).

REPORTS: There are two corroborated records of this species in Connecticut: a specimen was found at Stafford on June 3, 1976 (UCM No. 7479), and two were photographed at Mansfield from June 6 to June 24, 1989 (P. Coughlin, L. Bevier et al.). Nine sightings of this species in Connecticut have been published, three of which were before 1900: one was in the summer of 1861 (precise date not given) at Portland (Merriam 1877); one was on July 2, 1877, at Lyme (Merriam); and one was on June 16, 1889, at Saybrook (Sage et al. 1913). In this century the first sighting was on May 2, 1907, at Stamford by P. Howes (OO 45:70–96). On July 29 and 31, 1938, one was observed at Litchfield by S. Dillon Ripley (*Auk* 57:247). Two were sighted on May 26, 1940, at New Britain by Schmidt et al. (BMAS 25:42; HAS). One was seen on June 10, 1987, at Hamden by F. McBride et al. (CW 8:66), and another was observed on May 24, 1988, at Clinton by F. Sweet et al. (COAR).

COMMENTS: There is a vague report of two birds sighted in the spring of 1979, but exact dates, locations, and observers were not given (AmB 33:752). The authors do not assign any credence to this report, at least as published.

HISTORICAL NOTES: Merriam (1877), citing Samuel Williams's *The Natural and Civil History of Vermont* (1794), said it was "once not only common in New England, but actually wintered here." Although Bagg and Eliot (1937) stated that it "was more numerous, and ranged nearer us, in former times than now," there is no evidence it ever actually wintered in New England.

Bald Eagle (*Haliaeetus leucocephalus*)

STATUS: The Bald Eagle may occur in Connecticut at any time of the year. It is a rare to uncommon migrant from early August through October, less frequent in spring from early April to mid-May. It is a rare summer visitor. It is locally uncommon in winter, particularly at favored locations along the Connecticut River, Housatonic River, and large reservoirs. It is extirpated from Connecticut as a nesting species.

COMMENTS: Areas where eagles winter in Connecticut are susceptible to human disturbance that may adversely affect the birds (Craig, Mitchell, and Mitchell 1988).

HISTORICAL NOTES: The Bald Eagle was apparently a common and widespread resident in Connecticut in the early colonial period (Merriam 1877). In the 1840s Linsley mentioned active eyries at Hamden (Mt. Carmel), East Haven (near "Saltonstall Pond") and Bridgeport (Black Rock). On September 14, 1891, Trowbridge (1895) saw at least 12 individuals migrating by New Haven and reported that "a few pairs breed within the state" (*Auk* 12:265). An active nest was reported in April 1896 at Winchester by C. Williams, who also found another nest in the same town "some years" before (Job 1922). E. Chase noted that the Bald Eagle nested regularly at Kent up to 1933 (PLSNY 43/44:1). It reportedly nested at Colebrook to 1930, at Southbury to 1940, and at Hamburg Cove in Lyme into the 1950s (Milan Bull, pers. comm.). In the 1980s summering pairs have been observed, but nesting has not been proved. Bald Eagles presently nest at Quabbin Reservoir in central Massachusetts.

Into the 1940s the Bald Eagle became less frequent in all seasons in Connecticut—a decline largely attributable to pesticide poisoning, shooting, and habitat loss. By the early 1970s it was generally rare and unpredictable in winter and uncommon in fall migration. In the late 1970s sightings increased somewhat in migration and winter (AmB 32:322), more so since then. A statewide survey located 42 Bald Eagles on January 9, 1988 and 73 birds on February 13 (CW 8:64).

Northern Harrier (*Circus cyaneus*)

STATUS: an uncommon migrant from mid-August to early December; it is occasionally common to abundant at coastal locations during peak migration days from mid-September to mid-October. It is uncommon in spring from late March to May. It is apparently extirpated as a nesting species in the state; midsummer reports are very scarce. In winter it is rare except along the coast and floodplains of larger rivers, where a few occasionally linger; less numerous inland in all seasons.

HISTORICAL NOTES: This species was numerous in the 1800s. Linsley (1843a) said it "is the most common hawk found in our salt meadows and fields adjoining." In 1864 J. Allen said it was "by far our most common hawk" nesting in the Connecticut River valley north of Hartford (Bagg and Eliot 1937). Merriam (1877) called it a "tolerably common summer resident, especially about salt marshes, where it breeds." At the turn of the century it remained a "common" summer resident along the coast (Averill; Sage et al.; Wright 1897) and was abundant during migration (Trowbridge, *Auk* 12:265).

A significant decrease in its nesting population in the Connecticut River valley was noted by Morris (1901), who called it a "rare summer resident." Regarding this decline, Bagg and Eliot (1937) commented "hawk hatred had done its work in the forty years since Allen's time." In the 1920s some authors said it remained a "fairly common" breeder in coastal marshes (Howes; Forbush 1927), but habitat destruction restricted its nesting range. Its decline as a nester continued into the 1960s (Cruickshank; Bull 1964; NYBBA). In 1961 Mackenzie said one or two could be found on any summer day at Guilford. The last nesting in Connecticut is not known; it probably has not nested in the state since the mid- or late 1960s.

Sharp-shinned Hawk (*Accipiter striatus*)

STATUS: an uncommon migrant from late March to early May and a fairly common migrant from late August to early November; it is occasionally very abundant at hawk-watch locations on peak migration days from mid-September to mid-October. Individuals frequently linger through December—often at feeders; it is usually rare in midwinter. It is a rare and local nester in the northwest and northeast hills but increasing in recent years.

HISTORICAL NOTES: The Sharp-shinned Hawk was a "common" breeder into the 1890s (Merriam; Averill; Wright 1897), although Trowbridge said it "breeds sparingly" (*Auk* 12:265). In 1908, Job (1922) said, it was "a moderately common summer resident" at Litchfield County, and Sage et al. (1913) stated it was a "tolerably common summer resident." Howes (1928) called it a "fairly common" breeder in the Stamford area.

A steady decline began about 1920—particularly affecting the nesting population (Bent 1937, Griscom and Snyder; Bull 1964). Four nests were found in the Unionville (Farmington) area as late as 1934 (OO 51:94). In lower Fairfield County it reportedly last nested in 1947 (Hills 1978) and was virtually extirpated from Connecticut as a nesting species by the late 1950s. Since the late 1970s summer reports have increased; also, it has "increased substantially" in winter (AmB 41:254).

Cooper's Hawk (*Accipiter cooperii*)

STATUS: a rare to uncommon migrant from early April to early May and an uncommon to sometimes fairly common migrant from late August to mid-November. It is a rare nester in dense forests in the northwest hills south to Southbury and Greenwich; nesting is suspected but unconfirmed in the northeast hills. It is usually rare in midwinter.

HISTORICAL NOTES: This large accipiter substantially declined in numbers from the late 1800s to the late 1970s, especially as a nester. It was long persecuted by people because it preyed on chickens that roamed unprotected on farms. Bagg and Eliot (1937) noted that the Cooper's Hawk was "one of our most abundant birds of prey" before the mid-1800s, and it was called a "common" nester until the early 1900s (Merriam; Averill; Job; Wright 1897). Bent (1937) noted it was one of the most common nesting hawks north of Connecticut. Sage et al. (1913) said it was "tolerably common" in summer but added that it was "annually becoming rarer over most of the state." By the 1930s it had decreased to one third of its former numbers (Bent 1937). From the 1920s through the 1950s it was called "uncommon," "fairly common," or "rather common" (Forbush 1927; Griscom; Bagg and Eliot; Cruickshank; Griscom and Snyder; Bull 1964) and rarer than formerly (Howes 1928). It reportedly nested in New Haven County as late as 1949 (Mackenzie 1961) and in Fairfield County into the early 1960s (Hills 1978).

The decline continued into the 1970s, when it was nearly extirpated from Connecticut as a nesting species. From about 1970 it has been more frequently reported during fall migration (AmB 25:26). From the early 1980s, there have been more summer occurrences, and wintering numbers are up since 1978 (AmB 33:263).

COMMENTS: A study of environmental contaminants in eggs of eastern Cooper's Hawks showed that among five eastern states, only Connecticut had high DDE levels and eggshell thinning in 1980 (Pattee, Fuller, and Kaiser 1985).

Northern Goshawk (*Accipiter gentilis*)

STATUS: a rare to uncommon migrant from late February to May and from early September to early November, generally less numerous in spring. Migrations peak in mid-March and mid-October. It is a rare nester in dense forests in the northwest and northeast hills; more rarely south to northern New London and Fairfield counties. Numbers are variable in winter—it is usually rare, but may be locally uncommon.

HISTORICAL NOTES: The nesting range of this formidable raptor decreased as forests were cleared for agriculture and as the Passenger Pigeon became extinct (Bent 1937). In Connecticut it nested at Winsted (Winchester) in about 1893 (Job; Sage et al. 1913) and at Stamford in 1898 (Howes 1928). It was otherwise considered "casual" or "accidental" in summer into the 1930s (Bagg and Eliot; Forbush 1927).

This species has subsequently expanded its nesting range from western Massachusetts eastward and, more strikingly, southward. In 1962 it nested at Barkhamsted (AmB 17:393). By 1964, it was a "casual" nester in the northwest hills south to Litchfield and New Hartford (AFN 19:455, 19:528, 20:489; Bull). D. Finch reported in 1974 that this species "has been steadily increasing in New England for more than a decade" (AmB 29:747). At least 19 nests were located in the northwest hills in 1978 (AmB 32:978).

In the late 1800s W. Wood commented that it was "really common" in winter about once every 10 years. Marked flights occurred in the winters of 1859–1860, 1896–1897, 1906–1907, 1917–1918, and 1926–1927 (Bent 1937). Manter (1975) suggested that it was less frequent in winter than it had been in the 1890s.

Red-shouldered Hawk (*Buteo lineatus*)

STATUS: an uncommon migrant from late March to late May and from mid-September to early November. It is sometimes fairly common on peak migration days in late April and late October. An uncommon and very local nester inland in dense wooded swamps, more frequent east of the Connecticut River valley. It is not known to nest along the coast or in the Connecticut River valley. Normally rare in winter but sometimes uncommon.

HISTORICAL NOTES: This species has dramatically changed in status in historical times. Many of the wooded wetlands that it favored as breeding haunts have been drained or filled for housing developments or agricultural uses.

Merriam (1877) noted it was a "common resident . . . but more frequently seen in winter." In the early 1890s it nested more frequently than the Red-tailed Hawk (Averill 1892). Trowbridge (1895) reported that it "breeds abundantly" (*Auk* 12:265). Bagg and Eliot (1937) noted that after 1900 the Red-shouldered Hawk was the most abundant nesting hawk in north-central Connecticut, although Job (1922) said it "seldom" nested in Litchfield County. In 1908 Honeywill said this species was a "common permanent resident nesting in tall trees almost anywhere outside of the city" of New Haven. It was a "common resident" into the 1920s (Sage et al.; Forbush 1927; Howes 1928).

A nesting decline was noted in the late 1920s and 1930s (Forbush 1927; Bagg and Eliot; Cruickshank 1942) although Shipley (1931) said it continued to be more abundant in the 1930s near the western coast than the Red-tailed Hawk. In 1932 it was stated to be "the most common of the hawks" around Winsted (Winchester) (OO 49:93). Cruickshank (1942) noted it was a "fairly common" breeder southwest of Connecticut. By the late 1940s it dramatically declined as a result of wetland destruction and, later, pesticide poisoning. W. Smith (1950) aptly described its status as "formerly common" but "rare today." A substantial decline in wintering numbers was noted in the 1950s and 1960s (AmB 25:813), and it was nearly extirpated as a nesting species in Connecticut during the 1960s. Manter (1975) noted it was "uncommon" in migration and winter in the 1970s at the northeast hills.

Although five pairs nested in northern Windham County in 1977 (AmB 31:1111), this species has not appreciably recovered as a nester in the state.

Broad-winged Hawk (*Buteo platypterus*)

STATUS: a fairly common migrant from late August to mid-October and uncommon from mid-April to mid-May. It can be common at the peak of spring migration in late April. Fall migration peaks in mid-September, and on days with strong northwest winds, it is occasionally seen at hawk-watch locations in numbers that exceed 10,000. Accidental in winter with only one confirmed record: an immature was collected on January 12, 1929, at Stamford (D. Shipley, *Auk* 47:417). It is a widespread nester in mature deciduous forests throughout the state.

Earliest spring arrival: Mar. 11, 1927; Mar. 13, 1967; Mar. 17, 1920, 1945.

Latest fall departure: Nov. 11, 1972; Oct. 29, 1959, 1978; Oct. 28, 1959, 1973.

COMMENTS: This species has been reported on at least four Christmas Bird Counts since 1955. None of these reports was published with satisfactory details.

HISTORICAL NOTES: Linsley (1843a) called the Broad-winged Hawk "very rare" at a time when most of Connecticut's forests had been cleared for agriculture and when the shooting of hawks was a popular activity. Bagg and Eliot (1937) noted that it was "rare" throughout New England in the late 1860s. By the late 1870s regrowth of some forests began, and Merriam (1877) noted that it was a "rather rare resident, seldom seen in winter." Rev. C. Jones found his first specimen in 15 years in the Eastford area in 1884 (Manter 1975), and Trowbridge said in 1895 that it "breeds sparingly" (*Auk* 12:265). Bent (1937) reported that it first nested in southeast Massachusetts in 1899.

By 1908 it was a "common summer resident" in Litchfield County (Job 1922), although it was called a "comparatively rare transient visitant" in New Haven (Honeywill et al. 1908). It continued to be less than common elsewhere into the 1930s (Wright; Sage et al.; Howes; Forbush 1927; Griscom and Snyder 1955). Sage et al. (1913) commented that it bred "most abundantly" at relatively wooded Litchfield County. Bagg and Eliot (1937) reported an increase in north-central Connecticut. Subsequently, it has increased steadily as a nester.

Swainson's Hawk (*Buteo swainsoni*)

STATUS: an accidental vagrant from the west; it is a very rare migrant in New England in September, October, and November (Terres 1980; Conway).

RECORDS: The first confirmed record in the state was of one photographed at Madison on September 11, 1985 (R. Schwartz et al., CW 7:48; first published as September 9, 1985, CW 6:21). One was sighted on October 27, 1982, at East Haven by several observers (C. Taylor et al., CW 3:10). There are at least three other published sightings, but none of these is sufficiently corroborated (AmB 32:176, CW 1:5, CW 7:24). One sighted and later collected on April 5, 1934, at South Windsor was believed to be of this species but was not definitively identified, and the current location of the specimen is unknown (C. Vibert, HAS).

Red-tailed Hawk (*Buteo jamaicensis*)

STATUS: a fairly common migrant from late February to late April and common from mid-September to early November; migrations peak in early March and in October. It is a regular but uncommon nester inland. It is variable in winter but usually fairly common.

HISTORICAL NOTES: This conspicuous buteo has suffered a long-term decline in Connecticut until recently. Hill (1965) reported that it was "scarce in the early historic period when the land was mostly cleared" but added that it had increased somewhat with reforestation. In Massachusetts, Griscom and Snyder (1955) said it declined in migration after 1880. In 1895 Trowbridge called it a "common and widespread resident" in Connecticut (*Auk* 12:265). Job (1922) said it was a "common summer resident" in 1908 at Litchfield County, and Honeywill et al. (1908) reported it "formerly nested" in the New Haven area. Both Bagg and Eliot (1937) and Cruickshank (1942) noted a decline after the early 1920s. Griscom and Snyder (1955) said it was "steadily decreasing" as a nester in Massachusetts, and Bull (1964) noted a 30-year decline in the greater New York City area. Since about 1965 it has increased in winter and probably has stabilized in summer.

The Red-tailed Hawk was less abundant than the Red-shouldered Hawk in the 1880s (Bagg and Eliot 1937), the 1890s (Averill 1892), and the 1920s (Shipley 1931), paralleling somewhat the relationship of the Great Horned and Barred Owl. It decreased in the 1930s but to a lesser degree than the Red-shouldered Hawk (Bagg and Eliot 1937).

SUBSPECIES: Red-tailed Hawks in Connecticut in all-white plumage are probably leucistic and not the "Krider's" race *(B. j. krideri)* of the Great Plains. The "Western" race *(B. j. calurus)* is generally believed to be inseparable in the field from the nominate race.

Rough-legged Hawk (*Buteo lagopus*)

STATUS: a rare coastal and Connecticut River valley migrant and winter visitor from late October to April; it is occasionally uncommon at large open expanses of coastal marshes and tidal rivers. It is usually much less frequent elsewhere, particularly in forested parts of the state.

Earliest fall arrival: Sept. 7, 1936; Sept. 18, 1953; Sept. 22, 1917.

Latest spring departure: May 13, 1972; May 9, 1920; May 7, 1951.

HISTORICAL NOTES: The Rough-legged Hawk was once more numerous in the state than at present. It was reportedly an "abundant" winter visitor in the Connecticut River valley north of Middletown during the mid-1800s (Bergstrom 1960). Griscom and Snyder (1955) said it was "abundant" in the Connecticut River valley from 1870 to 1887, noting that 68 were killed in a single winter.

Reflecting the decrease of open land and the increase in "sport" shooting, a long-term decline began in the 1880s and 1890s (Bent 1937; Bagg and Eliot 1937) that continued into the 1960s (Griscom and Snyder; Bull 1964). In 1895 Trowbridge said it was "not very rare in the cold season" (*Auk* 12:266). Sage et al. (1913) said it was "rather uncommon," and Bagg and Eliot (1937) said it was "once locally common but now rare" in winter. Griscom and Snyder (1955) called it a "very rare" winter visitor in the Connecticut River valley. Apparently recovering somewhat, it was described by Bull (1974) as "variously rare to uncommon, occasionally fairly common" along coastal New York.

Golden Eagle (*Aquila chrysaetos*)

STATUS: a very rare migrant from late March through April and rare from mid-September to early December; rare but regular in winter. Accidental in summer: one on August 11, 1969, in Bethany (D. Finch, AmB 23:644). Reported more frequently west of the Connecticut River.

Earliest fall arrival: Sept. 15, 1974; Sept. 23, 1978; Sept. 30, 1973.
Latest spring departure: May 8, 1970; Apr. 23, 1949.

HISTORICAL NOTES: The Golden Eagle was possibly about as common in the early colonial period as it is now, although there was much confusion regarding the taxonomy and identification of eagles. Griscom (1923) said it was less "rare" than formerly, and Bagg and Eliot (1937) detected an increase in reports during the 1920s. An increase in the popularity of birding, especially hawk-watching, may account for the increase of sightings in recent years.

COMMENTS: There is a report published in 1932 (OO 49:93) of Golden Eagles "formerly" nesting in the Winsted (Winchester) area, but the report is vague and without details.

FALCONS (FAMILY FALCONIDAE)

American Kestrel (*Falco sparverius*)

STATUS: a fairly common migrant from September to late October, less frequent in spring from April to mid-May. It may be very common at hawk-watch locations on peak migration days in late April and from mid-September to mid-October. An uncommon and local nester throughout the state. Variable in winter, it is usually uncommon but can be rare.

HISTORICAL NOTES: During the late 1800s, this small falcon was a "rare" resident with only a "few pairs breeding in the state" (Merriam; Averill; Trowbridge; Bent 1938; Bagg and Eliot 1937). It increased slowly after 1900 (Hill; Griscom 1923). Job (1922) wrote that in 1908 it was "a rather uncommon summer resident" and listed only two midwinter records from Litchfield County. It was a "fairly common permanent resident" in New Haven in 1908 (Honeywill et al. 1908), and Rev. Jones reported the "first for many years" at Eastford in 1912 (Manter 1975). Sage et al. (1913) noted it was "tolerably common" and had increased during the preceding 10 years. At Stamford, Howes (1928) said it was absent in most years but was infrequently "fairly common." Shipley (1931) cited only 10 reports in the late 1920s at Stamford. The nesting population in the state remained stable from 1965 through 1979 (Robbins, Bystrak, and Geissler 1986), but the number of wintering birds has decreased in the 1970s and 1980s.

Merlin (*Falco columbarius*)

STATUS: an uncommon coastal migrant from early September to mid-November, less frequent from mid-April to mid-May. In winter it occurs chiefly along the coast; it is rare in December and very rare from January through March. Inland it is rare in migration and casual in winter.

Earliest fall arrival: Aug. 2, 1958; Aug. 17, 1988; Aug. 29, 1986.

Latest spring departure: May 25, 1882 (spec.); May 22, 1983; May 19, 1985.

HISTORICAL NOTES: C. H. Merriam (1877) was "strongly inclined to believe that a few pairs do occasionally breed in Connecticut." He noted that Dr. William Wood found it at "East Windsor Hill" (South Windsor) in May, June, and July (year not stated) but failed to locate any nest. Merriam added that he had recorded it in the state every month of the year. In 1895 Trowbridge said it was "rare at all times . . . no record of its nesting within the state" (*Auk* 12:266). Sage et al. (1913) mention no nesting records in the state. Bagg and Eliot (1937) mention several reports of suspected nesting in southern New England but added that many observers "confused [it] with the Sharp-shin."

By the mid-1980s winter sightings of this species have increased at coastal areas (AmB 41:255).

Peregrine Falcon (*Falco peregrinus*)

STATUS: a rare coastal migrant from late March to early May and from September to early November; it is occasionally uncommon on peak migration days in late September and early October. In winter it occurs primarily along the coast and is usually rare through mid-January; it is very rare to late March. Nonbreeding individuals occa-ᵢᵢᵢᵢᵢᵢᵢᵢᵢᵢᵢᵢᵢᵢ wander into the state in summer. Inland it is less frequent in all seasons.

HISTORICAL NOTES: The Peregrine Falcon was once a regular nester in Connecticut. The first confirmed nesting in New England was at Talcott Mt., Hartford, on May 25, 1861 (*Hartford Times,* June 29, 1861; Merriam 1877; Sage et al. 1913; Bent 1938; Bagg and Eliot 1937). Eyries were also located at Hamden to 1912 and 1914 (Mt. Carmel), Meriden (Castle Craig, Hubbard's Park), Berlin (west of Hart's Pond), and in the late 1800s at Guilford (Sage et al.; *Auk* 38:586; Forbush 1927; Mackenzie 1961).

The extirpation of this large falcon was dramatic. Bagg and Eliot chronicle the persecution of this species by collectors at several sites in Massachusetts and Connecticut in which hundreds of eggs and dozens of specimens were collected. They stated that in 1935 only one pair in Massachusetts successfully raised a complete brood. The devastation was so severe that several eyries were guarded by concerned citizens to protect nesting birds from the collector's guns (Bagg and Eliot). The Talcott Mt. site was deserted in 1942 because of the shooting of both adults and young by a game warden (*Auk* 59:176). The last nesting in Connecticut was in the late 1940s, when for several years a pair nested on the Travelers Insurance Building in Hartford (*Auk* 82:62).

Beginning before 1950, the nesting population elsewhere in the northeast states decreased rapidly (Bailey 1955), and by the late 1960s the eastern subspecies *P. f. anatum* was extinct. Several factors have contributed to an increase of peregrines since the mid-1970s: shooting and egg collecting have virtually stopped, DDT is no longer permitted for use in the United States, and restocking efforts with captive-bred birds have been successful. Most, if not all, recent peregrine sightings in Connecticut are of the arctic *P. f. tundrius* subspecies.

Gyrfalcon (*Falco rusticolus*)

STATUS: a very rare migrant and winter visitor, irregularly winters in eastern states south to New Jersey and Pennsylvania. It occurs from late October through March; most reports are in January and February. Of 17 published records since 1879, 11 are from coastal areas and 6 are from interior portions of the state.

Earliest fall arrival: Oct. 17, 1935 (spec.); Oct. 19, 1971; Nov. 11, 1984.

Latest spring departure: Apr. 7, 1988; Mar. 20, 1983; Mar. 19, 1937.

COMMENTS: This impressive hawk favors broad expanses of treeless open areas. Not surprisingly, four of the six inland records predate 1950, when many areas of the state were predominately open fields and pastures.

PHEASANTS, PARTRIDGES, GROUSE, TURKEYS (FAMILY PHASIANIDAE)

Gray Partridge (*Perdix perdix*)

STATUS: introduced and extirpated. This species was widely introduced in the early 1900s from Europe to southern Canada and northern United States to replace depleted populations of native upland game birds.

HISTORICAL NOTES: More than 3,000 birds were released in Hartford County from 1908 to 1910 (Bagg and Eliot; Bergstrom 1960), and in 1910 large numbers were released in Stamford and Norwalk (Hills 1978; Howes 1928). Initially, a few successfully acclimated, but most perished by the mid-1930s (Howes; Bagg and Eliot; Bergstrom 1960).

Ring-necked Pheasant (*Phasianus colchicus*)

STATUS: introduced. It is an uncommon resident in fields and thickets in less developed areas.

HISTORICAL NOTES: This species was widely introduced from Asia and England by a variety of hunting clubs in the 1890s; initially, these efforts were unsuccessful in establishing a viable population (Sage et al.; Forbush 1927). In 1913 Sage et al. said that "almost all have disappeared." Stocking continued, and it was "not uncommon" by the mid 1920s along the western coast (Howes 1928). In the 1930s, it was a "common resident" (Bagg and Eliot, Cruickshank 1942). After 1960 it was called "uncommon" (Mackenzie, Manter 1975), possibly reflecting a reduction in the amount of farmland and brushy areas. In recent years the state has released more than 25,000 individuals annually to be hunted, but relatively few birds survive the winter. It is now infrequent in parts of the state, particularly along the coast.

Ruffed Grouse (*Bonasa umbellus*)

STATUS: an uncommon to common resident inland in deciduous and overgrown forests, locally uncommon in wooded tracts along the coast.

HISTORICAL NOTES: The population of Ruffed Grouse in Connecticut has changed with the loss and later regrowth of the state's forests. Being well adapted to early successional stage forests, it quickly rebounded after farmlands were abandoned (NYBBA). Generally, it has increased since the early 1900s. In the 1980s, the loss of habitat through development and the aging of the forest appear to have resulted in a decrease in numbers (Dale May, pers. comm.). It is most readily located in areas where it is least hunted (Bull 1964). This species is known for dramatic fluctuations in numbers under natural conditions (Terres).

Ruffed Grouse

Greater Prairie Chicken (Heath Hen) (*Tympanuchus cupido*)

STATUS: extirpated. The subspecies *T. c. cupido,* now extinct, was formerly a nonmigratory resident from Massachusetts (possibly southern New Hampshire) south along the Atlantic seaboard to the Potomac River (Terres 1980).

HISTORICAL NOTES: Very little is known about the distribution and sequence of extirpation of the Heath Hen in Connecticut. It was probably extirpated from the state by Linsley's time (1840s). According to Forbush (1916) and others, it favored scrubby, stunted pine barrens and open areas with shrubs and grasses.

In addition to extrapolating its presence in Connecticut from its distribution in adjacent states, the following historical evidence supports its presence: Thomas Nuttall (1832) reported that the bird was found in "shrubby barrens" in Westford (Ashford), and Mrs. Blackburne was said to have had a specimen from Connecticut in her possession in England in about 1790. Interestingly, as the undeveloped commonland in Greenwich was subdivided into private parcels, three lots were laid out in an area called the "hen field" and "hen Plaine" in 1705, 1707, and 1731 (Town of Greenwich deed books, 3:598). Records of this kind probably lie undiscovered in the files of other towns.

The Heath Hen was last sighted on March 11, 1932, at Martha's Vineyard, Massachusetts (BL 35:189).

Wild Turkey (*Meleagris gallopavo*)

STATUS: extirpated and reintroduced; a local resident inland in larger forest tracts and wooded rural areas. Usually uncommon, it is occasionally fairly common in portions of the northwest hills; recently reported along the coast and in the Connecticut River valley.

HISTORICAL NOTES: The Wild Turkey was "abundant" and widespread throughout most of Connecticut during the early colonial period, but excessive hunting and habitat disruption caused a decrease in numbers. Josselyn (1672) wrote: "The English and the Indians having now destroyed the breed, so that 'tis very rare to meet with a wild Turkie in the woods." Such pressures continued, and its numbers throughout southern New England were noticeably reduced during the 1700s. By the late 1700s, it was largely restricted to hillier country west of the Connecticut River, although a few remained in the northeast hills (Forbush, 1916). After 1800 few were left in Connecticut; Linsley

(1843a) reported that the last record he was aware of in the state was of one shot at Northford (North Branford) in 1813.

By 1970 there had been unsuccessful attempts to reintroduce pen-raised birds. In spring 1975, 22 birds captured from wild New York State stock were released in Litchfield County. They increased rapidly and in the fall of 1976 were found 6 miles from the release site. Supplemented by releases in adjacent New York, the estimated population in the fall of 1977 was 350 birds, which doubled to about 700 in 1978 when its range expanded east and south to include Granby, Newington, New Milford, and Danbury. In 1978, 30 birds were released at north Ashford to develop a population east of the Connecticut River. From 1978 to 1987, 12 additional releases were sponsored by the Connecticut Department of Environmental Protection. These populations have steadily increased. In 1988 the estimated statewide population was 6,000 (Dale May, pers. comm.).

Northern Bobwhite (*Colinus virginianus*)

STATUS: an uncommon resident almost exclusively east of the Connecticut River. Released birds are occasionally found elsewhere in the state.

HISTORICAL NOTES: This species was "abundant" during the early 1800s, especially along the coast, after the southern New England forests were cleared for agriculture (Forbush 1916; Hill 1965). It was subject to periodic and occasionally widespread diebacks during severe winters. It decreased drastically during the winter of 1812–1813 and was called "no longer common" in New England by T. Dwight in 1821 (Forbush 1916). Also, Forbush noted that one bad snowstorm in the 1850s had destroyed the Bobwhite on Cape Cod; they were later replaced with imported southern birds. There were substantial restocking efforts in the late 1800s and early 1900s: from the 1870s to about 1920, it was called "common" (Merriam; Sage et al. 1913), and Sage et al. added: "Large numbers of Quail from the South and West have been released, so that it is now impossible to determine what proportion of Connecticut Quail are descendants from original stock." In the 1890s, Wright (1897) said it was the most "abundant of our game birds."

A long-term loss of fields and thickets and unregulated hunting have contributed to a decline in numbers. In 1908 Job wrote that "now very few can be found" in the Litchfield County area, adding "until the winter of 1903–1904 [it was] a common resident". Also in 1908,

Honeywill et al. said the Northern Bobwhite was "nearly exterminated" in the New Haven area and added that attempts to introduce south-western birds were unsuccessful. In the 1920s and 1930s, it remained "fairly common" at certain coastal locations but was practically extir-pated inland, except for localized introduced stock (Howes; Shipley; Bagg and Eliot 1937). It was noticeably reduced in the Guilford area in the early 1940s (Mackenzie 1961) and elsewhere by the 1950s when it became local and "rare" (Smith; Bergstrom; Bull 1964; Manter 1975). Several factors, including loss of habitat, changes in farming practices, hunting, severe winters and interbreeding with introduced less hardy subspecies have resulted in the decline of this species (Bagg and Eliot; Sage et al.; Mackenzie 1961).

RAILS, GALLINULES, COOTS (FAMILY RALLIDAE)

Yellow Rail (*Coturnicops noveboracensis*)

STATUS: a very rare migrant from September to November. Acciden-tal in spring from late March to late May: one was collected on April 17, 1880, at Milford (G. B. Grinnell, BCM No. 721); one was found dead in a snowdrift on March 24, 1888, at New Milford (*Auk* 5:319); one was collected in May 1912 at Portland (UCM No. 1513); one was collected on April 24, 1928, at Fairfield (BcM No. 1383).

Earliest fall arrival: Sept. 6, 1929; Sept. 8, 1894 (spec.); Sept. 15, 1922.
Latest fall departure: Nov. 10, 1913; Oct. 25, 1894; Oct. 23, 1928.

COMMENTS: Two spring sight records are not sufficiently corrobo-rated (May 21, 1959, South Windsor, HAS; March 21, 1978, Greenwich, AmB 32:978).

HISTORICAL NOTES: Merriam (1877) noted that this secretive species was "not common" in fall and related the experience of G. B. Grinnell and his brother, who collected eight birds in an hour by using a birddog near Milford on October 14, 1876. Most Connecticut records are from the late 1800s, when most observers used dogs to flush the birds. It has since been considered "rare" in fall (Bagg and Eliot; Bergstrom; Hill) and is less frequently reported since the early 1900s. This may reflect an actual decline in numbers, the loss of suitable habitat, the inability of dogless observers to locate it, or a combination thereof.

Merriam (1877) was informed by William Coe that the Yellow Rail nested at Middletown, where Coe collected it in 1874 and 1875. Sage et al. (1913) commented on this by saying, "A questionable record—probably a misunderstanding." There is no satisfactory evidence that this species ever nested in Connecticut.

Black Rail (*Laterallus jamaicensis*)

STATUS: a very rare visitor from late May to October; more than half of the reports are from August to early September. It is at the northeastern extension of its breeding range; the only published report of a potential breeder in recent years was of a territorial male calling in Cromwell, June 25 into July, 1980 (N. Proctor et al., photographed, AmB 34:876).

Earliest spring arrival: May 25, 1947; May 27, 1957; June 5, 1986.
Latest fall departure: Oct. 6, 1986; Oct. 3, 1983; Oct. 1, 1936 (spec.).

HISTORICAL NOTES: This secretive little rail was apparently an irregular nester along the Connecticut River in the 19th century. J. N. Clark found nests of this species at Saybrook in 1876 and at Great Island at the mouth of the Connecticut River in 1884 (*Auk* 1:393); he reported six nests in the vicinity of Saybrook and Old Lyme over a period of more than 50 years (Bergstrom 1960). It may have nested at Enfield along the Connecticut River in the 1860s or early 1870s (Beatty; Bagg and Eliot 1937).

Corn Crake (*Crex crex*)

STATUS: an accidental vagrant from Europe and Asia. One was collected by J. Clark at Saybrook on October 20, 1887 (OO 13:45; Forbush 1925) and a female was collected by D. Page at Orange on October 18, 1943 (YPM No. 950; *Auk* 61:471).

COMMENTS: This species has not been reported in North America in recent decades, and European populations are declining, so future records for Connecticut seem unlikely. Apparently, the last specimen record from North America was taken on Long Island at Orient, New York, on November 2, 1963 (Bull 1974).

Clapper Rail (*Rallus longirostris*)

STATUS: a fairly common visitor and nester in coastal marshes from mid-April to mid-December, less numerous in Fairfield County and east of Saybrook. Usually rare in winter; it may be absent during winters with extreme freezing of coastal marshes. Accidental inland: one was collected along the Connecticut River at Cromwell on Sept. 11, 1915 (Bagg and Eliot 1937).

HISTORICAL NOTES: Around the turn of the century the widespread draining and filling of coastal marshes and unregulated hunting contributed to a decline in the nesting population of this species in the state. Merriam (1877) noted that the Clapper Rail was "not common." Sage et al. (1913) considered it "rather rare" in summer and "occasional" in winter east to Saybrook; it was casual east to Massachusetts in the 1890s (Wright 1897). It increased noticeably from 1931 to 1944 after hunting restrictions were imposed, and it was more frequent in winter than previously (Saunders 1950). In 1950 it nested at Saybrook, Old Lyme, and Noank (AFN 4:266). Its range expanded east into Massachusetts, with the first nesting there in 1956 (Bergstrom 1960; Bull 1964). Bergstrom noted that it bred regularly east to Saybrook, and "probably occurs in Old Lyme." During the 1970s the numbers of nesting Clapper Rails declined on Long Island, possibly the result of the effects of Hurricane Belle in 1976 and two successive cold winters that killed wintering birds in the southeastern United States (NYBBA).

King Rail (*Rallus elegans*)

STATUS: a rare nester in marshes along the lower Connecticut River and its tributaries at Durham, Lyme, and Old Lyme and in estuaries and Stonington and Westbrook. It is a possible but unproven nester inland at large freshwater marshes. It is a rare migrant in April and from late September to mid November. Occasionally lingers to mid-December but is accidental in midwinter in coastal salt marshes: January 14, 1875 (Saybrook, Merriam 1877); December 28, 1968 to March 28, 1969 (Branford, D. Finch et al., AFN 23:459); November 23, 1983 to January 14, 1984 (Greenwich, MFN 11:6, 12:1).

COMMENTS: This species hybridizes with Clapper Rail along the coast in Connecticut (and elsewhere), and some authorities consider these two species to be conspecific (CW 8:61).

HISTORICAL NOTES: Connecticut is near the northern limit of the King Rail's range, and it has historically been a rare species in the state. Apparently, the first recorded nesting of this species in New England was in 1842 when Linsley discovered a nest at Stratford. It was collected at Stratford in 1868 by E. H. Austin (Averill 1892). Merriam (1877) noted it was "rather rare" in Connecticut; it was "rare" in the 1890s and early 1900s (Sage et al. 1913; Averill 1892), and "very rare" thereafter (Bagg and Eliot; Bull 1964; Manter 1975). Bergstrom (1960) reported it breeding in the late 1940s and 1950s inland at Bloomfield, Rocky Hill, and South Windsor and along the coast at Guilford.

Virginia Rail (*Rallus limicola*)

STATUS: a fairly common migrant in freshwater and brackish marshes from September to early December; it is uncommon from mid-April to late May. It is an uncommon nester at inland marshes except along the Connecticut River, where it is fairly common in Portland, Cromwell, Rocky Hill, Wethersfield, and South Windsor. In early winter it is often rare but occasionally uncommon on the coast; less frequent inland. A few spend the winter when marshes are not completely frozen.

HISTORICAL NOTES: There are indications that this species has decreased in population because of the loss of wetland nesting habitat (Zimmerman 1977). A review of the historical literature pertaining to Connecticut appears to support that view. Merriam (1877) said it was "a common summer resident, breeding plentifully in both salt and fresh-water marshes" and added that it was "quite abundant" in marshes along the Quinnipiac River.

Its population rapidly declined thereafter: Sage et al.(1913) said it was "a rather rare resident from May to October" but added that it remained a "tolerably common" fall migrant. Howes (1928) said it was "rare" at Stamford. Bagg and Eliot (1937) said it was "quite common in the bottomlands, uncommon in the hills," and Mulliken (1938) noted it was an "abundant migrant and breeder." In the 1960s, it was local and "uncommon" at Litchfield County (WMF), and Mackenzie (1961) said it was "unaccountably rare" in the Guilford area—he knew of no records prior to 1960. Bull (1964) noted it was an "uncommon to fairly common fall migrant" and a "locally common breeder." In the 1970s it was "irregular, rare" in summer in the Storrs area (Manter 1975).

Sora (*Porzana carolina*)

STATUS: an uncommon migrant in freshwater and coastal marshes from late August to mid-October; less frequent from early April to late May. It sometimes lingers through December but is very rare in midwinter. It is a rare nester in the northern portions of the state in large marshes; an uncommon nester in marshes along the Connecticut River in South Windsor, Cromwell, Portland, Rocky Hill, Durham, Lyme and Old Lyme—in brackish-water marshes in the two latter locations.

HISTORICAL NOTES: This species is becoming scarcer in many parts of its range as wetlands are destroyed or modified (NYBBA). Formerly, the Sora was quite numerous in Connecticut. Linsley (1843a) reported "hundreds" of birds during the peak of fall migration along the lower Housatonic River. Merriam (1877) noted it was an "abundant summer resident." In the 1880s Dr. Brewster said expert marksmen could shoot 100-150 Soras per day along the lower Connecticut River (Forbush 1916). Averill (1892) said it was "uncommon" in summer, although Wright (1897) noted it "bred freely" and was the "common rail of gunners."

Both Sage et al. (1913) and Forbush (1925) considered it a widespread nester, a "common" spring migrant, and "abundant" in fall. By the 1930s significant long-term disruption of nesting habitat was well under way in Connecticut, although the population remained stable in Massachusetts; it was "rare" in summer but was more common than all other inland rails in fall (Bagg and Eliot 1937). Mulliken (1938) said it was an "abundant migrant, and breeder." On January 3, 1950, the second winter record was recorded (*Auk* 68:374). In the 1950s Bailey reported a rapid decrease in numbers in southeastern New England. Mackenzie (1961) said it was "rare", and knew of no records at Guilford before 1950. In the late 1960s W. Bulmer estimated that 15 pairs nested at Great Meadows, Stratford, but added that the area had been subsequently disrupted by development and the species had stopped nesting (YPM records). In the 1970's Manter (1975) said it was a "rare" migrant in the Storrs area.

Purple Gallinule (*Porphyrula martinica*)

STATUS: a very rare visitor from April through early October; most occurrences are in May and June. Of 23 published reports since 1855, 16 are from coastal areas and 7 are inland in the Connecticut River valley (F. Gallo, CW 5:43–46). It breeds north along the Atlantic coast to Delaware and wanders north to southeastern Canada (Terres 1980).

Earliest spring arrival: Apr. 16, 1920; Apr. 22, 1963, 1977; May 5, 1932.

Latest fall departure: Oct. 11, 1924; Oct. 9, 1934.

HISTORICAL NOTES: a review of the published literature pertaining to Connecticut indicates that this southern species has historically been a very rare visitor in the state.

Common Moorhen (*Gallinula chloropus*)

STATUS: A rare to locally uncommon migrant and summer visitor in freshwater and brackish marshes from May to mid-October; lingering birds are very rare in November and December. Accidental in midwinter: one spent the winter of 1968–1969 at New Haven (D. Finch et al., AmB 23:459). It is a rare and infrequent nester at large inland marshes and coastal ponds; it nested in the 1980s at Stratford, North Haven, Litchfield, South Windsor and North Stonington.
Earliest spring arrival: Apr. 12, 1938; Apr. 22, 1916; Apr. 26, 1954.
Latest fall departure: Jan. 3, 1954; Jan. 2, 1972; Dec. 22, 1975.

HISTORICAL NOTES: Formerly called the Common Gallinule, this species is now less numerous and less widespread than in the early 1900s, probably because of the draining and filling of wetland areas (Strohmeyer 1977). It was called a "rather common summer resident" in the 1870s in the Milford area by G. B. Grinnell, who collected several (Merriam 1877). Subsequent authors have called it a "rare" or "locally uncommon" breeder (Wright 1897; Averill 1892; Sage et al. 1913; Bergstrom 1960; Bull 1964). It nested along the Housatonic River in 1891 (Wright 1897), and was first reported nesting at South Windsor in 1930 (BL 32:356, *Auk* 49:465). It nested at New Haven in 1940 (Bergstrom 1960) and at Stratford in the 1970s (Hills 1978).

American Coot (*Fulica americana*)

STATUS: a fairly common migrant from late October to early December, less numerous in spring from late March to mid-April. It may be very common at favored coastal locations during peak migration in mid-November. It is very rare in summer from late May to early September. In winter, it is variable and is usually uncommon to locally common at the coast, less frequent inland.
Earliest fall arrival: Sept. 1, 1983; Sept. 16, 1973; Sept. 19, 1893.
Latest spring departure: May 20, 1951; May 16, 1974; May 15, 1988.

HISTORICAL NOTES: Forbush (1916) wrote that this species was "formerly one of the most abundant waterfowl on the freshwaters of North America." Merriam (1877) said it was "common" in migration, especially in fall. Sage et al. (1913) said it was "much rarer than formerly" and added that it was "seldom seen in spring." The decline of this species has been attributed to the destruction of wetlands, overhunting, and occasional droughts that affected nesting success (Frederickson et al. 1977).

The first early winter record was on December 26, 1913 at East Haven (*Auk* 38:584); the second was on December 22, 1924, in New Canaan (W. Smith).

There are very few records of this species nesting in the state. It nested at South Windsor in 1931 (C. Vibert) and in 1941 (R. Beldon); probably there in other years (Bergstrom 1960). Bagg and Eliot (1937) suspected that nesting occurred at Berlin in 1935. Nesting has not been confirmed in recent decades.

CRANES (FAMILY GRUIDAE)

Sandhill Crane (*Grus canadensis*)

STATUS: a casual vagrant from the Midwest. It is most apt to appear from late August to late December.

RECORDS: There are two records supported by photographic evidence: one from August 24 to September 28, 1980, at South Windsor (P. Desjardins et al., AmB 35:158); another at Westport from December 31, 1983, to February 21, 1984 (F. Mantlik et al., CW 4:37).

HISTORICAL NOTES: Forbush (1916) wrote that it was "more or less common" in the northeast during the settlement period, with which Bagg and Elliot (1937) agreed. Although specimen evidence is lacking, various authorities believe that the Sandhill Crane may have been a regular migrant during colonial times and possibly a breeding bird in this region in postglacial times (AFN 21:487).

COMMENTS: A December 19, 1976, report by a single observer was incorrectly stated (AmB 31:306) as being sighted in Northampton, Connecticut. It was actually seen in Massachusetts. A report of three sighted on April 14, 1976, at Guilford (AmB 30:812) and a report of one May 20–21, 1987, at South Windsor (CW 7:53) lack sufficient corroboration.

PLOVERS (FAMILY CHARADRIIDAE)

Black-bellied Plover (*Pluvialis squatarola*)

STATUS: a fairly common coastal migrant from early April to late May and from early August to mid-November; less numerous in spring. It can be abundant at favored coastal locations during peak migration,

from late August into October. Nonbreeders occasionally linger through
June and July. In winter it is variable but may be uncommon at favored
locations. Inland it is usually uncommon in migration; not reported
otherwise.

Late June and early July reports are difficult to interpret; they may
be late spring migrants, early fall migrants, or lingering nonbreeding
individuals. Extreme fall departure and spring arrival dates are not listed
because of the proclivity of some birds to winter in the area

HISTORICAL NOTES: Nuttall (1832) said that this species was a very
abundant migrant in New England. It declined dramatically, probably
because of excessive shooting. It was less common than Lesser Golden-
Plover before the mid-1800s (Bent 1929). Remarkably, Merriam (1877)
never personally observed this species in the state and mentioned only
two post-Linsley records, the latest in 1873. In 1908 Honeywill et al.
said it was a "very rare late summer and fall migrant" in the New Haven
area. Sage et al. (1913) said young birds were "sometimes tolerably
common" but adults were "always rare." Bailey (1955) noted that it
remained less numerous than Lesser Golden-Plover and Red Knot about
1900.

It increased noticeably from 1910 to 1915 shortly after protective
laws were implemented (Griscom; Hill 1965), and became "common"
in the mid-1920s (Forbush 1925). Numbers stabilized from the mid-
1930's to the early 1940s (Hill; Bull 1964). By the early 1960s it was a
"very common to abundant coastal migrant, occasionally more numerous," with nonbreeders regular in summer and winter; rare inland (Bull
1964).

In New York it was first noted wintering in 1929 (Bull 1964) and
in Massachusetts in 1936–1937 (Bailey 1955). In Connecticut it was not
reported beyond late January until the 1960s. Nonbreeding summering
birds were first reported in Connecticut in 1934 (Bergstrom 1960).

Lesser Golden-Plover (*Pluvialis dominica*)

STATUS: an uncommon coastal migrant from mid-August to mid-
October; rare from mid-October into November. Fall migration is
chiefly over the ocean; this species is usually encountered in Connecticut after periods of strong easterly winds. It is rare in May; spring
migration is mostly along the Mississippi River flyway. Inland it is a
rare fall migrant.

Earliest spring arrival: Mar. 30, 1988; Apr. 16, 1984; Apr. 20, 1920,
1941.

One reported from "the beginning of March" to May 8, 1983, in the Stratford–Milford area was unusually early (CW 3:33).

Latest spring departure: June 5, 1926; May 30, 1926; May 28, 1967.
Earliest fall arrival: July 25, 1965; July 28, 1959; Aug. 17, 1966.
Latest fall departure: Nov. 20, 1917; Nov. 17, 1952; Nov. 15, 1958.

COMMENTS: Recent studies recommend treating Lesser Golden-Plover as two distinct species: American Golden-Plover (*P. dominica*) and Pacific Golden-Plover (*P. fulva*) (Connors 1983). The normal migration routes and winter areas of these two forms are very different, and studies have revealed no interbreeding where they overlap in Alaska. The American Golden-Plover is the species normally expected in Connecticut during migrations, but Pacific Golden-Plover has appeared in New England (Hayman et al. 1986). A golden-plover reported on December 8, 1958, at Marlborough (P. Isleib, BMAS 43:129) was not published with sufficient details to enable identification to species. Any winter record of golden-plover should be carefully studied to confirm the presence of *P. fulva* in Connecticut.

HISTORICAL NOTES: Before 1850 this species was a sporadically "common to abundant" fall migrant and "rare" in spring along coastal New England and New York (Forbush 1916; Hill; Bull 1964; Mackenzie 1961). It was shot in large numbers, particularly after 1860, paralleling the decline of the Passenger Pigeon (Forbush 1916). Merriam (1877) said it was "common" in migration, and Wright (1897) noted it was "fairly irregular." By 1900 it had declined 90% in numbers during the previous 15 years and was feared to be near extinction (Bent 1929; Forbush 1916; Bergstrom; Bailey 1955; Bull 1964). It increased very slowly after 1900 (Bergstrom; Shipley 1931), and Sage et al. (1913) called it a "very rare" fall migrant. It was "rare" in the 1920s (Forbush 1925). Unusual at the time was a report by R. Coles and L. Johnson of three birds on May 30, 1926, at Greenwich, which was thought to have been the first spring record in the greater New York City area since 1885 (*Auk* 44:99).

This species became more frequent at Cape Cod in the 1930s (Bailey 1968), and it was first found in winter in New York on Long Island in 1936–1937 (Bull 1964). By the 1940s, it was "more regular" and widespread in the region (Griscom and Snyder; Bull 1964; Bergstrom 1960). In 1955, 85 birds were found at South Windsor (HAS), and 45 were there on October 4, 1971 (P. Desjardins, pers. comm.), probably the largest concentrations in Connecticut in this century. In the 1960s, Bull noted that it was "uncommon" in fall and "rare" but regular since 1947 in spring.

Wilson's Plover (*Charadrius wilsonia*)

STATUS: a very rare coastal visitor from April to early September. Of more than 18 reports, 8 are from May and June and 3 from September. Spring reports are usually of "overshoots," and fall birds are normally storm-driven by strong southerly winds or hurricanes.

Earliest spring arrival: Apr. 7, 1950, 1951; Apr. 10, 1949; Apr. 30, 1948.

Latest fall departure. Sept. 10, 1957; Sept. 8, 1941; Sept. 4, 1954.

COMMENTS: There are at least two reports of sightings inland along the Connecticut River (HAS) that are not satisfactorily corroborated, at least as originally published.

HISTORICAL NOTES: This southern species has never been numerous in Connecticut in historic times. Linsley (1843a) reported this species at Stratford. Merriam (1877) added no additional Connecticut sightings other than Linsley's, and Sage et al. (1913) noted a report from Bridgeport in 1888.

From 1948 to 1951 this species regularly appeared in spring at Lyme and was apparently seen by knowledgeable observers (AFN 3:203, 4:235, 5:246). One observer wrote in 1958: "this species has been reported with varying regularity over many years at this particular spot and certainly must represent breeding somewhere in the vicinity" (AFN 12:335, 337). Not suprisingly, nesting was not confirmed, and reports from Lyme ceased soon after the above commentary was published. There is a vague and undocumented report of nesting at East Haven on June 2, 1950 (RNEB 6:125). In recent years this species has decreased at the northern edges of its range, and fewer birds have been sighted in New England.

Semipalmated Plover (*Charadrius semipalmatus*)

STATUS: a fairly common coastal migrant from early May to early June and from late July to mid-October; it is sometimes abundant during peak migration days in late August and early September. Inland it is uncommon along the shores of lakes, ponds, and larger rivers during migration. Nonbreeding stragglers are usually uncommon in June and early July.

Earliest spring arrival: Mar. 28, 1966; Apr. 26, 1981; Apr. 29, 1984.
Latest spring departure: June 21, 1984; June 14, 1939; June 13, 1977.
Earliest fall arrival: July 7, 1985; July 13, 1977; July 14, 1965.
Latest fall departure: Nov. 23, 1985; Nov. 17, 1975; Nov. 16, 1958.

HISTORICAL NOTES: This species was formerly "very abundant" along coastal New England (Forbush 1916). It was a popular game bird, and market hunting caused a rapid decline from about 1880 to 1910, after which it increased when protective laws were implemented (Forbush 1916; Bailey 1955). Sage et al. (1913) said it was "common." The population regained its mid-1800s level in about 1940 and has not changed significantly since (Hill 1965).

Piping Plover (*Charadrius melodus*)

STATUS: a rare to locally uncommon coastal migrant from mid-March to mid-May and from early August to early September, rarely into October. Inland it is a casual migrant from mid-July to late September. Nests very locally on undisturbed sandy beaches at Bridgeport, Stratford, Milford, West Haven, Madison, Old Saybrook, and Old Lyme, usually in association with colonies of Least Terns. At present it is federally listed as an endangered species.

Earliest spring arrival: Feb. 27, 1982; Mar. 11, 1985; Mar. 18, 1984.
Latest fall departure: Nov. 12, 1972; Nov. 4, 1941; Oct. 26, 1972.

Piping Plover

HISTORICAL NOTES: Alexander Wilson (1813) said it was "very abundant" on sandy shores, and Hill (1965) quoted Thoreau as calling it "abundant" on Cape Cod in the 1840s. Linsley (1843a) considered it "rare" in Connecticut and found it nesting at Stratford; Merriam (1877) reported it nesting at Saybrook. This species declined rapidly from 1880 to 1910, paralleling the decline of the Semipalmated Plover (Cruickshank; Bagg and Eliot; Bergstrom; Hill; Bull 1964). Sage et al. (1913) said it was "nearly extinct in the breeding season" and "very rare" in migration and listed only three reports from 1877 to 1913.

Protected from hunting after 1913, its numbers noticeably increased in the region during the 1920s (Forbush 1925; Bull 1964). It was seen at Westport in 1924 after an absence of 27 years, and it nested at Stratford in 1931 (A. Saunders, *Auk* 49:80). It nested at Westbrook in 1933 (*Auk* 50:444), at Guilford in 1952 (Mackenzie 1961), near Stratford in 1957 (AFN 11:391), at Westport in 1959 (AFN 13:420), at Sherwood Island (off Westport) in 1960 (Bull 1964), and at Stratford in 1961 (P. Spofford, pers. comm.). Bergstrom (1960) called it "quite common again." Subsequently, the increased recreational use of coastal beaches has disrupted the remaining nesting colonies and limited the number of available nesting sites. Recent protection efforts by the Connecticut Department of Environmental Protection and local conservation groups have benefited nesting colonies in Stratford, West Haven, and Milford, but its status remains precarious. According to the Department of Environmental Protection, only 27 pairs nested statewide in 1988.

Killdeer (*Charadrius vociferus*)

STATUS: a fairly common inland and coastal migrant from late September to mid-November; uncommon in spring from early March to late April. It is sometimes very common during peak migration in October. It nests in short grass fields, golf courses, and open areas with exposed soils throughout the state, occasionally on flat rooftops. Variable but usually uncommon in winter at the coast, less frequent inland.

HISTORICAL NOTES: Forbush (1916) stated that the Killdeer commonly nested in New England during the early 1800s. It decreased after 1850 (Bailey 1955, Hill) as agriculture declined and hunting was pervasive. Merriam (1877) said it was "not a very common summer resident" and added that it used to be "common" at Portland. Averill (1892) noted it was "formerly a common summer visitor" but was "now rare," with none seen by him in the Bridgeport area from 1881 to 1892.

Both Bagg and Eliot (1937) and Forbush (1916) considered it "practically extirpated" from Connecticut by about 1900. Job (1922) said it was a "rare" migrant in Litchfield County and noted that it nested at Winchester about 1890.

Sage et al. (1913) stated it was "a rather rare summer resident, apparently increasing during the last decade." This species became markedly more numerous after 1913 when hunting was prohibited (Howes; Bagg and Eliot; Bailey 1955; Saunders 1950); it returned to nest at Wilton, Stratford, and West Haven in 1916 (*Auk* 36:105, BL 19:89), and at Norwalk in 1917 (*Auk* 35:341). Shipley (1931) reported that it became "common" in the Stamford area after 1920, as did L. Porter (*Auk* 47:416). It nested at Darien in 1930 (*Auk* 47:416). Bagg and Eliot (1937) said it was "fairly common" in summer, although "rare" or absent in the hillier regions. Mackenzie (1961) reported that it resumed nesting in the Guilford area in 1948 and that a few could be found in winter. Smith (1955) said that it stayed into early winter in the Norwalk area, and Bergstrom (1960) noted that it was an "uncommon" winter resident at the coast. Bull (1964) remarked that it more frequently wintered in "fairly large numbers" along the Connecticut shore. Manter (1975) said it was "common" in summer and migration and "uncommon" in winter in the Mansfield area.

OYSTERCATCHERS (FAMILY HAEMATOPODIDAE)

American Oystercatcher (*Haematopus palliatus*)

STATUS: a rare coastal migrant from May to early June and from early July to early October. Although it may winter just to our south, it is accidental here in winter: one was seen on February 8, 1987, at Madison (AmB 41:255), and several attempted to overwinter in 1987–1988 at Westbrook, with one remaining to February 27 (CW 8:64). It nests very locally on offshore sandbars at Norwalk, Westbrook, and Stonington; nesting is suspected but unconfirmed at Old Lyme and Waterford.

Earliest spring arrival: Mar. 16, 1986; Mar. 26, 1982; Apr. 5, 1985.
Latest fall departure: Nov. 21, 1971; Oct. 27, 1985.

HISTORICAL NOTES: Forbush (1916) reported that Champlain found Oystercatchers in eastern Massachusetts in flocks "like pigeons" in July 1605. Linsley (1843a), at Stratford, Connecticut, wrote: "The oystercatcher is now rare here, but fifteen years since they were not very uncommon in autumn." Suffering from overhunting and egg collecting, this species was not reported again in Connecticut until November 21, 1971, when one was photographed at Milford (K. Gunther, J. de la Torre; MFCYM 1972:1), and next on June 4, 1972, when one was seen at Groton by H. Gilman and M. Laffarque (AmB 26:739).

Expanding its nesting range northward, it resumed nesting in New Jersey in 1947, in New York in 1957, in Massachusetts in 1967 or 1968, and in Rhode Island in 1978. It nested on Fisher's Island, New York, in 1977—only three miles from the Connecticut shore. It reportedly nested on islands off Mystic in 1980 (AmB 34:755). The first verified nesting in Connecticut was on June 12, 1981, at Ram Point, Mystic (R. Dewire et al., CW 1:52). It has since expanded its nesting range to other coastal locations west to Norwalk.

AVOCETS, STILTS (FAMILY RECURVIROSTRIDAE*)*

Black-necked Stilt (*Himantopus mexicanus*)

STATUS: an accidental coastal visitor from late May into September.

REPORTS: The first Connecticut record was on July 30, 1938, at Saybrook (W. Remington, *Auk* 56:77). W. Bulmer, P. Spofford et al. observed one at Stratford in 1959 (Hills, 1978). One was present on May 28, 1971, at Madison (W. Schultz et al., AmB 25:706). Three were reported at Greenwich on September 18, 1971 (P. Spofford, MFCYM 1971:11). One was at Guilford on May 27, 1979 (S. Sibley et al., photographed, AmB 33:752).

HISTORICAL NOTES: Regionally, this southern species was possibly more common in the early 1800s than in the late 1800s (Forbush 1916; Griscom; Cruickshank; Griscom and Snyder). It has been more frequently reported in the northeast since the mid-1950s (Bailey 1968).

American Avocet (*Recurvirostra americana*)

STATUS: a very rare fall visitor from mid August to November. Accidental in spring: a specimen was collected on May 16, 1966, at Stratford (F. Novak, BCM No. B1494); one was photographed at Stonington May 14–21, 1987 (D. Houghton et al., AmB 41:402); and one was seen on May 15, 1985, at Greenwich (J. Zeranski, CW 5:50).
Earliest fall arrival: Aug. 14, 1977; Aug. 24, 1970; Sept. 4, 1984.
Latest fall departure: Nov. 1, 1970; Oct. 27, 1951; Oct. 10, 1977.

HISTORICAL NOTES: This elegant shorebird may have once been a regular vagrant to southern New England; it bred in southern New Jersey into the late 1820s (Bull, 1964). The first known Connecticut record was in 1871 at the Old Lyme–Lyme border (Merriam 1877).

SANDPIPERS, PHALAROPES (FAMILY SCOLOPACIDAE)

Greater Yellowlegs (*Tringa melanoleuca*)

STATUS: a fairly common coastal migrant from early April to early June and from mid-July to early November; less numerous inland on mudflats along streams and ponds. It is sometimes very common during peak migration in late April and late August. Individuals infrequently linger through December. Nonbreeding stragglers are uncommon along the coast and rare inland in summer. Rare in winter from December to late March.

HISTORICAL NOTES: Merriam (1877) said the Greater Yellowlegs was a "common" migrant. Cruickshank (1942), Bull (1964), and Hill remarked that this species decreased from "abundant" to "rare" or "very rare" during the late 1800s as the result of excessive hunting. In 1908 Honeywill said it was a "rare spring" and "late summer and fall migrant" in the New Haven area. Sage et al. (1913) termed it a "tolerably common spring and more common fall migrant" but it was "becoming rarer." The species increased thereafter (Hill), and Forbush (1925) noted that it again was a "common" migrant in New England. By the 1960s it had become a "very common" or "abundant" coastal migrant (Mackenzie; Bergstrom; Bull 1964). The first winter reports from Massachusetts and New York were in the 1930s and in Connecticut in 1955. Christmas Bird Count data suggest it became more frequent in December and early January in the 1970s and 1980s.

Lesser Yellowlegs (*Tringa flavipes*)

STATUS: an uncommon inland and coastal fall migrant from mid-July into October; less numerous in spring from mid-April to mid-May. It can be common during peak migration days in August. Although most fall migrants depart by late October, a few occasionally linger into November and December.
Earliest spring arrival: Mar. 12, 1966; Mar. 16, 1986; Apr. 2, 1954, 1960.

Latest spring departure: June 9, 1976; May 30, 1970; May 27, 1957.
Earliest fall arrival: June 20, 1982; June 22, 1950; June 23, 1987.
Latest fall departure: Jan. 2, 1972, 1977; Dec. 26, 1964; Dec. 16, 1979.

HISTORICAL NOTES: Forbush (1916) stated that this species was formerly as abundant as the Lesser Golden Plover and Red Knot. Hunting caused a decline from the 1870s to the 1920s, when it was a "common" fall migrant (Merriam 1877; Averill 1892; Sage et al. 1913; Forbush 1925). In 1908 Honeywill said it was more common in fall than Greater Yellowlegs. Sage et al. (1913) listed only two spring records: one each in 1877 and 1897.

Lesser Yellowlegs increased rapidly after protection from hunting was implemented: Forbush (1925) called it "one of the most common migrant shorebirds." Cruickshank (1942) said it was "more numerous than the greater yellowlegs" in the early 1940s. Bergstrom (1960) noted that it was more frequently reported in spring after 1950 than previously and added that it was "common" in fall and "regular" in spring. Recent data suggest it is more frequently reported in October and November than formerly.

Spotted Redshank (*Tringa erythropus*)

STATUS: an accidental vagrant from Europe and Asia. One state record: a female in winter plumage at New Haven on November 15, 1969, collected by D. Parsons (*Auk* 89:677, AFN 24:24; YPM No. 85719).

Solitary Sandpiper (*Tringa solitaria*)

STATUS: an uncommon migrant from late April to late May and from late July to late September. It prefers mudflats and grassy margins of freshwater ponds and streams.
Earliest spring arrival: Apr. 6, 1985; Apr. 10, 1950; Apr. 11, 1982.
Latest spring departure: May 31, 1954; May 28, 1967; May 27, 1987.
Earliest fall arrival: June 20, 1986; July 4, 1966; July 7, 1986.
Latest fall departure: Oct. 28, 1986; Oct. 26, 1952, 1974; Oct. 24, 1940.

HISTORICAL NOTES: Unlike other shorebirds, this inland migrant apparently did not appreciably decline in the early 1900s (Forbush 1916), probably because of its tendency to migrate inland in more dispersed numbers.

Willet (*Catoptrophorus semipalmatus*)

STATUS: a rare to locally uncommon coastal migrant from late July to early October; rare in spring from late April to late May. Inland it is a very rare fall migrant in August and September. It nests very locally along the coast from Guilford east and has recently attempted to nest at Stratford.

Earliest spring arrival: Apr. 7, 1964; May 1, 1983; May 4, 1945.

Latest fall departure: Dec. 21, 1985; Dec. 17, 1977; Dec. 16, 1978.

HISTORICAL NOTES: Alexander Wilson (1832) said it nested in "great numbers along the shore of New York," and Audubon (1870) found it nesting near New Bedford, Massachusetts. Linsley (1843a) said it nested at Stratford. Relentless hunting during the 1800s caused a marked decrease in nesting along the Atlantic coast north of Virginia (Bent 1929; Forbush 1916; Bailey 1955). The last nesting in Connecticut in the 19th century was reported by W. Coe at Madison on June 5, 1873 (Merriam 1877).

Sage et al. (1913) listed only two specimens after 1877: one on August 12, 1887, at West Haven and one on August 9, 1888, at Stratford. Protection from hunting caused a gradual increase in the 1920s along the coast (Cruickshank 1942), but inland sightings remained scarce: one was seen at Meriden on July 24, 1904; another there on September 23, 1913; one at Cheshire on October 15, 1915 (*Auk* 38:466); one at Farmington on June 3, 1951 (AFN 5:247); and one at South Windsor on September 12, 1954 (HAS). Hill (1965) detected a decrease after 1950 in fall migrants, which largely consisted of the western race *C. s. inornatus*, while spring migrants, consisting mainly of the eastern race *C. s. semipalmatus*, became somewhat more numerous. It was confirmed as a nester in 1978 at both Madison and Old Lyme (AmB 32:155) although suspected of nesting there the previous 2 years. It has subsequently regularly nested there and in Norwalk.

Spotted Sandpiper (*Actitus macularia*)

STATUS: a fairly common migrant from early May to early June and from late July to early October; very rarely lingers into November and December. It nests locally throughout the state near inland streams and ponds, and, more rarely, along tidal creeks at the coast. It prefers to feed along the gravelly and stony margins of ponds and lakes. Unreported in midwinter.

Earliest spring arrival: Apr. 10, 1950; Apr. 16, 1916, 1980; Apr. 17, 1976.

Latest fall departure: Jan. 2, 1966; Dec. 30, 1972; Dec. 15, 1973.

HISTORICAL NOTES: This species undoubtedly benefited from the numerous farm ponds present in the state during the 1800s. Merriam (1877) wrote that it was found "wherever there is a pond or small stream" and called it a "common summer resident." Infrequently shot by hunters, it remained "common" in summer through the 1930s (Sage et al.; Wright; Job; Griscom; Howes; Forbush 1925; Bagg and Eliot; Shipley; Cruickshank). Griscom and Snyder (1955) detected a slight decrease after 1940. In the 1960s it was "common" and "widely distributed" throughout the state (WMF; Bull 1964; Mackenzie; Bergstrom 1960) but nested more infrequently, possibly due to the decline in the number of ponds with undisturbed grassy edges.

Upland Sandpiper (*Bartramia longicauda*)

STATUS: a rare to locally uncommon migrant from mid-July to late September, less numerous in spring from mid-April to mid-May. A rare nester in Hartford County; only about 14 pairs nested in 1988.

Earliest spring arrival: Mar. 13, 1938; Mar. 17, 1945; Mar. 26, 1939.

Latest fall departure: Oct. 24, 1963; Oct. 9, 1971; Oct. 8, 1944, 1947.

HISTORICAL NOTES: This species may have initially prospered after the early settlers cleared the land. Forbush (1916) and Bailey stated that it was a "common summer breeder and abundant migrant" during the mid-1800s, but decreased therafter as farms were abandoned and fields returned to deciduous forest. Linsley (1843a) said it nested at Stratford. Merriam (1877) called it a "common summer resident." Bagg and Eliot (1937) noted that it was "rare" in the Connecticut River valley in the 1880s, as did Averill (1892) and Wright (1897) in the 1890s in Fairfield County. It last nested in the Stamford area in 1897 and in Stratford in about 1892 (Howes 1928). In 1908 Honeywill et al. said it was "now becoming rare" in the New Haven area.

In 1908 Job said that it was "once quite common, but now scarce" and noted that it last nested in Litchfield County at Torrington in 1902. Sage et al. (1913) wrote that it was "formerly a common summer resident . . . now a rare spring and fall migrant," and they reported that the last nesting in the state occurred in 1904. Subsequently, it continued to nest in the Connecticut River valley in small numbers (Bergstrom

1960). After the 1920s it was "very rare" in summer and was a "rare but occasionally common" migrant (Howes; Bagg and Eliot; Forbush 1925). It nested at Glastonbury in 1948, Suffield in 1959, and Fairfield in 1966 (YPM records).

Eskimo Curlew (*Numenius borealis*)

STATUS: very close to extinction. Formerly, it was a fall migrant along the northern Atlantic coast south to Long Island, from which it migrated south over the ocean to eastern South America. In Connecticut it was formerly found after easterly storms, especially during early September.

HISTORICAL NOTES: In the early 1800s, the Eskimo Curlew was an "abundant" fall migrant in New England, and was most frequently seen on the outer coastal areas (Bailey 1955; Hill). Subjected to relentless hunting, it decreased markedly in southern New England after 1870 and, more rapidly, from the late 1880s to the early 1890s. Thereafter, it was never again seen in the large numbers formerly present (Forbush 1925; Hill).

In Connecticut, Linsley (1843a) collected one at Stratford (AMNH No. 299,436). Merriam (1877) said it was "not common." Averill (1892) called it "rare" and mentioned a specimen collected in the summer of 1886 at Stratford. Sage et al. (1913) wrote that it was "formerly an accidental visitor in the fall migration." Apparently, the last record for Connecticut was a specimen taken on September 12, 1889, at the Quinnipiac marshes, New Haven, by E. Munson (SMNC No. 46.87.56).

Whimbrel (*Numenius phaeopus*)

STATUS: a rare to locally uncommon coastal migrant from mid-July to mid-September; very rare in spring from late April into early June. Accidental inland: one was captured in the Eastford area, August 15, 1893 (Manter 1975), one was seen at Barkhamsted on July 21, 1946 (Bergstrom 1960), and one was seen at Mansfield on August 5, 1976 (AmB 31:228).

Earliest spring arrival: Apr. 9, 1984; Apr. 13, 1970; Apr. 27, 1973.
Latest spring departure: June 5, 1943; June 4, 1886; June 1, 1940.
Earliest fall arrival: July 1, 1972; July 3, 1982; July 10, 1965.
Latest fall departure: Oct. 24, 1940; Oct. 23, 1971; Oct. 5, 1947.

HISTORICAL NOTES: Thomas Nuttall (1832) described "dense flocks" of this species in coastal Massachusetts that covered several acres. Merriam (1877) said it was a "rare" migrant in Connecticut, although Hill (1965) and Griscom and Snyder (1955) said it was "common" prior to 1900 in Massachusetts. The population of this species declined; Sage et al. (1913) listed only 11 reports from 1853 to 1911 and called it a "rare straggler in spring and fall." It increased somewhat when protection from hunting was implemented in 1908 (Hill 1965; Bailey 1955; Cruickshank 1942), but it remains a scarce visitor in Connecticut.

COMMENTS: An unusually large concentration of 23 birds occurred on August 20, 1979, at Guilford (AmB 34:140).

Long-billed Curlew (*Numenius americanus*)

STATUS: an accidental vagrant from western North America. Although no photographs or specimens are extant, this species was formerly recorded in Connecticut as a fall migrant. It is now accidental on the Atlantic coast north of South Carolina.

HISTORICAL NOTES: This species was a regular fall migrant on coastal Long Island in the 1840s (Bull) and a "common" fall migrant in eastern Massachusetts before 1850 (Hill). It declined rapidly thereafter, and it was "rare" by the 1880s (Bagg and Eliot; Cruickshank; Griscom and Snyder). It has been "accidental" since 1900 (Griscom and Snyder; Bull 1964). This dramatic and continuing decline may result from the destruction of its Midwest nesting grounds for agricultural use since the mid 1800s (Bull 1964).

In Connecticut, nearly all of the published reports of this species are from the 1800s. Linsley collected a specimen at Stratford on August 3, 1841 (present whereabouts unknown). Merriam (1877) vaguely stated: "Not particularly rare during migrations, but excessively shy" and quoted Capt. O. Brooks of Faulkner's Island as saying, "Not plenty; occasionally one stops here in the fall." Merriam also stated that it had been collected near Hartford but failed to list any specific date. George Bird Grinnell, an observer familiar with this species, reported one at Milford during the summer of 1873 (Merriam). In 1892 one was collected at Stratford by E. Austin (Averill 1892), but its present location is not known. More recently, W. Bulmer reported one at Stratford on July 19, 1968 (Dater 1968). In 1975, P. Buckley wrote that it "has increased in the southeast U.S. in recent years" (AmB 29:954).

Hudsonian Godwit (*Limosa haemastica*)

STATUS: a rare coastal migrant from late August to late October; it occasionally lingers into November. Accidental in spring: one was reported on May 15, 1914, at Meriden (*Auk* 38:466); one was seen on May 23, 1971, at Milford (AmB 25:712); and one was seen on May 22, 1988, at Stratford (L. Bevier et al.) Accidental inland: a pair were shot near Middletown on October 25, 1845 (HAS); one was shot at Middletown on October 11, 1897 (Sage et al.; HAS); there was the above-referenced sighting at Meriden in 1914; and one was seen at New Canaan October 6–7, 1985 (MFN 13:6). It is most apt to be found after prolonged easterly winds.

Earliest fall arrival: July 18, 1972; Aug. 10, 1988; Aug. 20, 1971.

Latest fall departure: Dec. 1, 1983; Nov. 19, 1966; Nov. 11, 1967.

HISTORICAL NOTES: Forbush (1916) stated that this species was "quite abundant" in the early 1800s. One was taken at Stratford before 1843 (Linsley 1843a). Sage et al. (1913) noted that this species was collected in Connecticut only in 1845, 1852, and 1897. Hill (1965) noted a regional decline that continued into the early 1900s. A gradual increase was first noted after 1910 (Hill; Cruickshank; Bull 1964), and continued into the 1960s (AmB 18:11, 25:834).

Marbled Godwit (*Limosa fedoa*)

STATUS: a very rare coastal migrant from mid-August to early October. Accidental in spring: a female was collected on May 21, 1968, at Stratford (BcM No. B1384). Accidental in winter: a male was collected on February 10, 1955 at New Haven (YPM No. 6431); this bird may have been the same one observed at the same location December 12–31, 1954 (RNEB 10:311). Not reported inland.

Earliest fall arrival: Aug. 15, 1977, 1987; Aug. 19, 1986; Aug. 20; 1971.

Latest fall departure: Oct. 7, 1985; Oct. 6, 1985; Sept. 29, 1985.

HISTORICAL NOTES: Audubon (1870) said "immense flocks" of this large shorebird were present in fall along the Atlantic coast from Massachusetts south. Linsley noted "large flocks" at Stratford in August 1842. Suffering from the loss of nesting habitat in the northern prairie states and from shooting, it declined strikingly in the late 1800s (Hill); it was a "rare" migrant in the early 1870s (Merriam 1877) and was a "very rare fall migrant" in the 1880s (Forbush 1916; Cruickshank; Hill).

Sage et al. (1913) reported only one record (August 26, 1909) from the 1840s to 1913. Bent (1927) said it was a "straggler" before the 1930s, after which it increased slowly (Hill; Bull 1964). This species was a regular fall migrant on the south shore of Long Island, occasionally in flocks of up to 10 birds, in the 1940s (Cruickshank 1942). Bull (1964) noted it was a "rare to uncommon, but regular fall migrant" and "very rare in spring" on coastal Long Island.

COMMENTS: A spring report on May 15, 1977, at Stratford (AmB 31:974) was not satisfactorily corroborated, at least as published.

Ruddy Turnstone (*Arenaria interpres*)

STATUS: a common coastal migrant from mid-May to early June and from late July to mid-October; uncommon in winter. Nonbreeding stragglers are regular in summer. Inland it is very rare at any time. It prefers to feed along kelp-strewn beaches and rocky shores.

HISTORICAL NOTES: Forbush (1916) said the Ruddy Turnstone was a "very abundant" migrant through the mid-1800s. Merriam (1877) noted that it was "common," and Averill (1892) reported that it was "tolerably common." As it declined rapidly, Honeywill et al. (1908) said it was "not ordinarily to be found" in the New Haven area. Sage et al. (1913) said it was "a rather rare migrant" and listed only nine records from 1880 to 1910. It increased markedly after protection from hunting was implemented (Hill). A. Saunders found it in flocks of "a dozen to fifty or more" in the spring of 1918 (*Auk* 36:105), and it was again a "common" migrant by the 1920s (Forbush 1925). Its numbers stabilized by 1940 (Cruickshank; Hill); it was a "very common to occasionally abundant coastal migrant" and "rare in winter" in the New York City area in the early 1960s (Bull 1964).

It was first reported wintering in Massachusetts and New York in the 1930s (Bailey 1955; Bull 1964). Connecticut's first midwinter report was on January 22, 1950, at Madison (Bergstrom 1960). Winter reports have subsequently become regular (Bailey 1955; Bull 1964; CW).

Red Knot (*Calidris canutus*)

STATUS: an uncommon coastal migrant from late April to early June and from late July to late November; less numerous along the western Sound. It is occasionally very common at favored coastal locations during peak migration in late August. It is very rare in winter. Nonbreeding stragglers occasionally summer along the coast. Unreported inland. It favors flat beaches and mudflats.

HISTORICAL NOTES: Hill (1965) said this species was "one of the most abundant of the shorebirds until 1850." In Connecticut, Merriam noted that it was "common during migrations" in the 1870s, but overshooting caused noticeable declines; Sage et al. (1913) reported only six records from 1874 to 1900. After protection, slight increases were observed from 1915 to 1930 (Hill; Bull 1964). I. Gabrielson reported in 1916 what he believed was the first spring Connecticut record (*Auk* 34:462). In the early 1940s, it was again a "common" migrant at eastern Long Island, New York, but was uncommon westward along Long Island Sound (Cruickshank 1942). Bull (1964) said it occasionally occurred along the shores of the Sound in "small numbers—up to a dozen or so" and added that it had not attained its former numbers. It has increased gradually since.

Sanderling (*Calidris alba*)

STATUS: a fairly common coastal migrant from early April into June and from mid-July to late November; it is sometimes very common on peak migration days in September. It is regular but uncommon along the coast in winter. Nonbreeding individuals are occasionally reported in summer. Accidental inland: one was sighted at South Windsor on September 3, 1935 (BL 37:464). It favors sandy beaches; it is much less numerous on mudflats.

HISTORICAL NOTES: Linsley (1843a) wrote: "The sanderling is also rare here. I have obtained but one specimen." However, Merriam (1877) said it "occurs during migrations, and is extremely abundant in fall." It declined noticeably from the 1880s to about 1920, largely the result of excessive hunting. Sage et al. (1913) said it was "formerly an abundant spring and fall migrant; now rare, and occurring regularly only in the fall." It increased after protection from hunting was instituted.

Semipalmated Sandpiper (*Calidris pusilla*)

STATUS: a fairly common to abundant migrant from early May to early June, and from mid-July to early October; it occasionally lingers into November. It is frequent on coastal mudflats and occurs in small numbers inland along the shores of rivers, lakes, and ponds. Nonbreeding stragglers are frequent in summer.

Earliest spring arrival: Apr. 24, 1955; Apr. 26, 1984; Apr. 29, 1956.
Latest fall departure: Nov. 18, 1967; Nov. 9, 1983; Nov. 4, 1950.

COMMENTS: Early winter reports, of which there are several from Connecticut, are questionable because winter specimens from the northeast are apparently all Western Sandpipers (A. Phillips, AmB 29:799).

HISTORICAL NOTES: Griscom and Snyder (1955) said this species in the 1860s was "always a common transient, but never reported in flocks of as many as 1,000 birds." Forbush (1916) said it was "abundant" throughout the 1800s. Merriam (1877) said it was "common along the shore during migrations." Averill (1892), Wright (1897), and Sage et al. (1913) described it as "abundant" after 1890. Somewhat diminished by market hunting (Hill), its numbers recovered rapidly after hunting laws were implemented and then stabilized in the 1940s (Cruickshank; Hill).

Western Sandpiper (*Calidris mauri*)

STATUS: an uncommon fall migrant from late July to mid-October; sometimes fairly common at favored coastal location during peak migration days from late August to mid-September. Rare after mid-October; it occasionally lingers into December. It is rare in spring migration in May and rare inland at any time.

Earliest spring arrival: May 14, 1982; May 19, 1956; May 22, 1985.
Latest spring departure: June 10, 1971; June 7, 1984; June 2, 1955.
Earliest fall arrival: July 20, 1972; July 23, 1961; July 24, 1960.
Latest fall departure: Dec. 29, 1984; Dec. 20, 1973; Dec. 5, 1937.

HISTORICAL NOTES: This species was not distinguished from Semipalmated Sandpiper by early authorities with sufficient accuracy to enable any detection of significant population changes.

Least Sandpiper (*Calidris minutilla*)

STATUS: a fairly common coastal migrant from early May to early June and from early July to October. It is less frequent inland but is more numerous than Western and Semipalmated Sandpipers. Nonbreeding stragglers are rare in June and early July.

Earliest spring arrival: Apr. 18, 1984; Apr. 23, 1975; Apr. 24, 1977.
Latest spring departure: June 14, 1984; June 11, 1987; June 10, 1975.
Earliest fall arrival: June 29, 1986; July 4, 1977; July 5, 1968.
Latest fall departure: Nov. 3, 1929; Oct. 26, 1952; Oct. 12, 1963.

HISTORICAL NOTES: Bagg and Eliot (1937) reported it as "rare" inland before 1890. Hill (1965) said it had increased slightly since 1940.

White-rumped Sandpiper (*Calidris fuscicollis*)

STATUS: a rare to uncommon coastal migrant from mid-August to late October; usually rare in spring from mid-May to early June. It occasionally lingers to late November. Very rare inland at any time.

Earliest spring arrival: May 5, 1984; May 8, 1968; May 13, 1967.
Latest spring departure: June 14, 1953; June 11, 1987; June 7, 1985.
Earliest fall arrival: July 24, 1972; July 29, 1930; Aug. 10, 1972.
Latest fall departure: Nov. 28, 1986; Nov. 27, 1971; Nov. 19, 1967.

HISTORICAL NOTES: Forbush (1916) said that this species decreased before the early 1900s during the period of unlimited shooting. Sage et al. (1913) called it a "tolerably common" fall migrant along the coast, yet reported only one spring record. Its numbers increased somewhat after protection in 1913, and its population stabilized by 1940 (Hill).

COMMENTS: An unusually large number of White-rumped Sandpipers were present on September 18, 1987, when more than 120 were counted at Westport during a storm (F. Mantlik, CW 8:40).

Baird's Sandpiper (*Calidris bairdii*)

STATUS: a rare coastal migrant from early August to October; it is most frequently reported in late August and early September. It is casual inland. It favors short-grass wetlands, golf courses, and mudflats along tidal ponds.

Earliest fall arrival: July 11, 1967; Aug. 2, 1972; Aug. 7, 1972.
Latest fall departure: Nov. 3, 1888 (spec.); Oct. 28, 1887 (spec.); Oct. 24, 1972.

COMMENTS: Spring reports of this species in the state lack sufficient documentation, at least as published (BL 30:269; Bagg and Eliot; CW 5:51).

HISTORICAL NOTES: The first Connecticut record was on October 28, 1887, when a female was collected by L. Woodruff at New Haven (*Auk* 7:89). It was next reported on November 3, 1888, at Stratford by J. Averill (*Auk* 6:189).

Pectoral Sandpiper (*Calidris melanotos*)

STATUS: an uncommon coastal migrant in fall from early August to October; it sometimes lingers to late October and early November. It is occasionally common at favored coastal locations during peak migration days in September. Rare to uncommon in spring from mid-April to mid-May; it infrequently lingers to late May. It is less frequent, but regular, inland. It prefers wet fields and mudflats along ponds and reservoirs.

Earliest spring arrival: Mar. 24, 1963; Mar. 28, 1971; Apr. 1, 1972.
Latest spring departure: June 6, 1971; June 5, 1966; May 30, 1955.
Earliest fall arrival: July 22, 1934; July 24, 1967; July 27, 1968.
Latest fall departure: Nov. 22, 1956; Nov. 10, 1940; Nov. 19, 1950.

HISTORICAL NOTES: Forbush (1916) noted that this species was locally "abundant," with great flocks migrating along the coast during the mid-1800s, and that it declined from 1870 on. Merriam (1877) reported that it was "common" in fall migration. It remained common through the 1890s (Averill 1892; Wright 1897) and into the early 1900s (Sage et al. 1913). The first spring record in Connecticut was on May 13, 1916, at East Haven (Auk 35:341). Forbush (1925) said it was regionally a "common" fall migrant and "rare" in spring. Bagg and Eliot (1937) said it occurred "fairly often in spring as well as fall" in the upper Connecticut River valley.

COMMENTS: An exceptionally large number were present on April 6, 1986, when 51 were counted at South Windsor (CW 6:50).

Sharp-tailed Sandpiper (*Calidris acuminata*)

STATUS: an accidental vagrant from Asia. In North America it occurs rarely along the Pacific coast from Alaska south to California (Terres 1980); it is casual on the Atlantic coast. An immature bird was discovered at Norwalk on October 15, 1985 (F. Mantlik, CW 6:15, 7:48). It was photographed, banded and released the next day. (The dates reported in CW 6:21 are incorrect.)

COMMENTS: There is a spring sight report of one at Milford on May 8, 1977 (AmB 31:974), which, if correctly identified, would be the only spring record for eastern North America.

Purple Sandpiper (*Calidris maritima*)

STATUS: an uncommon coastal migrant and winter visitor on breakwaters, jetties, and offshore rocks from November to mid-May; it is sometimes very common during peak migration days in late November and late April. Accidental inland: one was seen near Hartford on November 3, 1928, by G. T. Griswold (Bagg and Eliot 1937). Accidental in summer: August 21, 1940, (Fairfield, A. Saunders; Auk 67:253); July 26, 1980, (Faulkner's Island, Guilford; S. Sibley, AmB 35:158).

Earliest fall arrival: Sept. 8, 1983; Sept. 13, 1964; Sept. 23, 1985.

Latest spring departure: June 5, 1943; May 29, 1966; May 28, 1962, 1967.

HISTORICAL NOTES: Merriam (1877) noted that this species was "not uncommon during the migrations . . . many winter on the islands near the coast." However, Sage et al. (1913) listed only 14 reports from 1876 to 1900 and called this species "a rare fall migrant" and an "occasional winter resident," which suggests that a significant decline occurred after the 1870s. Increases noted in the 1930s and 1940s (Griscom and Snyder 1955) were probably the result of protection from hunting and the construction of many stone jetties along the coast. After an absence of many years it was found at Fairfield in 1936 (*Auk* 67:253). Bull (1964) said it was "locally, a very common winter visitant."

Dunlin (*Calidris alpina*)

STATUS: a fairly common coastal migrant from October to early December and from late March to late May; uncommon to locally common in winter. Occasionally abundant on sandbars and mudflats during peak migrations in October and April. Nonbreeding stragglers are rare in summer. Inland it is rare but regular in fall; very rare in spring.

Earliest fall arrival: Sept. 10, 1967; Sept. 14, 1978, 1986; Sept. 17, 1966.

Latest spring departure: June 17, 1984; June 12, 1987; June 8, 1954.

HISTORICAL NOTES: Forbush (1916) noted that Dunlin were formerly "abundant" but declined after 1890. Merriam (1877) said it was a "common migrant" in fall, adding that "a few may winter"; but in 1908 Honeywill et al. stated that it was a "very rare spring and fall migrant" in the New Haven area. Sage et al. (1913), perhaps too generously, noted it was a "rare spring and tolerably common late fall migrant." It recovered rapidly after protection from hunting (Hill 1965). Forbush (1925) said it was a "rare spring and uncommon to common fall migrant." Winter reports increased in the 1940s and 1950s (Cruickshank 1942; Bull 1964; Hill), and it became a regular winter visitor in coastal Fairfield County in the 1950s (Bull 1964). During the early 1960s, it was a "common to locally abundant migrant and winter visitor" in the greater New York City area (Bull 1964).

Curlew Sandpiper (*Calidris ferruginea*)

STATUS: a very rare coastal visitor. Regionally, this species is a regular spring migrant in May and June, less frequent in fall, chiefly in August and September. July reports may be of summer stragglers or early fall migrants (Bull 1964). It may linger into December; a specimen was taken just off our shore at Fisher's Island, New York, on December 19, 1923 (Bull 1964).

HISTORICAL NOTES: This Eurasian vagrant was first reported in Connecticut on October 3, 1859, at Hartford (Merriam 1877). However, Sage et al. (1913) state that sightings in June 1874 and September 1886 at New Haven listed by Merriam and others were actually Stilt Sandpipers and not Curlew Sandpipers; this casts some doubt on the accuracy of the 1859 record. One in breeding plumage was seen May 31 and June 1, 1958, at New Haven by E. Stephenson et al. (RNEB 14:3) but apparently was not photographed. The first confirmed state record was of an individual photographed by D. Finch et al. June 9–10, 1971, at New Haven. What was possibly the same bird was seen at Milford, June 6, 1971, and later at Milford and New Haven July 7–11, 1971 (MFCYM 8/71; AmB 25:838).

The only reliable inland report, excluding the dubious 1859 record in Hartford noted above, was one at Chesire October 23–25, 1965 (D. Finch et al., YPM records).

Stilt Sandpiper (*Calidris himantopus*)

STATUS: a rare to uncommon coastal migrant from late July to October; very rare in May. Very rare inland, it prefers muddy shores of tidal ponds; infrequently reported on coastal mudflats.

Earliest spring arrival: Apr. 17, 1977; May 6, 1971; May 8, 1983.

Latest spring departure: May 30, 1894 (spec.); May 28, 1921; May 21, 1988.

Earliest fall arrival: July 17, 1983; July 21, 1985; July 23, 1982.

Latest fall departure: Oct. 31, 1983; Oct. 19, 1935; Oct. 15, 1955.

HISTORICAL NOTES: Forbush (1925) wrote that this species was "once common to abundant," although Hill (1965) said it was "overlooked in New England until 1868." It suffered a marked decline around the turn of the century (Forbush 1916). Sage et al. (1913) described it as a "rare straggler" and listed four fall and two spring reports, the first in

June 1874 in North Haven. After protection from hunting in 1913, this species increased gradually.

COMMENTS: The largest concentration in recent years was 38 individuals seen at Stratford on August 26, 1979 (AmB 34:140).

Buff-breasted Sandpiper (*Tryngites subruficollis*)

STATUS: a rare coastal migrant from late August into early October; most frequently reported in early September; not reported in spring. It prefers short-grass wetlands and occasionally dry sandy fields along the coast. It is very rare away from the coast.

Earliest fall arrival: Aug. 28, 1983; Aug. 29, 1939, 1950; Aug. 30, 1973.

Latest fall departure: Oct. 15, 1935; Oct. 5, 1977, 1973; Oct. 3, 1918.

HISTORICAL NOTES: A. C. Bent (1929) quotes Professor W. Rowan: "Like the American golden plover and Eskimo curlew [the Buff-breasted Sandpiper] used to exist in millions and was slaughtered in uncountable numbers." Merriam (1877) said it was "not common" in fall. Sage et al. (1913) listed only two reports from the 1880s to 1910, and Forbush (1925) and Cruickshank (1942) called it a "rare" and "very rare" migrant, respectively. In the 1940s and 1950s, slight increases were noted in Massachusetts (Hill; Bailey 1955). Bull (1964, 1974) said it was a "rare, but regular" fall migrant on Long Island and noted that increases occurred in the early 1970s.

Ruff (*Philomachus pugnax*)

STATUS: a very rare coastal visitor from late March to November. Of 19 published reports of sightings in Connecticut, 13 are in spring from late March through May; all are from the coast.

Earliest spring arrival: Mar. 24, 1979; Mar. 29, 1978 (spec.); May 2, 1986.

Latest fall departure: Nov. 9, 1983; Oct. 31, 1934; Aug. 22, 1986.

HISTORICAL NOTES: The Ruff was a rare straggler along the northeast Atlantic coast before 1940 (Forbush 1925; Hill; Bull 1964); it increased thereafter, even more so after 1950 (*Auk* 83:473; Bull 1964). The first Connecticut report was by F. Stebbins and A. Bowen on October 31, 1934, at Bridgeport (Bagg and Eliot 1937), and the second was May 25–30, 1946, at Westport by A. Saunders et al. (*Auk* 64:137).

Short-billed Dowitcher (*Limnodromus griseus*)

STATUS: a fairly common to occasionally abundant coastal migrant from July to late September, uncommon in spring from late April into June. Nonbreeding stragglers are occasionally reported throughout June. Accidental in early winter: one was seen and heard on December 21, 1980, at Greenwich (AmB 35:280). Inland it is a rare but regular migrant. This species favors tidal mudflats but also occurs in marshes and on sandbars.

Earliest spring arrival: Apr. 15, 1971; Apr. 18, 1985; Apr. 25, 1967.
Latest spring departure: June 13,1977; June 10, 1974; June 7, 1984.
Earliest fall arrival: July 1, 1983; July 2, 1984; July 3, 1966.
Latest fall departure: Oct. 27, 1966; Oct. 21, 1973; Oct. 16, 1981.

HISTORICAL NOTES: Forbush (1925) said this species was "abundant" in eastern Massachusetts before 1860. As with most other shorebirds, market hunting caused a severe decline (Bent 1927). Forbush (1916) reported a 75% decline in numbers in the 40 years from 1860 to 1900, although Merriam (1877) said it was "not rare during the migrations."

Short-billed Dowitcher

Sage et al. (1913) noted that it was "very rare, now merely an accidental fall migrant" and listed seven reports of only 17 birds from 1874 to 1897.

Slight increases were noticed after 1913, but sightings remained infrequent: A. Saunders reported four birds at Norwalk in May 1918 and said these were the first spring sightings in Connecticut (*Auk* 36:104). Howes (1928) called it "extremely rare and accidental" in western Connecticut. It increased rapidly by the early 1940s when Cruickshank (1942) called it "one of the most abundant transient shorebirds in our region" but added that it "becomes progressively less common westward along the Sound."

Long-billed Dowitcher (*Limnodroma scolopaceus*)

STATUS: a rare to occasionally uncommon coastal fall migrant from August to early November, very rare in May. Accidental in winter: one was present at Milford in January and February 1982 (CW 2:25). Not reported inland. Like the Short-billed Dowitcher, this species prefers tidal mudflats.

Earliest fall arrival: July 11, 1974; July 29, 1974; Aug. 3, 1981.

Latest fall departure: Nov. 24, 1983; Nov. 14, 1951; Nov. 5, 1986.

HISTORICAL NOTES: As with many other shorebirds, this species was very scarce in the late 1800s and early 1900s: the only published reports from that period were in 1886 (Sage et al. 1913), 1894, and 1913 (*Auk* 38:582).

Common Snipe (*Gallinago gallinago*)

STATUS: an uncommon migrant from late March to mid-May and from early August to mid-December; it is sometimes fairly common during peak migration days in early April and in October. Rare to locally uncommon in winter, usually near the coast. This species favors wet thickets and meadows.

HISTORICAL NOTES: Forbush (1916) said this species was "very common in New England" during the early 1800s, but noted that it declined around the turn of the century, mainly because of excessive hunting. Merriam (1877) noted that it was "common during migrations; sometimes breeds" but did not provide details about nesting locations. Job wrote in 1908 that it was "not common" in Litchfield County during migration. Sage et al. (1913) called it "tolerably common" in migration, adding that it was "rapidly decreasing in numbers." In the 1920s and 1930s, this species was called a "common" or "tolerably common" migrant (Forbush 1925; Howes, Bagg and Eliot 1937). Bull (1964) described it as a "variously uncommon to very common migrant."

The paucity of published nesting reports suggests that the Common Snipe was never a widespread nester in Connecticut. Forbush (1916) noted that it nested at Wethersfield and Fairfield in the 1860s or 1870s, and a nest with three eggs was found at Portland on May 13, 1874 (Merriam 1877). A nest with four eggs was found in New York, just over the state line from Kent, in 1936 (*Auk* 53:441). There are no acceptable nesting records in the 1970s and 1980s.

COMMENTS: Notable was a sighting of 30 Common Snipe on April 6, 1986, at Waterford (M. Szantyr, CW 6:50).

American Woodcock (*Scolopax minor*)

STATUS: an uncommon migrant from early March to mid-April and from early October to early November. In winter it is rare to locally uncommon and usually confined to coastal areas. It nests throughout the state and is locally fairly common in fields and short-grass wetlands adjacent to moist woodlands, as well as in alder and willow thickets.

HISTORICAL NOTES: Bailey (1955) said that the Woodcock was "abundant" during the mid-1800s, and Bull (1964) notes that "hundreds" were shot by hunters in a single day in the late 1800s. Merriam (1877) called it "common" in summer and "regular" in winter. Market hunting caused a marked decline in the 1880s and 1890s (Bagg and Eliot; Bull 1964). In 1908 Job wrote that it nested "sparingly," and Sage et al. (1913) said that it bred less frequently than formerly, although it was "common" in summer and "very common" in migration. Forbush (1916) noted that its numbers were "diminishing." After shorter hunting seasons and reduced bag limits were initiated, American Woodcock eventually increased (Bull 1964). Forbush (1925) described it as a "common to abundant migrant" and a "rather common local summer resident and rare winter resident." The population stabilized in the 1930s (Hill). Bull (1964) remarked that they have "not regained anything like their former numbers."

Wilson's Phalarope (*Phalaropus tricolor*)

STATUS: a rare fall migrant along the coast from mid-August to early September. Casual in spring: there are 10 reports, mostly from inland areas (all of single birds). It is very rare inland.

Earliest spring arrival: May 2, 1984; May 5, 1960; May 7, 1970.
Latest spring departure: June 2, 1987; May 26, 1968.
Earliest fall arrival: Aug. 7, 1971; Aug. 11, 1988; Aug. 14, 1948.
Latest fall departure: Sept. 18, 1973; Sept. 15, 1933; Sept. 10, 1971.

HISTORICAL NOTES: Linsley (1843a) collected a specimen at Bridge-port. Apparently this species was not reported again in the state until September 1, 1928, when R. Burdsall et al. found three at Greenwich (P. Spofford, pers. comm.) It was an accidental fall migrant until about 1935, when an increase was noted (Hill; Bailey 1955). The first inland *and* spring record was at Mansfield on May 5, 1960, by J. Slater (Manter 1975). It has been reported annually since the mid-1960s.

COMMENTS: A large concentration of this species was noted on August 24, 1975, when nine birds were counted at Stratford (AmB 30:32).

Red-necked Phalarope (*Phalaropus lobatus*)

STATUS: a very rare coastal migrant from mid-August to late September; casual in spring in May and early June. It is most often reported after storms with strong easterly winds. Casual inland.
    Earliest spring arrival: Apr. 24, 1931; May 3, 1929; May 9, 1969.
    Latest spring departure: June 8, 1987; June 3, 1932; May 29, 1955.
    Earliest fall arrival: Aug. 4, 1886; Aug. 13, 1932; Aug. 18, 1962.
    Latest fall departure: Nov. 17, 1986; Oct. 30, 1950; Sept. 30, 1971.

COMMENTS: Of 17 published sightings in Connecticut, 10 are from coastal areas, 5 are from the Connecticut River valley, and 2 are from other inland areas. Although Bull (1964) noted that this species is observed more frequently in spring, only five of the Connecticut reports are in the spring.
    On May 3, 1929, between "500 to 1000" were seen at East Haddam following a major spring storm on April 16 of that year (BL 31:267).

Red Phalarope (*Phalaropus fulicaria*)

STATUS: a very rare migrant in May and from late September to November; occurs both along the coast and inland. It is normally reported after storms with strong easterly winds; it usually migrates offshore.

Earliest spring arrival: May 5, 1958 (spec.); May 9, 1969; May 10, 1924.

Latest spring departure: June 4, 1954; May 30, 1981; May 24, 1894 (spec.).

Earliest fall arrival: Sept. 18, 1971; Sept. 22, 1946; Sept. 25, 1908.

Latest fall departure: Nov. 24, 1895 (spec.); Nov. 8, 1953; Oct. 23, 1936.

COMMENTS: About 70% of the published sightings in Connecticut are in the fall, and the remainder are in spring. Forty percent of the published reports are from the coast, 40% are from the Connecticut River valley, and the balance are from upland areas. Although Bull (1964) stated that Red-necked Phalarope is more frequently reported inshore than is the Red Phalarope, both species are reported in Connecticut in similar numbers.

An unusual summer occurrence was noted when one was seen on August 18, 1962, at Litchfield by M. Van Winkle (AFN 23:570). On May 9, 1969, 70 Red Phalaropes were reported at Stonington (AmB 23:570), representing an unusually large concentration.

JAEGERS, GULLS, TERNS (FAMILY LARIDAE)

Parasitic Jaeger (*Stercorarius parasiticus*)

STATUS: a very rare fall visitor on Long Island Sound from late August to November; most reports are in September. Regionally, it is an uncommon pelagic migrant from early May to early June, and from late July to November.

RECORDS: There are several accounts of specimens taken in the state—the only known extant one was taken on September 10, 1903, at Noank (Groton) by C. Graves (Sage et al., UCM No. 1977). One was seen at Fairfield on August 22, 1933, and found dead there on August 27, 1933 (*Auk* 53:445); one with a broken wing was found at Fairfield on November 1, 1942, by A. Saunders (BNEBL 6:(11)91)—the current locations of these two specimens are not known.

Earliest fall arrival: Aug. 22, 1933; Aug. 25, 1943, 1979.

Latest fall departure: Nov. 1, 1942 (spec.); Oct. 12, 1948; Oct. 11, 1970.

COMMENTS: The Parasitic Jaeger reported by Sage et al. (1913) as collected at Portland in the "fall of 1875" was recently reexamined and found to be a juvenile Long-tailed Jaeger (L. Bevier, pers. comm.). One reported on April 12, 1984 (CW 4:64), if correctly identified and corroborated, would represent the only spring record in Connecticut and an unprecedented early arrival date for New York and New England.

HISTORICAL NOTES: In 1970 D. Finch wrote that this species was "regular in the mouth of Long Island Sound" but added that in the "Sound itself, it is rare" (AmB 25:28).

Long-tailed Jaeger (*Stercorarius longicaudus*)

STATUS: an accidental migrant. Regionally, it is the most pelagic and least common of the jaegers; reported mostly in August and September, less frequently from late May through June.

RECORDS: Two specimens are extant: one, originally identified as a Parasitic Jaeger, was collected by John Sage at Portland in "fall of 1875" (reidentified by L. Bevier, UCM No. 9265); and one, also first identified as a Parasitic Jaeger, was found at Eastern Point, Groton, on September 30, 1979, (reidentified by L. Bevier, UCM No. 7815). Merriam (1877) reported that a specimen (present location unknown) was taken by W. Lane at Wallingford on August 30, 1873.

Laughing Gull (*Larus atricilla*)

STATUS: a fairly common coastal migrant from early April to mid-May and from late August to November; it is sometimes abundant on peak migration days in early May and September. Inland it is uncommon during migration along the Connecticut River and very rare on large lakes. It is a regular summer visitor along the coast but does not nest. In winter it is rare to uncommon along the coast in December, very rare in January.

HISTORICAL NOTES: This species was once very scarce in the state. Pressures from the millinery trade and commercial egg collecting had greatly reduced its numbers all along the east coast of the United States during the 1800s (Buckley, Gochfeld, and Buckley 1978). Linsley (1843a) noted that "some summer." Merriam (1877) said it was "not common" and reported, without details, that it may nest. Griscom and Snyder (1955) and H. Hathaway (*Auk* 30:546) reported an increase in Massachusetts from about 1900, and Sage et al. (1913) said it was "at present an accidental summer visitor" in Connecticut and listed only two records, in 1876 and 1904.

Laughing Gull

A. Saunders noted an increase in the Fairfield area beginning in 1914 (*Auk* 35:340). Several were reported in early summer of 1915 in New Haven, and it was reportedly "common" there by late summer of 1917 (*Auk* 38:582). In 1917 W. Smith spoke of an "increase in the last few years" (*Auk* 34:462, BL 19:89). Howes (1928) did not mention it for western Long Island Sound, Forbush (1925) called it "rare," and Griscom (1923) noted only four New York City area records. Shipley (1931) recorded a "recent big increase" in the Stamford area. Cruickshank (1942) detected an increase in New York since 1923, stating that it was "a fairly common spring and abundant fall migrant" and was "more common on Long Island Sound than on the south shore of Long Island." A decline in Massachusetts in the mid-1960's was attributed to competition with Herring Gulls (Hill). Bull (1964) noted an increase in the New York City area.

It was first reported in early winter in the 1920s and was reported as regular but rare in that season since the 1950s in Massachusetts and New York (Bailey 1955; Bull 1964).

COMMENTS: Nesting colonies are known in Nova Scotia, Massachusetts, New York, and New Jersey (NYBBA, Bull 1974). A major factor limiting the expansion of its nesting range is competition with larger gulls, notably the Herring Gull, that prey on eggs and young of the Laughing Gull (NYBBA). The poor quality of remaining salt marsh nesting habitat may also be a factor (Buckley et al., 1978).

Franklin's Gull (*Larus pipixcan*)

STATUS: an accidental vagrant from the Great Plains and Canadian prairies, very rare on the Atlantic coast from Massachusetts south to Virginia (Terres 1980).

RECORDS: There are two records: one was photographed on June 12, 1972, at New Haven (D. Finch, AmB 26:835), and one was sighted on August 14, 1971, at New Haven (D. Finch, AmB 25:838).

Little Gull (*Larus minutus*)

STATUS: a rare migrant and visitor on Long Island Sound. Most reports are from mid-August to January and from early March to May. It usually associates with Bonaparte's Gulls.

HISTORICAL NOTES: This species was first collected in North America on September 15, 1887, at Fire Island, New York (Bull 1964). It was first reported in Connecticut on February 12, 1955, at Guilford (Mackenzie 1961) and first confirmed on June 20, 1968, when a female was collected at Stratford (UCM No. 1999, Bulmer). This species was regionally considered an accidental winter visitor before 1960. Since the late 1960s, it has been reported virtually annually in Connecticut. Apparently, the largest number ever reported in the state was nine on May 19, 1974, at New Haven by G. Daniels and T. Burke (AmB 28:781).

COMMENTS: Two reportedly observed on July 29, 1973, at Milford and New Haven (AmB 27:850) are not satisfactorily corroborated.

Common Black-headed Gull (*Larus ridibundus*)

STATUS: a rare migrant and winter visitor on Long Island Sound; most reports are from November through mid-April. Accidental in midsummer: one was seen on July 23, 1960, at Waterford (RNEB 16:6); one was observed on July 8, 1985, at New Haven (AmB 27:850, CW 6:12); and an immature was sighted at Stratford on June 24, 1987, (CW 8:67). Like the Little Gull, it usually associates with Bonaparte's Gulls.

    Earliest fall arrival: Aug. 12, 1967; Aug. 26, 1967; Sept. 9, 1968.
    Latest spring departure: May 19, 1974; May 13, 1967; Apr. 17, 1966.

HISTORICAL NOTES: Linsley (1843a) stated that J. H. Trumbull occasionally reported this species at Stonington. These reports are questionable, although it is possible that small numbers may have been present at that time. The first North American specimen was taken in 1930, in Massachusetts (BL 32:135). The first New York report was at Montauk in 1937 (Bull 1964). Regionally, it was considered an accidental visitor through the 1940s, but it increased markedly in the 1950s, particularly at sewer outlets (Bull 1964). The first corroborated record of this species in Connecticut was on December 27, 1964, at New London (AFN 19:117); R. Emery reported one at Waterford on July 23, 1960, but provided no details (BMAS 45:34).

Bonaparte's Gull (*Larus philadelphia*)

STATUS: a fairly common coastal migrant and winter visitor from early October to mid-May, generally uncommon on western Long Island Sound. It is sometimes abundant at favored estuaries during peak migration days in early April. Stragglers, mostly immatures, are rare in summer from late May to September. It is very rare inland at any season.

Earliest fall arrival: Aug. 1, 1842, 1987; Aug. 6, 1966; Aug. 11, 1891 (spec).

Latest spring departure: June 7, 1982; June 4, 1966; June 2, 1934.

HISTORICAL NOTES: Linsley (1843a) collected a Bonaparte's Gull on August 1, 1842, at Stratford. In the 1870s it was a "tolerably common fall migrant" at Faulkner's Island (Merriam 1877). Wright (1897) said "it sometimes winters" at Fairfield. In 1908 Honeywill et al. said it was a "rare fall migrant" with "no recent records." Sage et al. (1913) noted it was a "rather rare late fall migrant and occasional winter resident . . . rare inland" and listed three summer records. In 1917 W. Smith reported a flock of 15 at Stratford (BL 19:89). Howes (1928) called it a "very rare migrant" along the western coast in the 1920s. Elsewhere in southern New England, it was considered a "common" migrant and a regular resident in mild winters in the 1930s and 1940s (Griscom and Snyder 1955).

Maximum counts for this species include 1,240 observed on January 7, 1967, at New Haven and 1,100 sighted on March 10, 1967, at Saybrook (YPM records).

Mew Gull (*Larus canus*)

STATUS: a hypothetical winter vagrant: an adult was well described at Madison November 4–7, 1973, by F. Sibley et al. (AmB 28:30); but unfortunately, it was not photographed. Other sight reports include one at Milford, November 12 and December 11, 1965 (D. Finch et al., YPM). The nominate race *L. c. canus* nests from Iceland across northern Europe and has been recorded in eastern North America (Lauro and Spencer, AmB 34:111; Terres 1980).

COMMENTS: The gull described in CW 5:1 and CW 5:34 was actually a Ring-billed Gull, not a Mew Gull as claimed. The excellent paper by A. Lauro and B. Spencer (1980, AmB 34:111) describes in detail identification of subspecies and separation from Ring-billed Gull.

Ring-billed Gull (*Larus delawarensis*)

STATUS: a common to very abundant coastal migrant and winter visitor from late August to May, generally uncommon inland. Non-breeding individuals are uncommon to common in summer along the coast.

HISTORICAL NOTES: Merriam (1877) said the Ring-billed Gull was "not rare" and added that "the young . . . may be frequently seen in winter." This species declined markedly in the late 1800s throughout much of its range, primarily due to excessive egg collecting (Bent 1921). In 1908 Honeywill et al. said it was "not ordinarily to be found." Sage et al. (1913) described it as "a rare fall migrant" and listed only six records from 1893 to 1908, all from mid-October to early December. In 1916 W. Smith found several in spring and one in mid-September, calling it "fairly common, though not generally found" (BL 19:89). The first winter report in this century was in 1917–1918 at Norwalk (*Auk* 35:340). Howes (1928) noted that it was a "very rare fall migrant" in the Stamford area. Forbush (1925) said it was "not common" in migration and "irregular" in winter in the southern New England area.

A rapid increase was noted after 1935 in Massachusetts (Hill). Bull (1964) said "the tremendous increase in the breeding population in upstate New York waters is reflected by an equally great increase within our area" in migration and winter. Since the 1950s, it has replaced the Herring Gull as the most frequent winter and spring gull (AmB 27:753). By the early 1960s, it was reported at Guilford in every month of the year except June (Mackenzie). It was first reported in the Storrs area in 1958 (Manter 1975), and since 1982 it has increased there in spring. Robbins et al. (1986) noted a significant increase in nesting in Ontario and New York from 1965 through 1975. Recent Christmas Bird Count data suggest that this species is continuing to increase in winter along the coast.

Herring Gull (*Larus argentatus*)

STATUS: a very common to very abundant resident, most abundant in winter when local populations are augmented by individuals from the north. Largest concentrations are at the coast and Connecticut River valley north to Hartford, particularly at large garbage dumps. Smaller numbers visit large inland lakes and rivers. It nests locally in colonies along the coast.

HISTORICAL NOTES: The Herring Gull was a regular visitor to Connecticut in the 1800s but apparently did not nest here. Linsley (1843a) said this species was "very abundant" in winter and spring. In the 1870s Merriam (1877) said it was an "abundant" visitor from October to May. A report written in 1892 stated that it was primarily a winter visitor, arriving in late August and early September and leaving in the first half of April; a few remained until early June (*Auk* 9:221). Sage et al. (1913) reported arrival dates as early as mid-August, and in 1914 W. Smith noted numerous flocks of 10 to 20 individuals summering along the coast in Fairfield and New Haven counties (BL 16:357, 405) but did not find evidence of nesting. In 1916 I. Gabrielson similarly found summering birds at Norwalk, Old Lyme, and at the mouth of the Connecticut River (*Auk* 34:461).

The first modern nestings in the region occurred in Massachusetts in the late 1920s; in New York at Orient, Long Island, in 1931; and at Fisher's Island in 1933 (Hill; Bull 1964). It first nested in Connecticut in 1943 at Stonington (BL 45:II:2). Its nesting range extended west to Sheep Rocks, Norwalk, in 1962, where R. Clement found 50 nests with at least 85 young. Increasing as a nester in the 1960s, this species was described by Bull (1964) as a "very abundant" year-round resident. Robbins et al. (1986) noted that Herring Gull nestings remained stable in southern New England from 1965 to 1979.

Iceland Gull (*Larus glaucoides*)

STATUS: a rare to uncommon winter visitor along the coast and inland along the Connecticut River from October to late April, less frequent along the western coast. It is sometimes reported at large inland lakes and reservoirs. Nonbreeding stragglers are accidental in summer along the coast: one was at Milford July 5–16, 1986, and was found dead there on August 1 (CW 7:10); and one was at East Haven on June 3, 1967 (RNEB 23:6). The majority of sightings are of first- or second-winter immatures; adults normally stay north of the state.

Earliest fall arrival: Sept. 6, 1954; Oct. 2, 1972; Oct. 4, 1983.

Latest spring departure: May 7, 1933; Apr. 26, 1987; Apr. 23, 1967.

HISTORICAL NOTES: Neither Linsley (1843a) nor Merriam (1877) mentioned this species. In Massachusetts it was first reported in 1880 (Bailey 1955). Apparently, the first Connecticut record was a specimen taken at Stamford on February 16, 1894 by L. Porter (*Auk* 12:76). Forbush (1925) wrote that it was "very rare in Connecticut." The second record for the state was on November 26, 1926, at Fairfield (*Auk* 49:84). Increases were noted after 1940 (AFN 24:488, Bull 1964).

Lesser Black-backed Gull (*Larus fuscus*)

STATUS: a rare winter visitor from September through April. It is usually reported from the coast and inland at large garbage dumps but sometimes from inland reservoirs. Accidental in summer: one was reported on June 29, 1978, at Groton (AmB 32:1138), and one summered in 1979 at Greenwich (AmB 33:752, 846).

Earliest fall arrival: Sept. 3, 1982; Sept. 12, 1983; Sept. 13, 1978.

Latest spring departure: June 6, 1983; May 14, 1978.

HISTORICAL NOTES: In New York this species was unreported before 1934 but reported annually since 1954 (Bull 1964). It was first recorded in Connecticut on February 28, 1970, at New Haven (D. Finch, AFN 24:488) and has been reported annually since 1978. In the winter of 1987–1988 several large dumps were regularly visited by a number of birds: three at Shelton, two at East Hartford, two at Hartford, and two at West Haven.

Glaucous Gull (*Larus hyperboreus*)

STATUS: a rare but regular winter visitor along the coast from mid-October through April; less numerous along the western coast and inland along the Connecticut River and large lakes. Nonbreeding stragglers are very rare in summer, from early June through September. It frequents large garbage dumps. Most sightings are of immatures.

Earliest fall arrival: Oct. 15, 1988; Oct. 18, 1970; Oct. 29, 1981.

Latest spring departure: May 20, 1967; May 12, 1968; Apr. 29, 1967.

HISTORICAL NOTES: Bull (1964) notes that this gull was more numerous than Iceland Gull prior to 1900 but subsequently has become less numerous. Bailey (1955) described an increase in numbers in Massachusetts during the 1920s.

This species was not reported by Linsley, Merriam, or Sage et al. Apparently, it was first reported in Connecticut on March 18, 1916, at New Haven by H. Job (*Auk* 38:582) and not again until April 20, 1933, at New Haven (Bagg and Eliot 1937). A. Saunders mistakenly thought his January 12, 1936, record at Fairfield was the second state record (*Auk* 67:253)—it apparently was the third. It has been reported annually since about 1960.

Great Black-backed Gull (*Larus marinus*)

STATUS: a fairly common resident along the coast, sometimes very common in winter and migration. Inland it is generally uncommon and local along larger rivers and lakes. It nests locally in small colonies on islands along the coast.

HISTORICAL NOTES: Hill (1965) suggested that the Great Black-backed Gull suffered a rapid decline soon after settlement. Linsley (1843a) mentioned only one record at Stratford. Merriam (1877) said it was "not rare" in winter and added that two or three individuals were frequently seen at New Haven. Averill (1892) said it was "uncommon" in the Bridgeport vicinity. In 1908 Honeywill et al. said it was "rare" in the New Haven area. It was present only from November to early April in the early part of this century (Sage et al. 1913; Forbush 1925). Protected from hunting in 1915 (Hill), it increased after 1920 (Griscom; Griscom and Snyder; Bull 1964), rapidly so after 1955 (Bull 1964).

After 1920 the breeding range of this species steadily expanded south along the New England coast. Nesting resumed in Maine in 1928, in Massachusetts in 1931 (Griscom and Snyder 1955), and in New York in 1942 (*Auk* 61:653). In Connecticut it summered and possibly nested at Guilford in 1952; young were found there in 1961 (Mackenzie 1961). Its nesting range expanded westward, and colonies were established at the Norwalk Islands in 1971 and in Greenwich in 1983.

Inland it was first reported at Hartford in 1931 (Bagg and Eliot 1937) and in the Mansfield area in 1950 (Manter 1975). It was an "uncommon winter visitor" in the vicinity of Hartford in the mid-1960s (HAS).

Black-legged Kittiwake (*Rissa tridactyla*)

STATUS: a very rare migrant and winter visitor on Long Island Sound from October into early April; most sightings are in November and March. It is accidental inland: one was sighted at Norwich on April 2, 1880 (G. Holbrook, OO 5:31), and a specimen (current whereabouts unknown) was taken at Eastford on December 16, 1898, after "the great gale of November 27" (C. Jones). It is more frequently reported from the eastern coast than from west of New Haven.

Earliest fall arrival: Sept. 3, 1943; Sept. 8, 1983; Sept. 11, 1938.

Latest spring departure: May 12, 1955; Apr. 18, 1979; Apr. 11, 1944.

HISTORICAL NOTES: The Black-legged Kittiwake has been a very rare visitor to Connecticut waters in historic times. Linsley (1843a) found this species at Stonington, and Merriam (1877) said it was "not common." Sage et al. (1913) said it was "a very rare winter visitant on the coast." This species was unreported at Guilford by Mackenzie (1961).

COMMENTS: An unusually large number of Black-legged Kittiwakes were present on October 21, 1988, when nine were observed at Greenwich (CW 9:41).

Ross' Gull (*Rhodostethia rosea*)

STATUS: an accidental winter visitor. There is one record: an adult was discovered on April 11, 1984, at West Haven by D. Varza and R. Schwartz. The bird stayed until April 22 and was seen by several hundred observers (CW 4:19, 4:64, 7:48; photographed).

Caspian Tern (*Sterna caspia*)

STATUS: a rare coastal migrant from mid-May to mid-June and from August to early October. Summer wanderers are rare but regular in late June and July. Not reported from inland areas.

Earliest spring arrival: Apr. 19, 1984; May 4, 1982; May 5, 1945.

Latest fall departure: Nov. 16, 1936 (spec.); Oct. 28, 1945; Oct. 27, 1984.

HISTORICAL NOTES: Before the late 1870s Caspian Terns regularly migrated along the New England coast (Griscom 1923; Cruickshank; Hill). It was not recorded in Connecticut, however, by Linsley, Merriam, or Sage et al. Griscom (1923) reported it annually in New York after 1915, and Cruickshank (1942) said it was "rare even on the eastern half of the Sound." It was "regular" in Massachusetts after 1939 (Bailey 1955); Hill (1965) reported a slow increase after 1950.

Apparently, the Caspian Tern was not reported in Connecticut until June 3, 1928, when J. Kuerzi observed one at Greenwich (PLSNY 41:1322). The next record was by C. Beardslee at Waterford on June

27, 1931 (*Auk* 49:85). It was reported six times from 1936 to 1953 (Mackenzie; Saunders 1950) and annually since the early 1970s.

Royal Tern (*Sterna maxima*)

STATUS: a rare to uncommon coastal visitor from June to mid-September; it is most frequently reported from August into early September. Not reported inland

Earliest summer arrival: May 24, 1988; June 3, 1976; June 20, 1975.
Latest fall departure: Sept. 25, 1971; Sept. 22, 1972; Sept. 13, 1982.

COMMENTS: One reported on April 19, 1984, at Milford (CW 4:64) represents, if correctly identified, an unprecedented early arrival date for New England.

HISTORICAL NOTES: This large tern was very rare in New England during the 1800s. There is speculation that it may have nested at Massachusetts in 1874 (Griscom and Snyder 1955). Only two specimens were taken in New York in the 1800s (Bull 1964). It was considered accidental by Griscom (1923) and Cruickshank (1942). A slight increase was observed in New York in the mid-1920s, and more so after 1940 (Cruickshank). It was reported annually in Massachusetts by the mid-1960s (Hill). Bull (1964) reported that it was increasing on the south shore of Long Island and cited great increases in southern populations as the cause.

In Connecticut the Royal Tern was not recorded by Linsley, Merriam, or Sage et al. The first record may not have occurred until the mid-1960s. By the mid-1970s it was reported annually.

Roseate Tern (*Sterna dougallii*)

STATUS: a rare migrant along the eastern coast in May and uncommon in fall, from late July to late September; very rarely reported on western Long Island Sound. It is strictly coastal; not reported inland. It is locally common near its nesting colonies on Faulkner's and Tuxis islands at Guilford during the summer. Eight to ten pairs nested at Westbrook in 1987 (CW 8:69) and two in 1988 (CW 9:11). Because of the limited world population and relatively small number of nesting localities, this species was declared an endangered species in 1988.

Earliest spring arrival: May 6, 1945; May 7, 1938; May 12, 1935.
Latest fall departure: Oct. 24, 1954; Sept. 29, 1966; Sept. 20, 1953.

Roseate Tern

HISTORICAL NOTES: This species suffered a striking decline during the plume-hunting era from the late 1800s into the early 1900s. Merriam (1877) said it was an "abundant summer resident" at the coast. In the same period W. Hoyt reported it as "common" in the Stamford area (Sage et al. 1913). Wright (1897) considered it a "rare summer resident" at Fairfield. By the early 1900s it was "very rare" and "no longer common anywhere along the coast" (Sage et al. 1913). It was not reported from 1888 through 1929 in Fairfield (A. Saunders, *Auk* 49:84).

This species recovered somewhat after hunting laws were implemented. Forbush (1925) called it a "common local migrant" in the region, and Cruickshank (1942) said it was "slowly increasing." In the spring of 1931 it was at times "equal in numbers to the Common Tern" (*Auk* 49:84). In 1938, F. Novak said it had become the "commonest tern along the Fairfield shore" (Shipley 1931), and on August 14, 1940, 500 birds were reported at Fairfield (Hills 1978). In August 1960 about 1,000 migrants were present at West Haven and Milford (AFN 22:592), and 2,311 were counted at West Haven and Milford on September 9, 1968 (Hills 1978).

This species has declined in the 1970s and 1980s, probably from competition with gulls, predation, encroachment of vegetation at nesting sites, coastal development, and market hunting on its wintering grounds in South America (NYBBA).

It nested at Goose Island, Guilford, in the 1870s (Merriam 1877). This colony was nearly wiped out by a single taxidermist in 1884 (Sage et al. 1913). In 1901 about 500 pairs nested at Goose and Faulkner's Islands, Guilford and at least 1,600 pairs nested there in 1941 (Bull 1964). Afterward, only small numbers bred there to about 1952 (Mackenzie 1961). Nesting resumed at Faulkner's Island in 1959 (Mackenzie). It nested at Branford in 1949 and 1951 (Mackenzie) and at the Norwalk Islands in 1962 (Bull 1964).

Common Tern (*Sterna hirundo*)

STATUS: a fairly common coastal migrant from late April to late May and from late August to October; it is sometimes abundant on peak migration days in September, casual in November and December. It nests locally in colonies on offshore islands and is regularly observed feeding in coastal waters. Inland it is a very rare summer visitor along the Connecticut River.

Earliest spring arrival: Apr. 21, 1976; Apr. 25, 1984; Apr. 26, 1983.

Latest fall departure: Dec. 15, 1973; Dec. 10, 1967, 1984; Nov. 29, 1967.

HISTORICAL NOTES: The Common Tern was "abundant" in the early 1800s (Cruickshank 1942). Merriam (1877) said it was a "common summer resident" and reported that it nested on Goose Island, Guilford, although outnumbered there by Roseate Terns. It continued to nest there until ousted by Herring Gulls in 1958 (Mackenzie 1961).

The Connecticut Common Tern population was decimated by extensive shooting before the turn of the century. Wright (1897) wrote that it was "very plentiful twenty years ago," and Griscom (1923) feared that it was nearing extinction. Sage et al. (1913) noted it was "rather rare" and mentioned the government's 1898 effort to construct a military fortification at Great Gull Island, New York which displaced about 7,000 terns, forcing them to disperse to smaller coastal islands.

Slowly, new nesting colonies were established, and older ones grew in size. In 1914 it nested off Madison (BL 16:405). After an absence of many years, it nested briefly at the Norwalk Islands in 1926 (fide W. Smith, BL 16:405). In Stamford, Shipley (1931) said it was "rare" in the 1920s. It nested at Westbrook in 1933 (*Auk* 50:444). Since the 1940s loss of nesting habitat and competition by Herring Gulls have pressured many nesting colonies (Mackenzie 1961). Nevertheless, its nesting range expanded westward, reaching the Norwalk Islands in 1962 (Bull 1964) and Greenwich by 1973 (MFN 1:4).

An unusually large concentration of migrants was present at West Haven in late August, 1968, when 10,000 were counted (AFN 22:592). Other high counts include 6,000 at West Haven on September 20, 1971 (AmB 26:40), and 5,000 on October 14, 1972 at Milford (AmB 27:33).

Arctic Tern (*Sterna paradisaea*)

STATUS: a hypothetical fall vagrant on Long Island Sound.

RECORDS: One specimen (present location unknown) was reportedly taken at Saybrook in the fall of 1876 by J. N. Clark, who wrote: "I have an undoubted specimen of the fall plumage of the young" (Merriam 1877). There is a vague account of a "young" Arctic Tern collected on Goose Island, Guilford, on July 9, 1931, by T. James (YPM No. 10,256), but its location was not determined after a search by the authors. There have been at least seven sight reports since 1936; two in fall and five in spring. From August 25 to September 10, 1939, one to four birds were reported at Fairfield, and A. Saunders surprisingly stated "the Arctic Tern is a regular migrant here in late August and early September" (BNEBL 3:9). The only Connecticut sight record by more than three observers was of a single bird at Milford on May 14, 1977 (AmB 31:975).

COMMENTS: Bull (1964) writes: "Although there are a number of alleged sight reports for our area, including some published, field identification is extremely difficult. Most of these reports were made in the summer or fall, when the bird is likely to be in nonbreeding plumage. At this time it is highly variable, both as to plumage characters and soft part colors." He adds an anecdote about a bird seen off Jones Beach in May 1960, thought by some experienced observers to be an Arctic Tern, which when collected, was revealed to be a Common Tern, and the individual was in *breeding plumage*. Bull concludes his passage with a question: "If specimens in museums are misidentified, as they most certainly have been, then how can one be sure in the field?"

There is a vague and undocumented report of nesting at Branford in 1945 (RNEB 1:173).

Forster's Tern (*Sterna forsteri*)

STATUS: an uncommon fall visitor along the coast from August to late November; it is sometimes fairly common on peak migration days in October. Not reported inland.

Earliest fall arrival: July 6, 1966; July 17, 1984; July 25, 1944.
Latest fall departure: Nov. 29, 1952; Nov. 22, 1970; Nov. 14, 1982.

COMMENTS: Two sighted at Milford on April 19, 1984 (CW 4:64), if correctly identified, would be an unprecedented spring record for New England. Forster's Terns in our area are probably derived from breeding populations along the southern Atlantic coast (north to New Jersey) and from inland colonies west of the Mississippi River (Griscom and Snyder; Bull 1964).

HISTORICAL NOTES: The southern nesting population of this species expanded north to New Jersey in the 1850s (Griscom 1923). It nested for the first time in New York in 1981 (NYBBA). It was not reported in Connecticut by Linsley, Merriam, or Sage et al. Cruickshank (1942) said it was reported annually at Long Island after 1925, and Hill (1965) reported it annually at Cape Cod since 1936. Possibly overlooked in earlier years, Forster's Tern was first recorded in Connecticut on November 4, 1945, when 20 birds were sighted at Fairfield (A. Saunders). Increasing in numbers, it was regularly observed in fall at coastal New Haven County during the 1960s.

Least Tern (*Sterna antillarum*)

STATUS: an uncommon coastal migrant and summer visitor from May to September; it is sometimes common during peak migration days in August. Accidental inland: one was collected at Mansfield on October 19, 1891 (Manter 1975). It nests in colonies on open sandy shores at Old Lyme, Westbrook, Madison, West Haven, Milford, Stratford, and Greenwich. The largest colony by far is at West Haven, where 500 pairs fledged 400 young in 1987.
Earliest spring arrival: May 6, 1965; May 8, 1966, 1972, 1973, 1975, 1983.
Latest fall departure: Oct. 19, 1891(spec.); Oct. 2, 1971; Sept. 9, 1975. The latest departure dates recorded in Massachusetts and New York are October 1 and October 10, respectively (Griscom and Snyder; Bull 1974). The authors view with considerable skepticism sightings in late October (RNEB 10:256) and November (AmB 28:30), at least as published.

HISTORICAL NOTES: This species was a regular summer visitor to Connecticut during the 1800s. Linsley (1843a) recorded this species at Stratford. Merriam (1877) said that this species was "not very common" generally, but was "sometimes quite abundant . . . during migrations."

The Least Tern was practically annihilated in the late 1800s by professional hunters for the millinery trade, with up to 1,200 birds killed in a day along the Virginia coast and as many as 100,000 killed in a season (Bent 1921). Sage et al. (1913) said it was "formerly common in certain localities along the coast. No recent records." Forbush (1925) said it was a "rare migrant and resident" in Connecticut. It came back strongly in the New York City area in the 1920s after protection laws were implemented (Bull), but apparently did not resume nesting in Connecticut until the 1940s (W. Smith; Mackenzie).

COMMENTS: Destruction of nesting habitat and disturbance of the few remaining colonies by recreational activities is a present and serious threat.

Sooty Tern (*Sterna fuscata*)

STATUS: a very rare visitor from late July to early October, with most reports in September, usually after tropical storms. It ranges widely in the nonbreeding season over tropical and subtropical seas; reported north to Nova Scotia after hurricanes.

RECORDS: There are at least 18 occurrences of Sooty Tern in Connecticut, and of those 12 are specimens. The major incursions occurred in 1876, 1878, 1938, and 1979. About September 20, 1876, a large storm resulted in the capture of five specimens at four locations (Merriam 1877). After the hurricane of September 12, 1878, that resulted in numerous sightings throughout the northeast, a young male was killed with an oar at Stamford on September 16 (Sage et al.; Bull 1964; the year stated in *Auk* 12:86 is incorrect). On September 15, 1938, following the Great Hurricane, an adult was picked up dead at Branford (MacKenzie 1961). The current whereabouts of the above-noted specimens is not known.

On September 12, 1960, after Hurricane Donna, one was captured at Westport by F. Carral (BCM No. B1386). The largest invasion in Connecticut occurred after Hurricane David on September 7, 1979; a specimen was obtained at Bridgeport (BCM No. B1346), at Ledyard (UCM No. 7725), at Orange (BCM No. B1347), and at Waterford (UCM No. 7809); and there were at least 10 individuals seen along the Connecticut shore (AmB 34:140).

Inland records include one taken at Granby in 1876, one at Torrington in October 1891 (Job 1922), and the two records from Orange and Ledyard noted above.

Black Tern (*Chlidonias niger*)

STATUS: a rare migrant along the coast from late July to late September; less numerous in spring from mid-May to early June. Inland it is a very rare spring migrant; it is usually sighted over open-water marshes or lakes and rivers.

Earliest spring arrival: Apr. 29, 1937; Apr. 30, 1938, 1956; May 3, 1953.

Latest fall departure: Oct. 16, 1954; Sept. 23, 1972; Sept. 20, 1953, 1971.

HISTORICAL NOTES: This species has historically been rarely observed in the state, and apparently has not nested here in historic times. Merriam (1877) said that the Black Tern was a "rare visitor" to Connecticut, occurring chiefly in fall. Sage et al. (1913) termed it "a rare visitor, usually late in August."

Cruickshank (1942) said that the Black Tern was "casual" before 1920 but added that it increased somewhat by the early 1940s. Increases at New York nesting colonies were noted into the early 1970s (NYBBA). However, Black Tern numbers have declined in the 1980s, probably the result of increased human disturbance and habitat loss as a result of draining of marshes for agriculture or development, or raising of water levels (NYBBA).

Apparently, the first spring record in Connecticut was not recorded until May 24, 1916, when one was seen at Norwalk by I. Gabrielson (*Auk* 34:462), and the second was on May 30, 1932, at Fairfield (*Auk* 50:105). An increase in spring sightings since the 1950s coincided with the extension of its breeding range eastward (Hill) into northern Vermont, central Maine, and New Brunswick.

COMMENTS: An unusually large concentration of Black Terns, consisting of about 40 birds, was observed at Milford on August 24, 1893, during a strong gale and again on August 29 near New Haven (*Auk* 11:74). A flock of 50 birds was seen at Branford on September 14, 1960, of which five were collected for Yale Peabody Museum (Mackenzie 1961).

Black Skimmer (*Rynchops niger*)

STATUS: a rare coastal visitor from mid-May into October; sometimes fairly common after tropical storms. There is one confirmed nesting record: in June–July 1982, J. Bova et al. photographed a nest on Bluff Island, Greenwich (AmB 36:956, CW 2:47). Nesting was suspected but not confirmed at Waterford in July 1967 (AmB 22:588) and at Norwalk in 1987 (AmB 41:403). Accidental in early winter: one was seen on January 1, 1945, at Lyme (fide A. Brockway, *Auk* 62:460); and one was seen on December 20, 1971, at New Haven (AmB 25:556).

Earliest spring arrival: May 2, 1971; May 8, 1968; May 16, 1981.

Latest fall departure: Oct. 29, 1986; Oct. 23, 1954; Oct. 9, 1938.

HISTORICAL NOTES: This unusual species undoubtedly nested in Massachusetts in colonial times up to the 1830s (Forbush 1925; Hill; *Auk* 63:594) but was "rapidly eliminated" (Hill). In the late 1800s it was a "very rare vagrant, except for invasions after hurricanes" (Hill). In Connecticut late 19th-century records include one bird taken at New Haven on about June 16, 1883, and another killed at Saybrook in the first week of November 1894 (Sage et al. 1913).

Regionally, it increased in New York after 1924 and nested there from 1934 (Cruickshank; Bull 1964). It was regular visitor to Massachusetts after 1936 and has nested there irregularly since 1946 (*Auk* 63:594). Two days after the hurricane of September 14, 1944, "not less than sixty-five" were seen at Fairfield, some remaining to the 18th (*Auk* 62:312). Steadily increasing in the region after 1940, it was not regularly reported in Connecticut before the early 1960s.

AUKS (FAMILY ALCIDAE)

Dovekie (*Alle alle*)

STATUS: a very rare winter visitor from early November to February. There have been more than 70 sightings and at least 21 specimens preserved since 1849. About two thirds of the records are from the month of November after storms with strong easterly winds. It is occasionally found well inland after such storms—usually exhausted and severely emaciated.

Earliest winter arrival: Oct. 29, 1932 (spec.); Nov. 2, 1960; Nov. 4, 1966 (spec.).

Latest winter departure: Mar. 11, 1945; Feb. 17, 1945; Feb. 16, 1894.

HISTORICAL NOTES: On November 19, 1932, following a raging northeast gale, a tremendous flight of Dovekies occurred off the Atlantic coast that extended as far south as Florida and Cuba (*Auk* 50:325, Bull 1964). From November 19 to November 23 there were no fewer than 25 reports and at least 6 specimens taken throughout Connecticut—

from Greenwich to Stonington and some far inland at Meriden, Bristol, and Simsbury (*Auk* 50:325, BL 35:12).

A notable flight occurred in the region November 20–23, 1970; there were at least 35 inland reports from Massachusetts and one from Connecticut at Willimantic (AmB 25:29); there were several sightings along the coast, and one bird was collected at Milford (AmB 25:34).

Thick-billed Murre (*Uria lomvia*)

STATUS: a very rare winter visitor from November to February. About half of the records are from the coast; the remainder are inland on large lakes and on the Connecticut River. Most frequently reported in December following strong easterly gales. Accidental in spring: one was seen on May 2, 1956, at Guilford (Mackenzie 1961), and one was photographed on May 27, 1973, at Stonington (B. Kleiner et al.; AmB 29:750, BcM photo No. 3).

Earliest winter arrival: Nov. 18, 1893 (spec.); Nov. 21, 1901; Nov. 23, 1900.

Latest winter departure: Mar. 20, 1944 (spec.); Feb. 19, 1878; Feb. 6, 1964.

HISTORICAL NOTES: This alcid was not reported by Linsley. In the northeastern United States it was found in most winters from 1890 to 1902 (*Auk* 24:364). In Massachusetts, Hill (1965) said it was "fairly common, occasionally abundant" in the late 1800s, but that it "decreased steadily" in the early 1900s. The first known specimen in Connecticut was taken by Capt. O. Brooks about 1869 "near Faulkner's Island" off Guilford (Merriam 1877); the second was taken by J. Clark on February 19, 1878, at Saybrook (Sage et al., 1913). Sage et al. described it as an "irregular and probably accidental winter visitor to Long Island Sound; found occasionally on the ponds in the interior." On December 31, 1916, A. Saunders found four together at Norwalk (*Auk* 35:340). Bull (1964) noted that it "has been consistently rare in our area the past 30 years," adding that there have been several years when it was not reported at all.

In Connecticut there have been six distinct incursions: 1884, 1890–1891, 1901, 1926, 1932, and 1976. The largest of these was "the great invasion of 1890–91," when D. Sanford reported "thousands" from Penfield Reef in Fairfield to the mouth of the Saugatuck River in Westport, where "hundreds were shot" (*Auk* 8:307). W. Hoyt reported that they were "plentiful," and he obtained 14 specimens at Stamford from

December 20, 1890, to February 10, 1891; they also were seen in large numbers at Stratford (*Auk* 8:307). W. Davis said that "hundreds could be seen from the 1st to the 10th of January" at Branford (*Auk* 8:307). More recently, a large invasion in eastern Massachusetts on December 17, 1976, following a storm with winds exceeding 60 mph yielded three Connecticut records: one at Niantic on December 24, one at Milford on December 25, and one picked up alive but emaciated on the Connecticut Turnpike in Darien on December 31 (AmB 31:307, UCM No. 7490, MFN 4:11).

Razorbill (*Alca torda*)

STATUS: a hypothetical visitor; winters south to Long Island, more rarely to New Jersey, from December to April. There are three sight reports without photographic or specimen evidence: one was seen on April 8, 1978, at Niantic (East Lyme) by P. Alden, T. Parker, R. Ridgely, et al.; one was observed on January 2, 1966, at Groton (RNEB 22:9); and one was reportedly present in late December 1960 at New London (AFN 15:114).

HISTORICAL NOTES: Merriam (1877) termed this species "a rare winter visitor in the Sound" but provided no details of any sightings or specimens.

Black Guillemot (*Cepphus grylle*)

STATUS: an accidental winter visitor along the coast. This species nests along the North Atlantic coast from Greenland south to Maine. It winters mainly near its nesting areas and, rarely, moves south to Long Island and New Jersey.

There is one specimen record: a male was collected at Stony Creek (Branford) in December 1887 by G. Trumbull (*Auk* 7:283) and is now at the University of Connecticut Museum (No. 9416). On January 1, 1934, numerous observers saw one on the Connecticut River at Hartford (HAS, BMAS 20:(8)4–5); several more were seen the next day upriver in Massachusetts. There are at least five undocumented and uncorroborated sight reports by single observers (AmB 35:197, 280, 436; AmB 35:802; Bagg and Eliot; Hills 1978; Shipley 1931).

HISTORICAL NOTES: Bull (1964), referring to the New York City area, said "it was unknown in our area before 1918."

Atlantic Puffin (*Fratercula arctica*)

STATUS: an accidental winter vagrant: an immature was shot by a hunter at Penfield Reef, Fairfield on November 19, 1947 (*Auk* 67:254, BcM No. 1487), and an immature was captured and photographed on November 10, 1968, at East Haven by Mrs. J. Wilkinson (AmB 23:26). Also, Yale Peabody Museum has an alcohol specimen (No. 7740) of a female collected at New Haven on October 7, 1968, by D. Paronno.

COMMENTS: This species nests along the north Atlantic coast from Greenland south to Maine and winters in open water near nesting areas And, rarely, south to New Jersey (Terres 1980); apparently the least migratory of the Atlantic alcids (Bull).

PIGEONS, DOVES (FAMILY COLUMBIDAE*)*

Rock Dove (*Columba livia*)

STATUS: introduced. A year-round resident throughout the state and common to abundant in most places near human habitation. It nests on building ledges, under railroad and highway bridges, and on rock cliffs. Eggs may be laid in any month of the year but in New England are usually laid from March to June and from August to November.

HISTORICAL NOTES: It was first introduced in North America by the French in 1606 at Port Royale, Nova Scotia; at Virginia, about 1621; and in Massachusetts, about 1642 (Terres 1980).

Band-tailed Pigeon (*Columba fasciata*)

STATUS: hypothetical. There are two sight reports: November 7, 1982, East Haven (C. Taylor, B. Wheeler, L. Mallers, R. Schwartz; CW 3:20) and one from December 1984 to March 1985 at a Portland feeder (S. and J. Mitchell et al., CW 7:49). Unfortunately, photographs were not taken in either instance.

White-winged Dove (*Zenaida asiatica*)

STATUS: hypothetical. There is one sight report: November 18, 23, and 25, 1973, at Milford by R. English, K. Gunther, D. Hudson, A. Jenks, and N. Proctor. "Regretably, word was not sent out until two weeks later" (D. Finch, AmB 28:618); photographs were not taken.

This species is accidental in northeastern United States; it has wandered to Nantucket, Massachusetts; Water Mill and Riis Park, Long Island; and Maine (Terres; AmB 28:618; Bull 1974).

Mourning Dove (*Zenaida macroura*)

STATUS: a fairly common migrant and nester throughout the state; it is sometimes abundant during peak migration days in March and October. Generally more common near the coast than inland. It is uncommon to fairly common in winter. It nests in a variety of settings, including agricultural lands and residential areas.

HISTORICAL NOTES: Forbush (1916) said this species was abundant in southern New England before 1850. However, it was hunted extensively and suffered a striking decline during the late 1800s. Merriam (1877) said it was "rare" in summer and "irregular" in winter. Sage et al. (1913) listed only seven records from 1882 to 1911 and remarked that numbers were decreasing. Job (1922) said in 1908 that it was "rather scarce" in summer at Litchfield County with an "occasional individual or pair in Kent." Also in 1908, Honeywill et al. said it was an "occasional summer resident: rare in this [New Haven] region."

Protected from hunting in 1908, the population stabilized by 1920 (Hill 1965), and slow growth followed (Howes 1928). In 1924 the first in 20 years were seen in East Granby (OO 51:82). Griscom and Snyder (1955) noted more vigorous growth of its numbers during the 1930s. Winter numbers increased markedly in the 1950s (AFN 11:251, Bull 1964, Pink and Waterman). Robbins et al. (1986) noted that "significant increases" of the nesting population occurred in New England from 1965–1979.

Passenger Pigeon (*Ectopistes migratorius*)

STATUS: extirpated, extinct. At the beginning of colonization, the Passenger Pigeon might have been the most numerous bird species in North America, numbering from 3 to 5 billion (Schorger 1955). The extinction of any species is tragic, but the tale of the Passenger Pigeon is particularly noteworthy in the most ominous sense. It migrated and nested in vast, concentrated flocks and was subjected to intense hunting, trapping, and netting at its nesting colonies and along its migratory path. In one Michigan nesting colony in 1874, more than 700,000 were netted in one month for the market (Schorger).

There are numerous accounts of hunting events in which thousands of birds were shot in a single day (Sage et al.; Bent, Bull 1964). This kind of destruction, in addition to the cutting of oak and beech forests for agriculture, doomed this species (Terres 1980; Bull 1974).

The Passenger Pigeon was a species whose existence seemed to depend on close association in large numbers with others of its kind. Once the enormous colonies had been reduced, with remnants separated and scattered in small flocks, there seemed unable to reproduce, for reasons not known, in sufficient numbers to survive (Terres 1980).

FORMER STATUS: It presumably nested in many wooded sections of Connecticut before and during the early 1800s. Before the 1870s, it nested in large colonies in the northwest hills, beginning in April and May (Merriam; Bull 1964), and irregularly south to Bethel (1874) and east to Portland (1875) (Sage et al. 1913). In spring it migrated mostly west of the Appalachian Mountains and was rarely seen in large numbers in Connecticut (Sage et al. 1913), although flocks might occasionally appear from mid-March to early June (Bent 1932; Forbush 1927; Bull 1964). Fall migration began as early as late August and continued into mid-October (Bent 1932); most passed through the state in late September (Bull 1964). The fall movement was concentrated inland, although strong northwest winds would push flocks to the shore (Bull 1964). Small numbers lingered into December. Very few would winter: several birds were reported in the winter of 1882–1883 near Hartford (Bent 1932); and a specimen was taken at Milford by G. B. Grinnell during the winter of 1873 (BcM). Bull (1974) noted no definite winter occurrence in New York.

HISTORICAL NOTES: A decline in the Passenger Pigeon population was noted within 50 years of the settlement of the Plymouth Colony in Massachusetts (Forbush 1916). An ongoing and accelerating decline followed. It had become very rare in Connecticut by the late 1880s (Bent 1932, Bull 1964). The last large flock containing more than 1,000 birds was seen at the New London–Groton area in 1876, and several smaller flocks of several hundred birds each were reported in 1883 at Guilford (Sage et al. 1913). Reportedly, "quite a number" were still present in eastern Connecticut around buckwheat fields in the early 1880s (OO 39:87). What was probably the last specimen collected in the state was taken in 1897 at Stamford by W. Hoyt (Shipley 1931). Although Schorger (1955) believed the last wild bird was shot on March

24, 1900, at Pike County, Ohio, Sage et al. reported that a flock of 27 was seen in September 1902 at Bethel by G. Hamlin. A sighting in May 1918 at Stonington was one of many unverified reports that were published periodically and probably resulted from confusion with Rock Doves or Mourning Doves (*Auk* 36:158).

The well-published "1906" specimen collected in north Bridgeport (*Auk* 38:274) is in question. (Forbush [1927] incorrectly said "north Bridgewater.") Bent (1932) felt that the date, which was written on the mounted specimen, was far too late to be the collection date and actually signifies when the bird passed from one collector to another, not when the bird was collected in the field.

CUCKOOS (FAMILY CUCULIDAE)

Black-billed Cuckoo (*Coccyzus erythropthalmus*)

STATUS: an uncommon migrant and breeder from mid-May to October; numbers vary depending on degree of caterpillar infestation. It favors forested areas with dense understory shrubs. It is more numerous than Yellow-billed Cuckoo in the hillier areas away from the coast.

Earliest spring arrival: Apr. 23, 1886; Apr. 30, 1953; May 1, 1928.
Latest fall departure: Oct. 27, 1950; Oct. 22, 1971; Oct. 21, 1975.

HISTORICAL NOTES: A slight decrease of the nesting population in southern New England from 1965 to 1979 was noted by Robbins et al. (1986).

Yellow-billed Cuckoo (*Coccyzus americanus*)

STATUS: a rare-to-uncommon migrant and breeder from mid-May to late September; as in the preceeding species, numbers vary considerably depending on caterpillar infestations. It is very secretive in its habits and is much less numerous away from the coast.

Earliest spring arrival: May 4, 1980; May 5, 1923; May 7, 1895, 1986.
Latest fall departure: Oct. 29, 1979; Oct. 24, 1954; Oct. 18, 1980.

HISTORICAL NOTES: Pink and Waterman (1965) noticed an increase in numbers after the late 1930s, although this may have been related to local caterpillar outbreaks. More significantly, Griscom and Snyder (1955) noted an expansion of its breeding range northward, and it currently nests in southern Ontario and Quebec, Canada. Robbins et al. (1986) said that Breeding Bird Survey data showed a slight decline in numbers of this species in Connecticut from 1965 to 1979.

OWLS (FAMILIES TYTONIDAE [BARN OWLS] AND STRIGIDAE)

Barn Owl (*Tyto alba*)

STATUS: a rare resident; largely absent in interior areas away from coastal areas and large river valleys. Very rarely observed away from known nest sites in Milford, Old Lyme, Middletown, and Sharon or away from known winter roosts. Nest sites are mainly in urban areas in abandoned buildings and church steeples and, more rarely, near farms.

HISTORICAL NOTES: The Barn Owl is a very difficult species to locate, and many individuals have certainly escaped detection over the years. Therefore, its historic population change, if any, is imperfectly understood. Linsley (1843a), Merriam (1877), Sage et al. (1913), and Howes (1928) all list this species as "accidental," principally along the coast and large river valleys. Although first confirmed nesting in Connecticut in 1892 at Winchester (Job 1922), it was not until about 1920 that its range extended northward through Connecticut (Griscom; Bagg and Eliot; Cruickshank; Bull 1964).

Eastern Screech-Owl (*Otus asio*)

STATUS: an uncommon resident in the southern and western portions of the state, generally rare east of the Connecticut River and in the northwest hills. It nests locally in forested residential areas, wooded parks, and rural areas, particularly near orchards and wetlands. In winter it generally disperses to coastal areas.

HISTORICAL NOTES: There is some evidence that this species has declined in this century in Connecticut and elsewhere (Robbins et al., NYBBA). The reversion of farmland to forest may have adversely affected this species, since this owl seems to favor smaller woodlots, orchards, and open areas (DeGraff et al., 1980). Van Camp and Henny (1975) found that cutting of forests seemed to increase its abundance in northern Ohio (NYBBA).

Eastern Screech-Owl

Great Horned Owl (*Bubo virginianus*)

STATUS: an uncommon resident throughout the state. It nests in mature deciduous and mixed evergreen forests in rural areas, rarely in outskirts of larger towns, in larger suburban parks, and along the coast. In winter it often disperses to coastal areas.

HISTORICAL NOTES: Linsley (1843a) said this large owl was "much less numerous than formerly"—a decline possibly caused by excessive shooting and the clearing of forests for agriculture. From about 1870 to 1920 its status was stated as "not rare" or "uncommon" (Merriam; Averill; Sage et al.; Forbush 1927). In 1908 Job (1922) said that it was most frequent "in the wild, mountainous sections." In 1918 A. Brockway said that it was "fast nearing extermination . . . as a permanent resident" (*Auk* 35:351).

The Great Horned Owl has increased in this century as woodlands have expanded and matured (Griscom; Hill; Bull 1964).

SUBSPECIES: The nominate race breeds in Connecticut. The Arctic Horned Owl (*B. v. wapacuthu*) has been recorded in Connecticut (January 1919 in the New Haven area; Bull 1964). This pale subarctic form can be as white as the Snowy Owl, and it has pale gray facial disks unlike the chestnut brown of the nominate race (Peterson 1947). The Labrador race (*B. v. heterocnemis*) resembles the nominate race but has darker and heavily barred underparts; it has been recorded in western Connecticut (November 1917, *Auk* 38:586; and January 1928, *Auk* 47:94).

Snowy Owl (*Nyctea scandiaca*)

STATUS: a rare winter visitor along the coast from mid-November into early March, very rare inland. It is most frequently reported in December and January. This diurnal species favors flat open expanses and often perches on posts, buildings, light poles, rocks, and jetties— seldom in trees.

Earliest fall arrival: Oct. 13, 1983; Oct. 18, 1957; Oct. 26, 1987.

Latest spring departure: Apr. 12, 1950; Mar. 28, 1927; Mar. 20, 1972, 1983.

HISTORICAL NOTES: The Snowy Owl has presumably invaded southern New England in regular intervals throughout the historic period. Since 1833 flights have occurred about once every 5 years.

According to Dr. Wood, 15 to 20 were shot in Hartford County during the winter of 1858–1859 (HAS). During the 1800s it may have wintered in greater numbers than now. Farmlands undoubtedly provided a more favorable winter habitat than is currently available, even though it was subject to widespread shooting.

Northern Hawk Owl (*Surnia ulula*)

STATUS: an accidental winter visitor, reported from October to late January. It winters south to the Adirondacks and northern New England—irregularly to Massachusetts.

RECORDS: There are five reports for Connecticut, two of them specimens: one was collected at New Haven in November 1869 by Dr. F. Hall (Merriam 1877); and C. Jones received a specimen on November 12, 1902, thought to be from East Woodstock (Manter 1975). There are three credible sight reports: "one seen at a distance of twenty feet" by W. Hoyt near Stamford in winter 1879 (Sage et al. 1913); one seen at Rowayton (Norwalk) on September 24, 1924, by J. S. Hoyt (BL 26:404); and one seen at South Windsor on January 26, 1934, by G. T. Griswold (*Auk* 51:521). Several observers inexperienced in owl identification submitted an intriguing report of one at Stamford on October 12, 1972 (AmB 27:33), but this sighting was not corroborated.

HISTORICAL NOTES: This species is migratory at the northern portions of its range, and small numbers occasionally move south to southern New England in winter. "Flight" years were noted in 1867, 1884–1885, and 1922–1923 (Bent 1938; Griscom and Snyder 1955). Most reports of this species in southern New England occurred before 1890.

Burrowing Owl (*Athene cunicularia*)

STATUS: an accidental vagrant. There are two records: one was photographed at New Haven, December 19–28, 1980 (N. Proctor et multi al., AmB 34:254); and one was seen at Greenwich, May 24, 1981 (T. Baptist et al., AmB 34:756). These sightings were possibly of the same individual, which may have wintered along the intervening coast.

Barred Owl (*Strix varia*)

STATUS: an uncommon resident in dense wooded wetlands; much less numerous in coastal areas and the southwestern portion of the state. In winter it occasionally moves to the coastal region in small numbers.

HISTORICAL NOTES: This vociferous owl is at present less numerous than in previous years and is less common than the Great Horned Owl in many areas. The loss of large tracts of continuous forest has contributed to the decline of the Barred Owl in Connecticut.

This species was a "common" resident from the 1870s to the 1920s (Merriam; Averill; Sage et al.; Howes 1928). These same authors considered the Great Horned Owl "uncommon." In 1908, Job (1922) said it was "not an uncommon migrant, but scarce as a summer resident" in Litchfield County, and "commoner near the Sound." In 1908 Honeywill et al. wrote that it was a "permanent resident" and was "fairly common in any considerable wooded tract about the city" of New Haven. In the 1920s, Howes (1928), Forbush (1927), and Griscom considered the Barred Owl the commonest large owl. Bagg and Eliot (1937) considered it "fairly common" at the higher elevations.

Cruickshank (1942) noted a decrease since the late 1920s, and Griscom and Snyder (1955) said it was "steadily decreasing." In the New York City area, Bull (1964) said it was "uncommon to fairly common"—the same as the Great Horned Owl. By the 1980s this owl was no longer present in urban areas along the coast.

Great Gray Owl (*Strix nebulosa*)

STATUS: an accidental winter visitor; it winters south to the Adirondacks and northern New England, irregularly to Massachusetts.

RECORDS: There are three specimen records: Linsley collected one at Stratford on January 6, 1843; a male was collected at North Haven on January 18, 1893 (*Auk* 10:207; Sage et al. says January 22); and one was collected at Foot Haven in late March 1907 (*Auk* 27:468). There are three credible sight reports: one was seen on February 4, 1934, in the New Haven area by F. Loetscher (*Auk* 51:521); one was observed at Hartford on January 12, 1938, by G. T. Griswold, A. Powers et al. (*Auk* 55:533, CW 6:10); and one was reported in January 1944 at Lyme (C. Martin, HAS).

COMMENTS: There is a vague report of two birds sighted in the historic flight year of 1978–1979, but dates, locations, and observers were not given (AmB 33:264). Also, there is a published report of a sighting on December 27, 1958, at New London that is without corroboration (AFN 13:95).

HISTORICAL NOTES: Regionally, several marked incursions into areas well south of the normal winter range have occurred: the winters of 1842–1843, 1890–1891, and 1978–1979. The largest influx on record occurred in the winter of 1978–1979 when at least 92 individuals were reported in New England, New Brunswick, and Long Island (AmB 33:264, 269).

Long-eared Owl (*Asio otus*)

STATUS: a rare to occasionally uncommon winter visitor along the coast and Connecticut River valley, much less numerous inland. Usually arrives by early November and departs by mid-April. It is a very rare and infrequent nester in dense mature woodlands; the most recent nesting was in 1982 at Wethersfield (CW 2:40). It favors abandoned squirrel and crow nests 10 to 40 feet above the ground in pines, hemlocks, and spruces.

HISTORICAL NOTES: The Long-eared Owl was formerly far more numerous in the state than at present. Merriam (1877) said it was "a common resident" and cited nesting in "thick dark evergreen woods" at Berlin and in "clumps of low bushes near the coast." This species apparently declined as a nester in the state around the turn of the century. Sage et al. (1913) said it was a "common winter and rare summer resident," and listed nesting records for Ellington, Bristol, Woodbridge, and Northford. Forbush (1927) wrote that it was "formerly common." Griscom and Snyder (1955) described a steady decrease. Bull (1964) said it was locally fairly common in winter but did not list any nesting records for the state. It is presently found less frequently along the coast in winter than formerly, largely because of the loss of roost sites to development and of human disturbance.

Short-eared Owl (*Asio flammeus*)

STATUS: a rare coastal migrant and winter visitor from mid-October to April infrequently reported inland. Nonbreeding wanderers are very rare in summer. It favors large open marshes and meadows. Extirpated from Connecticut as a nesting species.

Earliest fall arrival: Sept. 7, 1955; Sept. 19, 1987; Sept. 27, 1987.
Latest spring departure: May 3, 1914; Apr. 29, 1916; Apr. 26, 1941.

HISTORICAL NOTES: There are accounts of Short-eared Owl nesting in Connecticut in the 1800s. Dr. W. Wood said the Short-eared Owl bred north of Hartford in the Connecticut River valley before the 1860s (J. A. Allen, 1865). Merriam (1877) said it was a "not uncommon" resident about the salt marshes near the coast but did not provide any specific details of nesting in the state. By 1900 it became less numerous and apparently stopped nesting in Connecticut (Sage et al.; Forbush 1927; Griscom). Eight wintered at Hartford in 1935 (Bagg and Eliot 1937). It is currently much less numerous in winter than formerly, reflecting a loss of inland marshes and meadows and coastal wetlands.

Boreal Owl (*Aegolius funereus*)

STATUS: an accidental winter visitor, reported from mid-November to mid-March. It winters south to northern New York, northern New England, and very rarely to Massachusetts. It favors coniferous forests.

RECORDS: There are three specimen records: Dr. W. Wood reported a specimen found in the winter of 1859–1860 at East Windsor (Merriam, Bagg and Eliot 1937); a male was found at Kent on November 12, 1906 (Job, YPM No. 1662); and a partial specimen was found in January 1923 at South Windsor by C. Vibert and identified by E. Forbush (Bagg and Eliot 1937). There have been several credible sight reports: one seen by C. Vibert and G. Griswold at South Windsor on December 2, 1932 (Bagg and Eliot); one seen at Hartford by R. Belden et al. on February 17,

1943 (BL 45:II:2; BMAS 27(4):126, 28(6):268); and one at West Hartford on December 15, 1946 by C. W. Catlin (AFN 1:124).

HISTORICAL NOTES: Incursions well south of its normal winter range were noted in the winters of 1859–1860 and 1922–1923. Griscom and Snyder (1955) said it "is now much rarer than formerly."

Northern Saw-whet Owl (*Aegolius acadicus*)

STATUS: a rare but occasionally uncommon winter visitor from late October to April. A rare nester; the most recent reported nesting was at Hartland in 1981 and at Sharon in 1986 (CW 7:11). It seems to prefer coniferous woods to deciduous forests and has nested in low wooded swamps with mixed hemlocks and maples.

Earliest fall arrival: Sept. 11, 1982; Sept. 23, 1950; Oct. 3, 1966.

Latest spring departure: May 22, 1960; May 2, 1983; Apr. 30, 1957.

HISTORICAL NOTES: The Northern Saw-whet Owl is the smallest of the state's owls and is very nocturnal in its habits. Nesting pairs are difficult to locate, a factor that should be considered when assessing its historical status in Connecticut. Linsley (1843a) said it was "very rare here; I have seen but two individuals." Merriam (1877) called it "resident, though rather rare," and noted that a set of five eggs had been collected from a nest at Portland. Sage et al. (1913) and Job (1922) list several old nesting reports: Chester, April 1894; Bridgeport, June 1896; and Winsted, June ca. 1895. It nested at Hadlyme in 1920 (*Auk* 40:330) and in Fairfield in 1925 (Hills 1978).

After many years without published nesting reports, it nested in July 1965 at Pleasant Valley (Barkhamsted)(AFN 19:528). It nested at Marlborough in April 1977 (photo, AmB 31:975). In 1978 three nesting pairs were found in the Sharon area and another at Mansfield (AmB 32:979). The Northern Saw-whet Owl may have suffered a decline in the 1970s and 1980s because of the increase in the Great Horned Owl population in Connecticut; the Great Horned Owl is known to prey on this species (Hill).

GOATSUCKERS (NIGHTJARS) (FAMILY CAPRIMULGIDAE)

Common Nighthawk (*Chordeiles minor*)

STATUS: a fairly common to occasionally abundant fall migrant from mid-August to late September and infrequently into October. Large migrating flocks are common in late afternoons and evenings in late August and early September along the coast and larger river valleys. It is uncommon to fairly common in spring in May, often occurring in small flocks; rarely reported in April. In Connecticut this species is a rare nester on flat tar and gravel rooftops of buildings, locally in coastal areas in larger towns and cities and very locally inland in rural areas.

Earliest spring arrival: Apr. 20, 1940, 1952; Apr. 21, 1956 (spec.).

Latest fall departure: Nov. 19, 1983; Oct. 26, 1974; Oct. 17, 1975.

HISTORICAL NOTES: The Common Nighthawk appears to have declined significantly in recent decades as a nesting species in the state. Linsley (1843a) said it was "common." Merriam (1877) said the Common Nighthawk was a "common" summer nester. Averill (1892) noted that it was "uncommon," and Job (1922) in 1908 said it had "notably declined in numbers" throughout the state. Sage et al. (1913) reported that it was generally "rare" but had once been "abundant" in summer. It has nested in historical times in open pastures but became increasingly scarce as farmland was lost to other uses. After the mid 1800s it began to nest on flat gravel and tar rooftops in urban areas (Sage et al. 1913). In the 1930s almost all nesting in the state occurred on rooftops (Howes; Bagg and Eliot 1937). By the 1960s, it was a very local nester throughout the state almost exclusively on urban rooftops. In 1982 S. Tingley wrote that "it seems that this species is genuinely on the decline in the region" (AmB 36:956).

Chuck-will's-widow (*Caprimulgus carolinensis*)

STATUS: a casual coastal spring visitor from mid-May to late June, accidental inland. Most reports are from the western coast.

RECORDS: The first record in the state was of a specimen captured on May 17, 1889, at New Haven by D. Morgan (Sage et al. 1913). Other specimen records: a female was found dead on June 26, 1969, at Stony Creek (Branford) by E. Morton (YPM No. 85435), and one was collected on May 11, 1980, at Faulkner's Island, Guilford (YPM No. 95108). There are ten sight reports since 1962, with arrival dates as follow: May 10, May 14 (three), May 15 (two), May 16, May 18, May 22, and June 2. One reported on the unusual date of September 18, 1984, at Branford (AmB 39:28) was not satisfactorily corroborated.

HISTORICAL NOTES: The specimen taken in 1889 at New Haven was for more than 70 years the only verified record for Connecticut.

Regionally, this species was considered an accidental visitor prior to the mid-1960s and has increased since.

It was reported regularly in Cape May County, New Jersey, since 1930 and first occurred in New York at Riverhead, Long Island, on May 2, 1933 (Bull 1964). It first nested in New York on May 24, 1975, at Oak Beach, Long Island (AmB 29:830). Nesting has not been documented in Connecticut.

Whip-poor-will (*Caprimulgus vociferus*)

STATUS: an uncommon nester on the eastern coastal plain and inland in the northwest and northeast hills; it is rare in the southwestern portion of the state. It favors dense, moist woodlands. Very rarely observed during migration, from late April to late May and from late August to late September; very nocturnal.

Earliest spring arrival: Apr. 5, 1933; Apr. 17, 1945; Apr. 19, 1927, 1941.

Latest fall departure: Nov. 2, 1950; Oct. 22, 1959, 1984; Oct. 11, 1966.

HISTORICAL NOTES: Before the 1920s, nearly all authorities considered this species to be a common summer nester (Linsley 1843a; Merriam; Averill; Sage et al.; Forbush 1927; Howes 1928). However, a steady decline in its population was observed since the 1930s (Hill; Cruickshank; Pink and Waterman). Bull (1964) said it was "fairly common to uncommon" and "much less numerous than formerly" in the greater New York City area. Currently, it has become even more restricted in the nesting season, particularly along the coast. The cause of the decline is unclear, but one hypothesis is that the decline results from the decrease in large Saturnid moths, a major part of its diet, as a result of industrial pollution and insecticide use (NYBBA; Robbins et al.).

SWIFTS (FAMILY APODIDAE)

Chimney Swift (*Chaetura pelagica*)

STATUS: a common migrant from late August to mid-September, rare after early October. Sometimes abundant on peak migration days in early September, hundreds can occasionally be found roosting in larger chimneys. Fairly common in spring from early May to June; rare before late April. It is an uncommon nester throughout the state in unused chimneys.

Earliest spring arrival: Mar. 29, 1945; Apr. 12, 1947; Apr. 14, 1876.
Latest fall departure: Nov. 20, 1969; Nov. 13, 1985; Nov. 7, 1907 (spec.).

HISTORICAL NOTES: Apparently, this species increased during the initial settling of Connecticut as the colonists built chimneys (Bent 1940). Both Merriam (1877) and Sage et al. (1913) said it was an "abundant" nester in chimneys. Bagg and Eliot (1937) termed it "very common" in the 1930s. Cruickshank (1942), referring to this species' pre-colonial nest sites, noted that it no longer nested in hollow trees. Bull (1964) said it was a "locally common" nester.

Apparently, this species began to decline in the 1960s and 1970s (Siebenheller; NYBBA). A decrease in available chimneys, or possibly a change in materials or structural design, may explain the decline of nesting swifts in Connecticut.

HUMMINGBIRDS (FAMILY TROCHILIDAE)
Ruby-throated Hummingbird (*Archilochus colubris*)

STATUS: an uncommon migrant from early May to June and from late August to late September, very rarely into October. Sometimes fairly common during peak migration days in September. Its nesting distribution in the state is widely dispersed and local; it is uncommon in the interior areas and is rare in the coastal region.

Earliest spring arrival: Apr. 20, 1973; Apr. 23, 1976, 1983; Apr. 25, 1953.
Latest fall departure: Nov. 22, 1978; Nov. 11, 1961; Nov. 1, 1950.

HISTORICAL NOTES: The Ruby-throated Hummingbird was a "common" nester in Connecticut into the 1930s (Merriam; Averill; Sage et al.; Forbush 1927; Griscom; Bagg and Eliot 1937). However, its nesting population has subsequently declined. Since the 1930s it has been called "uncommon," "fairly common," or "local" breeder (Cruickshank 1942; Griscom and Snyder 1955; Bull 1964; Pink and Waterman 1965; Manter). Its decline is continuing as the state's developed areas spread, and the species no longer nests in urbanized areas in Connecticut.

KINGFISHERS (FAMILY ALCEDINIDAE)
Belted Kingfisher (*Ceryle alcyon*)

STATUS: an uncommon migrant from March to mid-May and from late August to early October. In winter it is uncommon along unfrozen watercourses and near harbors in the coastal lowlands; it is less numerous inland. It nests throughout the state in exposed earthen banks, often along streams, ponds, and coastal bays.

HISTORICAL NOTES: A review of the published literature suggests that there has been little change in the historic status of this species.

WOODPECKERS (FAMILY PICIDAE)

Red-headed Woodpecker (*Melanerpes erythrocephalus*)

STATUS: a rare migrant from mid-April to late May and from late August to November, reported more often in fall. Very rare in winter. An accidental nester: a pair successfully fledged young at Suffield in 1984 (S. Kellogg, fide L. Bevier).

HISTORICAL NOTES: Dr. J. Whelpley said the Red-headed Woodpecker was "rare" at New Haven about 1808 (Merriam 1877). However, Professor B. Silliman noted that it was an "abundant" resident near that city until 1840 (Sage et al. 1913). Dr. W. Wood reported that it was as common as the flicker at East Windsor in the early 1840s, but "they entirely disappeared in 1847" (OO 6:78). Regionally, the population crashed between 1845 and 1850 (Sage et al.; Cruickshank 1942) for unknown reasons.

In the late 1870s the Connecticut River became the eastern limit of its range (Bagg and Eliot 1937). Continuing to decline, it was "rare" and erratic, although it still was occasionally "common" or even "abundant" in fall migration during the 1880s (*Auk* 12:261, Averill; Sage et al. 1913). It was "abundant" in the winters of 1872–1873 and 1881–1882 (Merriam; Sage et al. 1913), and large numbers were reported in the fall of 1914 (BL 76:449). However, nothing resembling those fall and winter concentrations has occurred since (Bull 1964).

The advent of the automobile and an increase in starlings in the 1890s, particularly after 1900, further contributed to the decline of this species; it regularly fed along roadways and was often killed by passing vehicles, and starlings aggressively competed for nest sites. It became rare and local east of the Hudson River after 1900 (Forbush 1927, Cruickshank; Howes; Shipley; Smith; Griscom and Snyder; Bull 1964; Pink and Waterman 1965).

Some last local nesting records in Connecticut prior to 1930 include the following: East Windsor until 1863, Guilford around 1875, Portland in 1882 (Sage et al. 1913); New Canaan in 1897 (OO 45:79); Litchfield

County until 1906 or 1907 (Job 1922); New Haven to 1916 (*Auk* 38:586); West Haven to 1916 (*Auk* 35:341); Stamford to about 1920, and Darien to 1927 (Howes 1928). Cruickshank (1942) called it "accidental" during the nesting season after 1930 in the New York City area, and Bagg and Eliot (1937) reported it as "rare" and sporadically nesting in the upper Connecticut River valley into the 1930s. Bull (1964) said it was a "rare to uncommon, but regular migrant" and "occasional in winter." He added that it regionally nested regularly only in parts of northern New Jersey.

Red-bellied Woodpecker (*Melanerpes carolinus*)

STATUS: an uncommon resident throughout most of the state; fairly common in Fairfield and New Haven counties. It is primarily found in dense deciduous woods; infrequently reported at elevations above 800 feet.

HISTORICAL NOTES: Linsley (1843a) observed a Red-bellied Woodpecker at Stratford on October 16, 1842, and said it was "the only specimen I ever saw." Later, Merriam (1877) and Bagg and Eliot (1937) called it an "accidental" straggler. Sage et al. (1913) mentioned only three records: in 1842 (from Linsley), in 1874, and one from Hartford (date unknown).

In the New York City area Bull detected an increase after 1956. Increasing in Connecticut, it was regularly reported in the 1960s along coastal Fairfield County. It reportedly nested at Farmington in 1962 after 9 years of sight records (AFN 17:993). It was noted at Old Lyme in 1969 (AFN 24:484). It was first reported in the Storrs area in 1969 and first wintered there in 1971 (AmB 26:579). In 1971 it nested at Greenwich (AmB 25:713). It was first observed at New London in 1971. By 1974 it had nested east to Old Lyme (AmB 29:749). By 1977 it had "apparently increased to the point where they are considered common and 10–15 are not unusual" along coastal Connecticut (AmB 33:753). By 1980 it regularly occurred north to Hartford and Mansfield (SCCC).

Yellow-bellied Sapsucker (*Sphyrapicus varius*)

STATUS: an uncommon migrant from mid-April to mid-May and from mid-September to mid-November; it is sometimes fairly common on peak migration days in April and October. Small numbers regularly winter in the coastal region and occasionally at inland areas. It is a rare nester in the northwest hills south to Litchfield, Harwington, and Kent and east to Granby, Barkhamsted, and Burlington.

HISTORICAL NOTES: The Yellow-bellied Sapsucker appears to have increased in historic times as a migrant, winter visitor, and nester. Merriam (1877) said it was "rare about New Haven" but cited various observers who said it was "abundant in fall," "not uncommon," and "very common both in spring and fall." In 1908 Job (1922) wrote that it was "not very common, but sometimes fairly common in the fall" in Litchfield County. Sage et al. (1913) said it was "a tolerably common spring and fall migrant" and added that it "rarely" wintered. Bagg and Eliot (1937) detected an increase, saying that it "is undoubtedly more numerous than it was fifty or even twenty-five years ago." Apparently, the first detailed winter record was in 1917 at Norwalk (*Auk* 35:341).

Although Merriam (1877) suspected that this species might nest in the northern portions of the state, the first published report of confirmed nesting was not until 1893, when G. Williams collected two nests at Winsted (Winchester) (Sage et al.; Job 1922). Bull (1964) wrote that it "breeds south to the Berkshires, more rarely to Litchfield Hills in northwestern Connecticut." Robbins et al. (1986) noted a decline in southern New England from 1965 to 1979 along Breeding Bird Survey routes. In 1976 seven nests were found in the Sharon area (AmB 30:929).

Downy Woodpecker (*Picoides pubescens*)

STATUS: a fairly common resident; it nests throughout the state in wooded areas. In winter it is fairly common in woodlands throughout the state and is a regular visitor to feeders.

HISTORICAL NOTES: The historical status of this woodpecker appears to have not changed noticeably over the years. Linsley (1843a) said it was "common." Merriam (1877) commented that it was "a common resident; found everywhere except in open fields devoid of stumps and fences." Sage et al. (1913) said it was "a common resident."

Hairy Woodpecker (*Picoides villosus*)

STATUS: an uncommon resident, less numerous than the Downy Woodpecker. It nests throughout the state in large tracts of mature woodlands, favoring those areas with large trees with dead limbs and branches. It is more frequently encountered in winter and often visits feeders.

HISTORICAL NOTES: Like the Downy Woodpecker, the Hairy Woodpecker apparently has not significantly changed in status in historic times. Linsley (1843a) observed this species in Stratford and New Haven. Merriam (1877) said it was "resident, but not common" and added it was "found chiefly in winter." Merriam cites W. W. Coe as saying it was common at Portland. Sage et al. (1913) said this species was "a tolerably common resident; apparently more numerous in winter." It is at present largely absent in urbanized areas, even in winter.

Black-backed Woodpecker (*Picoides arcticus*)

STATUS: a very rare fall visitor from late September to late December and in spring from early March to mid-May. It is casual in midwinter from January through February. It winters south to northern New York, New Hampshire, Vermont, and Maine—rarely to Massachusetts, Long Island, and northern New Jersey.

   Earliest fall arrival: Sept. 29, 1957, 1961; Oct. 5,1982; Oct. 8, 1923.
   Latest spring departure: May 14, 1961; May 5, 1924; May 3, 1958.

COMMENTS: This northern species usually occurs in the state during major winter incursions such as those of 1923–1927 and 1956–1961 (Bull 1964). Of about 30 records in Connecticut, 12 were from 1956 to 1958. About half of all records are in October and November; only six are from coastal areas. Summer sight reports in 1956 and 1957 (AFN 16:11; Hills 1978) lack satisfactory corroboration.

Northern Flicker (*Colaptes auratus*)

STATUS: a common migrant from late March to mid-May and from mid-September to late October. Uncommon in winter along the coast; less frequent inland in this season. The most numerous of the state's breeding woodpeckers, the Northern Flicker is a common nester in rural areas, including farmlands and woodland clearings, and in residential yards and parks.

HISTORICAL NOTES: This woodpecker has apparently declined in recent years. Significant declines were noted in 20 states and provinces, including Connecticut, on Breeding Bird Surveys from 1965 to 1979 (Robbins et al., 1986). Sage et al. (1913) speculated that the then recently introduced European Starling might compete with the flicker for nest sites, to the detriment of the flicker, a suspicion that has been borne out by recent studies (Robbins et al. 1986; Kilham 1983).

SUBSPECIES: The western race, Red-shafted Flicker (*C. a. cafer*), has been reported at least twice in the state (AmB 26:38; CW 9:47) but is not supported by a specimen or photograph. Dr. L. Short, referring to the western form, knew of none taken anywhere in the northeast, although he has examined specimens approaching "hybrid type" (Bull 1964).

COMMENTS: J. Audubon named this species *Picus ayresii* in honor of William Ayres (1817–1887), New Canaan native and early naturalist (*Connecticut Environment* 16(6):12).

Pileated Woodpecker (*Dryocopus pileatus*)

STATUS: an uncommon resident in mature forests throughout the state, less numerous along the coast. It is increasing as the state's woodlands mature.

HISTORICAL NOTES: The Pileated Woodpecker suffered a striking decline following the settlement of Connecticut as a result of land clearing for agriculture. Linsley (1843a) noted that it was present on the

Pileated Woodpecker

coastal plain at Stratford and New Haven but stated "once common here, is much more rare at present." Merriam (1877) said it was "a rare winter visitant; it was once common throughout the state, but is now almost exterminated and driven into the less civilized districts." Griscom and Snyder (1955) stated that the decline in the 1800s was caused by "civilization and logging." It was virtually extirpated from Connecticut in the 1880s (Averill; Griscom). W. Hoyt saw his last Stamford bird in 1879 (Shipley 1931).

Increasing somewhat in the 1890s, it was called "rare" in winter and spring (Sage et al.; Bailey 1955; Manter 1975), probably the result of the regrowth of some of the state's forests. In 1890 C. Jones found one at Ashford, his first in that area in many years (Manter). It was found at Granby in 1890 and 1894–1895 (*Auk* 10:371, 12:311). It reportedly nested near Litchfield in 1896 and at Torrington in 1901 (*Auk* 40:533). In 1908 Job (1922) said it was a "rare visitor . . . usually only in winter" in Litchfield County.

This species was a regular but very local nester by the 1920s, east to the upper Connecticut River valley (Griscom; Griscom and Snyder, Bagg and Eliot) but was a vagrant elsewhere. It expanded its range east and south during the 1930s and 1940s; it was first found at Unionville (Farmington) in 1934 (OO 51:98), Storrs in 1951 (Manter 1975) and southwest Fairfield County in the early 1950s (Smith 1950). In 1957 three nests were found in Litchfield County (AFN 11:392). By the early 1970s it was fairly common in most of the wooded portions of western Connecticut but was local south to the coast; it was much less frequent in the eastern and central portions of the state. In the mid-1970s it was increasingly reported in the areas east of the Connecticut River (SCCC).

TYRANT FLYCATCHERS (FAMILY TYRANNIDAE)

Olive-sided Flycatcher (*Contopus borealis*)

STATUS: an uncommon migrant from mid-May to mid-June and from late July to early September, normally reported only in small numbers. It is a very rare nester; the only recent nesting occurred at Norfolk. It is suspected of nesting at Barkhamsted.

Earliest spring arrival: May 5, 1958; May 6, 1956; May 8, 1972.

Latest fall departure: Oct. 1, 1950; Sept. 23, 1954; Sept. 20, 1969, 1981.

HISTORICAL NOTES: Before the 1920s the Olive-sided Flycatcher decreased as a migrant, and its nesting range retreated north from southern New England (Forbush 1927, Bagg and Eliot; Griscom and Snyder 1955). Merriam (1877) strongly suspected it nested in the northern hills, although he had no direct evidence. Job did not report nesting. However, it nested at Stamford in 1897 (Howes 1928), and a pair with young was observed in 1903 at Danbury (Sage et al. 1913). Since the late 1960s it has nested sporadically in the northern hills.

COMMENTS: Manter (1975) reports that young were being fed away from the nest in the Storrs area on June 5, 1968. This date is extremely early; Bent lists no New England egg dates before June 8. Since this species might be confused with Eastern Phoebe, the authors are inclined to doubt this record as published.

Eastern Wood-Pewee (*Contopus virens*)

STATUS: a fairly common migrant from mid-May to early June and from late August to October. Migrations peak in late May and in the first 2 weeks of September. It is a widespread nester throughout the state in mature forests and open woodlands.
 Earliest spring arrival: Apr. 22, 1986; Apr. 29, 1956; Apr. 30, 1955.
 Latest fall departure: Oct. 19, 1973, 1980; Oct. 18, 1959; Oct. 7, 1962.

HISTORICAL NOTES: The Eastern Wood Pewee has apparently been a common nesting species in the state in historic times. It was recorded by Linsley (1843a) on the coast at Stratford and New Haven. Merriam (1877) said it nested "in the heart of the city, near the farm house, and in the darkest swamps and most secluded forests." Sage et al. (1913) said it was "a common summer resident of woodlands and shade trees." This species has declined since the 1960s as a result of the spread of urbanized areas.

Yellow-bellied Flycatcher (*Empidonax flaviventris*)

STATUS: an uncommon migrant in late May and early June and from early August to mid-September, generally less numerous in spring. Spring migration peaks in late May, and fall migration peaks in late August. Accidental in midsummer: a singing male was present on July 2, 1973, at Easton but not observed thereafter (M. Breslau et al., AmB 27:851).

Earliest spring arrival: May 7, 1892; May 12, 1959; May 16, 1982.

Latest fall departure: Oct. 23, 1974; Oct. 6, 1966; Sept. 26, 1893 (spec.).

HISTORICAL NOTES: The status of this species in Connecticut appears to have not changed significantly since the mid-1800s. Merriam (1877) said it was "not common during migrations" and was "not known to breed." Sage et al. (1913) termed it a "rather rare spring and fall migrant" and did not mention any nesting records.

Acadian Flycatcher (*Empidonax virescens*)

STATUS: a rare to uncommon migrant from late May to mid-June and from late July to late September.

This species has a widely dispersed nesting range in the state. It is a rare nester in the southwestern portion of the state. It is uncommon but restricted along the Housatonic River in the northwest hills; in the lower Connecticut River valley at East Hampton, East Haddam, and Haddam; along the Thames River in Ledyard, Preston, Lisbon, Griswold, Centerbury and Plainfield; and along the Farmington River at Burlington, New Hartford, and Barkhamsted. Isolated nestings have been reported from Union, Willington, Ashford, and Mansfield. At certain locations, such as Ashford and East Haddam, it is fairly common. It favors moist mature hemlock ravines but is also found in wet deciduous woods.

Earliest spring arrival: May 10, 1979; May 12, 1980; May 13, 1935.

Fall dates are scarce because of the difficulty of identifying nonsinging individuals.

HISTORICAL NOTES: The first state specimen of Acadian Flycatcher was collected by E. I. Shores at Suffield in 1874 (Merriam 1877), and this species was first found nesting in the state in 1875 by W. Hoyt at Stamford (Sage et al. 1913). In the early 1900s nesting was mostly confined to the southwest corner of the state (Sage et al., Bull 1964) and nesting continued near there until about 1950, when the northern limit of its nesting range retreated south to New Jersey; it decreased in Connecticut after 1950 and became merely a very infrequent straggler (Bull 1964).

After years of absence, it was found nesting at Litchfield in 1962 (AFN 16:462) and at East Haddam in 1968 (AFN 22:588). Increasing in the 1970s, it nested at North Windham, Greenwich, and Stonington in 1977 (AmB 31:975). In 1978 it was said to have "firmly established itself in southern New England" (AmB 32:980).

Alder Flycatcher (*Empidonax alnorum*)

STATUS: a rare to uncommon migrant from mid-May to early June and from early August to mid-September, less numerous in eastern portions of the state.

It nests locally in the northwest hills from New Hartford and Torrington southwest to New Fairfield and Danbury. There are no confirmed nestings in the northeast hills. Nesting is suspected in the Connecticut River valley south of Hartford. It favors open marshes and wet alder thickets.

Earliest spring arrival: May 7, 1901; May 8, 1943; May 16, 1965.

Fall dates are scarce because of the difficulty of identifying nonsinging birds.

HISTORICAL NOTES: The former status of this species is difficult to determine because both Alder and Willow Flycatchers were once considered races of a single species—Traill's Flycatcher—and many authors did not differentiate between the two different song types. Color banding of Alder and Willow Flycatchers in the Litchfield area during the 1960s revealed no evidence of interbreeding (Gorski).

Willow Flycatcher (*Empidonax traillii*)

STATUS: an uncommon to fairly common migrant from mid-May to early June and from early August to mid-September; migrations peak in late May and late August. It is an uncommon nester in coastal and inland marshes and wet willow and alder thickets throughout the state; more numerous in the southern and western portions of the state.

Earliest spring arrival: May 13, 1952; May 15, 1954; May 16, 1982.

Latest fall departure: Sept. 29, 1976; Sept. 25, 1983; Sept. 18, 1980.

HISTORICAL NOTES: Like the Alder Flycatcher, the former status of this species is difficult to assess because many early authors failed to distinguish between the two species. In 1973 this species was reportedly "increasing in the New York area [and] in southwest Connecticut" as a nester (AmB 27:851).

Least Flycatcher (*Empidonax minimus*)

STATUS: an uncommon to fairly common migrant from early May to early June, and from early August to mid-September; migrations peak in mid-May and late August. It nests inland in rural areas, rarely in the coastal region. It prefers woodland edges and shade trees and edges of swamps and ponds.

Earliest spring arrival: Apr. 20, 1913; Apr. 21, 1880, 1912; Apr. 22, 1954.

Latest fall departure: Oct. 9, 1958; Oct. 7, 1984; Oct. 6, 1943.

COMMENTS: A bird reported to be a Least Flycatcher "flew into Mrs. Risley's kitchen" at East Windsor on the extraordinary date of December 14, 1942, and died the next day (HAS). However, measurements taken do not rule out various western *empidonax* flycatchers. The present location of the specimen is not known.

HISTORICAL NOTES: The Least Flycatcher declined dramatically after the late 1800s. Both Linsley (1843a) and Merriam (1877) said it was "abundant" in summer, the latter adding that it bred "abundantly throughout the city" of New Haven. In 1908 Honeywill et al. said that it "is quite domestic and nests readily among the houses" in New Haven. It was called a "common summer resident" in Stamford in 1928 (Howes 1928). However, it became less numerous from the 1930s to the 1960s, when it was generally uncommon or even rare. This decline was noted by Cruickshank (1942); Griscom and Snyder (1955) described the decrease as "slow but steady since the introduction of House Sparrows." In 1962 P. Spofford noted the continuation of a 7-year decline in southwest Connecticut, with only one bird recorded that year (AFN 16:462). In 1978 it was termed a "declining summer resident" in Fairfield County (Hills 1978).

Eastern Phoebe (*Sayornis phoebe*)

STATUS: a fairly common migrant from mid-March to mid-May, and from mid August to early November, rare before early March and after late November. It is locally common in summer and nests throughout the state, usually in less developed areas—under bridges, eaves and other man-made structures, upturned tree roots, ledges, and cliffs— chiefly near ponds and watercourses. It is very rare in early winter to early January and casual in midwinter.

HISTORICAL NOTES: The Eastern Phoebe was an "abundant" breeder before the late 1800s (Merriam 1877). Job (1922) also described it as "abundant" in rural Litchfield County in 1908. Averill (1892), Sage et al. (1913), Howes (1928), and Bagg and Eliot (1937), writing from the early 1890s to the late 1930s, reported it as "common" in summer.

Cruickshank (1942), referring to the New York City area, said it was "fairly common" into the early 1940s. It has subsequently decreased (Griscom and Snyder; Manter 1975).

The historic decline of this species in Connecticut is probably due to the loss of its preferred nesting habitat. The succession of farmland to woodland and, all too often, to developed land has resulted in the decline of appropriate habitat for it to nest in.

Say's Phoebe (*Sayornis saya*)

STATUS: an accidental fall vagrant.

RECORDS: There is one specimen record: an adult female was collected on December 15, 1916, at Gaylordsville (New Milford) by E. H. Austin (formerly in the Bishop Collection [*Auk* 38:586]; current location unknown).

COMMENTS: There is a vague and uncorroborated sight report by a single observer at Branford in the fall of 1980 (AmB 35:159).

Great Crested Flycatcher (*Myiarchus crinitus*)

STATUS: an uncommon migrant from May to early June and from mid-August to late September; it is sometimes fairly common during peak migration in mid-May and late August. It is an uncommon nester in tree cavities in mature woodlands throughout the state.

Earliest spring arrival: Apr. 25, 1961; Apr. 26, 1980; Apr. 28, 1911, 1986.

Latest fall departure: Oct. 23, 1982; Oct. 11, 1980; Oct. 3, 1977.

COMMENTS: One was reported on December 7, 1975 (AmB 30:33), which, if correctly identified, was extraordinarily late. Such late *Myiarchus* flycatchers deserve careful scrutiny—Ash-throated Flycatcher has occurred in New England in November and December.

HISTORICAL NOTES: The historical changes in the nesting population of this species reflect the loss and later regrowth of the state's woodlands. It was least numerous in the mid-1800s, when forested areas were diminished.

Western Kingbird (*Tyrannus verticalis*)

STATUS: a rare fall visitor from early September to December, primarily at the coast. About two-thirds of the published reports are coastal, and half of the others are from the Connecticut River valley. It is most frequently reported in September and October.

Earliest fall arrival: Sept. 5, 1978; Sept. 7, 1986; Sept. 8, 1982.

Latest fall departure: Dec. 23, 1949; Dec. 14, 1972; Nov. 29, 1962, 1979.

COMMENTS: One reported on April 10, 1977, at Falls Village (Canaan), which was reportedly "fully described" (AmB 31:975), represents an unprecedented spring occurrence for New England. Bull (1974) lists only two spring records for New York: June 3 and June 16. The earliest spring records for Iowa, which is of similar latitude to Connecticut and where Western Kingbird is a common nester, are April 21 and May 1 (Dinsmore et al. 1984). Griscom and Snyder (1955) listed no spring records in Massachusetts. The authors feel there is cause to doubt this report as published.

HISTORICAL NOTES: There were only four records of this species north of Washington DC from the mid-1800s to 1900 (Bagg and Eliot 1937). It was first reported in Connecticut on November 4, 1921, at Meriden, by L. Smith (*Auk* 39: 270). Into the 1930s it was an "accidental" straggler in southern New England (Griscom and Snyder; Hill). It has been reported more frequently since the 1940s, coinciding with an eastward extension of its nesting range and an increase in the popularity of birding (Bull 1964).

In Connecticut there was one published report in the 1930s, four in the 1940s, four in the 1950s, and nine in the 1960s; it has been reported virtually every year since the mid-1970s.

Eastern Kingbird (*Tyrannus tyrannus*)

STATUS: a fairly common migrant from late April to June and common from late August to late September; migrations peak in early May and early September. It nests locally throughout the state in open woodlands, farmland, and suburban parks, often near open water.

Earliest spring arrival: Apr. 9, 1984; Apr. 21, 1961; Apr. 22, 1985.

Latest fall departure: Oct. 13, 1985; Oct. 12, 1951; Oct. 10, 1959.

COMMENTS: One was reported on the extraordinarily late date of December 15, 1973, at New Haven, but the report was published without details (AmB 28:219).

HISTORICAL NOTES: This conspicuous species has apparently not significantly changed in status in Connecticut in historic times. On

September 1, 1940, A. Saunders found 150 of these birds at Fairfield "sitting on wires" (BNEBL 4:70), a concentration that has not been matched in recent years.

Gray Kingbird (*Tyrannus dominicensis*)

STATUS: an accidental vagrant. In the United States it nests along the Gulf Coast to Alabama and from South Carolina south to Florida. It has wandered north to Massachusetts, Long Island, and British Columbia.

RECORDS: The only record for the state is of an immature bird, October 9 and 10, 1974, at Old Lyme, photographed by W. Burt (AmB 29:32).

Scissor-tailed Flycatcher (*Tyrannus forficata*)

STATUS: an accidental vagrant. It is usually reported in April and May. There is a single fall report: one was observed on October 11, 1983, at Madison (C. Taylor et al., CW 4:26, 7:49).

RECORDS: The first Connecticut record was about April 27, 1876, at Wauregan (Plainville), where C. Carpenter collected one (current location of specimen unknown, BNOC 2:21). One was photographed on May 25, 1974, at Old Lyme by W. Burt (AmB 29:128).

There are several uncorroborated single-person sight reports published without sufficient details: May 17–22, 1977, at Old Lyme (AmB 34:975); an immature on May 2, 1980, at Branford (AmB 34:756); and April 17, 1983, at Guilford (CW 3:33).

LARKS (FAMILY ALAUDIDAE*)*

Horned Lark (*Eremophila alpestris*)

STATUS: an uncommon coastal migrant and winter visitor from late October to April; it is sometimes very common during peak migration days in the fall, flocks of 100 birds or more are occasionally reported. It is usually uncommon away from the coast. It is a rare nester along the shore in open and barren areas, in the Connecticut River valley in tobacco fields, and in short-grass areas at airports.

Earliest fall arrival: Oct. 11, 1984; Oct. 12, 1982; Oct. 14, 1951.

Latest spring departure: May 19, 1984; May 18, 1983; May 9, 1916.

SUBSPECIES: The "Prairie" Horned Lark *E. a. praticola*, a western subspecies, extended its nesting range eastward and southward into New

England in the 1880s (*Auk* 21:81). It nested at Torrington in 1891, at Watertown in 1904, at Litchfield in 1905, at Washington in 1906 (BL 9:174), at Danbury in 1908 (*Auk* 22:420, 23:461, 67:254; BL 5:129), at Fairfield in 1941, at Bridgeport from 1941 to 1945 (Job; Cruickshank; Forbush 1927), at Mansfield in 1947 (Manter 1975), at Guilford in 1960 (Mackenzie 1961), and at Windham in 1978 (AmB 32:980). It increased regionally as a nester, migrant, and winterer since the early 1930s (Bull 1964; Hill; Cruickshank 1942). It has wintered at Milford since the 1960s, and at Stratford since the 1970s.

The northern subspecies, Hoyt's Horned Lark (*E. a. hoyti*), was named in 1895 by L. Bishop after William Hoyt of Stamford (*Auk* 13:129) and has been reported in Connecticut at least twice (*Auk* 58:408; Honeywill et al. 1908).

HISTORICAL NOTES: The Horned Lark did not always nest in Connecticut. The clearing of the forests of the eastern United States in the 1800s enabled the nesting range of this species to move eastward. Its first recorded nesting in New York was at Buffalo in 1875 (NYBBA). Merriam (1877) did not mention any nestings in Connecticut. Job (1922) reported nesting at Torrington in 1891, probably the first record for Connecticut. From 1965 to 1979 a decline in nesting was noted in New England (Robbins et al. 1986), probably caused by the reduction of tree-less expanses.

SWALLOWS (FAMILY HIRUNDINIDAE)

Purple Martin (*Progne subis*)

STATUS: a rare migrant from late April to June and from late July to mid-September. It is a very restricted nester and not normally seen away from its nesting colonies. There are several colonies along the coast at Westport, Milford, and from Guilford east to Stonington. Inland, colonies are generally decreasing, and nesting is known at New Milford, Kent, Sharon and Cornwall and in the northeast hills at Pomfret, Woodstock, Thompson, and Putnam.

Earliest spring arrival: Mar. 14, 1964; Mar. 26, 1982; Mar. 28, 1965.
Latest fall departure: Oct. 28, 1979; Oct. 25, 1983; Oct. 2, 1971.

HISTORICAL NOTES: Before Connecticut was settled, the Purple Martin was probably an uncommon nester. The clearing of forests during the 1800s undoubtedly aided this species, as did the placement of man-made nestboxes in farms and villages. Linsley (1843a) said this species was common, and Merriam (1877) said it was locally "abundant."

However, the introduction of the English Sparrow and European Starling in the late 1800s resulted in a striking decline in the number of Purple Martins in the state. Unusually cold temperatures in June 1904 caused significant mortality and nesting failure (BMAS 23(3):5). Sage et al. (1913) said it was "formerly an abundant summer resident . . . now rapidly decreasing throughout the state" and called the English Sparrow its "worst enemy." Its population dropped more rapidly than that of the Cliff Swallow—then undergoing a similar decline (Bagg and Eliot; Sage et al.; Forbush 1927). After an absence of many years it appeared at Hartford in 1911 and nested there in 1913 and 1914 (BL 16:449). In 1923 A. Bagg said of the Connecticut River valley that it "nested abundantly in former years throughout most of its length, but a few scattered . . . colonies remain" and that they "began to decrease in the 1880s" largely due to competition with House Sparrows (*Auk* 40:264). By the 1920s, with wet meadows and open lands steadily reduced, it had become "very local" in southern New England (Forbush 1927).

Tree Swallow (*Tachycineta bicolor*)

STATUS: a fairly common migrant from late March to late May and common in fall from mid-August to late October, sometimes very abundant at the coast on peak migration days in mid-September; flocks of 2,000 or more birds are occasionally reported. It rarely lingers to late December; casual in January and February. It nests locally throughout the state in nest boxes and tree cavities in fields, meadows, marshes, and open wetlands.

There are no less than 10 late December and January reports of this species in the state. Notable among these are a flock of 100 birds sighted on December 23, 1965, at New London, eight remaining there until December 28 (AFN 20:402); a flock of 20 birds observed on January 11, 1953, at Niantic, which dwindled to 4 birds on February 17, with none reported thereafter (RNEB 8:12, 31). There are four February reports: 10 were sighted on February 19, 1919, at Jewett City (Griswold); 6 were seen on February 5, 1938, at Saybrook, with 1 remaining until February 22 (BNEBL); 10 were observed on February 1, 1954, at Waterford (RNEB 10:38); and 1 was observed on February 28, 1971, at New Haven (AmB 25:554).

Earliest spring arrival: Mar. 7, 1961, 1988; Mar. 11, 1956; Mar. 14, 1982. Birds that appear in February and early March probably wintered just south of Connecticut and arrived in the state as a result of warm midwinter weather.

HISTORICAL NOTES: Merriam (1877) said the Tree Swallow was a "common summer resident." It declined as a nesting species in the state during the early part of this century, paralleling the decrease of agricultural lands. In 1908 Job (1922) said it was "locally common or scarce, not found in anything like the abundance of former years" in Litchfield County. Sage et al. (1913) noted that it was a "rare summer resident but more common in Litchfield county." Most observers have called it a "common" breeder since, although there has probably been a slight increase after the 1930s (Bagg and Eliot; Pink and Waterman 1965; Manter 1975). "Significant increases" in nesting were noted in New England from 1965 to 1979 (Robbins et al. 1986). The placement of nesting boxes has aided the nesting population in Connecticut.

COMMENTS: A flock of 20,000 birds on September 21, 1958, at Rocky Hill was extraordinarily large (AFN 13:16).

Northern Rough-winged Swallow (*Stelgidopteryx ruficollis*)

STATUS: a fairly common migrant from mid-April to June and common in fall from late July to September, sometimes very common during peak migration in early August. It nests throughout the state singly or in small groups near water under bridges, in holes and pipe openings in concrete abutments, and, less frequently, in earthen banks and bluffs.

Earliest spring arrival: Mar. 3, 1888 (spec.); Mar. 30, 1980; Apr. 1, 1979.

Latest fall departure: Oct. 15, 1983; Oct. 13, 1980; Sept. 26, 1976.

HISTORICAL NOTES: The Northern Rough-winged Swallow has extended its range northward in historical times and was first reported in New England in 1851 and next in 1874, when a female was collected at Suffield, Connecticut, by E. Shores (Bagg and Eliot 1937). Merriam (1877) said it was a "rare summer visitor." It first nested in 1876 at Westport (Bagg and Eliot). By 1900 it nested east to Ledyard (*Auk* 17:389). In 1901 a total of 10 pairs nested at eight coastal locations (*Auk* 19:93). Sage et al. (1913) considered it a "tolerably common summer resident" along the coast although only mentioning areas in and west of New Haven. They also noted that it was "much rarer in the interior." It nested north to Portland in 1888 (Sage et al.), northwest to Litchfield in 1905 (Job 1922), at Kent by 1908, and north of Hartford by 1917, which was also the first year it nested in Rhode Island (Bagg and Eliot). Its range expansion continued slowly but steadily through the early 1940s (Cruickshank 1942) and the early 1960s (Bull 1964).

Bank Swallow (*Riparia riparia*)

STATUS: an uncommon migrant from late April to June and from late July to early September; it is sometimes fairly common during peak migration days in mid-August. It nests in colonies near lakes and rivers in earthen banks at scattered locations throughout the state; some colonies contain more than 50 pairs.

Earliest spring arrival: Apr. 14, 1938, 1972, 1978; Apr. 16, 1988; Apr. 17, 1882, 1931.

Latest fall departure: Oct. 4, 1947; Sept. 25, 1891; Sept. 23, 1906, 1953.

HISTORICAL NOTES: The Bank Swallow digs its nest holes in the soft banks of ponds, lakes, and rivers or nearby gravel quarries. Since this specialized habitat is unevenly distributed in Connecticut, the Bank Swallow is locally common in some areas and completely absent from others. This pattern of distribution in Connecticut appears not to have changed in historic times. Sage et al. (1913) said it was "abundant locally where suitable banks occur along the larger rivers, but absent through much of the state except as a migrant." Nesting sites for this species have declined since the mid-1900s as gravel-excavation operations have become less common in many areas of the state.

Cliff Swallow (*Hirundo pyrrhonota*)

STATUS: a rare migrant from early May to June and rare to uncommon from early July to September. A very local colonial nester inland, mostly west of the Connecticut River from Stamford north through the northwest hills; active colonies are known at New Milford, Sharon, Cornwall, Colebrook, and Barkhamsted. In the east it is known to nest only at Columbia.

Earliest spring arrival: Apr. 21, 1906, 1972; Apr. 22, 1956; Apr. 23, 1967.

Latest fall departure: Oct. 23, 1971; Oct. 10, 1987; Oct. 8, 1984.

HISTORICAL NOTES: Using buildings as nesting sites, this species may have expanded its nesting range into southern New England in the early 1800s (Bagg and Eliot 1937). A "large colony" was at Windsor in 1830 (Merriam 1877). In the 1870s it was termed a "common summer resident, breeding abundantly under the eaves of barns" (Merriam).

Competition with House Sparrows and a change in architectural styles of outbuildings caused a decline (Forbush 1927). Bagg and Eliot (1937), referring to the north-central portion of the state, noted a decline from the 1880s, and Bull (1964) described its decline in the southwestern area from the 1890s. Job (1922) said it was "locally common" in Litchfield around 1900. In 1908 Honeywill et al. said that "a few breed" in New Haven although it was "formerly common." It remained a locally "common" nester in the northwest and northeast hills to the mid-1930s (Bagg and Eliot), and even increased somewhat (PLSNY 42, 43). It was very local and scarce along the coastal plain at that time. Continuing its decline, it had become a very local nester in Litchfield County and the Storrs area by the 1960's (Manter 1975). Beginning in the 1970's, its nesting population increased to a limited extent and has slowly extended its range southward, nesting mostly on masonry structures.

Barn Swallow (*Hirundo rustica*)

STATUS: a common migrant from mid-April to June, and very common in fall from late July into October; migrations peak in mid-May

Barn Swallow

and late August. It is sometimes very abundant on peak migration days in late August, and flocks of more than 2,000 birds are occasionally reported. It is a common nester throughout the state in sheds, barns, old buildings and, occasionally, under bridges.

Earliest spring arrival: Mar. 30, 1929; Mar. 31, 1952; Apr. 3, 1938.
Latest fall departure: Nov. 12, 1983; Nov. 8, 1982, Nov. 7, 1981.

HISTORICAL NOTES: The Barn Swallow has historically been one of the state's most common summer residents. Linsley (1843a) considered it common and Merriam (1877) said it bred "abundantly under the roofs of barns." Sage et al. (1913) called it an "abundant summer resident."

CROWS, JAYS, RAVENS (FAMILY CORVIDAE)

Gray Jay (*Perisoreus canadensis*)

STATUS: a hypothetical winter visitor from early November to early May; no photographs or specimens taken in Connecticut are known. It is casual and irregular in winter south to central New York and Massachusetts.

COMMENTS: The published reports of sightings in Connecticut are surprisingly recent: the first was at Colebrook on December 30, 1944, by R. Morrill (*Auk* 62:457). In the fall of 1957, there was an incursion of Gray Jays into western New England. In early November at Washington, Niantic and Lime Rock (Salisbury) five birds were noted by the Hartford Bird Study Club (AFN 12:265). Most stayed briefly, but one remained to at least December 28 (AFN 12:84). On May 14, 1958, one was sighted by M. French and E. Bergstrom at West Hartford (AFN 12:338, RNEB 14:11, HAS). Another incursion into western New England occurred during the winter of 1965–1966. One bird was reported from mid-January to February 1, 1966, at Litchfield by R.Buyak (AFN 20:405). On December 16, 1973, two birds were reportedly seen by many observers at Sharon (AmB 28:218) and reportedly photographed, but the location of the photographs is not known. On October 7, 1982, one was sighted at Harwinton by R. Belding (CW 3:11).

Blue Jay (*Cyanocitta cristata*)

STATUS: a common resident throughout the state. In migration, steady streams of small flocks have been observed flying at tree-top level from mid-September to early November, and from mid-March to mid-May. In winter, there are occasional fluctuations of numbers from year to year. It nests commonly in wooded areas throughout the state.

COMMENTS: On September 29, 1983, 701 migrating Blue Jays were counted over the Quaker Ridge Hawk Watch site in Greenwich (CW 4:25).

HISTORICAL NOTES: In the 1800s, the Blue Jay was chiefly a bird of the less settled areas (Bagg and Eliot 1937). However, the Blue Jay's range expanded into cities during the 1920s (Bagg and Eliot), possibly because of a change in urban vegetation, protection from hunting, and an increase in feeding stations. Nesting Blue Jays along Breeding Bird Survey routes in southern New England decreased from 1965 to 1979 (Robbins et al. 1986).

Eurasian Jackdaw (*Corvus monedula*)

STATUS: an accidental vagrant. One was present at West Haven from February 16 to March 16, 1988 (F. Gallo et al.; CW 8:66, 8:84, 8:87). The bird was observed by many and photographed.

COMMENTS: Eurasian Jackdaw has appeared in eastern North America several times in the 1980s. Authorities differ as to the origins of these individuals. It appears that these occurrences are natural rather than human-assisted.

American Crow (*Corvus brachyrhynchos*)

STATUS: a common resident throughout the state. In migration it is common to abundant from early September to late November and common from early March to early May. Occasionally very abundant in winter when large numbers congregate at roosts—particularly near garbage landfills along the coast and larger river valleys. It is a common and widespread nester in open woodlands.

HISTORICAL NOTES: This conspicuous species has successfully adapted to historical land-use changes in Connecticut. It was "common" in the early 1800s (Linsley 1843a) and an "abundant resident" in the late 1800s (Merriam 1877), and the early 1900s (Sage et al. 1913). An increase in the number of nesting American Crows was noted in southern New England from 1965 to 1979 (Robbins et al.).

COMMENTS: In the winter of 1932–1933, the Connecticut Board of Fisheries and Game began a campaign to reduce numbers of crows in winter roosts, citing the potential danger to game, song, and insectivorous birds! The objective was to perform a "thinning out" of the roosts. At that time there were 50,000 birds at one Hartford roost "known to exist for at least 100 years," 7,000 birds in New London County, 3,000 birds in Windham County, 5,000 birds in Middlesex County, and 5,000 birds in New Haven County. The program was abandoned after 1,000 birds were shot because the birds simply dispersed from the roosts and formed new ones elsewhere, thus outnumbering the men performing the killing (BL 35:132).

Fish Crow (*Corvus ossifragus*)

STATUS: an uncommon to fairly common coastal migrant from March to mid-May and from late July to November; locally uncommon to fairly common in early winter along the coast and inland along the Connecticut River. Small numbers can be found locally through the winter season. It nests locally along the coast and inland along large rivers.

HISTORICAL NOTES: This species was reported at Stratford in the early 1800s (Linsley), and Merriam (1877) called it "a rare summer visitor." The first confirmed nesting was in 1888 at New Haven (C. Trowbridge), and next at Fairfield in 1892 (*Auk* 10:90). It was first seen at Springfield, Massachusetts, in 1896 (*Auk* 14:100). The first winter record was in 1902 at New London (*Auk* 19:93) and next in 1903 at North Haven (Sage et al. 1913). In 1908 Honeywill et al. said it was a "common summer resident" at New Haven and added that it was also found there in winter. By 1913 it was "resident" along the coast east to Niantic, north along the Housatonic River to New Milford and in the Connecticut River valley (Sage et al.; Bagg and Eliot 1937). From the 1870s to the early 1920s it had been called, in succession, "rare" (Merriam; Averill 1892), "not rare" (Sage et al. 1913), "uncommon" and "lingering later into the fall" (Howes 1928).

In the mid-1940s it was recorded three times in the Hartford area (HAS). Its range expanded east along the coast to Rhode Island by 1946 (Bent 1946) and by the mid-1950s north along the Connecticut River into Massachusetts, where it was "occasionally reported" (Griscom and Snyder 1955). Increases were noted along Breeding Bird Survey routes in southern New England from 1965 to 1979 (Robbins et al.). It returned to the Hartford area in 1976 after an absence of many years (AmB 30:814), and it wintered there by the early 1980s (CW 2:25). By the early 1980s, nesting had been reported well inland from salt and brackish waters in Connecticut.

Common Raven (*Corvus corax*)

STATUS: a rare winter visitor in the northwest and northeast hills from October to late April, accidental elsewhere. Increasing, it has been reported annually since 1983 in Litchfield County; there have been several sightings elsewhere in the state. Nesting was suspected on Canaan Mountain in 1986 and was reportedly confirmed there in 1987 (D. Rosgen, pers. comm.). A pair was believed to have nested in 1987 in the northeast hills at Ashford (L. Bevier, AmB 41:403), and a nest was observed there by many in 1988 and 1989 (pers. obs.).

HISTORICAL NOTES: Common Ravens were reportedly "numerous" in eastern Massachusetts in the 1600s (Forbush 1927) and were probably present in our state and extirpated shortly after settlement (*Auk* 62:1; Griscom and Snyder; Hill). In the 1840s it may still have been occasional on Long Island (Cruickshank 1942). Nesting may have occurred in northeast Massachusetts as late as the 1870s (Bagg and Eliot 1937).

It has historically been a very rare visitor in Connecticut. One was shot by O. Hagenaw on September 18, 1890, at south Manchester (HAS). On May 25, 1919, one was seen along the coast at the Norwalk–Westport border (*Auk* 36: 572). On October 12, 1921, four were reported from central Connecticut (OO 39:29). Reports on March 11, 1942 (BL 44:II:3) and April 2, 1943 (BNEBL) are questionable as published. On February 29, 1948, one was reported at Bethany (AFN 2:134). One was reported at Wilton from mid-January to late March 1958 (AFN 12:265).

Reports in southern New England were irregular but increasing during the 1940s (*Auk* 67:104). Increases were noted in western Maine and northern New Hampshire in the early 1960s, when it was "definitely more frequent" (AFN 15:452). Its range has expanded in the Adirondacks, Catskills, and Berkshires since the mid-1960s (AFN 22:510). The first nesting in New York since colonial times occurred in 1967 (AFN 22:570). Since the mid-1970s its range has extended into western Massachusetts and northern Connecticut (AmB 22:128). It was reportedly a fall migrant in the extreme northwest corner of Connecticut since 1977 (AmB 32:178, 33:15). In 1983 B. Nikula noted that they "continue to expand south" (AmB 37:848), and in 1985, they "continued to increase" (AmB 39:22).

TITMICE (FAMILY PARIDAE)

Black-capped Chickadee (*Parus atricapillus*)

STATUS: a common and widespread resident. It is occasionally very common in fall and winter as young birds emigrate from interior areas to the coast. It is a fairly common nester in tree cavities throughout the state's woodlands.

HISTORICAL NOTES: The population of Black-capped Chickadees in Connecticut apparently has not changed significantly in historical times. Linsley (1843a) said it was "common." Merriam (1877) said it was "a common resident" and added that it was "gregarious except during the breeding season." Sage et al. (1913) said it was "a common resident; keeping in family flocks except in the breeding seasons, and venturing into the cities in the fall and winter."

COMMENTS: Important studies on the demography of this species in the Litchfield area have been conducted by Gordon Loery and his co-workers (Loery and Nichols 1985; Loery et al. 1987).

Boreal Chickadee (*Parus hudsonicus*)

STATUS: an irregular and very rare winter visitor from late October to mid-April; absent most years but may be numerous during certain winters.

Mainly resident from the tree limit in northern Canada south to northern United States (Terres 1980), winter invasions south to Long Island and northern New Jersey occur rarely. It was first recorded in Connecticut at New Haven on November 13, 1875 (Merriam 1877); recent eruptions occurred during the winters of 1954–1955, 1962–1963, and 1965–1966. The last, and possibly the largest, invasion occurred in the winter of 1975–1976 (MFN 3:9–11, 4:1–4; AmB 30:679, 694).

Earliest fall arrival: Oct. 6, 1983; Oct. 16, 1974; Oct. 19, 1986.

Latest spring departure: May 1, 1955; Apr. 19, 1970; Apr. 15, 1976.

HISTORICAL NOTES: There is insufficient evidence to suggest that any significant change in its occurrence here has taken place in historic times.

Tufted Titmouse (*Parus bicolor*)

STATUS: a fairly common resident, somewhat less numerous in the northeast and northwest hills. It is a fairly common nester in tree cavities in woodlands throughout the state.

HISTORICAL NOTES: The Tufted Titmouse was a very rare straggler in Connecticut in the 1800s and early 1900s. Linsley (1843a) recorded this species at New Haven. Merriam (1877) said it was "a rare visitor from the south" and listed sightings in Lyme and Hartford in addition to Linsley's report. A pair reportedly nested for two years at Putnam in about 1888 and 1889 (*Auk* 60:106). Sage et al. (1913) called it "a very rare visitor" and listed no additional records other than those stated by Merriam.

Forbush (1929) termed it a "mere straggler in New England." According to A. Saunders, there were only five records of this species in Connecticut prior to 1934 (*Auk* 67:254). A single bird was reported in 1938 at Wilton (PLSNY No. 50, 51:71). Cruickshank (1942) called it "extremely uncommon east of the Hudson River."

Expanding its range northward, the Tufted Titmouse was reported annually in Connecticut beginning in 1942. Two birds wintered at Norwalk in 1942–1943 (BL 45:II:3). The first nesting in this century in the state occurred at Westport in 1949 (AFN 3:230) (although Bull [1964] says Weston) and the next at Westport by B. Brown in 1953 (Bull 1964; Smith 1950). Increasing, it was resident in Fairfield County by the early 1950s; a large incursion occurred in the winter of 1954 (AFN 22:423). By the late 1950s it was seen annually east to Guilford, north to Mansfield and the northwest hills; in 1961 it nested at the two latter locations (Mackenzie; Pink and Waterman 1965; Manter 1975). In 1962 it nested at West Hartford (AmB 17:393). By the 1970s it was a widespread and common resident throughout the state (Robbins et al. 1986).

NUTHATCHES (FAMILY SITTIDAE)

Red-breasted Nuthatch (*Sitta canadensis*)

STATUS: an uncommon migrant from mid-April to mid-May and from early September to early December; it is sometimes fairly common on peak migration days in October. It is variable in numbers from year to year but is usually uncommon. A very local nester in the northwest hills, with 16 reports in the 1980s, and, more rarely, in the northeast hills. There is a report of an isolated nesting near the shore at Branford in 1986.

Earliest fall arrival: Aug. 13, 1972; Aug. 14, 1977; Aug. 15, 1957.
Latest spring departure: May 26, 1978; May 23, 1976; May 21, 1939.

HISTORICAL NOTES: There are only two published nesting records of this species in Connecticut prior to 1900, both from the northwest hills. The first was found by Mr. Williams in 1876 at Winsted (Job 1922) and the second in 1896 at Norfolk (Sage et al. 1913). Nesting was unreported into the 1930s (Bagg and Eliot 1937). In 1943 a pair nested at Bethany (BL 45:II:3). By the 1960s it bred locally south to Litchfield (AFN 15:454). Unusual was a report of nesting at Waterford in 1968 (AFN 22:588). By 1973 it nested south to East Haddam (AmB 27:1023). Nesting was noted in the Mansfield area in 1975 (Manter).

White-breasted Nuthatch (*Sitta carolinensis*)

STATUS: a fairly common and widespread resident; it is usually more conspicuous in winter. It nests in tree cavities in woodlands throughout the state.

White-breasted Nuthatch

HISTORICAL NOTES: The White-breasted Nuthatch has been a numerous resident in historic times. Linsley (1843a) said it was "common," and Merriam (1877) simply called it a "resident." Sage et al. (1913) called it "a tolerably common resident" but added that it was "less common than formerly in southern Connecticut." This species is a bark-gleaning bird of deciduous woodlands, and it has somewhat expanded its distribution since the early 1900s with the regrowth of the state's forests.

CREEPERS (FAMILY CERTHIIDAE)
Brown Creeper (*Certhia americana*)

STATUS: an uncommon migrant from March to late May and from late September to early December; it is sometimes fairly common in mid-April and early November. In winter it is variable in numbers but is usually uncommon. An uncommon and local nester in mature, moist woodlands, it is most frequent in the northwest hills but very scarce near the coast.

HISTORICAL NOTES: This species declined in Connecticut as the forest was cut during the settlement period. It increased after the mid-1800s as the forests gradually returned. Merriam (1877) wrote that it nested, but provided no details. Neither Sage et al. nor Job listed any nesting records. Forbush (1927) called it an "uncommon" summer resident. E. Rowland thought that it probably nested at Norwich in 1928 (Bagg and Eliot 1937). It was found summering at Kent in 1934 by J. Kuerzi (PLSNY No. 43:1–13), but nesting was not confirmed until May 30, 1936, when J. and R. Kuerzi found a nest at Kent (PLSNY No. 48:98). It nested at Wallingford in 1954 (AFN 8:336). Expanding its nesting range south and east by the early 1960s, it nested regularly in the northwest hills but was less frequent south to Greenwich (AFN 15:454). It has nested since 1965 in the Mansfield area (Manter 1975). Robbins et al. (1986) noted an increase of nesting birds on Breeding Bird Survey routes in southern New England from 1965 to 1979. It is now a fairly widespread but not numerous nester in the northeast hills.

WRENS (FAMILY TROGLODYTIDAE)
Carolina Wren (*Thryothorus ludovicianus*)

STATUS: an uncommon migrant from late March to late May and from September to mid-November. In winter it is usually rare, but its numbers vary from year to year, and it is sometimes uncommon. It nests locally in a wide variety of settings, including coastal thickets, old fields, wooded ravines, moist forests, and even buildings. It is less numerous at higher elevations in all seasons.

HISTORICAL NOTES: The Carolina Wren was not recorded in Connecticut in the early and mid-1800s. Apparently, the first occurrence in the state was on November 25, 1878, when one was collected at Old Saybrook by J. Clark (BNOC 4:61). Noted by many observers only since 1891 (*Auk* 26:263), this species was first reported nesting in the state in 1895 at Bridgeport (E. Eames and H. Taylor, *Auk* 13:84). Nesting occurred at Norwalk in 1900 (Smith 1950) and at Chester in 1901 (*Auk* 19:90). There was a notable influx in 1908 (*Auk* 26:263). This species is subject to decimation by winter cold spells with heavy snows but recovers after successive mild winters. Its range has gradually extended northward in this century (Bent 1948; Griscom and Snyder 1955). Robbins et al. noted an increase in nesting Carolina Wrens on Breeding Bird Survey routes in Connecticut from 1965 to 1979.

House Wren (*Troglodytes aedon*)

STATUS: a fairly common migrant from late April to late May and common from mid-August to mid-October; migrations peak in mid-May and in mid-September. It is very rare in November and December, and lingering birds are accidental in January. Very few survive the winter: one spent the winter of 1929–1930 at a Stamford feeder (BL 32:205). It is a common nester throughout the state in rural and suburban areas in thickets, wet woodlands, orchards, and gardens.

Earliest spring arrival: Apr. 1, 1986; Apr. 2, 1952; Apr. 4, 1953.
Latest fall departure: Jan. 28, 1973; Jan. 27, 1985; Jan. 8, 1983.

HISTORICAL NOTES: The House Wren declined from the late 1800s into the early part of this century. Linsley (1843a) said it was "common," but Merriam (1877) said it was "not abundant." Sage et al. (1913) said it was "not abundant anywhere, and apparently decreasing in numbers." A similar decline during this period was noted elsewhere in New England and New York (Ellison 1985), and the decline has been attributed to competition with House Sparrows and European Starlings. By 1930 the number of House Wrens in Connecticut had rebounded (Bagg and Eliot; Manter; Griscom and Snyder 1955).

Winter Wren (*Troglodytes troglodytes*)

STATUS: an uncommon migrant from late March to early May and from late September to mid-October. It is usually uncommon in winter but is less numerous inland at higher elevations. It nests locally in the northwest and northeast hills, rarely near the coast and larger river valleys. It prefers moist, wooded ravines.

HISTORICAL NOTES: The Winter Wren has historically been a regular migrant and winter visitor in Connecticut. Linsley (1843a) recorded it at New Haven and Stratford, and Merriam (1877) said it was "a winter resident; rather common during migrations." Sage et al. (1913) termed it a "tolerably common fall migrant" but added that it was "much rarer" in winter and spring.

The nesting status of this species in the 1800s and early part of this century is unknown. There are no known nesting records in the 1800s. Job reported two pairs, with males in full song, in early July at Salisbury in 1906. Sage et al. (1913) said it "very rarely breeds in this state." Reports of nesting increased during the 1930s and 1940s. It probably nested at Canaan in 1936 (PLSNY 48:98). East of the Connecticut River, breeding was recorded at Ashford in 1939, regularly there since 1960 (Manter 1975). Its nesting range extended south to northern Fairfield County by the early 1960s (Bull 1964). It nested at northern Stamford and Greenwich by 1974 (MFN 2:7) and at Old Lyme in 1975 (AmB 29:749).

Sedge Wren (*Cistothorus platensis*)

STATUS: a very rare migrant in May and June and from early September to late October. This elusive species is most apt to be found in mid-May and in October. It is extirpated from Connecticut as a nesting species. There are two winter records: a male was collected on February 7, 1953, at North Haven (D. Parsons, YPM No. 16029), and one was seen on January 1, 1955, at Saybrook (R. T. Peterson, AFN 9:245).

Earliest spring arrival: Apr. 29, 1935; May 2, 1902; May 5, 1914.
Latest fall departure: Oct. 30, 1976; Oct. 25, 1971; Oct. 22, 1932.

HISTORICAL NOTES: The Sedge Wren has been scarcely reported in the state in historic times. Linsley (1843a) reported it at New Haven, and it nested at South Windsor sometime prior to 1864 (Bagg and Eliot). Merriam (1877) said it was "a rather rare summer resident; breeding in suitable localities along our southern border and in the Connecticut Valley." It nested in the Bridgeport area in the 1890s (Averill 1892). Sage et al. (1913) called it a "rare summer resident" throughout the state, although it may have been more common locally in Litchfield

County; nesting was also reported at Warren, Bethel, and Danbury. It nested at South Windsor for several years up to 1916 (*Auk* 34:465).

Suffering from loss of habitat, it was declining by 1900 (Bagg and Eliot 1937). Continuing to decrease in the early 1940s (Cruickshank; Griscom and Snyder 1955), it was a "very rare" migrant and a local and "sporadic" nester by the early 1960s (*Auk* 67:254, Bull 1964; Manter 1975). Robbins et al. (1986) noted a continental decline in nestings along Breeding Bird Survey routes from 1966 to 1979. The last recorded nestings in the state were at Danbury in 1972 (C. Hills et al., AmB 26:840) and at Salisbury in 1975 and 1976 (R. Dewire, AmB 31:231). There were at least two attempted nestings since 1978 (HAS, MFN 7:6).

Marsh Wren (*Cistothorus palustris*)

STATUS: an uncommon coastal migrant from late April to June and uncommon to locally common from September to mid-November; it is very rare into early January. Although wintering birds are known from New York and New Jersey, it is not known to have survived the winter in Connecticut. Inland it is usually rare in migration. An uncommon to fairly common nester in brackish and salt marshes along the coast and along the Connecticut River in South Windsor, Cromwell, and Portland, it is usually rare inland in freshwater marshes at Goshen, Litchfield, and Barkhamsted. It favors marshes that contain narrow-leaved cattail *Typha angustifolia* (*Auk* 39:257).

Earliest spring arrival: Apr. 4, 1976; Apr. 13, 1983; Apr. 27, 1913.

Latest fall departure: Jan. 7, 1952; Jan. 4, 1986; Jan. 3, 1953.

HISTORICAL NOTES: Merriam (1877) wrote that it was "a common summer resident; breeds abundantly in the brackish marshes bordering the Quinnipiac River" and "also breeds in suitable fresh water marshes throughout the state." Sage et al. (1913) said it was "abundant" along the coast in summer, whereas Job (1922) in 1908, referring to Litchfield County, said it was "a rather rare migrant." It has declined inland with the destruction of freshwater marshes.

SUBSPECIES: Two subspecies of Marsh Wren may be found in the state. For many years the Prairie Marsh Wren (*C. p. disseptus*) has nested inland, including marshes along the Connecticut River at South Windsor (Bagg and Eliot 1937) and has been recorded as a fall coastal migrant (*Auk* 38:589). Declining since the late 1800s with the destruction of inland marshes, it became an increasingly local nester. The protection of coastal and inland wetlands since 1972 has resulted in a modest stabilization of its population. This form is larger than the nominate race, has reddish-brown upper parts, and is buffy or brownish-white underneath (Bent 1948).

The nominate race *T. p. pulustris* nests along the Connecticut coast and has white on its breast, belly, and chin with dusky brown upper-parts (Bent 1948). Separation of the two forms in the field is difficult.

KINGLETS, GNATCATCHERS, THRUSHES
(FAMILY MUSCICAPIDAE)

Golden-crowned Kinglet (*Regulus satrapa*)

STATUS: an uncommon to fairly common migrant from late March to May and from early October to mid-November; migrations peak in mid-April and late October. It is usually uncommon in winter but is occasionally fairly common. It is a rare to locally uncommon nester in the northwest and northeast hills, very rare and irregular elsewhere. Apparently, it has slowly expanded its nesting range southward. It favors stands of mature conifers, especially planted spruce groves.

Earliest fall arrival: Sept. 13, 1980; Sept. 20, 1954; Sept. 22, 1970.

Latest spring departure: May 18, 1975; May 16, 1958; May 13, 1978.

HISTORICAL NOTES: The Golden-crowned Kinglet has histori-cally been a common migrant and winter visitor in Connecticut. Interestingly, nesting is not mentioned by Merriam, Job, or Sage et al. Apparently, the first confirmed nesting in Connecticut was at Salis-bury in June 1934, although individuals were noted there the previous summer (J. Kuerzi, PLSNY 1934: No. 43). Another pair was present at Sharon during the summer of 1936 (PLSNY No. 48). More recently, it nested at Litchfield in 1973 (AmB 27:851). Nesting was confirmed at Union in 1974 (AmB 29:749) and was suspected at Hartford in 1975 (AmB 29:831).

Ruby-crowned Kinglet (*Regulus calendula*)

STATUS: a fairly common migrant from early April to mid-May and from mid-September to late November; it is sometimes common during peak migration days in late April and mid-October. Individuals regularly linger along the coast to late December; it is rare in January. It nests south to northern New York and northern New England (NYBBA;

Terres 1980). There are no corroborated nesting records from Connecticut.

Earliest spring arrival: Mar. 17, 1921; Mar. 18, 1956; Mar. 20, 1937.
Latest spring departure: May 27, 1969; May 25, 1982; May 22, 1981.
Earliest fall arrival: Aug. 29, 1981; Sept. 2, 1953; Sept. 3, 1974.
Latest fall departure: Jan. 31, 1955; Jan. 19, 1951; Jan. 15, 1984.

HISTORICAL NOTES: The Ruby-crowned Kinglet has historically been a common migrant in Connecticut. Linsley (1843a) reported numbers of this species at Stratford. Merriam (1877) called it "common during its migrations," and Sage et al. (1913) said it was a "common" migrant. Neither Merriam nor Sage et al. listed any winter records beyond November. This kinglet has increased in abundance in this century (NYBBA). In 1965 it was noted that "certainly this species has been increasing in winter and is less of a prize on a Christmas Count than formerly" (AFN 19:364).

Blue-gray Gnatcatcher (*Polioptila caerulea*)

STATUS: an uncommon migrant from late April to mid-May and from late July to late September; it is sometimes fairly common during peak migration days in early May. It very rarely lingers into October and November; it is accidental in December. One was seen by six observers December 16–17, 1984, at Stamford (MFN 12:7); a different bird was sighted at Greenwich on December 7, 1984 (MFN 12:7). It nests along the coastal plain and larger river valleys; scattered elsewhere.

Earliest spring arrival: Apr. 9, 1985; Apr. 10, 1988; Apr. 11, 1982.
Latest fall departure: Nov. 13, 1972; Nov. 12, 1972; Nov. 3, 1923, 1964.

COMMENTS: Two December single-observer sightings lack sufficient corroboration (RNEB 9:286; CW 6:39).

HISTORICAL NOTES: The status of this species has changed dramatically since the mid-1800s. It was observed by Linsley at Stratford before 1843 and was next recorded in 1883 at Portland (BNOC 8:179). It was generally regarded as a "casual" visitor before the 1920s, chiefly occurring in spring along the coast (Averill; Griscom; Forbush 1929). Sage et al. (1913) noted only seven records in the 1800s. It was increasingly reported in spring and fall during the 1920s and 1930s; it was possibly an annual visitor by the late 1930s (Bagg and Eliot 1937). In 1942 Cruickshank said it was annual but "rare to uncommon" just west of Connecticut.

The major expansion of its range into Connecticut occurred in the 1940s—particularly after 1947, and it has slowly increased since. The first attempted nesting in the state was at Fairfield in 1947 (*Auk* 67:255), but the first successful nesting occurred in 1950 at Weston (Bull 1964). Other unusually large spring flights were noted in 1954 and 1956 (Bull 1964). Increasing in the 1950s, by 1959 there were at least five nesting records in southern Fairfield County (Bull 1964). It was reported in the Guilford area in 1950 and 1956 (Mackenzie 1961) and was first found (and nested) at Mansfield in 1957 (*Auk* 75:352; Manter 1975). In 1972 this species was cited as nesting "north to southwest Connecticut" (AmB 26:840). In 1973 six birds were reported in spring at West Hartford (AmB 27:753). From 1965 through 1979 increases were noted along Breeding Bird Survey routes in southern New England north to New Hampshire and Vermont (Robbins et al.).

Northern Wheatear (*Oenanthe oenanthe*)

STATUS: a casual fall vagrant; it is most apt to occur in September and October. Accidental in spring: there are two records in May. Most occurrences are from coastal areas.

RECORDS: it was first found in Connecticut on September 9, 1965, at Stonington by G. Bissell, S. Dana et al. (AFN 20:12, RNEB 21:21, CW 3:18). Other records, all of single birds:

May 30–31, 1968	Guilford	M. Gallagher et al. (ph.)	AFN 22:593
Sept. 7–11, 1976	Stonington	R. Dewire et al.	AmB 31:230
May 17–27, 1980	Guilford	P. Desjardins et al.	AmB 34:756
Aug. 29, 1982	Madison	F. Whitney et al.	CW 2:46
Oct. 10, 1982	New Canaan	R. Gilbert et al. (ph.)	CW 3:18
Sept. 5–10, 1985	Madison	R. English et al.	CW 6:22
Sept. 28–30, 1986	Westport	R. Souffer et al.	CW 7:26
Sept. 27–29, 1987	Clinton	J. Zickefoose et al.	CW 8:42

COMMENTS: An uncorroborated report by a single observer on February 15, 1981, at North Branford (CW 3:18) would represent an unprecedented winter occurrence for the United States if it had been verified (see B. Bruun, AmB 34:310).

Eastern Bluebird (*Sialia sialis*)

STATUS: an uncommon migrant from March to mid-April and uncommon to locally common from September to late October. Variable in

Eastern Bluebird

winter, but usually uncommon. It nests locally in rural areas with open fields, orchards, and low thickets; it does not nest along the coast and in the southern Connecticut River valley.

HISTORICAL NOTES: The Eastern Bluebird was probably uncommon throughout most of Connecticut when the first settlers arrived and the land was mostly forested (NYBBA). As the settlers cleared the land, this species apparently increased. Linsley (1843a) said it was "common," and Merriam (1877) said it was an "abundant" nester and was "generally evenly distributed and everywhere a common species." However, this species decreased significantly in the late 1800s and early 1900s, probably the result of competition with House Sparrows, a series of severe winters, and the loss of nesting habitat (Manter; Bagg and Eliot 1937). Sage et al. (1913) said it was "almost exterminated in the winter of 1895 by the long continued cold weather in the South . . . yet it had regained its former abundance by 1898." In 1908 Job (1922) said it was "a common summer resident" in Litchfield County.

About 1910 a decrease in the House Sparrow population resulted in a slight recovery, but an expanding European Starling population and the pervasive loss of nesting habitat soon curtailed this increase (Bagg and Eliot; Forbush 1929). By about 1940 it was "fairly common" to "abundant," but by the 1960s it was called "rare," "uncommon," or "fairly common" (Bull 1964; Manter 1975). Nesting box placement programs have helped stabilize its numbers since the 1950s and have in some cases resulted in an increase (Griscom and Snyder 1955; Pink and Waterman 1965; Manter 1975). However, decreases were noted from 1965 to 1979 along Breeding Bird Survey routes in Connecticut (Robbins et al.).

Its wintering population in rural areas of Connecticut increased in the 1970s (Pink and Waterman 1980; Manter; SCCC, MFN).

Townsend's Solitaire (*Myadestes townsendi*)

STATUS: a hypothetical vagrant from the western North America. There are two sight reports: one was reported at Hartford May 7– 8, 1939, by M. Hoffman et al. (HAS), and one was reported at Bethel November 12 and 24, 1983, by T. Lofgren (CW 7:49). Unfortunately, there is no specimen or photographic evidence to support these reports, and thus they are here termed hypothetical.

Veery (*Catharus fuscescens*)

STATUS: a fairly common migrant from May to early June and from late August to October. It is occasionally common on peak migration days in mid-May and mid-September. Accidental in winter: one was present at Greenwich, January 2–8, 1980 (photographed, P. Lehman, J. Dunn et al., MFN 8:1). It is a common and widespread nester throughout the state in mature forests.

Earliest spring arrival: Apr. 19, 1935; Apr. 21, 1921; Apr. 29, 1951, 1981.

Latest fall departure: Oct. 27, 1984; Oct. 24, 1974; Oct. 16, 1986.

HISTORICAL NOTES: Linsley (1843a) recorded this species at Stratford and New Haven, and Merriam (1877) said it was "common in the immediate vicinity of New Haven." Sage et al. (1913) said it was "a common summer resident of damp woodland throughout the state." Certainly, the Veery has increased in population since the mid-1800s as a result of the regrowth of the state's forests. However, recent studies suggest that this species may now be declining around urban and suburban areas caused by the fragmentation of deciduous woods (NYBBA).

Gray-cheeked Thrush (*Catharus minimus*)

STATUS: a rare migrant from mid-May to June and from September to early October; it is sometimes uncommon on peak migration days in late May and late September.

Earliest spring arrival: May 1, 1965; May 3, 1973; May 6, 1923, 1983.

Latest spring departure: June 9, 1935 (spec.); June 3, 1906, June 1, 1907, 1900.

Earliest fall arrival: Aug. 17, 1967; Aug. 20, 1966; Aug. 27, 1981.

Latest fall departure: Oct. 29, 1955 (spec.); Oct. 27, 1975; Oct. 22, 1921.

HISTORICAL NOTES: Although the Gray-cheeked Thrush is now infrequently encountered during migration, several early accounts seem to indicate that it was once more numerous in the state. Merriam (1877) indicated that it was "more common" in migration than the Swainson's Thrush in the vicinity of New Haven. Sage et al. (1913) noted that the Gray-cheeked Thrush was "a common spring and fall migrant."

Swainson's Thrush (*Catharus ustulatus*)

STATUS: a fairly common migrant from mid-May to early June and from late August to late October; it is occasionally common on peak migration days in September.

It very rarely lingers to late December; there are at least 10 sightings of this species on Christmas Bird Counts since 1958, but none is corroborated by specimen or photographic evidence. In view of the difficulty of some observers in distinguishing this species from Hermit Thrush, the authors feel that most of these sightings are questionable as published. The only verified late December record was one photographed on December 26, 1983, at Greenwich (D. and J. Bova, CW 4:38-39).

Earliest spring arrival: Apr. 27, 1957; Apr. 30, 1972; May 1, 1974.

Latest spring departure: June 7. 1987; June 2, 1967; June 1, 1940.

Earliest fall arrival: Aug. 15, 1972; Aug. 31, 1966; Sep. 6, 1914.

Latest fall departure: Nov. 12, 1952; Nov. 11, 1937; Nov. 10, 1906.

HISTORICAL NOTES: The Swainson's Thrush has apparently not changed in abundance in historic times. Merriam (1877) said it was "common during its migrations," and Sage et al. (1913) called it "a tolerably common spring and fall migrant."

Hermit Thrush (*Catharus guttatus*)

STATUS: a fairly common migrant from early April to mid-May and from late September to late November; it is sometimes common on peak migration days in late April and late October. It occasionally lingers through early January, particularly along the coast, is very rare in mid- and late winter. It is an uncommon to locally fairly common nester at higher elevations in northwest and northeast hills, rarely on higher trap-rock ridges in New Haven County.

Earliest spring arrival: Mar. 10, 1933, 1953; Mar. 14, 1916; Mar. 16, 1907.

Fall departures are difficult to assess because of the tendency of individuals to linger into January.

HISTORICAL NOTES: The Hermit Thrush has expanded its nesting range in Connecticut in historic times. Apparently, the first reported nesting in the state was in 1893 at Norfolk (*Auk* 10:371) and next in 1910 (*Auk* 27:451), although Sage et al. (1913) said it "nested regularly in the northwestern part of the state." By the 1920s it nested elsewhere in the northwest hills with records for Salisbury, Canaan, Litchfield, and at several towns in Hartford County (Job 1922; Forbush 1929). From 1905 to 1913 it increased as a nester in Rhode Island (*Auk* 30:558), and during the 1920s its nesting range expanded in central Massachusetts (Bagg and Eliot 1937). In 1934 it was reported summering at Kent and Cornwall (Bagg and Eliot). Reports of summering pairs without confirmation of nesting were noted as far south as Greenwich in the late 1950s (Bull 1964) and at Guilford in the mid-1960s (Mackenzie 1961). Nesting was reported south to mid-Fairfield County by the early 1970s (Hills 1978). A decline was noted along Breeding Bird Survey routes in southern New England from 1965 to 1979 (Robbins et al.).

Wood Thrush (*Hylocichla mustelina*)

STATUS: a fairly common migrant from May to early June and from late August to mid-October; it is sometimes common on peak migration days in mid-May and mid-September. Very rare in November and accidental in December: one was reported on December 27, 1964, at New London about which A. Cruickshank said, "an unquestionable observation . . . within a few feet" (AFN 19:II:2, 19:117), and one was apparently photographed on January 2, 1988, at Hartford (CW 8(3):66; AmB 42:664). It is a widespread and common nester throughout the state's forests.

Earliest spring arrival: Apr. 20, 1954; Apr. 21, 1976; Apr. 25, 1959.
Latest fall departure: Nov. 21, 1965; Nov. 14, 1973; Nov. 11, 1947.

HISTORICAL NOTES: The Wood Thrush has been a common nester in Connecticut at least since the mid-1800s. Linsley (1843a) recorded this species at Stratford and New Haven, and Merriam (1877) said it was "a common summer resident; breeds." Similarly, Sage et al. (1913) said it was "common . . . throughout the state" and "abundant" along the southern border. Its population has probably increased since the mid-1800s as woodlands have spread and matured. A "significant increase" was noted along Breeding Bird Survey routes in New England from 1965 to 1979 (Robbins et al.).

Fieldfare (*Turdus pilaris*)

STATUS: a hypothetical spring vagrant.

RECORDS: One was collected in April 1878 near Stamford by J. Schaler (OO 14:44), but the current disposition of the specimen is unknown. Referring to this record, Sage et al. wrote: "This specimen is now in the collection of Hoyt, and from the condition of its plumage and feet had certainly not been recently in captivity." Its condition and the time of year it was captured (which coincides with that time of year when the species is likely to occur) suggest it may have been a wild bird. However, this species is believed to have been kept at that time as a caged pet, so the origin of the specimen remains in question, and the species is treated here as hypothetical.

American Robin (*Turdus migratorius*)

STATUS: a common migrant from late March to late May and from September to early November; it is sometimes abundant on peak migration days in late April and October. Variable, but usually rare to uncommon in winter. It is a widespread and common nester throughout the state.

HISTORICAL NOTES: The American Robin, the state bird of Connecticut, has probably always been numerous. Its original use of forest habitats would have made it well adapted for breeding in Connecticut's presettlement wilderness (NYBBA). Most historical accounts call this species an "abundant" nester throughout the state (Merriam; Sage et al.; Forbush 1929). It has remained abundant by shifting its habitat use to open parklike settings and short-grass lawns now prevalent in urban and suburban parts of the state. Excessive spraying with pesticides has decreased some local populations (Bull 1974), and mortality attributed to diazinon and organophosphates continues to be reported, particularly where these pesticides are applied to lawns (NYBBA; Stone and Gradoni 1985, 1986).

COMMENTS: An unusually large number of this species was noted on October 23, 1977, when 20,000 were estimated at Old Lyme (AmB 32:178).

SUBSPECIES: The black-backed race *T. m. nigrideus* nests in northern Quebec, Labrador, and Newfoundland. It does not show contrast between the head and upper back and is identifiable in the field probably only in the spring. It migrates through the state and may also be present in winter.

Varied Thrush (*Ixoreus naevius*)

STATUS: a very rare fall and winter vagrant; most apt to be seen from mid-December to late March, with most reports in December and January. It sometimes overwinters at feeding stations.
   Earliest fall arrival: Nov. 8, 1985; Dec. 9, 1964; Dec. 12, 1960.
   Latest spring departure: Mar. 24, 1960; Mar. 15, 1972.

HISTORICAL NOTES: The first record of this species in Connecticut was of an individual at Ridgefield from mid-February to March 24, 1960 (R. Belden, RNEB 16:10, AFN 14:372), and the second was at Newtown from December 21, 1960, to February 4, 1961 (photographed, RNEB 16:13, 17:11). There are at least 16 published accounts of this species in the state.

MOCKINGBIRDS, THRASHERS (FAMILY MIMIDAE)

Gray Catbird (*Dumetella carolinensis*)

STATUS: a common migrant from late April to June and from late August to late October; it is sometimes very common during peak migration days in mid-May and early September. Variable, but usually uncommon along the coast and Connecticut River valley to late December and rare from January to early April. Birds that arrive in March and early April probably wintered just south of Connecticut. It is a common and widespread nester throughout the state in thickets, old fields, and shrubby forests.

Earliest spring arrival: Mar. 19, 1959; Mar. 24, 1973; Mar. 27, 1951.

Fall departure dates are difficult to determine because of its tendency to linger into winter.

HISTORICAL NOTES: The Gray Catbird has been a common breeder in Connecticut in historic times. Linsley (1843a) said it was "common," and Merriam (1877) called it "an abundant summer resident." Similarly, Sage et al. (1913) said it was "abundant" and added that it wintered "accidentally." Several authors termed it "very common" into the 1960s (Forbush 1929; Bagg and Eliot; Griscom and Snyder; Bull 1964). More recently, it has been called "common" (Mackenzie 1961; Manter 1975). A slight increase was noted in New England states along Breeding Bird Survey routes from 1965 to 1979, and Connecticut had the highest mean counts of nesting catbirds on the continent (Robbins et al.).

Northern Mockingbird (*Mimus polyglottos*)

STATUS: a widespread and fairly common resident throughout the state. It is a common migrant, particularly along the coast, from early April to late May and from September to early November. In winter it generally retreats from higher elevations to the larger river valleys and coast. It nests commonly in fields, shrubby wetlands and thickets, and suburban yards and parks.

HISTORICAL NOTES: Few species have increased in Connecticut as dramatically as the mockingbird. Most accounts written in the 1800s list it as "rare" (Merriam 1877). Linsley recorded it along the coast before 1843. In 1867 Samuels said it was an "exceedingly rare . . . accidental visitor" in New England. It nested at Hartford in about 1860 (Bagg and Eliot 1937), at Jewett City (Griswold) in 1884 (Sage et al. 1913), and at Winchester sometime before 1900 (Job 1922). Around the turn of the century it was a "very rare" visitor, with only eight records from 1873 to 1913 (Sage et al.). It overwintered in 1910–1911 (*Auk* 38:412). Apparently, numbers increased slightly until the severe winter of 1919–1920, and thereafter reports were fewer (Forbush 1929).

A northward expansion into New Jersey and New York occurred in the 1930s and 1940s (Bent 1948), and sightings in Connecticut increased in the 1950s. By 1957 a few were regularly reported in Connecticut in winter (Bull 1964). This expansion has been attributed to the introduction of multiflora rose (*Rosa multiflora*) in the northeast, which provides berries for wintering birds (AmB 36:358). During this range expansion the first nestings in the state were in 1958 at Weston and Westport

(Bull 1964). In Hartford County it first nested in 1963 at Simsbury (AmB 17:451) and at Mansfield (Manter). In the 1960s it increased from a rare and local resident (chiefly along the western coast) to a widespread resident virtually throughout the state (AmB Connecticut Christmas Bird Counts, 1960–1970). From 1965 to 1979 significant increases were noted in Connecticut along Breeding Bird Survey routes (Robbins et al.).

Brown Thrasher (*Toxostoma rufum*)

STATUS: an uncommon to fairly common migrant from mid-April to late May and from late August to late October; migrations peak in early May and in early September. In December and January its numbers vary, but it is usually rare along the coast and very rare inland; it is very rare anywhere in the state in February and March. It is an uncommon nester throughout the state in thickets and old fields, less numerous at higher elevations.

Earliest spring arrival: Mar. 14, 1959, 1973; Mar. 15, 1983; Mar. 28, 1879.

Fall departure dates are difficult to determine because of the number of early winter records.

HISTORICAL NOTES: The Brown Thrasher probably increased in Connecticut as abandoned farms turned to thickets and shrubs. Linsley (1843a) and Merriam (1877) both called this species "common." Sage et al. (1913) said it was "a common summer resident . . . winters accidentally." Through the early 1960s the Brown Thrasher decreased somewhat and was generally called "fairly common" (Bagg and Eliot; Bull 1964; Manter 1975). In recent years it has been reported less frequently, probably the result of many old-field areas reverting to forest. A significant downward trend was noted along Breeding Bird Survey routes in southern New England from 1965 to 1979 (Robbins et al.). Recent Christmas Bird Count data suggest a decline in wintering numbers (SC-CC).

PIPITS (FAMILY MOTACILLIDAE)

American Pipit (*Anthus rubescens*)

STATUS: This species is erratic in its occurrence in the state, and its numbers fluctuate from year to year. It is usually a rare to locally uncommon migrant from mid-March to May and uncommon from late

September to early December; migrations peak in early April and mid-October. It infrequently lingers along the coast to late December and is very rare in midwinter.

This species favors beaches, short-grass lake and river shores, plowed fields, and filled areas, where it feeds on seeds and insects (Terres 1980).

Earliest fall arrival: Sept. 8, 1983; Sept. 9, 1916; Sept. 15, 1964, 1980.
Latest spring departure: May 19, 1971; May 16, 1888; May 12, 1935.

HISTORICAL NOTES: A review of the published literature does not indicate that any substantial change in population has occurred, but its favored habitat has declined in this century as farmlands reverted to forest or have been developed.

COMMENTS: Unusually large was a flock containing 200 individuals at Middlebury on October 21, 1984 (CW 5:22). This species was formerly called Water Pipit.

WAXWINGS (FAMILY BOMBYCILLIDAE)

Bohemian Waxwing (*Bombycilla garrulus*)

STATUS: a very rare and irregular winter visitor from early December to early April. Most reports are from the northern portions of the state. It winters south to southern Canada and rarely to northern New England; very rare south to Long Island and New Jersey.

RECORDS: Two specimens apparently have been taken in Connecticut, but the present whereabouts of each is unknown. One was shot at East Windsor during the winter of 1859–1860 by Dr. Wood (*Auk* 38:69). Another was shot from a flock of Cedar Waxwings in the fall of 1899 at Torrington (Job 1922). There are at least 13 published sightings, of which most are prior to 1950 and the majority are uncorroborated.

Cedar Waxwing (*Bombycilla cedrorum*)

STATUS: a fairly common migrant from early April to early June and common to occasionally very common from September to mid-November; migrations peak in late May and mid-October. Its numbers are variable in winter, but they are usually fairly common in December, becoming uncommon in January and February. It is an uncommon nester in mixed and deciduous second-growth forests, usually near water; generally less frequent along the coast.

HISTORICAL NOTES: There have been periodic fluctuations in its wintering population but no documented long-term changes. It is possible that the changing composition of the state's forests may make such areas less suitable for this species.

SHRIKES (FAMILY LANIIDAE)

Northern Shrike (*Lanius excubitor*)

STATUS: a rare and irregular winter visitor from November to late March; often several years pass without any sightings. It prefers thickets, open fields, and pastures in agricultural areas and, along the coast, open areas with shrubby growth.

Earliest fall arrival: Oct. 12, 1952; Oct. 20, 1929; Oct. 24, 1928.

Latest spring departure: Apr. 18, 1885; Apr. 15, 1972; Apr. 4, 1936.

HISTORICAL NOTES: The Northern Shrike was clearly more numerous in winter in the late 1800s than at present. Merriam (1877) said it was "very abundant in some years, and equally scarce in others." Sage et al. (1913) wrote that it was "not nearly as common at present as twenty years ago." Howes (1928) said it was "not at all a common winter resident." In the 1920s and 1930s this species was recorded in small numbers on the majority of Christmas Bird Counts in the state. Subsequently, it was noted to be "irregular" (Forbush 1929; Bagg and Eliot; Manter 1975), thus indicating that a persistent decrease has occurred.

Marked incursions of this species in late fall and winter have occurred irregularly over the years. During the winters of 1921–1922, 1926–1927, 1930–1931, and 1949–1950 large numbers were reported in southern New England (Cruickshank 1942; Bull 1964).

Loggerhead Shrike (*Lanius ludovicianus*)

STATUS: a rare fall migrant from late August to early November; the majority of fall reports are from coastal areas. It is casual in spring migration (March), very rare in winter.

Earliest fall arrival: Aug. 12, 1968; Aug. 13, 1985; Aug. 18, 1903.

Latest spring departure: Apr. 11, 1900 (spec.); Apr. 10, 1914; Apr. 4, 1935.

COMMENTS: Two midsummer sightings lack sufficient corroboration (CW 2:46, RNEB 22:7).

HISTORICAL NOTES: The Loggerhead Shrike apparently has been a rare migrant in Connecticut in historic times. This species was not mentioned by Linsley (1843a). Merriam (1877) said it was "a rare visitor from the south and west" and listed only one definite record—one collected in November 1876 at Portland. Sage et al. (1913) called it "a rare and irregular fall migrant and winter resident . . . occurring chiefly near the salt marshes along the coast." It was apparently first reported in winter on February 1̇3, 1902 (Sage et al. 1913) and next on February 17, 1905, at Norwalk (*Auk* 22:211). In the 1930s and 1940s it was regular in fall along the coast (Bagg and Eliot; Griscom and Snyder 1955); the increase in sightings probably resulted from the increase in the number of birders. It decreased as a migrant and winter visitor in the 1970s and 1980s, and its nesting range retreated westward to western New York state (NYBBA).

The only definite nesting record in Connecticut was of a nest with five eggs, found by C. Williams in an apple orchard in late May about 1893 at Winchester (Job 1922). E. Schmidt observed a bird on June 7, 1908, at New Britain but "could not locate its probable nest" (Bagg and Eliot 1937).

STARLINGS (FAMILY STURNIDAE)

European Starling (*Sturnus vulgaris*)

STATUS: introduced; a very common to very abundant resident throughout the state. In winter it congregates in large roosts in evergreen groves, under bridges along the coast and inland along rivers, and elsewhere. A widespread nester in tree cavities and in crevices and holes in man-made structures, it is the most numerous bird in the state.

HISTORICAL NOTES: The entire North American population of this species is believed to have descended from two different flocks of birds released in Central Park, New York City. The first was a flock of 20 liberated on March 16, 1890, and the second was a flock of 40 released on April 25, 1891. By 1900 it was reported from Norwalk, Stamford, and North Haven. By 1901 it was reported from New Haven; by 1904, from Bridgeport; by 1906, from Wethersfield, Danbury, New London, and Stonington; by 1907, from Bethel, Watertown, and Middletown; and by 1908, from Portland (BL 9:207; Sage et al. 1913). Along the Connecticut River valley, about 100 were released at Springfield, Massachusetts, in 1897 (*Auk* 26:84), and one was collected in 1908 north of Hartford, where small flocks were encountered in 1911 and 1912 (Bagg and Eliot 1937). It was first recorded in the northeast hills in 1914 (Manter 1975).

It apparently first wintered in Connecticut in 1902–1903 in New Haven, and it first nested in 1900 near Norwalk (Bent 1950). By 1906 its breeding range covered about half of the state (Bent 1950). A flock of 1,500 was seen in the fall of 1906, and it was called "an increasingly common resident" although "not yet numerous in the interior of the state" (Sage et al. 1913). In the mid-1920s much of the nesting population migrated south by "November 10" (Forbush 1929), and by the late 1930s it was considered a permanent resident in the north although most numerous along the coast and larger river valleys, where large winter roosts were located (Bagg and Eliot). By the early 1960s it was an abundant resident and "here to stay" (Bull 1964).

VIREOS (FAMILY VIREONIDAE)

White-eyed Vireo (*Vireo griseus*)

STATUS: an uncommon migrant from May to early June and from mid-August to early October; migrations peak in mid- to late May and in mid-September. It is an uncommon to occasionally fairly common nester in overgrown fields and wet thickets but is much less numerous at higher elevations.

Earliest spring arrival: Mar. 24, 1984 (banded); Apr. 14, 1979; Apr. 25, 1941.

Latest fall departure: Oct. 21, 1984; Oct. 16, 1983; Oct. 8, 1936, 1979.

HISTORICAL NOTES: The White-eyed Vireo is near the northern limit of its range in Connecticut and has regularly nested in the state in historic times, although its distribution has periodically contracted and expanded. Merriam (1877) said this species was "not particularly common except along southern Connecticut, and in the Connecticut Valley, where it is common all the way up to the Massachusetts line." From 1880 to the early 1900s this species retreated south from the northern and higher portions of its range in southern New England and became more localized and uncommon, especially along the coast (Griscom; Bagg and Eliot; Griscom and Snyder; Bull 1964). In 1908 it was "rare" in Litchfield, with only two nesting records known to H. Job.

Its nesting range expanded somewhat in the late 1910s, and a slight increase was detected after the mid-1930s (Griscom and Snyder,

Bagg and Eliot 1937). A summering pair was observed at Kent in 1935, and nesting was confirmed there in 1937 (PLSNY 48, 50, 51). Bull (1964) said this species has "decreased considerably since before 1900 . . . , and has not shown any signs of increasing." However, Robbins et al. (1986) indicated that this species significantly increased in Connecticut from 1965 to 1979. It first nested at Mansfield in 1982 (CW 2:46).

Solitary Vireo (*Vireo solitarius*)

STATUS: an uncommon migrant from late April to late May and from mid-September to late October; migrations peak in early May and late September. It is an uncommon nester in the northwest hills south to New Milford, Bethlehem, and Watertown and east to Plymouth, Burlington, and Granby. In the northeast hills it nests west to Enfield, Coventry, and Lebanon and south to Franklin, Preston, and North Stonington. There are scattered nesting reports south to Wilton, Trumbull, Woodbridge, and North Branford.

Earliest spring arrival: Apr. 7, 1957; Apr. 11, 1941; Apr. 15, 1984.

Latest fall departure: Nov. 16, 1980; Nov. 14, 1976, 1979; Nov. 11, 1937.

HISTORICAL NOTES: The Solitary Vireo clearly suffered from the cutting of the state's forests after the arrival of settlers. Linsley (1843a) collected one in Stratford and said it was "extremely *rare*" (emphasis in original). As the state's farmlands began to revert to forest in the mid-1800s, this species gradually increased. Bagg and Eliot (1937) noted that the increase began about 1860, and Merriam (1877) said it was "not uncommon during the migrations," adding that "a few breed." It apparently increased as a nester in the northern portions of the state in the 1880s until 1895, when a severe winter in the southern United States killed many birds (Bagg and Eliot 1937; Griscom and Snyder 1955). Nesting was noted south to Bethel and Stamford in 1897 (Bull 1964). In 1908 it was "rare" in summer at Litchfield (Job 1922). Sage et al. (1913) said it was "a very rare summer resident." An increase in the 1920s was followed by a decline in the 1940s—possibly the result of forest damage caused by the Great Hurricane of 1938 (Cruickshank, Griscom and Snyder). Numbers stabilized in the 1950s (Griscom and Snyder 1955), but it was called a "very rare and local breeder" by the early 1960s (Bull 1964). Manter (1975) said it was a "regular fairly common migrant and less common" nester at Mansfield in the early 1970s.

Yellow-throated Vireo (*Vireo flavifrons*)

STATUS: an uncommon migrant from early May to June and from mid-August to late September; migrations peak in mid-May and mid-September. It nests locally throughout the state in open deciduous woods except along the coast.

Earliest spring arrival: Apr. 9, 1973; Apr. 20, 1972; Apr. 26, 1889.
Latest fall departure: Oct. 30, 1985; Oct. 13, 1952; Oct. 12, 1906.

HISTORICAL NOTES: The Yellow-throated Vireo may have been more numerous in Connecticut in the 1800s than in recent decades. This species was recorded by Linsley (1843a) in Stratford and New Haven. Merriam (1877) said it was "a tolerably common summer resident; particularly abundant in spring and fall." In 1908 Job (1922) called it a "not common summer resident" in Litchfield County. Honeywill et al. (1908) said it was a "common summer resident" in New Haven. Sage et al. (1913) similarly noted that it was "a tolerably common summer resident of the orchards, shade trees, and more open woodland." A striking decline began about 1910 (Bagg and Eliot, Griscom and Snyder 1955), probably because of increased pesticide use (Bagg and Eliot; Cruickshank; Bull 1964). The nesting population of this species continued to decrease into the early 1960s (Bull 1964; Griscom and Snyder 1955), and such decline may be exacerbated by the fragmentation of deciduous forests and related brood parasitism by Brown-headed Cowbirds (NYBBA).

Warbling Vireo (*Vireo gilvus*)

STATUS: an uncommon migrant from early May to June and from early August to early September; migrations peak in mid-May and late August. It nests in river valleys throughout the state, favoring large shade trees, open woods, and forest edges; it is less frequent near the coast.

Earliest spring arrival: Apr. 20, 1898; Apr. 26, 1908; Apr. 28, 1985.
Latest fall departure: Oct. 7, 1954; Oct. 1, 1890; Sep. 26, 1936.

HISTORICAL NOTES: This species was apparently quite numerous in Connecticut during the 1800s. Linsley (1843a) collected several specimens at Stratford and New Haven, and Merriam (1877) described it as "a common summer resident, breeding in orchards." Sage et al. (1913) said it was "a common summer resident of the shade trees of the villages and cities . . . , but rare elsewhere in the state." A long-term decline caused by widespread spraying of diseased elms began about 1900 in New York (Bull) and continued into the 1960s. Forbush (1929) noted in Massachusetts that in "recent years [it] has become rare or local." Mackenzie (1961) said it "definitely does not nest" in Guilford. A significant increase was noted along Breeding Bird Survey routes in Connecticut from 1965 to 1979 (Robbins et al.).

Philadelphia Vireo (*Vireo philadelphicus*)

STATUS: n rare migrant in May and rare to occasionally uncommon from late August to late September; fall migration peaks in mid-September.

Earliest spring arrival: May 7, 1934; May 9, 1941; May 11, 1983.

Latest spring departure: May 29, 1967, 1973; May 25, 1965; May 23, 1966.

Earliest fall arrival: Aug. 23, 1942; Aug 30, 1973; Sep. 1, 1975, 1976.

Latest fall departure: Oct. 11, 1982; Oct. 10, 1954, 1980; Oct. 6, 1928.

COMMENTS: Confusion with Warbling Vireo or female Tennessee Warbler make assessment of early spring arrival dates difficult.

HISTORICAL NOTES: This species was apparently overlooked by ornithologists in Connecticut before the early 1900s (Bagg and Eliot 1937). Merriam (1877) said it "undoubtedly occurs within our limits, as a rare, or accidental, visitant, but as yet no record of its capture has appeared." Sage et al. (1913) said it was "a very rare spring and fall migrant." This species has increased during the migrations since the 1920s (Cruickshank; Griscom and Snyder 1955).

Red-eyed Vireo (*Vireo olivaceus*)

STATUS: a fairly common migrant from early May to June and from mid-August to mid-October; it is sometimes common on peak migration days in mid-May and early September. It is a widespread and common nester in moist deciduous forests throughout the state.

Earliest spring arrival: Apr. 20, 1976; Apr. 26, 1896; Apr. 29, 1933.

Latest fall departure: Oct. 25, 1900; Oct. 24, 1980, 1988; Oct. 23, 1969.

HISTORICAL NOTES: There are indications that the Red-eyed Vireo has suffered a slow decline as a nesting species in this century. It was considered "abundant" into the 1920s (Merriam; Sage et al.; Howes). In the 1930s, it was called "almost abundant" (Bagg and Eliot 1937). In the early 1940s Cruickshank said it was steadily decreasing in New York adjacent to Connecticut. By the 1960s it had become a common summer resident (Bull), although in some northern portions of the state it was still called "very common" in the mid-1970s (Manter 1975). The decline of this species has been attributed to the fragmentation of the forest and increased brood parasitism by Brown-headed Cowbirds (NYBBA).

WARBLERS, TANAGERS, GROSBEAKS, SPARROWS, ETC. (FAMILY EMBERIZIDAE)

Wood Warblers (Subfamily Parulinae)

Blue-winged Warbler (*Vermivora pinus*)

STATUS: a fairly common migrant from late April to early June and from early August to late September; it is occasionally common during peak migration days in early to mid-May and in early September. It is a common nester throughout the state in overgrown fields, orchards, and wet thickets at the edges of deciduous forests, less numerous at higher elevations.

Earliest spring arrival: Apr. 23, 1977; Apr. 24, 1976; Apr. 27, 1908, 1985.

Latest fall departure: Oct. 31, 1987 (banded); Oct. 20, 1984; Oct. 18, 1961.

HISTORICAL NOTES: This species apparently first appeared in Connecticut during the late 1800s, probably originating from populations along the lower Hudson River valley (Gill 1980). Merriam (1877) called this species a "summer resident in southern Connecticut and in the Connecticut Valley" and added that it was "not common at New Haven" and that it bred in "considerable numbers" at Saybrook. Expanding its range along the coast and inland along the major river valleys, it was "common" in the 1890s (Averill; Wright 1897), was first reported in the northeast hills in 1901 (Manter 1975), and was a "rare summer resident" in 1908 in Litchfield County (Job 1922). It began to supplant the Golden-winged Warbler from New Britain by 1908 (Bagg and Eliot 1937).

Sage et al. (1913) said the Blue-winged Warbler was an "abundant summer resident of southern Connecticut . . . outnumbering any other warbler with the possible exception of the ovenbird; rarer farther north." Sage et al. added that this species was "very abundant . . . from Bridgeport to New Haven," "rare" in Stony Creek and Guilford, and "abundant again" at the mouth of the Connecticut River; it was found in smaller numbers north to New Preston and Portland. Increasing, it was regularly found after 1924 in southern Massachusetts along the Connecticut River valley (Bagg and Eliot 1937) and was "almost common" there by the late 1930s (Griscom and Snyder 1955), although it remained unreported in the highlands of Kent and Litchfield (PLSNY 43/44). It has since continued its expansion northward.

Golden-winged Warbler (*Vermivora chrysoptera*)

STATUS: a rare migrant from early to mid-May and from late August into early September, less frequently reported from the coast and areas east of the Connecticut River. It is a rare nester in Sharon, Cornwall, Kent, and New Milford; very rare and sporadic in the northeast hills at Mansfield, Chaplin, Hampton, and Windham. During the nesting season it favors wet overgrown fields, woodland clearings, and shrubby wetlands with few trees.

Earliest spring arrival: May 1, 1968; May 2, 1915, 1970; May 3, 1896, 1960.

Latest fall departure: Oct. 3, 1967; Sept. 27, 1918; Sept. 15, 1946, 1972.

HISTORICAL NOTES: The expansion of the range of the Golden-winged Warbler into Connecticut is imperfectly understood. This expansion began before that of the Blue-winged Warbler and has extended to higher altitudes and latitudes (NYBBA; Gill). Although Linsley (1843a) had "no knowledge of their being found living in this state," he stated vaguely that "there is good evidence of their occasional visits during migration seasons." Apparently, the earliest documented occurrence in the state was of one collected in May 1875 (Merriam). From 1876 to the early 1900s it was a "rare" nester in the northern part of the state (Merriam) south to Danbury, Bethel, and Portland (Sage et al.). It nested at Suffield in 1876 (Merriam), at Stamford in 1897 (Howes 1928), at Bridgeport in 1892 (*Auk* 10:208, Bent 1953), Bethel in 1905 (a male with a female Blue-winged Warbler, *Auk* 23:104), and at New Haven before 1908 (Bent). It experienced a short-lived increase at New Britain to 1902 and was "rare" there after 1909 (Bagg and Eliot 1937). Similarly, an increase was noted at Portland in the early 1890s, but it was recorded only "in small numbers" there in 1913 (Sage et al.). Referring to Litchfield County, R. Kuerzi wrote: "abundant in spring migration, 1933 [and] breeds relatively sparingly on both slopes of Housatonic Valley" (PLSNY 43/44:7).

This species has since declined statewide, both in migration and as a nester (CW 5:23–26). The northern limits of its nesting range continue to expand, but this species is losing much of its southern range (NYBBA). In 1983 it was reportedly "disappearing from the Berkshires" in Massachusetts (AmB 37:848).

Hybrid Warblers (*Vermivora Chrysoptera X Pinus*)

"Brewster's Warbler" (*Vermivora "leucobronchialis"*)

STATUS: a rare to locally uncommon hybrid of the Blue-winged and Golden-winged Warbler; occasionally observed during migration from late April to June and from early August to late September. Recognizable intergrades are infrequently observed during the breeding season, mostly reported from Litchfield, Windham, and Tolland counties.

The first record in Connecticut was on May 25, 1875, at Wauregan (Plainfield) by C. Carpenter (BNOC 3:99).

"Lawrence's Warbler" (*Vermivora "lawrencei"*)

STATUS: a rare and infrequently encountered hybrid of the Blue-winged and Golden-winged Warbler. Almost never seen in migration; it is much less numerous than "Brewster's Warbler." Very rare in the breeding season; mostly reported from Fairfield, New Haven, and New London counties.

The first record in Connecticut was an adult male collected at Stamford on May 12, 1886, by W. Hoyt (*Auk* 54:234).

Tennessee Warbler (*Vermivora peregrina*)

STATUS: a fairly common migrant from early May to June and from late August to mid-October; very rare in November. Migrations peak in mid-May and in mid-September.

Earliest spring arrival: Apr. 28, 1985; May 1, 1955; May 5, 1981.

Latest spring departure: June 9, 1917; June 8, 1875 (spec.); June 5, 1984.

Earliest fall arrival: Aug. 5, 1984; Aug. 14, 1975 (banded), 1979.

Latest fall departure: Nov. 26, 1979; Nov. 22, 1976; Nov. 12, 1983.

HISTORICAL NOTES: This species was apparently an irregular migrant in the 1800s, often fluctuating widely in numbers (Forbush 1929, Bagg and Eliot 1937), but was generally "rare" (Bull 1964). Job (1922) referring to Litchfield County, indicated that it was "generally a rare migrant, but sometimes numerous in migratory bird-waves."

Sage et al. (1913) said the Tennessee Warbler was "rare" and listed only 13 records from 1876 to 1909. Increasing from 1912 to 1915, it was "common" or "almost common" (Forbush 1929, Bagg and Eliot 1937). L. Bishop found his first spring record in 1916 (*Auk* 38:588). In 1917 A. Saunders said it had "greatly increased in numbers in the past few years" and had become "one of the most abundant of migrant warblers." A decline was noted after 1920 (Griscom and Snyder 1955), and both Forbush (1929) and Howes (1930) called it "late." Bagg and Eliot indicated that it was "rather uncommon" from 1922 to 1937. A moderate increase was noted after 1950 (Griscom and Snyder), and Bull (1964) said it was ordinarily rare to uncommon but sometimes common.

Orange-crowned Warbler (*Vermivora celata*)

STATUS: a very rare migrant from late April to late May and rare from late September to late November, most frequently reported in October. It rarely lingers into early January. Unusually late were three birds at Greenwich on January 6, 1935, one of which was singing (A. Cruickshank et al., PLSNY 48:90; Bull 1964). Accidental in mid- and late winter: one was present at a Hamden feeder from March 1 to April 15, 1951 (RNEB 6:56, 84), and one visited a Glastonbury feeder from January 10 to late April 1955 (RNEB 11:18, 88).

Earliest spring arrival: Apr. 28, 1985; Apr. 29, 1981; May 2, 1948.
Latest spring departure: May 26, 1956, 1965; May 21, 1977.
Earliest fall arrival: Aug. 21, 1984; Sept. 2, 1986; Sept. 4, 1968.
Latest fall departure: Jan. 6, 1935; Jan. 2, 1982; Dec. 27, 1981.

HISTORICAL NOTES: The first Connecticut record of this inconspicuous warbler was on May 8, 1888, when a male was shot at East Hartford (*Auk* 5:323). Cruickshank (1942) reported a slight increase in birds passing through the New York City area during the 1920s. It reportedly decreased in eastern Massachusetts in the late 1940s (Hill).

Nashville Warbler (*Vermivora ruficapilla*)

STATUS: an uncommon migrant from early May to June and from late August to mid-October. In some years it is fairly common during peak migration days in mid-September. It rarely lingers into November, very rarely into December. It is a very rare nester at higher elevations in the northwest hills south to Litchfield and Harwinton and east to New Hartford, Burlington, and Canton.

Earliest spring arrival: Apr. 23, 1977; Apr. 26, 1938, 1964; Apr. 27, 1985.

Latest fall departure: It has been recorded at least eight times in December; the latest dates are Dec. 18, Dec. 17 (2), Dec. 16 (2).

HISTORICAL NOTES: This species expanded its range into New England from areas west of the Appalachians in historical times, possibly appearing as recently as the 1830s (Bagg and Eliot; Griscom and Snyder 1955). Linsley (1843a) reported it at Stratford and New Haven. Merriam (1877) said it was an "abundant" migrant and added that it bred "sparingly throughout the state." From the 1870s to about 1910, nesting was reported east to Windham County (Manter 1975) and in small numbers south to Bridgeport, Seymour (with 5–6 nesting pairs in 1892, *Auk* 10:90), New Haven, Deep River, and Norwich (Sage et al.; Bent 1953). In 1908 it was called a "common migrant and very rare summer resident" at New Haven (Honeywill et al.).

Declining as a nester shortly after 1900, its nesting range retreated northward to higher elevations (Bent 1953; Griscom and Snyder 1955). In the early 1930s it was a "fairly common summer resident" in Litchfield County (R. Kuerzi et al., PLSNY 43/44:7). Three pairs nested at Norfolk in 1959 (AFN 13:421). Also declining as a migrant, it was reported as generally "common" by Sage et al. (1913), Bagg and Eliot (1937), and Job (1922), but by the 1960s it was called "uncommon" (Bull 1964).

Northern Parula (*Parula americana*)

STATUS: a fairly common migrant in May and from early September to mid-October; it is occasionally common during peak migration days in mid-May and mid-September. Nesting is suspected, but unconfirmed, at Norfolk and Salisbury.

Earliest spring arrival: Apr. 20, 1985; Apr. 27, 1954, 1971; Apr. 28, 1957.

Latest fall departure: Dec. 14, 1877; Nov. 28, 1901 (spec.); Nov. 19, 1986.

HISTORICAL NOTES: The nesting status of the Northern Parula has dramatically changed since 1890. Merriam (1877) termed this species "one of our most common migrants" and noted that it nested at Portland and near New Haven. In the late 1880s, 30 nesting pairs were discovered in a swamp at Norwich (OO 13:1). Job (1922), referring to

Litchfield County, wrote that it was "breeding in small numbers, sometimes in straggling colonies, in swamps or tracts where the gray *Usnea* moss hangs from trees" and added that there was "quite a colony in Litchfield." Sage et al. (1913) reported that "*Usnea* covered trees" and that breeding Northern Parulas had both declined near New Haven after the early 1890s. It was also reported nesting at Bridgeport (Wright 1897), Stratford, and Fairfield (Averill 1892) in the 1890s.

The *Usnea* lichen was extirpated from the state by the 1920s as a result of increased air pollution, and there was a corresponding decrease in the Northern Parula nesting population as this species is almost entirely dependent on the "beard moss" for its nest materials. Subsequently, the Northern Parula has been virtually extirpated as a nesting species in the state; it remains a very rare and irregular breeder in the northwest hills.

Yellow Warbler (*Dendroica petechia*)

STATUS: a common migrant from late April to June and from mid-August to late September: it is sometimes very common on peak migration days in mid-May and early September. It is a common to very common nester throughout the state in old fields, wet meadows, thickets, marshes, and shrubby swamps.

> *Earliest spring arrival:* Apr. 21, 1986; April 22, 1979; Apr. 25, 1981.
> *Latest fall departure:* Oct. 13, 1976; Oct. 6, 1977; Oct. 4, 1959.

COMMENTS: One reported on the extraordinary date of December 7, 1958, at New Canaan (AFN 13:16) was not satisfactorily corroborated.

HISTORICAL NOTES: The Yellow Warbler appears to have declined in recent years near areas of dense human populations (NYBBA). This decline may be the result of the loss of suitable habitats to suburban sprawl, the excessive spraying of pesticides, or brood parasitism by cowbirds (NYBBA). This species may decrease further as brushy thickets continue to revert to woodland.

Chestnut-sided Warbler (*Dendroica pensylvanica*)

STATUS: an uncommon to fairly common migrant in May and from mid-August to mid-September; migrations peak in mid-May and early September. A common but somewhat restricted nester throughout the state in drier settings, favoring edges of overgrown fields, thickets and shrubby woods.

Earliest spring arrival: Apr. 25, 1921; Apr. 26, 1913; Apr. 27, 1925, 1938.

Latest fall departure: Oct. 16, 1963; Oct. 13, 1956; Oct. 1, 1951.

COMMENTS: One was reported at the extremely late date of November 18, 1962 (AFN 17:17) but was not corroborated.

HISTORICAL NOTES: In the early 1800s the Chestnut-sided Warbler was apparently a very scarce migrant in the state, but it increased from 1835 to 1860 as the forests were cleared (Bagg and Eliot 1937). It was first reported breeding in New England in 1839 (Bagg and Eliot), and J. Whelpley reported it was "often extremely numerous" at New Haven in spring migration (Linsley 1843a). It was "common" in summer through the mid-1930s (Merriam; Sage et al.; Howes; Job; Forbush 1929). Cruickshank (1942) mentioned a nesting decrease along the western coast in the early 1940s. It probably increased in the northern portions of the state in the 1950s (Pink and Waterman 1965).

Magnolia Warbler (*Dendroica magnolia*)

STATUS: an uncommon to fairly common migrant from early May to June and from late August to mid-October; migrations peak in mid-May and in mid-September. It is a very rare nester in areas of hemlocks and spruces in elevations above 1,000 feet in the northwest hills south to Kent, Litchfield, and Harwinton and east to Canton and Granby.

Earliest spring arrival: Apr. 24, 1950; Apr. 29, 1981; Apr. 30, 1983.

Latest fall departure: Nov. 5, 1967; Nov. 4, 1965; Oct. 28, 1979.

COMMENTS: One was reported on the remarkable date of January 1, 1972, at New Fairfield. It reportedly was present from "late October" (AmB 26:202) but apparently was not corroborated.

HISTORICAL NOTES: The Magnolia Warbler expanded its nesting range eastward and southward in New York and Massachusetts during the first three decades of this century as a result of the regrowth of coniferous woods at higher elevations (Bagg and Eliot; NYBBA). In Connecticut, Job (1922) suspected it was breeding at Litchfield in 1891, as did Kuerzi and Kuerzi (1934) in 1931–1933. However, nesting was not confirmed in the state until 1934 when Kuerzi and Kuerzi found an adult feeding several young at Mohawk State Forest in Goshen (PLSNY 43:7). In 1966 four territorial males were found at Litchfield (AFN 20:556), and in 1977 a territorial male was noted at Hampton in the northeast hills (AmB 31:1113).

Cape May Warbler (*Dendroica tigrina*)

STATUS: This species is known for its fluctuating numbers. In some years it is fairly numerous; in others, very scarce. It is usually an uncommon migrant from mid- to late May and from late August to early October; it is sometimes fairly common during peak migration days in mid-September. Although most depart by early October, stragglers sometimes linger into November. It is accidental in December: one was sighted on December 2, 1968, at Marlborough (P. Isleib, HAS); one lingered to December 16, 1973, at West Hartford (P. Desjardins, AmB 28:217); and one was observed on December 16, 1979, at Mansfield (AmB 34:406).

Earliest spring arrival: Apr. 27, 1972; May 3, 1967; May 4, 1887 (spec.).

Latest spring departure: June 1, 1940; May 29, 1917, 1967; May 28, 1876 (spec.).

Earliest fall arrival: Aug. 22, 1973; Aug. 23, 1951, 1965; Aug. 27, 1966.

Latest fall departure: Nov. 18, 1971; Nov. 17, 1951; Oct. 24, 1985.

COMMENTS: On June 15, 1929, a pair of Cape May Warblers were reportedly observed "at leisure" in Simsbury by a group of observers who, citing the behavior of the adults, felt "positive" a nest was there (HAS). The area was a "cut-off portion of the forest now covered with scrub oak about four feet high"; no nest was found. The authors doubt this report; this species nests almost exclusively in spruce forests, and the closest known nestings to Connecticut are in the Adirondacks in northern New York and the White Mountains of Vermont and New Hampshire. The 1929 sighting was probably of a pair of Prairie Warblers.

HISTORICAL NOTES: The Cape May Warbler was considered a "very rare" migrant in Connecticut prior to 1900 (Merriam; Averill; Job; Bull 1964), and Sage et al. (1913) listed only 13 records between 1883 and 1909—all but two in the spring. Sightings increased in 1916 and 1917 (*Auk* 35:343), and in 1920 L. Bishop wrote that sightings had increased "in recent years" (*Auk* 38:388). However, a decrease was detected from the early 1920s to the late 1930s (Griscom; Forbush 1929; Bagg and Eliot). It increased again, mostly as a fall migrant, until about 1950, when its numbers stabilized (Bull 1964; Hill).

Black-throated Blue Warbler (*Dendroica caerulescens*)

STATUS: an uncommon to fairly common migrant from early May to June and from late August to mid-October; migrations peak in mid-

May and mid-September. It is a very restricted, but increasing, nester in the northwest hills south to Kent and Morris and east to Harwinton, Canton, and Granby; most numerous on Mt. Riga in Salisbury. In the northeast it nests in Stafford, Willington, Ashford, Somers, Woodstock, and Mansfield.

Earliest spring arrival: Apr. 22, 1945; Apr. 23, 1977; Apr. 27, 1985.
Latest fall departure: Nov. 16, 1971; Oct. 31, 1943; Oct. 28, 1962.

HISTORICAL NOTES: This species apparently nested less frequently in southern New England during the early 1800s than during the late 1800s. C. Jones found two nests at Eastford in 1874 (BNOC 1:11; Merriam; Manter 1975) and one there in 1881 (Sage et al. 1913). It nested in Stamford in 1898 (Howes 1928). It reportedly nested south to coastal Connecticut and along the lower Connecticut River valley by the early 1900s (Bagg and Eliot 1937). Job (1922), referring to Litchfield County, said it was "locally common as a summer resident, breeding in the woods of the higher slopes, especially where there is mountain laurel undergrowth." It nested at Ledyard in 1918 (*Auk* 36:294) and at Cornwall in 1931 (*Auk* 51:526).

Nesting increased in southern Massachusetts after 1919 (Bagg and Eliot 1937), and it was "regular and usually fairly common around and above 700–800 feet" in Litchfield County in the early 1930s (PLSNY 43/44:8). It nested infrequently south to Hadlyme before 1937 (Bagg and Eliot 1937). It has declined to the northwest of Connecticut in Dutchess County, New York, since around 1950 (Pink and Waterman, 1965). It was called "common" as a nester in Litchfield in the mid-1960s (WMF).

Yellow-rumped Warbler (*Dendroica coronata*)

STATUS: a common migrant from mid-April to late May and from late August to early November; it is sometimes abundant during peak migration days in early May and early October. It is uncommon during the winter months along the coast and Connecticut River valley; rare inland. It is a rare and local nester at higher elevations in the northwest and northeast hills; there are scattered reports of nesting elsewhere.

HISTORICAL NOTES: This species was not reported nesting by Linsley (1843a), Merriam (1877), Job (1922), or Sage et al. (1913). In Massachusetts its nesting range moved south in the 1920s to near the Connecticut line (Bagg and Eliot 1937). Forbush (1929) suspected that it nested in northern Connecticut but provided no details. It was reported in early summer in 1936 near Winchester but not confirmed (PLSNY 48:98). The date of the first confirmed nesting is unknown, but in 1961 nesting was reported at Litchfield (AFN 15:454), and adults were observed feeding young there in 1963 (AFN 17:451).

SUBSPECIES: The eastern race, Myrtle Warbler *(D. c. coronata)*, was considered until recent decades to be a distinct species. The western race, Audubon's Warbler *(D. c. auduboni)* was first collected in the state in May 1893 at New Haven (*Auk* 10:305).

Black-throated Gray Warbler (*Dendroica nigrescens*)

STATUS: a hypothetical vagrant from the west.

REPORTS: A male was observed October 4, 25, and 27, 1967, at Waterford (G. Bissell, R. Dewire et al., CW 7:49; RNEB 23:10). Two separate sightings by single observers are not satisfactorily corroborated (Hills 1978; AmB 35:803).

Hermit Warbler (*Dendroica occidentalis*)

STATUS: a hypothetical vagrant from the west. A male was seen by several experienced observers May 1 and 2, 1977, at New Haven (R. English, J. Souther et al., AmB 31:976; CW 7:49–50) but unfortunately was not photographed.

Black-throated Green Warbler (*Dendroica virens*)

STATUS: an uncommon to fairly common migrant from late April to June and from early September to mid-October; it is occasionally common during peak migration days in mid-May and mid-September. It is very rare in November and early December. It nests locally in the northwest and northeast hills in moist hemlock forests and is common in certain locations in Ashford and Union.
   Earliest spring arrival: Apr. 17, 1927; Apr. 18, 1985; Apr. 20, 1938.
   Latest fall departure: Dec. 5, 1981; Nov. 23, 1943; Nov. 22, 1974.

HISTORICAL NOTES: The nesting range of this species appears to have decreased in Connecticut during this century. Merriam (1877) wrote that it nested along the Connecticut River at Portland and Old Saybrook. Sage et al. (1913) said it was a "common summer resident of the hemlock groves throughout the state." Along the coast, Clark recorded it at Old Saybrook in the 1880s, and Howes (1928) found it to be "fairly common" in 1928 at Stamford and Darien. By about 1960 it was generally "rare" along the western coast in the nesting season (Bull 1964), whereas it was "locally common" inland at higher elevations (WMF; Manter 1975).

Blackburnian Warbler (*Dendroica fusca*)

STATUS: an uncommon to fairly common migrant in May and from late August to early October; migrations peak in mid-May and early September. It is usually a rare nester in hemlocks and spruces at higher elevations in the northwest and northeast hills but is locally common at certain locations in Union, Ashford, and Mansfield.

Earliest spring arrival: Apr. 27, 1988; Apr. 29, 1911, 1956; Apr. 30, 1908, 1955.

Latest fall departure: Oct. 17, 1971; Oct. 14, 1974; Oct. 10, 1954.

COMMENTS: Remarkably, one lingered at a Greenwich feeder to November 29, 1973 (AmB 28:31) and was well described. Another was reported on November 24, 1983, at Guilford (CW 4:26).

HISTORICAL NOTES: The nesting population of this species has increased somewhat in the 1970s and 1980s as a result of the maturation of stands of evergreens. Job (1922) wrote in 1908 that it was "a rare summer resident" and noted that territorial males were collected in late June in 1879, 1904, and 1905 in Litchfield County. Sage et al. (1913) wrote that "a few spend the summer in the pine groves of the northern part of Litchfield County, and doubtless breed there." Nesting was confirmed at Cornwall and Canaan in the 1930s (PLSNY 43/44:8). Regionally, it was reported to have declined after the Great Hurricane of 1938 (Griscom and Snyder) but experienced a range extension after 1950 (Pink and Waterman 1965, Manter 1975).

Yellow-throated Warbler (*Dendroica dominica*)

STATUS: a very rare coastal migrant from mid-April to late May. It is accidental in fall: a male was "found dead in dooryard" on October 31, 1952 at Hamden by N. Peters (YPM No. 6189) and identified by D. Finch as *D. d. albilora*.

Earliest spring arrival: Apr. 6, 1953; Apr. 19, 1952, 1972.

Latest spring departure: May 26, 1987; May 21, 1987; May 18, 1925.

SUBSPECIES: The Eastern Yellow-throated Warbler (*D. d. dominica*) nests along the Atlantic seaboard. The interior race, the Sycamore Yellow-throated Warbler *(D. d. albilora),* was first found in Connecticut on May 18, 1925, when a male was collected at Fairfield by F. Novak (*Auk* 43:248). This record was also the first for New England (*Auk* 46:553). Field identification of the two races is possible but is not without difficulties (Parkes 1953). The typical interior race can be distinguished at close range by the white lores and chin, whereas *D. d. dominica* has yellow lores and chin.

HISTORICAL NOTES: Merriam (1877) listed an account of several specimens collected at Hartford (Dr. D. Crary) and adds that it was seen at New Haven (Dr. E. Thompson), but he did not provide specific dates or locations. Bull (1964) speculated that an increase in sightings after 1951 is largely the result of an increase in birders.

Pine Warbler (*Dendroica pinus*)

STATUS: a rare to uncommon migrant in April and early May and from mid-September to early November; it is rarely reported in March and very rarely lingers into December and January. It is a very local nester in pine groves in the northwest and northeast hills. In the east it nests to the coast in pitch pine *(Pinus rigida)* stands. There are reports of isolated nesting at Stamford, New Canaan, Redding, Weston, Shelton, and Southington.

Earliest spring arrival: Mar. 8, 1953; Mar. 14, 1982; Mar. 19, 1927.
Latest fall departure: Jan. 16, 1955; Jan. 13, 1971; Jan. 6, 1982.

COMMENTS: One was observed on the unusual date of February 18, 1987, at Milford (CW 7:37) but was not corroborated by other observers or a photograph. The only other known midwinter occurrence was on February 24, 1953, at Mystic (Stonington) (RNEB 9:33).

HISTORICAL NOTES: The nesting range of the Pine Warbler in Connecticut has decreased as the state has been developed. Linsley (1843a) wrote that it was "common," possibly indicating that it nested in coastal stands of pitch pine, which are now nearly absent from our coastal areas. In 1889 L. Bishop described it as "generally common along the coast" (*Auk* 6:192). Bull (1964) considered it less numerous than formerly, both as a migrant and a nester.

Prairie Warbler (*Dendroica discolor*)

STATUS: an uncommon migrant from late April to late May and from mid-August to late September; it is occasionally fairly common during peak migration days in mid-May and early September. It is a widespread but scattered nester along dry fields, road cuts, powerline right-of-ways, and other similar second-growth areas throughout the state.

Earliest spring arrival: Apr. 20, 1976; Apr. 23, 1979; Apr. 26, 1986.
Latest fall departure: Oct. 17, 1904; Oct. 9, 1960; Oct. 6, 1984.

HISTORICAL NOTES: The Prairie Warbler is a southern species, and Connecticut is near the northern limit of its range. This species has increased its nesting population in the state in historic times as a result of open farmfields reverting to brushy thickets (Bent; Hill). Linsley (1843a) wrote that it was "rare," and Merriam (1877) said it "breeds sparingly." By about 1900 it was "common" in the southern half of the state and was "uncommon" in the northern portions (Sage et al. 1913). It was first collected at Suffield in 1875 by E. I. Shores, who wrote "it is not rare about Enfield" (Bagg and Eliot 1937), and was first collected in the Eastford area in 1902 (Manter 1975). It was first reported at New Britain in 1908 (Bagg and Eliot 1937). In the early 1900s it continued to increase throughout southern New England (Bent 1953). By 1932 it had nested north to West Cornwall, Sherman, and Kent (PLSNY 43/44:8).

Palm Warbler (*Dendroica palmarum*)

STATUS: an uncommon to fairly common migrant from early April to mid-May and from mid-September to late November; it is sometimes common during peak migration days in late April and mid-October. It rarely lingers into December and early January.

Earliest spring arrival: Mar. 8, 1953; Mar. 23, 1925; Mar. 24, 1890.
Latest spring departure: May 25, 1952; May 15, 1982; May 14, 1983.
Earliest fall arrival: Aug. 21, 1982; Aug. 30, 1971; Sept. 4, 1893.
Latest fall departure: Jan. 5, 1966; Jan. 4, 1987; Jan. 3, 1953.

COMMENTS: Although this species is known to survive mild winters along coastal Massachusetts (Griscom and Snyder 1955) and Long Island, New York (Bull 1974), there are apparently no records of individuals spending the entire winter in Connecticut.

SUBSPECIES: Two races of Palm Warbler occur in the state. The Yellow Palm Warbler *(D. p. hypochrysea)* is the more frequently encountered of the two races in spring migration. It has bright yellow underparts.

The Western Palm Warbler *(D. p. palmarum)* breeds in central Canada south to central Michigan and is more frequent in fall and winter than the preceding race. It arrives earlier in spring and departs later in fall than the Yellow Palm Warbler and favors coastal areas. Unlike the Yellow Palm, it has bright yellow only on the undertail coverts and (in spring) has a dull yellow wash on the breast. Also, its eye-stripe is whitish compared to the yellow eye-stripe of the Yellow Palm Warbler (Peterson 1947).

Bay-breasted Warbler (*Dendroica castanea*)

STATUS: an uncommon to fairly common migrant from mid-May to early June and from late August to early October; it is sometimes common on peak migration days in late May and mid-September.

Earliest spring arrival: May 2, 1964; May 6, 1959, 1960; May 7, 1932, 1950.

Latest spring departure: June 6, 1882; June 2, 1912, 1982; May 31, 1984.

Earliest fall arrival: Aug. 1, 1953; Aug. 9, 1984; Aug. 14, 1975 (banded).

Latest fall departure: Oct. 25, 1986; Oct. 20, 1984; Oct. 13, 1979.

HISTORICAL NOTES: Merriam (1877) wrote that this species was "sometimes quite abundant during the spring migration; at other times extremely rare, if occurring at all." Job (1922) described its status much as Merriam had 30 years earlier. Sage et al. (1913) considered it rarer in fall than in spring and listed only eight fall records from 1876 to 1911. A. Saunders noted an increase in 1916–1917 and wrote that it was "one of the most abundant migrant warblers, particularly late in the season" (*Auk* 35:343). It has been generally more numerous since 1900 (Griscom).

Blackpoll Warbler (*Dendroica striata*)

STATUS: a fairly common migrant from mid-May into early June and from late August to mid-October; it rarely lingers into November. It is sometimes common during peak migration days in late May and in late September.

Earliest spring arrival: Apr. 29, 1908; May 1, 1915; May 2, 1914, 1972.

Latest spring departure: June 19, 1977, 1983; June 17, 1907, 1957.

Earliest fall arrival: Aug. 16, 1942, 1978; Aug. 22, 1943; Aug. 28, 1976.

Latest fall departure: Nov. 30, 1949; Nov. 22, 1934; Nov. 18, 1980.

HISTORICAL NOTES: According to Linsley (1843a), the Blackpoll Warbler was "often extremely numerous at New Haven in the month of May." Merriam (1877) said it was "one of our most abundant migrants." Similarly, Sage et al. (1913) said it was an "abundant spring and fall migrant."

Cerulean Warbler (*Dendroica cerulea*)

STATUS: a rare migrant from mid-May to June, very rare in July and August. It is infrequently observed away from its nesting sites, and there are surprisingly few records of fall migrants moving through the state. It is a rare nester in the northwest hills along the Housatonic River and along the Connecticut River in Haddam and East Haddam; often colonial. Elsewhere, nonbreeding territorial males are occasionally found through June. It prefers mature, moist deciduous forests near rivers, streams, and lakes.

Earliest spring arrival: May 1, 1983; May 3, 1982; May 5, 1981.
Latest fall departure: Sept. 29, 1957; Aug. 19, 1986; Aug. 11, 1987.

HISTORICAL NOTES: Before the early 1900s, this species was a very rare spring visitor in the state. Linsley collected one at Stratford in April, 1841, and Sage et al. (1913) listed only three records from 1875 to 1900. It was sighted more frequently in the 1930s (Bagg and Eliot 1937), and nesting was suspected by M. Crosby at Winchester in 1933 (PLSNY 43/44:8). After 1950 it was regularly reported in the New York City area, but it remained "an extremely rare bird anywhere east of the Hudson River south of Dutchess County" (Bull 1964).

Reports increased in the 1960s, and it probably bred at Newtown in 1968, where four to six territorial males were found (AmB 22:510). Nesting was confirmed at Canton in 1972 by P. Carrier and W. Williams, apparently the first for New England (AmB 26:837,840). In 1977, a brief search of a colony with 11 singing males at Kent revealed at least one nest (J. Souther et al., AmB 31:1113). In 1978 three territorial males were found at Windham (AmB 32:980).

Black and White Warbler (*Mniotilta varia*)

STATUS: a fairly common migrant from late April to late May and from early August to late October; migrations peak in mid-May and early September. Accidental in winter: one was seen on February 15, 1982, at South Windsor (AmB 36:274); one was present on December 27, 1958, at New London (AFN 13:95); one was observed December

Black and White Warbler

13–16, 1984, at Greenwich (MFN 12:7); and one was observed December 5–6, 1953, at West Hartford (HAS). It is a common and widespread nester in deciduous forests throughout the state.

Earliest spring arrival: Apr. 11, 1954; Apr. 14, 1948; Apr. 15, 1979.

Latest fall departure: Oct. 31, 1937; Oct. 30, 1953; Oct. 26, 1980.

HISTORICAL NOTES: The nesting population of this species in the state has increased since the mid-1800s as the forests have returned and matured.

American Redstart (*Setophaga ruticilla*)

STATUS: a fairly common migrant from early May to early June and from early August to mid-October; it very rarely lingers into November. It is often very common on peak migration days in mid-May and early September. It is an uncommon nester in deciduous forests throughout the state but is much less numerous along the coast.

Earliest spring arrival: Apr. 26, 1953, 1984; Apr. 28, 1941; Apr. 29, 1974.

Latest fall departure: Nov. 27, 1958; Nov. 25, 1949; Nov. 19, 1988.

HISTORICAL NOTES: Writing in 1945, A. Gross described this species as "one of the most common warblers in New England, perhaps second in abundance only to the Yellow Warbler" and added that it was more frequently seen than the Ovenbird (Bent 1953). This statement no longer reflects the status of this species; it is now less frequent in many areas, particularly near the coast, where urban sprawl has eliminated its habitat.

Prothonotary Warbler (*Protonotaria citrea*)

STATUS: a very rare migrant in April and May; most reports are in the first two weeks of May. It is accidental in fall: remarkable was a young female found dead on the late date of November 27, 1911, at New Haven by M. Jennings (BL 14:109); and one was banded on August 17, 1982, at Fairfield and recaptured there on August 30 (CW 2:46).

This species has apparently been found nesting in the state only once: a pair was feeding young at Fairfield on May 30, 1946 (R. Birdsall, F. Novak, and P. Spofford)—a first not only for Connecticut but for east of the Hudson River (Bull 1964). Of note were two males present from April 29 to June 10, 1945, at Fairfield, but nesting was not proved (*Auk* 67:255). A singing male at Westport June 1–23, 1971, was apparently unattached (D. Finch, R. Dewire et al., AmB 25:840).   One was at Hartford June 17–24, 1984 (J. Kaplan et al., CW 5:10).

Earliest spring arrival: Apr. 7, 1974; Apr. 18, 1987; Apr. 19, 1971.

Latest spring departure: June 11, 1946; June 10, 1945; May 25, 1946.

HISTORICAL NOTES: Bagg and Eliot (1937) wrote that this species was "accidental . . . before the middle 1880s" in New England. Apparently, the first Connecticut record was of one seen on May 14, 1910, at Glastonbury by L. Ripley (Sage et al. 1913). By the 1930s it was sighted nearly every spring in New England (Bagg and Eliot 1937). Bull (1964), referring to the New York City area, called it a "rare but regular spring migrant; very rare in fall."

Worm-eating Warbler (*Helmitheros vermivorus*)

STATUS: a rare to uncommon migrant from early May to June and from early August to September; migrations peak in mid-May and late August. It is an uncommon nester in mature deciduous forests with dense understory vegetation; it is less numerous along the coast and in the northwest hills.

Earliest spring arrival: Apr. 17, 1976; Apr. 28, 1973; May 1, 1929, 1974. *Latest fall departure:* Sept. 30, 1888 (spec.); Sept. 29, 1973; Sept. 24, 1959.

HISTORICAL NOTES: The nesting population of this species increased in Connecticut as farmlands were abandoned and reverted to forest (Bagg and Eliot 1937; Griscom and Snyder 1955). Dr. J. Whelpley observed this species at New Haven (Linsley 1940.), and Merriam (1877) said it was "a late summer resident" citing several records from Suffield, New Haven, and Saybrook. Apparently the first nesting in Connecticut was in June 1879 at New Haven (W. Nichols, BNOC 5:116). Increasing in the late 1800s, this species was termed by Sage et al. (1913) to be a "tolerably common summer resident along the coast; occurring rarely in the interior as far north as Kent and Portland." Job (1922), in 1908, said it was "a rare summer resident" at Litchfield.

By 1918 it nested at Hartford (BL 20:95). In 1936 it nested north to New Britain and was found east along the coast to the Thames River (Bagg and Eliot 1937). By the 1960s it was "rare" at Mansfield and first nested there in 1972 (Manter 1975). It has increased there since. In 1983, this species was reported to be "continuing . . . northward expansion" (AmB 37:848).

Ovenbird (*Seiurus aurocapillus*)

STATUS: a fairly common to common migrant from early May to June and from early August into October; migrations peak in mid-May and mid-September. It is a common and widespread nester in deciduous forests throughout the state. Accidental in winter: one was present at Mansfield from December 29, 1971, to January 13, 1972, and was viewed by many and banded (AmB 26:580); one was sighted on January 3, 1978, at Milford (AmB 32:324); one was present December 12–30, 1967, at Greenwich and found dead on December 31 (AFN 22:133); and one was present December 11–16, 1962, at Pleasant Valley (Barkhamsted) and viewed by many (AFN 17:3).

Earliest spring arrival: Apr. 19, 1981; Apr. 23, 1919, 1985; Apr. 24, 1910.

Latest fall departure: Oct. 28, 1944; Oct. 20, 1954, 1981; Oct. 19, 1982.

HISTORICAL NOTES: Despite substantial changes in the state's forests in historic times, the status of the Ovenbird appears to have not changed significantly. Linsley (1843a) called this species "common," and Merriam (1877) termed it a "common summer resident" that "breeds abundantly." In 1913 Sage et al. noted that it was "an abundant summer resident of woodland." In this century the Ovenbird has probably increased as abandoned farmlands have reverted to forest, except in suburban and urban areas, where development has reduced and fragmented the amount of undisturbed forest.

Northern Waterthrush (*Seiurus noveboracensis*)

STATUS: an uncommon migrant from late April to late May and from late July to late September; migrations peak in mid-May and in early September. It is an uncommon nester in shrubby swamps and wet thickets in the northwestern and northeastern portions of the state; absent at this season along the coast and Connecticut River valley. Accidental in early winter: one was seen from December 30, 1984, to January 2, 1985, at Milford (D. Varza, CW 5:34), and one was seen on December 21, 1985, at New Haven (D. Sibley, AmB 40:673, CW 6:8).

Earliest spring arrival: Apr. 16, 1973, 1988; Apr. 18, 1951; Apr. 19, 1957.

Latest fall departure: Oct. 24, 1937; Oct. 21, 1979; Oct. 9, 1966.

HISTORICAL NOTES: Apparently, this species was "rarely encountered" prior to the mid-1800s (Bagg and Eliot 1937), although the lack of reports may have been the result of confusion with Louisiana Waterthrushes (Bent 1953). Merriam (1877), Job (1922), and Sage et al. (1913) said it was a "common" migrant, and Merriam added that "possibly a few occasionally remain and breed." Neither Job nor Sage et al. make reference to nesting. Increasing north of Connecticut after 1900 (Griscom and Snyder 1955), it was undoubtedly overlooked here as a nester until 1932 and 1933, when J. Kuerzi et al. found territorial pairs at Cornwall (PLSNY No. 43/44; Bagg and Eliot 1937). Its nesting range expanded south in Massachusetts and nearby New York in the 1950s and 1960s (Griscom and Snyder 1955; Bull 1964).

The range expansion of Northern Waterthrush in Connecticut is poorly documented. It nested at Norfolk in 1953 (AFN 9:369) and was a "fairly common" nester east to Mansfield by the early 1970s (Manter 1975). Territorial males were found south to Newtown and Redding by the late 1970s. Nesting was confirmed in 1977 in Pound Ridge, New York, only 1 mile west of New Canaan, Connecticut (MFN 5:6), but nesting has not been confirmed in southwest Fairfield County.

Louisiana Waterthrush (*Seiurus motacilla*)

STATUS: an uncommon migrant from late April to mid-May and from late July to mid-August. It is an uncommon but increasing nester along watercourses and streams in mature forests throughout the state.

Earliest spring arrival: Mar. 30, 1945; Mar. 31, 1958; Apr. 6, 1928, 1955.

Latest fall departure: Oct. 2, 1950; Sept ?8, 1937, Sept. 28, 1962. One was reported on October 23, 1985 (CW 6:22) which, if correctly identified, is an unprecedented late date for New England.

COMMENTS: There is an old record of one collected on the extraordinary date of February 15, 1882, at Deep River by H. Flint (Sage et al. 1913). Details concerning its identification are unknown. Its current location is unknown.

HISTORICAL NOTES: Prior to the mid 1800s, the nesting range of this species expanded northeast from southern New York (Bagg and Eliot 1937). Merriam (1877) noted that it was "not rare in southern Connecticut, where it breeds regularly, and probably in considerable numbers." Expanding northward in the early 1900s (Griscom and Snyder 1955), it nested at Litchfield, where Job (1922) said it was "a rather scarce summer resident." In Litchfield County, by 1934 it was "little if any rarer than in Putnam or Westchester Counties, N.Y." and had been found "along all mountain streams investigated at Kent, Macedonia [and] Canaan Mountain" (PLSNY 42/43:80). Spreading northeast in the 1930s (Griscom and Snyder), it was first recorded nesting at Mansfield in 1958 and was "uncommon" (but widespread) there by the mid-1970s (Manter 1975).

Kentucky Warbler (*Oporornis formosus*)

STATUS: a rare migrant from mid-May to mid-June and very rare from late July to September. It is a rare nester in the coastal lowlands in moist deciduous forests with dense understory shrubs; very rare elsewhere. It has recently been confirmed nesting at Stonington and inland at Litchfield.

Earliest spring arrival: Apr. 23, 1977; Apr. 27, 1972; May 4, 1976.
Latest fall departure: Sept. 26, 1942; Sept. 25, 1983; Sept. 22, 1944.

HISTORICAL NOTES: This species was a rare and irregular visitor to southern New England during the late 1800s (Averill; Bagg and Eliot; Bull 1964). New England's first record was obtained on August 16,

1876, by E. Shores at Suffield, Connecticut (Merriam; Bagg and Eliot 1937). The first Connecticut—and New England—nesting was on July 10, 1892, at Greenwich (C. Voorhees, *Auk* 10:86). In the early 1900s its nesting range retreated south to western New Jersey (Bull), and it became very irregular here in spring. In the late 1950s, reports increased (Bull 1964; Manter 1975), and it nested at Hartford in 1962 (AFN 16:464). Nesting was suspected at Greenwich in 1979 (MFN 7:5) and elsewhere along the coast by the early 1980s.

Connecticut Warbler (*Oporornis agilis*)

STATUS: a rare fall migrant from late August to mid-October, most frequently reported in the last week of September and the first week of October. Very shy and difficult to observe, it is most apt to be found in low wet thickets with dense patches of raspberries (*Rubus* sp.) or Jewelweed (*Impatiens* sp.). Accidental in spring: a female was collected on May 30, 1879, by G. Woolsey at New Haven (BNOC 5:117), but its current disposition is unknown; and one was banded on May 27, 1980, at Sharon (fide A. Gingert, AmB 34:756).

    Earliest fall arrival: Aug. 19, 1987; Aug. 21, 1988; Aug. 24, 1987.

    Latest fall departure: Oct. 31, 1958; Oct. 23, 1974 (banded); Oct. 21, 1926.

COMMENTS: Reliable spring records of this species in the east are few and far between. The May 30, 1888, record from Connecticut mentioned in Forbush's *Birds of Massachusetts* is in error—the reference cited is solely concerned with a Kentucky Warbler. Two single-person sight reports lack sufficient corroboration (RNEB 6:109; AFN 17:394).

HISTORICAL NOTES: The "type specimen" of this species was obtained by Alexander Wilson near Hartford in early October 1808. This specimen was possibly acquired from Richard Alsop (1761–1815) of Middletown, who apparently was an active collector and student of birds (BMAS 37(2): 67). The nest of this species was first discovered in 1883 in Manitoba by Connecticut resident Ernest T. Seton (*Auk* 1:192; Bent 1953).

    The Connecticut Warbler was more numerous in the state before 1910 than afterward and has not regained its former abundance (Bull). In 1908 Job (1922) said it was a "regular but not common migrant in fall" in Litchfield County. Sage et al. (1913) called it a "tolerably common fall migrant." From the mid-1920s to the early 1940s it was "uncommon to rare" (Forbush 1929; Cruickshank 1942), although it was "uncommon to common" in the upper Connecticut River valley and adjacent upland areas as late as 1937 (Bagg and Eliot 1937). Prior to the late 1930s it was considered more numerous than the Mourning Warbler (Sage et al.; Griscom; Bagg and Eliot; Cruickshank 1942). According to Bagg and Eliot (1937), it was less common than the Tennessee Warbler but more common than the Canada, Black-throated Blue, Wilson's, Blackburnian, and eight other regular fall warblers! Subsequently, it continued to decline at least through the mid-1930s (Griscom and Snyder 1955).

Mourning Warbler (*Oporornis philadelphia*)

STATUS: a rare but regular migrant from mid-May to early June and during September, most apt to be seen in late May and mid-September. This species is difficult to observe; it favors low dense thickets and shrubby woodlands; in spring it is most often located by its song.

Earliest spring arrival: May 3, 1951; May 8, 1885; May 10, 1959, 1964.

Latest spring departure: June 17, 1907; June 12, 1986; June 10, 1928.

Earliest fall arrival: Aug. 24, 1984; Aug. 26, 1986; Aug. 29, 1982.

Latest fall departure: Oct. 9, 1974; Oct. 2, 1955; Sept. 28, 1948, 1963.

HISTORICAL NOTES: The Mourning Warbler was rarely encountered by the pioneering ornithologists of the early 1800s (NYBBA). This species was not listed by Linsley in his 1843 catalog. Merriam (1877) said it was "a rare migrant but probably more abundant than commonly supposed" and added that he had seen it only in spring. Sage et al. (1913) called it "a rare late spring and fall migrant" and listed only 10 records from 1882 to 1913. Bagg and Eliot (1937) listed numerous sightings in the 1920s and 1930s, and Griscom and Snyder (1955) said this species was "formerly very rare, now increasing." Possibly, the Mourning Warbler is more common today than in Linsley's time, a beneficiary of the widespread clearing of forests between 1800 and 1850 and subsequent regrowth to successional shrubland (NYBBA).

Common Yellowthroat (*Geothlypis trichas*)

STATUS: a fairly common migrant from late April to June and from mid-August to late October; it is occasionally very common during peak migration days in early May and late September. Although most depart by November, a few regularly linger into December; it is very rare in January. It is a common and widespread nester throughout the state in wetlands, fields, and forests with dense thickets and shrubs.

Common Yellowthroat

Earliest spring arrival: Apr. 12, 1973; Apr. 18, 1974; Apr. 20, 1982.
Latest fall departure: Jan. 22, 1983; Jan. 20, 1968; Jan. 7, 1967.

HISTORICAL NOTES: The Connecticut population of Common Yellow-throat has not changed significantly in historic times. Linsley (1843a) said this species was "common," as did virtually all other authors concerned with the state's avifauna, for example, Merriam (1877) and Sage et al. (1913). Since about 1950 the number of early winter reports has markedly increased (Bull 1964; SCCC).

Hooded Warbler (*Wilsonia citrina*)

STATUS: a rare to uncommon migrant from early May to June and rare from late July to September; it is infrequently observed away from its nesting areas. It is an uncommon nester in moist deciduous forests, mostly in the coastal areas inland to Danbury, Newtown, North Branford, East Haddam, Lebanon, Hampton, and Killingly. There are a few isolated nestings well inland at Torrington and Kent.
   Earliest spring arrival: Apr. 28, 1969; Apr. 29, 1984; Apr. 30, 1983.
   Latest fall departure: Sept. 28, 1972; Sept. 21, 1952; Sept. 20, 1897 (spec.).

HISTORICAL NOTES: The Hooded Warbler was apparently fairly common, although locally distributed, in the 1800s. Linsley (1843a) said that it "probably" nested in the New Haven area and cited a June record by Dr. J. Whelpley. Merriam (1877) said that it nested in the Connecticut River valley and along the "southern border" of Connecticut. Merriam also noted that it nested "abundantly" at Saybrook. From about the late 1800s to the late 1930s it was a "common" nester along the coast and, to a lesser degree, north along the Housatonic River to Newtown and Winchester, the Connecticut River north to Suffield, and the Thames River north to Preston (*Auk* 16:360, Bent; Bagg and Eliot 1937). It was a "very rare" nester elsewhere (*Auk* 10:89; Sage et al.; Job; Forbush 1929; Howes; Bagg and Eliot 1937). It first nested in Massachusetts in 1901 (*Auk* 18:397). This species was reported more frequently in the 1940s and 1950s in southern New England (Griscom and Snyder; Hill). In 1985 the Hooded Warbler was "common in the Naugatuck area . . . regular elsewhere in the southwest part of the state, and increasing in the eastern half" of Connecticut (AmB 39:888).

Wilson's Warbler (*Wilsonia pusilla*)

STATUS: This species often varies in numbers from year to year but is usually an uncommon migrant from mid-May to June and from late August to late September. It is occasionally fairly common during peak spring migration days in mid-May. Accidental in winter: January 16–17, 1932, an adult male was observed at Fairfield (F. Novak, A. Saunders, *Auk* 49:355); one was present at a feeder at Oxford to December 20, 1971 (AmB 26:205); and one was seen on December 16, 1978, at Woodbury (AmB 33:265).

Earliest spring arrival: Apr. 28, 1984; Apr. 29, 1961; May 3, 1911.

Latest spring departure: June 14, 1973; June 6, 1971; June 5, 1915, 1948.

Earliest fall arrival: Aug. 5, 1973; Aug. 15, 1980; Aug. 16, 1979.

Latest fall departure: Nov. 20, 1962; Nov. 3, 1950; Oct. 25, 1972.

HISTORICAL NOTES: The status of Wilson's Warbler in Connecticut appears to have been relatively constant in historic times. This species was not listed by Linsley in his 1843 catalog. Merriam (1877) said it was "a tolerably common spring migrant" and added that it was "by no means so common here as it seems to have been formerly." In 1913 Sage et al. called it a "usually rather rare" migrant, and "most often seen in spring." Bagg and Eliot (1937) said it was "rather common in spring, less common in fall," and added that "unquestionably its numbers vary from year to year." In 1955 Griscom and Snyder (1955) said it was "usually uncommon" in spring and "almost rare" in fall.

Canada Warbler (*Wilsonia canadensis*)

STATUS: a fairly common migrant from mid-May to June and from early August to late September; migrations peak in late May and early September. It is an uncommon nester in the northwest and northeast hills, with scattered reports south to Greenwich, New Canaan, Trumbull, and Naugatuck in the west. It favors moist deciduous woods with a dense understory of shrubs—particularly mountain laurel *(Kalmia latifolia);* it is mostly absent from coastal areas and the Connecticut River valley. It is most numerous at Salisbury and Thompson at the northern corners of the state.

Earliest spring arrival: Apr. 29, 1962; May 1, 1905; May 2, 1973.
Latest fall departure: Oct. 17, 1973; Oct. 15, 1977; Oct. 14, 1974.

HISTORICAL NOTES: Increasing as old farmlands returned to forest, this species became a more frequent and widespread nester after the 1880s. In 1843 Linsley said it was a "very rare" visitor to Stratford and New Haven. Merriam (1877) noted that it was a "common" migrant and "doubtless breeds about Portland." Sage et al. (1913) said it "undoubtedly breeds more or less regularly in the northwestern portion of the state, although few nests have been taken." In 1937 Bagg and Eliot said it was an "increasing summer resident" and added that it was "now common" in northwestern Connecticut during the nesting season.

Yellow-breasted Chat (*Icteria virens*)

STATUS: a rare migrant from early May to June and from early September to early October; it regularly lingers into late December and early January but is very rare in midwinter. It is a very rare nester in shrubby, overgrown fields.

Earliest spring arrival: May 2, 1899, 1908; May 3, 1974; May 4, 1971. Birds arriving in March probably wintered just south of the state.

Fall departure dates are difficult to assess because of the number of early winter records.

HISTORICAL NOTES: Historically, the Yellow-breasted Chat moved into areas cleared of forest cover but declined as open areas reverted to forest. This species was present in Connecticut in the early 1800s. Linsley (1843a) recorded it at New Haven, where Dr. Whelpley said it "haunts the vicinity of springs, and builds in watered hollows." Bagg and Eliot (1937) state that its numbers historically "wax and wane with the vicissitudes of the species' general fortunes" and quote Dr. E. Emmons of Williamstown, Massachusetts, who in 1833 said it was "occasional" there. Merriam (1877) said it was a "common resident, breeding in dense undergrowth." In 1908, Job (1922) said it nested commonly in low altitudes in Litchfield County "as along the Housatonic River" but was "rather rare on the higher parts." In 1913 Sage et al said this species was a "common summer resident . . . breeding in brush lots throughout the state, but most abundantly in the southern portion."

From the late 1920s to the early 1940s it decreased in the upper Connecticut River valley to a "rare" and irregular nester (Bagg and Eliot 1937) and in the southern portions of the state to "fairly common" and "local" (Griscom; Cruickshank). This decrease has continued statewide, and it has become a very infrequent nester, reflecting the decrease of overgrown fields. The last confirmed nesting in the state was at Greenwich in 1985 (MFN 13:4). Elsewhere in the 1980s, nesting was suspected but unconfirmed at Hamden, Watertown, Waterford, Groton, and Stonington (CW 7:11).

In winter W. Smith observed one at Norwalk from December 24, 1911, to February 22, 1912—perhaps the first state winter record (BL 14:114). Regionally, winter reports increased after 1950 (Bull 1964; Hill). Like the Northern Oriole and Dickcissel, the Yellow-breasted Chat normally winters in the tropics, but individuals occasionally linger in Connecticut through the winter.

Tanagers (Sub-family Thraupinae)

Summer Tanager (*Piranga rubra*)

STATUS: a very rare migrant from late April to early June; it is most frequently reported in mid-May. The only midsummer report is of one collected on July 21, 1876, at Suffield (Sage et al. 1913). Accidental in fall from late August to mid-October: one was observed on September 8, 1964, at Kensington (Berlin) (AFN 19:21), and there is a unique report of one from November 29 to December 10, 1977, at a Cheshire feeder (N. Proctor et al., AmB 32:180). It is usually observed in coastal areas; casual inland.

Earliest spring arrival: Apr. 8, 1886 (spec.), 1984; Apr. 21, 1947; Apr. 27, 1895 (spec.).

Latest spring departure: June 21, 1968; June 12, 1968; June 10, 1973.

HISTORICAL NOTES: This species was possibly more numerous in the early 1800s than later. Linsley (1843a) recorded this species at Stratford and New Haven. During the mid-1800s it nested north to New Jersey, and it regularly wandered north into southern New England (Griscom; Cruickshank 1942). Apparently, there were no corroborated reports of this species in Connecticut from 1895 (*Auk* 12:306) to 1947; reports in New York increased after 1926 (Cruickshank). Nesting resumed in New Jersey in 1955.

Scarlet Tanager (*Piranga olivacea*)

STATUS: an uncommon to fairly common migrant in May and from early August to early October; migrations peak in mid-May and mid-September. It is an uncommon to fairly common nester in mature deciduous forests throughout the state.

Earliest spring arrival: Apr. 23, 1955; Apr. 28, 1935; Apr. 29, 1946.
Latest fall departure: Nov. 11, 1958; Nov. 1, 1965; Oct. 27, 1971.

COMMENTS: An injured male was reportedly captured on the incredible date of January 12, 1953, at West Hartford (HAS, RNEB). The published accounts of this record do not include sufficient information to enable proper evaluation. If accurate, this record represents an unprecedented mid-winter occurrence in New England.

HISTORICAL NOTES: This species probably declined through the mid-1800s with the loss of the state's forests during the period of extensive agricultural activity (Forbush 1929) but since the 1920s has rebounded with the return of deciduous woodlands (Bagg and Eliot; Hill).

Western Tanager (*Piranga ludoviciana*)

STATUS: a casual fall vagrant from the west, reported from August into January. There is one spring report: May 1924 at Hartford by Mrs. H. J. Pratt (Bagg and Eliot 1937).

RECORDS: The first record in Connecticut was an immature male collected on December 15, 1892, at New Haven by H. Flint (*Auk* 10:86). Other reports, all of single birds, include the following:

Sept. 26, 1933	New Haven	F. W. Loetscher	Bagg and Eliot
Jan. 22, 1950	Hamden	Wells	RNEB 6:13
July 31, 1973	Sharon	G. Komorowski	AmB 28:31
Sept. 30–Oct. 1, 1973	Madison	N. Proctor et al.	AmB 28:31
Aug. 11, 1979	Cornwall	fide A. Gingert	AmB 34:141

Dec. 15, 1979	New Haven	R. Ridgely	AmB 34:255
Nov. 24, 1984	Greenwich	D. Bova	CW 5:22

Several reports published with incomplete details include one sighted at Stratford on December 29, 1979 (AmB 34:406), and one seen at Milford on January 1, 1980 (AmB 34:255).

Cardinals, Grosbeaks, etc. (Sub-family Cardinalinae)

Northern Cardinal (*Cardinalis cardinalis*)

STATUS: a common resident throughout most of the state; it is uncommon to fairly common in the northwest and northeast hills. It nests in a variety of settings including open woodlands, shrubby swamps, thickets, and suburban yards.

HISTORICAL NOTES: The status of this species has dramatically changed in the last 50 years (Beddall 1963). It was irregularly reported and possibly decreasing after the 1830s in the Connecticut River valley (Bagg and Eliot 1937). Linsley (1843a) found it at New Haven. Merriam (1877) called it a "very rare and accidental visitor from the south," and Sage et al. (1913) listed only two records from 1880 to 1900. Apparently first wintering in 1916–1917 (*Auk* 35:342), it remained a "rare" visitor through the 1920s (Wright; Forbush 1929; Bagg and Eliot; Griscom and Snyder 1955).

Sightings increased somewhat after 1930 (Griscom and Snyder, Bull 1964). By 1941 it nested regularly, though sparsely, in northern New Jersey and in southern Westchester and Rockland counties east of the Hudson River (Bull 1964; Cruickshank 1942). Expanding rapidly, it first nested in Connecticut in 1942 at Greenwich (Bull 1964). By 1943 it had expanded east along the coast to Westport (Smith 1950) and to Stratford by 1944 (*Auk* 67:253). In the 1950s, it was described as "not abundant, . . . by no means rare" in Fairfield (A. Saunders, *Auk* 67:253). Also in the 1950s it was first found at Guilford (Mackenzie 1961) and in the Mansfield area (Manter 1975). It wintered widely in 1950–1951, even to Canaan and Glastonbury (AFN 5:196). By the early 1960s its range included all of the state (AFN 22:423; Bent et al. 1968).

Rose-breasted Grosbeak (*Pheucticus ludovicianus*)

STATUS: a fairly common migrant from early May to June and from late August to mid-October; migrations peak in mid-May and mid-

Rose-breasted Grosbeak

September. It very rarely lingers to late December. Accidental in mid-winter; an immature male was at Mansfield January 11–14, 1971 (J. MacDonald et al. AmB 26:581); a young male was seen at a Darien feeder from February 16 to 23, 1976 (A. Schulman, MFN 4:2); one was at Willington in February 1981 (photo at UCM); and one was at Greenwich on January 13, 1983 (CW 4:38). It nests throughout the state in mature deciduous woods, wooded swamps, and occasionally in large shade trees along fields, edges of woods, and rural roads.

Earliest spring arrival: Apr. 12, 1972; Apr. 25, 1942; Apr. 27, 1985.
Latest fall departure: Dec. 24, 1951; Dec. 23, 1972; Dec. 20, 1981.

HISTORICAL NOTES: This species was apparently very scarce in New England prior to the 1840s; T. Nuttall (1832) said it was known only as a cage bird (Bagg and Eliot 1937). Linsley (1843a) wrote that it was found at Middletown in 1841—the first record, to his knowledge, for the state. However, he added the questionable statement that "they are common at Hartford, where they breed." Merriam (1877) contradicts this statement by writing "Mr. J. Hammond Trumbull tells me that it was almost unknown about Hartford thirty-five years ago." Rarely reported, this species was added to the list of protected songbirds in

1849 by the Connecticut legislature (Sage et al. 1913). A significant increase began in the 1870s, when it became a "common summer resident" (Merriam). Its numbers increased through the early 1940s (Averill; Wright; Sage et al.; Howes; Forbush 1929; Bagg and Eliot; Cruickshank 1942). In Massachusetts, Griscom and Snyder described a decrease in the mid-1950s. Since then it has been called "locally common" (Bull 1964) and "not common" (Mackenzie 1961) along the coast and "fairly common" inland (Manter 1975).

Black-headed Grosbeak (*Pheucticus melanocephalus*)

STATUS: a casual visitor from the west; chiefly occurs from November through March with a few overwintering at feeders and lingering to May.

RECORDS: It was first reported in the state on January 10–March 19, 1953, at Glastonbury by D. Snyder; this record was also the first for New England (AFN 7:206). Other records, all of single birds, include the following:

Feb. 20– Apr. 19, 1954	imm.m New Canaan	Grierson, Poor et al.	AFN 8:242
Jan. 12– Feb. 13, 1957	banded Glastonbury	R. Belden et al.	AFN 11:252
Apr. 24– May 3, 1957	m.ph. Greenwich	L. Chamberlain et al.	Bull (1964)
Oct. 31, 1959– Mar. 18, 1960	S. Windsor	P. Isleib	AFN 14:294, 373;15:19
Sep. 1–3, 1962	Glastonbury	fide O. Rhines	HAS
Dec. 8, 1973	New Britain	B. Kleiner et al.	HAS
Nov. 27, 1977– Mar. 1978	m.sp. Guilford	N.Proctor et al.	AmB 32:324
Mar. 18, 1978	m.sp. Ledyard	UCM No. 7726	CW 1:55
Dec. 20, 1980	Branford	N. Proctor et al.	CW 9:23

Published reports containing incomplete details include one at Wethersfield on January 19, 1963 (HAS), one in late December 1965 at Waterbury (AFN 20:131), and one at Windsor on January 22, 1977 (AmB 31:309).

Blue Grosbeak (*Guiraca caerulea*)

STATUS: a very rare migrant from mid-April through May and from mid-September to mid-October. It is most apt to be present in May. Accidental in summer: hundreds of miles from the closest known nesting, a pair summered in 1927 at South Windsor, but nesting was not proved (C. Vibert; Bagg and Eliot 1937); a pair was at Kent in late

May 1962 and appeared to be preparing to nest before the brushy field they frequented was cleared (AFN 16:463); and a singing male was at Greenwich in late June 1979 (AmB 33:846). Accidental in early winter: one was banded December 30, 1961, at Greenwich (AFN 16:102); and one was observed at a feeder from December 21 to 29, 1960, at New London (AFN 15:114).

Earliest spring arrival: Apr. 4, 1957; Apr. 20, 1982; Apr. 23, 1986.
Latest spring departure: May 29, 1982; May 27, 1985; May 25, 1932.
Earliest fall arrival: Aug. 16, 1944; Sept. 3, 1971; Sept. 18, 1976.
Latest fall departure: Oct. 30, 1951; Oct. 19, 1946; Oct. 16, 1982.

COMMENTS: There is a vague and uncorroborated report of one on March 16, 1956, at West Hartford (HAS) that is questionable, at least as published.

HISTORICAL NOTES: This species was accidental in New England prior to the 1920s (Forbush 1929; Bagg and Eliot 1937). Sight reports increased to the mid-1940s (Bull 1964; Hill), and it was regular after 1948 in the New York City area (Bull 1964). In the mid-1950s its nesting range extended north into New Jersey, and it appeared more frequently in both spring and fall migrations in Connecticut, mainly along the western coast (Bull 1964). Nesting was first confirmed in New York on Staten Island in 1982 (NYBBA). Since the mid-1970s it has been reported in Connecticut nearly every year.

Indigo Bunting (*Passerina cyanea*)

STATUS: an uncommon migrant from early May to June and from early September to early October, sometimes fairly common during peak migration days in mid-May and mid-September. An uncommon nester throughout the state at edges of deciduous woods, along powerline cuts, and in overgrown fields and thickets.

Earliest spring arrival: Apr. 17, 1984; Apr. 18, 1982; Apr. 19, 1956, 1969.
Latest fall departure: Oct. 26, 1958; Oct. 23, 1966; Oct. 20, 1979.

COMMENTS: One was reported in February and March 1967 at New London (RNEB 23:3); this report is viewed with considerable skepticism.

HISTORICAL NOTES: The Indigo Bunting frequently nested in Connecticut during the 1800s, and undoubtedly benefited from the clearing of the forests. Linsley (1843a) said this species was "very common," and Merriam (1875) termed it "a common summer resident." Sage et al.

1913 and Job 1922 both called this species "common" in the first decade of this century. Griscom and Snyder (1955) said this species declined between 1890 and 1930 and increased in the 1950s. Mackenzie (1961) noticed an increase in the Guilford area in the 1950s. In the 1960s and 1970s, the urbanization of many areas and the spread of suburban sprawl reduced nesting habitat.

Painted Bunting (*Passerina ciris*)

STATUS: an accidental migrant; most apt to appear in May. It nests along the Atlantic coast north to North Carolina and has wandered north to Massachusetts in spring.

RECORDS: The only definite record in the state is of a female banded and photographed at Chimon Island, Norwalk, on May 26, 1982, by C. Trichka and P. Marra (CW 3:21). There are several published but unconfirmed sight reports by single observers (e.g., CW 3:22, 3:35), but none is adequately corroborated.

Dickcissel (*Spiza americana*)

STATUS: a rare migrant from late September to mid-November and casual from late April to late May. It is rare in winter, when it is normally found at feeding stations, usually near the coast.

Earliest spring arrival: Apr. 3, 1972; Apr. 23, 1965; Apr. 27, 1983.

Latest spring departure: May 27, 1971; May 23, 1974; May 20, 1966.

Earliest fall arrival: Aug. 14, 1956; Aug. 24, 1954, 1965; Aug. 28, 1966.

Latest fall departure: Difficult to determine because of the large number of winter records.

COMMENTS: Since 1970 there have been at least 20 reports of individuals visiting feeding stations during the winter, from December through March. These wintering Dickcissels are in a category similar to the Yellow-breasted Chat and Northern Oriole; all three species winter in the tropics, but certain individuals remain far north of their usual range, almost always at feeders (Bull). Unusual was a pair that wintered in a brushy field at Stamford from December 16, 1984, to late March 1985, independent of any feeding station (MFN 12:7). Possibly, many of the spring reports, particularly those in March and early April, are of individuals that wintered locally.

HISTORICAL NOTES: The Dickcissel's nesting population in New England dramatically declined before 1850, possibly the result of a change in farming practices or the eastward expansion and increased nest parasitism by Brown-headed Cowbirds. It was an "abundant" or "very abundant" nester before 1840 (Sage et al., Bagg and Eliot 1937), and Linsley (1843a) described it as "very common" at New Haven. By the 1860s it was virtually extirpated as a nesting species (Griscom; Forbush 1929; Bagg and Eliot; Bull 1964). Samuels (1867) said it was an "extremely rare summer visitor," and it went unreported until 1922 (Forbush 1929). In the 1920s its nesting range expanded eastward into the southeastern Atlantic states, and reports of stragglers in the northeast increased (*Auk* 73:66). It became more numerous in Connecticut as a coastal fall visitor after the mid-1940s; also, it was reported more often in winter and spring (Bent). Inland, reports increased after the mid-1950s (Manter 1975; Pink and Waterman 1965).

Towhees, Sparrows, Longspurs, etc. (Sub-family Emberizinae)

Rufous-sided Towhee (*Pipilo erythrophthalmus*)

STATUS: a common migrant from mid-April to late May and from mid-August to mid-October; migrations peak in early May and in mid- and late September. It is rare to locally uncommon in winter, mostly along the coast and near feeding stations. It is fairly common to common nester in woodlands and dense thickets throughout the state; somewhat less numerous at higher elevations in the northeast and northwest hills.

HISTORICAL NOTES: The distribution and abundance of this species in Connecticut apparently has not changed significantly since the late 1800s. Merriam (1877) said it was "a common summer resident, breeding on the ground, in undergrowth, and in the woods" and noted only one winter record. In 1913 Sage et al. called it "common" in summer and "a rare winter resident" and listed six winter records between 1882 and 1905. Bull (1964) noted an increase in winter reports beginning in the late 1940s and attributed the increase to "the great increase in feeding stations" and a trend toward milder winters.

American Tree Sparrow (*Spizella arborea*)

STATUS: a fairly common migrant and winter visitor from late October to mid-April; migrations peak in mid-November and early March. It prefers open areas and brushy fields.

Earliest fall arrival: Oct. 10, 1890; Oct. 15, 1906; Oct. 16, 1900, 1953.
Latest spring departure: May 10, 1971; May 3, 1973; Apr.28, 1907.

There are published reports of earlier and later occurrences of this species that are not included here because of the difficulty some observers have in distinguishing this species from other sparrows — notably Field Sparrow and Chipping Sparrow.

HISTORICAL NOTES: The Tree Sparrow was a "very abundant" winter visitor in southern New England in the early and mid-1800s (Hill). Merriam (1877) said it was a "common winter resident, but more numerous in spring and fall." Similarly, Sage et al. (1913) wrote that it was "common" in winter and "very abundant" during migration in November and March. The number of Tree Sparrows wintering in Connecticut has probably decreased since the 1940s and 1950s as old fields have been lost to development or reverted to forest.

Chipping Sparrow (*Spizella passerina*)

STATUS: a common migrant from mid-April to mid-May and from late August to mid-November; migrations peak in early May and mid-October. It is very rare in early winter, mostly in coastal areas. It is a common and widespread nester throughout the state in areas with lawns, gardens, fields, and low, dense shrubs.

Earliest spring arrival: Mar. 12, 1954; Mar. 18, 1983; Mar. 28, 1902.

Latest fall departure: difficult to determine because of the number of early winter records.

Winter records: Although this species is easily confused by some observers with American Tree Sparrow, several winter reports are believed to be correct. Two were present at a feeder from early November 1981 to late February 1982 at Sherman (CW 2:25). One was observed by the authors at a Greenwich feeder from December 20, 1981, to January 16, 1981. There is an old record of one on February 23, 1887, by G. B. Grinnell (Sage et al. 1913). Special care must be taken when identifying Chipping Sparrows in fall and winter.

HISTORICAL NOTES: Nearly all references in Connecticut ornithological literature refer to the Chipping Sparrow as common, abundant, or very abundant during the nesting season.

Clay-colored Sparrow (*Spizella pallida*)

STATUS: a casual migrant from mid-September into November, accidental in spring from mid-April to mid-May. Most records are from coastal areas and the Connecticut River valley. The first spring report was of a male collected on April 9, 1956, at East Haddam (YPM No. 6873, AmB 28:32). Other spring records include May 7–19, 1973, at Suffield (AmB 27:754), May 15, 1975, at Mansfield (Manter 1975), and May 10–12, 1981, at New Canaan (AmB 35:803; MFN 9:4). Interestingly, all spring records are from inland areas.

Earliest fall arrival: Sept. 8, 1985; Sept. 10, 1978; Sept. 30, 1970; 1987.

Latest fall departure: Nov. 26, 1961; Nov. 18, 1955; Nov. 3, 1984.

HISTORICAL NOTES: After 1950 sightings of this species increased in the region, in both spring and fall, as its nesting range moved eastward into western New York state (Bull 1964; NYBBA).

Field Sparrow (*Spizella pusilla*)

STATUS: a fairly common migrant from mid-March to late May and from late August to November; migrations peak in early May and early October. In winter it is uncommon to fairly common but is much less numerous at higher elevations. It is a fairly common but scattered nester in open areas with brushy fields and thickets.

HISTORICAL NOTES: The Field Sparrow undoubtedly benefited from the clearing of the state's forests during the colonial period. This species was an "abundant" nester before about 1915 (Merriam; Wright; Sage et al. 1913) but has decreased since. The decline of the Connecticut nesting population of Field Sparrow can be attributed to the annihilation of its old-field habitat by development and regrowth of forests (NYBBA). The number of individuals lingering into the winter months has increased as feeding stations have become popular, particularly since the late 1940s.

Vesper Sparrow (*Pooecetes gramineus*)

STATUS: a rare to uncommon and very local migrant from mid-April to mid-May and from mid-September to December; fall migration peaks in late October. Very rare in winter; some years it is not present at all. It is an accidental nester inland at dry fields and pastures; it nested at Torrington in 1985. Also, nesting was suspected, but not proved, at Ellington in 1985.

Earliest spring arrival: Mar. 29, 1950; Mar. 31, 1953; Apr. 3, 1963.

Latest spring departure: May 30, 1983; May 22, 1971; May 10, 1972.

Earliest fall arrival: Sept. 30, 1954; Oct. 1, 1950; Oct. 5, 1968.

Latest fall departure: difficult to determine because of the number of winter records.

HISTORICAL NOTES: The Vesper Sparrow has significantly changed in status in Connecticut during the last 100 years. Presumably, this species increased as a breeder in the 1600s and 1700s as the state was settled and developed into farms. It was an "abundant" or "very abundant" nester throughout the state in the mid- and late 1800s (Merriam; Sage et al.; Bagg and Eliot; Griscom and Snyder; Hill). In 1913 Sage et al. said this species was "now rare over most of the state, none being found in places along the coast where they were common a few years ago" and added that it "seems never to have recovered from the great freeze of 1895, when so many thousands of birds perished in the southern states, and has become rarer annually since that date." The Vesper Sparrow remained "rare" along the coast and "fairly rare" inland during the 1920s and 1930s (Griscom; Howes; Forbush 1929; Hill). By the 1960s and early 1970s it was mostly restricted to the northern agricultural uplands, where it was occasionally "common" (WMF; Pink and Waterman 1980). There was no evidence of breeding in the Mansfield area in the late 1960s and 1970s. Its nesting range has continued to shrink rapidly in the 1970s and 1980s (NYBBA; Robbins et al.).

Lark Sparrow (*Chondestes grammacus*)

STATUS: a casual fall migrant and early winter visitor from September into January; most sightings are from coastal areas. It has successfully wintered in the state at least once: one was at a Guilford feeder from early February to April 7, 1968 (RNEB 24:24). It is an accidental spring migrant, with four sight reports: May 31, 1961, at Greenwich (P. Spofford, AFN 15:396); April 19, 1964, at Waterford (R. Dewire, RNEB 20:4); April 29 to May 12, 1966, at New Haven (Mulholland, RNEB 22:4); and April 7, 1968 (from February) at Guilford (Mackenzie et al., RNEB 24:4).

Earliest fall arrival: Aug. 27, 1951; Sept. 4, 1968; Sept. 23, 1949.

Latest fall departure: Jan. 14, 1987; Dec. 29, 1979; Dec. 27, 1980.

HISTORICAL NOTES: Its nesting population expanded eastward in historical times as the forests were cleared (Bull; Bent), and sightings in New England increased after about 1930 and, more dramatically, after 1950 (Griscom and Snyder; Hill).

COMMENTS: This species allegedly nested at Stamford in June 1912. P. Howes withdrew this report and stated that it was not properly verified (OO 29:348; Bagg and Eliot; Forbush 1929).

Lark Bunting (*Calamospiza melanocorys*)

STATUS: an accidental vagrant from western prairies.

RECORDS: The only definite record was a male banded and photographed October 8–25, 1978, at East Haven (J. Spendelow et al., AmB 33:158). There are two uncorroborated sight reports (HAS; AmB 39:148; CW 5:34).

Savannah Sparrow (*Passerculus sandwichensis*)

STATUS: a fairly common migrant from late March to June and from early September to late November except along the western coast, where it is uncommon. It is sometimes very common during peak migration days in late April and early October. It is rare to locally fairly common in winter along the central coast and the Connecticut River valley. It is a rare nester inland in extensive open areas with short grass, very rarely along the coast at the upland fringes of beach areas.

SUBSPECIES: Four races of this species occur in Connecticut. The nominate race *P. s. savannah* is a local nester. The "Ipswich" Sparrow (*P. s. princeps*) is rare along the coast in winter and has decreased in Connecticut in recent years. The Labrador race (*P. s. labradorius*) may winter and migrate along the coast. The "Churchill" race (*P. s. oblitus*) also may winter.

HISTORICAL NOTES: This species presumably increased as the forests were cleared during the settlement period. As the forests returned, it declined, initially and most severely in the southwest portions of the state. It was an "abundant summer resident" in the 1870s (Merriam), and from the 1890s to 1913 it was a "common" nester near the border of large salt marshes and inland in open fields and pastures (Averill; Wright; Job; Sage et al. 1913). In the 1920s it remained "common" (Forbush 1929), and a slight increase was noted in the 1930s in the western portions of the state (Bagg and Eliot 1937). Its overall decline continued through the 1960s and early 1970s, when it was termed "uncommon" or "fairly common" in the northern portions of the state (WMF; Manter 1975) and very local at lower elevations.

Grasshopper Sparrow (*Ammodramus savannarum*)

STATUS: a very rare migrant in late April and May and from mid-September to late October; most apt to be present in early October. It occasionally lingers to late December. Accidental in mid- and late winter: one was present March 2–23, 1970, at Stonington (G. Bissell et al., AmB 26:581), and an individual survived from January 6 to early April 1900 at a Greenwich feeder (P. Purnell in al., MPH 0.1, 2, 9). It is a very rare and local nester at Simsbury and Windsor Locks, where 20 singing males were found in 1987 (CW 8:70). Unattached singing males are occasionally encountered elsewhere in summer.

Earliest spring arrival: Apr. 20, 1971; Apr. 22, 1888; Apr. 24, 1913, 1915.

Latest spring departure: June 7, 1968; May 31, 1967; May 30, 1940, 1952.

Earliest fall arrival: Sept. 2, 1987 (banded); Sept. 11, 1949 (banded); Sept. 18, 1891.

Latest fall departure: Jan. 1, 1968; Dec. 29, 1962; Dec. 26, 1974.

HISTORICAL NOTES: As with other grassland sparrows, this species probably increased as forests were cleared during the settlement period. It was an "abundant" nester into the 1870s (Merriam 1877) but decreased somewhat thereafter. It remained "locally abundant" in the Connecticut River valley (Bagg and Eliot 1937) but was "not common" in Litchfield County in 1908 (Job) and "common" elsewhere into the 1930s (Averill; Wright; Sage et al.; Howes; Forbush 1929; Griscom and Snyder 1955). It has steadily declined since (Robbins et al. 1986) as dry grassy uplands reverted to forest or were consumed by development.

Henslow's Sparrow (*Ammodramus henslowii*)

STATUS: a very rare migrant in May and from late September to late October; it is most apt to be seen in late September and early October. Accidental in early winter: one was seen on December 28, 1965, at New London and was observed "twice during the day ... by five competent observers" (AFN 20:132; 20:II:5); and one was seen on November 20, 1982, at Madison (CW 3:11). Extirpated from the state as a nesting species; nonbreeding singing males have been reported in July in 1968 and 1985 (Manter, CW 6:13).

Earliest spring arrival: Apr. 26, 1951; Apr. 27, 1905; Apr. 28, 1983.

Latest fall departure: Nov. 7, 1965; Oct. 27, 1888 (spec.); Oct. 23, 1983.

HISTORICAL NOTES: Merriam (1877) said that the Henslow's Sparrow was "a rare summer resident" and commented that he knew of only one specimen taken in the state (July 18, 1873, at Killingworth). Nesting was reported at Eastford, where it increased in the late 1870s (Bagg and Eliot). In the 1890s nesting continued at Eastford (Manter) and was reported at Stamford (Howes). In 1908 Job said it was "a rather rare summer resident" and noted that it nested at Litchfield and Warren. E. Woodruff wrote in 1908 that "Henslow's Sparrow, though generally considered a rare bird in New England, is a regular and not uncommon summer resident in the vicinity of Litchfield" (BL 10:111). In 1913 Sage et al. wrote that it was "common locally in Litchfield County, rare elsewhere." Unusual was a report of nesting along the coast at Fairfield in 1921 (*Auk* 31:264). Two pairs reportedly nested at West Hartford in 1939 (RNEB 3:7,8). An increase in reports occurred in the 1930s and 1940s, but subsequently observations became less numerous.

COMMENTS: A report of one at a Killingworth feeder in January 1960 (Mackenzie) is viewed with considerable skepticism; it is not clear from the published account whether this sighting was corroborated by an experienced observer.

Le Conte's Sparrow (*Ammodramus leconteii*)

STATUS: an accidental vagrant.

RECORDS: There is one definite record: one was photographed at Canton from December 27, 1987, to January 9, 1988 (J. Kaplan et multi al.; CW 8:25, AmB 42: 231).

Sharp-tailed Sparrow (*Ammodramus caudacutus*)

STATUS: a rare to uncommon coastal migrant from late April to late May and from early September to November; it is very rare to early January and casual in midwinter. It is an uncommon to locally common nester in salt marshes. Seldom found inland; in addition to numerous sight reports (most from before 1940), there are at least three specimen records: 14 were collected October 4–13, 1890, at Portland (*Auk* 9:115); one was shot at Litchfield on September 28, 1906 (Job 1922); and one *A. c. caudacutus* was found dead at Mansfield on June 12, 1973 (Manter 1975).

HISTORICAL NOTES: This species became locally extirpated as salt marshes were filled and destroyed, particularly along the western shore. Linsley (1843a) recorded this species at Stratford and New Haven, and

Merriam (1877) said it was a "common summer resident" in coastal marshes. In 1913 Sage et al. said it was "abundant" in salt marshes. The fragmentation of once continuous marshes has contributed to the decline of this species (NYBBA).

SUBSPECIES: Four subspecies of Sharp-tailed Sparrow may be found in the state. The nominate race *A. c. caudacutus* is relatively readily separable from the other subspecies. It arrives in late May, nests in coastal marshes, and departs by late October, although it might winter (WB 54:107). The following subspecies are indistinguishable from one another in the field: "Nelson's" Sharp-tailed Sparrow (*A. c. nelsoni*) is a very rare inland migrant in late September and October (*Auk* 9:115); the "Acadian" race (*A. c. subvirgata*) breeds coastally from Maine north and migrates through Connecticut in late May into mid-June and from late September to mid-October—it may winter; the "James Bay" race (*A. c. altera*) may be found from late September through mid-October.

Seaside Sparrow (*Ammodramus maritimus*)

STATUS: a rare to uncommon coastal migrant from mid-April to June and from mid-September to mid-November, very rare before mid-April and after mid-November. It is casual in early and midwinter. It is an uncommon to locally fairly common nester in saltwater marshes, generally less numerous than Sharp-tailed Sparrow (*A. caudacutus*).

HISTORICAL NOTES: As with the preceding species, the Seaside Sparrow's nesting population in Connecticut has suffered from the destruction of salt marshes. Linsley (1843a) recorded this species at Stratford and New Haven, and Merriam (1877) said it bred "abundantly" in salt and brackish marshes. In 1896 it extended its range northeast into Rhode Island and Massachusetts (*Auk* 14:219). Sage et al. (1913) termed it an "abundant" nester and listed six winter records from 1882 and 1892.

Fox Sparrow (*Passerella iliaca*)

STATUS: an uncommon migrant from mid-March to mid-April and from late October to late November; migrations peak in early April and early November. It is a rare to uncommon winter visitor.

Earliest fall arrival: Oct. 8, 1980; Oct. 17, 1890, 1893, 1953; Oct. 18, 1955.

Latest spring departure: Apr. 26, 1875; Apr. 25, 1907, 1975; Apr. 22, 1956, 1974, 1978.

HISTORICAL NOTES: The Fox Sparrow was apparently more frequently encountered in the 1800s than in recent decades. Linsley (1843a) recorded it at Stratford and New Haven, and Merriam (1877) said it was "common during the migrations" and noted that it was "gregarious." In 1913 Sage et al. said it was "common" during migrations but "rarely" occurred in winter.

Song Sparrow (*Melospiza melodia*)

STATUS: a common migrant from early March to early May and from mid-September to late November; it is sometimes very common during peak migration days in late March to early April and in mid-October, especially along the coast. It is fairly common in winter, generally uncommon inland at higher elevations. It is a common and widespread nester throughout the state.

HISTORICAL NOTES: Virtually all references in historical literature pertaining to Connecticut birds refer to the Song Sparrow as common or abundant. In the late 1800s its overall population was reduced by competition with the House Sparrow, but it had rebounded by about 1920 (Bagg and Eliot 1937). Prior to the early 1900s it was apparently irregular in winter or only "occasional" away from the coast (Job; Sage et al.; Bagg and Eliot 1937) but is now regular inland during that season.

Lincoln's Sparrow (*Melospiza lincolnii*)

STATUS: a rare migrant in May and from late September to late October. It is sometimes uncommon during peak migration days in mid-May and early October.
   Earliest spring arrival: Apr. 25, 1982; May 3, 1972 (banded); May 6, 1968.
   Latest spring departure: May 30, 1917; May 25, 1976; May 24, 1966, 1983.
   Earliest fall arrival: Sept. 8, 1976; Sept. 11, 1988; Sept. 13, 1972.
   Latest fall departure: Nov. 28, 1972; Nov. 21, 1976; Nov. 5, 1972.

COMMENTS: Most early winter reports are viewed skeptically; there are at least 10 reports of this species on Christmas Bird Counts in the state, and the authors are unaware of any substantiated by photograph or specimen evidence. Similarly, it has been reported without verification during the summer months. This species is apt to be confused with the immature Swamp Sparrow by less-active observers.

HISTORICAL NOTES: During the 1800s and the first two decades of this century, the Lincoln's Sparrow was seldom reported in Connecticut (Merriam; Sage et al.; Bagg and Eliot 1937).

Swamp Sparrow (*Melospiza georgiana*)

STATUS: an uncommon migrant from late March to late May and occasionally common from mid-September to mid-November; migrations peak in early May and mid-October. In winter it is uncommon to locally fairly common in coastal areas and along the Connecticut River, less numerous elsewhere. It is an uncommon to fairly common nester in freshwater marshes throughout the state.

HISTORICAL NOTES: According to Bagg and Eliot (1937), the nesting range of the Swamp Sparrow extended southward into Massachusetts and northern Connecticut in the mid-1800s. Such a range expansion was not noticed in New York, where it "has always been considered a common, if elusive and local, breeding bird" (NYBBA). In 1913 Sage et al. said it was a "tolerably common" nester in the northern parts of the state but was only known to breed in the Quinnipiac Marshes and near Bridgeport in the southern portions of the state. This species increased throughout the state by the 1940s (Bagg and Eliot 1937). Winter reports increased after 1950 (Hill).

White-throated Sparrow (*Zonotrichia albicollis*)

STATUS: a common migrant from early March to late May and from mid-September to mid-November; it is sometimes very common during peak migration days in mid-April and mid-October. It is rare after May and before mid-September except in those areas where it nests. It is fairly common in winter along the coast and the Connecticut River valley, less numerous inland.

It is an uncommon to fairly common nester in the northwest hills south to Kent, Warren, and Litchfield and east to Harwington, Canton, and Granby. In the northeast hills it is uncommon to locally fairly common west to Somers, Vernon, and Bolton and south to Columbia, Windham, Griswold, and Voluntown.

HISTORICAL NOTES: Before 1900 the White-throated Sparrow was a "rare" breeder in western Massachusetts, and its range expanded southward into Connecticut after 1915 (Bagg and Eliot 1937). Sage et al. mentioned summer records at Salisbury in 1904, Winsted in 1905, and Salisbury in 1906. Territorial males were noted by Job (1922) in 1906 at Litchfield and by Kuerzi and Kuerzi (1934) in 1933 and 1934 in Canaan, but breeding remained unconfirmed. The first confirmed nesting in the state is unknown, but four to five singing males were reported at Litchfield in 1963 (M. Van Winkle, AFN 17:451). It nested south to Ridgefield in 1972 (AmB 26:840) and in the northeast hills in 1974 (Manter 1975).

White-crowned Sparrow (*Zonotrichia leucophrys*)

STATUS: variable but usually an uncommon migrant in May and from late September into December; it is occasionally fairly common during peak migration days in mid-May and early October. Rare in winter, it sometimes frequents feeders through the winter months. March and April reports are probably of birds that wintered locally.

Earliest spring arrival: Apr. 15, 1977; Apr. 28, 1951, 1953; May 3, 1970, 1972.

Latest spring departure: May 30, 1943; May 26, 1935, 1978; May 24, 1953.

Earliest fall arrival: Sept. 18, 1954; Sept. 21, 1976; Sept. 22, 1976.

Latest fall departure: difficult to determine because of the number of winter reports.

COMMENTS: summer occurrences of this species have not been documented; those by single persons lack sufficient corroboration (CW 5:10).

SUBSPECIES: The nominate race, *Z. l. leucophrys*, is the subspecies that occurs most frequently in the state. The western race, *Z. l. gambelii*, may be found during migration and in winter (May 3, 1972, AmB 27:35). It is distinguished from the nominate race by white or grayish lores, compared to the black lores of *Z. l. leucophrys*.

HISTORICAL NOTES: Formerly accidental in winter, this species has been reported more frequently since about 1947 (AmB 20:404; Bull 1964).

Harris' Sparrow (*Zonotrichia querula*)

STATUS: a casual migrant and winter visitor; it has been reported from October to May but is most apt to be seen in December and January at feeders. This species winters east to Tennessee and Louisiana (Terres 1980) and is casual along the Atlantic seaboard (Bull 1974).

RECORDS: The first state record was December 11–17, 1945, at Hamden (*Auk* 63:448). The following are other published records, all of single birds:

Oct. 10, 1951	Glastonbury	L. J. Whittles	AFN 6:9
Apr. 1– May 3, 1964	Guilford	Telling et al.	RNEB 20 (4, 5)
Dec. 9, 1973 Apr. 1, 1974	Bridgewater	A. Jenks et al.	AmB 28:223, 8:11
Jan. 10– Mar. 1, 1974	Madison	sp. N. Proctor et al.	AmB 28:620
Jan. 1– May 8, 1976	Windham	ph. W. Gaunya et al.	AmB 30:815
Jan. 2– Feb. 25, 1978	Milford	ph. F. Mantlik et al.	AmB 32:324
Dec. 27, 1986	South Windsor	P. Lescault et al.	CW 7:50

Published reports lacking adequate corroboration include one at Westport on December 28, 1963 (AFN 18:109), and one at Madison on April 15, 1976 (AmB 30:815).

Dark-eyed Junco (*Junco hyemalis*)

STATUS: a fairly common to very common migrant from mid-March to May and from late September to mid-November; migrations peak in early April and mid-October. In winter it is fairly common throughout the state.

An uncommon nester in the northwest hills south to Sherman, New Milford, and Bethlehem and east to Harwington, Canton, and Granby, it is most numerous on Mt. Riga in Salisbury. In the northeast hills it nests west to Somers, Tolland, and Coventry and south to Windham, Canterbury, and Sterling. Nesting may occur south to Danbury, Southbury, and Farmington.

Earliest fall arrival: Sept. 11, 1980; Sept. 14, 1963; Sept. 15, 1975.

Latest spring departure: May 24, 1981; May 21, 1950; May 15, 1975.

SUBSPECIES: The Oregon Junco (*J. h. oreganus*) normally winters east to South Dakota and Nebraska but occasionally wanders farther east. It is very rare here. Observers should be alert to intergrades appearing in the state.

HISTORICAL NOTES: In the 1880s a few Dark-eyed Juncos nested in western Massachusetts, and by the 1920s it nested regularly there (Bagg and Eliot 1937). In 1908, Job (1922) wrote that it was "common

Dark-eyed Junco

as a migrant, and it occasionally winters" in Litchfield. This species apparently first nested in the state in 1922 at Hadlyme (A. Brockway, *Auk* 40:330). Several nests were found in Litchfield County in the early 1930s (Bagg and Eliot 1937). Increasing, it was a locally "uncommon" nester there by the early 1960s (WMF). In the northeast hills it nested at Union in the early 1960s (Bent et al. 1968). In 1970 it nested at East Haddam (AmB 24:665), and in 1971 it nested at Ashford (Manter 1975). In 1972 nesting was reported at West Hartford (AmB 26:840).

Lapland Longspur (*Calcarius lapponicus*)

STATUS: a rare winter visitor from late October to April; the majority of reports are from coastal areas, but it occurs inland in agricultural fields and pastures. Coastally, it favors drier portions of beaches and short-grass fields. It often occurs in large flocks of Horned Larks.

Earliest fall arrival: Oct. 5, 1987; Oct. 8, 1950; Oct. 9, 1988. Unusually early was one reported on Sept. 24, 1983, at Stratford (CW 4:26).

Latest spring departure: May 9, 1975; May 8, 1985; Apr. 22, 1973.

COMMENTS: A review of the literature reveals that flocks of 20 or more birds are exceedingly rare in Connecticut. On December 26, 1953, a flock of 75 birds was counted at Wethersfield (RNEB 9:292). A flock of 20 was observed on March 30, 1930, at Stratford (BL 32:200); about 24 were present in February 1975 at Stamford (MFN 3:2), and about 35 were at Milford on October 30, 1987 (CW 8:43).

HISTORICAL NOTES: This species has apparently not occurred in the state with any regularity in the last 100 years. Merriam (1877) said that the Lapland Longspur "occurs as a winter visitant," but added that "no record of its capture [in Connecticut] has yet been published." Sage et al. (1913) called this species "a rare and probably accidental late fall migrant."

Smith's Longspur (*Calcarius pictus*)

STATUS: an accidental vagrant from the west.

RECORDS: There are two definite records for Connecticut: a female was collected on March 23, 1968, at Stratford by W. Bulmer (UCM No. 6618; *Auk* 96:345); and a female was photographed on May 2, 1982, at Madison by P. Desjardins (AmB 36:831; CW 2:48).

Chestnut-collared Longspur (*Calcarius ornatus*)

STATUS: an accidental vagrant from the west.

RECORDS: There is one record for Connecticut: a specimen was collected at Stratford on August 29, 1968, by W. Bulmer (UCM No. 6614; WB 82:225). Sight reports on October 1, 1967 (RNEB 23), and October 19, 1973 (AmB 28:32) are not satisfactorily detailed as published.

Snow Bunting (*Plectrophenax nivalis*)

STATUS: variable but usually an uncommon winter visitor from early November to late February; it is most apt to be seen in mid-November along the coast on the drier portions of beaches, short-grass fields, and open areas near coastal estuaries; much less numerous inland. In some winters it may be locally abundant, with flocks larger than 100 birds; whereas in other winters, it may be very scarce. It is very rare in October and after early March.

Earliest fall arrival: Oct. 11, 1986; Oct. 13, 1985; Oct. 20, 1934.
Latest spring departure: Apr. 5, 1966; Apr. 3, 1937; Mar. 24, 1987.

HISTORICAL NOTES: Linsley (1843a) wrote "Large flocks of the Snow Bunting were repeatedly seen here [at Stratford] in the winters of 1840, 1841 and 1842. Previous to that period, I had not seen one here in eighteen years." It was a "common winter visitor" in the 1870s (Merriam 1877). In 1908, Job (1922) wrote that it was "less irregular than the Crossbills and others, it is found nearly every winter in flocks, but is not common inland, though quite so on the coast."

Blackbirds, Orioles, etc. (Sub-family Icterinae)

Bobolink (*Dolichonyx oryzivorus*)

STATUS: an uncommon to fairly common migrant from mid-May to June and from mid-August to mid-October; it is sometimes common during peak migration days in mid-May and early September.

The Bobolink is declining in the state as a nesting species. It is an uncommon to locally common nester in lush fields in the northwest hills south to Sherman, Washington, and Litchfield and east to Harwinton, Barkhamsted, and Hartland. It also nests in the northeast hills west to Stafford, Mansfield, and Windham and south to Scotland, Plainfield, and Sterling. It nests in the Connecticut River valley at South Windsor, Glastonbury, and Rocky Hill. Nesting is suspected but unproved in Durham.

Earliest spring arrival: Apr. 27, 1891; Apr. 28, 1935, 1957; Apr. 29, 1945.

Latest fall departure: Nov. 13, 1983; Nov. 11, 1979; Nov. 3, 1966.

It is acidental in December: one was seen on December 20, 1969, at New Haven (AFN 24:151); one was present from November 30 to December 7, 1968, at East Haven (AFN 23:28); and one was observed by the authors at a feeder in Greenwich from early October to December 1, 1974 (MFN 7:12).

HISTORICAL NOTES: This species was a "common" and widespread nester before 1875; it declined as fields were mechanically cut in June and again in late summer to produce two crops (formerly limited to one in mid-July), thus severely disrupting nesting birds (Linsley 1843a; Merriam; Averill; Sage et al.; Griscom; Forbush 1927; Bagg and Eliot; Pink and Waterman 1965; Bent 1958). After 1920 a dramatic decline occurred as agriculture decreased, especially along the coast where Bobolinks nested locally (Cruickshank; Bagg and Eliot 1937). By the late 1930s the decline had stabilized somewhat in the northeast (Griscom and Snyder; Bull 1964; Mackenzie; Manter 1975) but only after its nesting range in the state was severely reduced.

Red-winged Blackbird (*Agelaius phoeniceus*)

STATUS: a common migrant from late February to early May and from mid-September to mid-November; it is sometimes abundant during peak migration days in early April and mid-October, when large flocks pass through the state. In winter it is uncommon to fairly common along the coast from Fairfield east to Stonington and along the lower Connecticut River valley, rare to uncommon along the western shore and inland. It is a common and widespread nester in coastal and inland marshes throughout the state.

HISTORICAL NOTES: The Red-winged Blackbird has been considered common, abundant, or very abundant since the mid-1800s by ornithologists in Connecticut. However, wetlands have been among the fastest disappearing habitats because they were frequently drained for housing, industry, and agriculture, especially along the coast (NYBBA). A vast amount of wetland has been destroyed in Connecticut in the last 50 years, so possibly the Red-winged Blackbird has correspondingly declined.

The first winter record was apparently not until 1891, when L. Bishop collected one at Stratford (*Auk* 38:582).

Eastern Meadowlark (*Sturnella magna*)

STATUS: an uncommon migrant from early March to late May and from early August to early November. It is uncommon in early winter along the coast near marshes and open areas from Stratford east to Stonington, generally rare elsewhere. Declining as a nester, its range is now restricted as suitable nesting habitat has been lost; it remains occasionally fairly common in grassy fields and pastures, mostly in the interior of the state.

HISTORICAL NOTES: This species has markedly decreased in recent times, mainly the result of the decline of agriculture and the development of open areas. It was "abundant" to "very abundant" to 1890 (Merriam; Griscom and Snyder; Hill). It declined thereafter, partially caused by earlier summer mowings of its nesting areas and several reportedly severe winters to our south (Bagg and Eliot; Griscom and Snyder 1955). The nesting population in the state declined during the 1930s, when it was called "hardly common" or "generally uncommon" (Forbush 1927; Howes 1928). It has steadily become even more localized since then (Bull 1964). In the 1960s it was reported more frequently in winter than in the 1920s (Bull 1964).

Yellow-headed Blackbird (*Xanthocephalus xanthocephalus*)

STATUS: a very rare visitor from the west. Most reports are in the fall and early winter, from September to January. It sometimes overwinters at feeders and lingers into May.

RECORDS: There are at least 15 published reports from the state, 3 of which are old specimen records: the first was taken in June 1878 near New Haven (*Auk* 18:195); one was collected from a flock of Red-winged Blackbirds in July 1884 at Hartford (*Auk* 4:256; Sage et al. 1913); and an adult female was taken on August 13, 1888, at Stamford (Bull 1964).

Fall records include three birds seen in a flock of Red-winged Blackbirds on November 11, 1956, at Wethersfield (AFN 11:252), one on November 22, 1979, at Windsor Locks (P. Desjardins, pers. comm.), and a vague report of two seen in the fall of 1978 (date, location, and observers not stated; AmB 33:158). It has been recorded on Christmas Bird Counts four times: a male "present from mid-December" was tallied at New London on December 28, 1969 (AFN 24:152), and remained to January 31, 1970 (AFN 24:485); one was present at Storrs (Mansfield) from December 21 to 29, 1975 (AmB 30:694); a male was present on the Stratford–Milford count from mid-December to January 3, 1978 (AmB 32:324); and one was recorded at New London during "count period" in December 1980 (AmB 35:280, 437).

Winter reports include an immature male seen on January 29, 1952, at Glastonbury (AFN 6:188), one seen at Tolland on March 19, 1976 (AmB 30:694), one at South Windsor from February to the first week of March 1985 (CW 5:51), and one at New London February 7–20, 1986 (CW 6:39). Spring reports include three birds on April 1, 1950, at Putnam (RNEB 6:75), one on May 14 and June 2, 1966, at East Haven (YPMR), a male at a Stratford feeder from April 7 to 23, 1983 (photographed, CW 3:35), and one at Stratford from February to April 25, 1985 (CW 5:51).

The only summer record this century was of one that visited a feeder from July 6 to October 12, 1973, at Guilford (photographed, AmB 28:31, 119). Before 1900 a female specimen was obtained in July 1884 at Hartford (*Auk* 4:256; Sage et al. 1913), and another female was found on August 13, 1888, at Stamford (O&O 13:189; AMNH No. 71952).

Rusty Blackbird (*Euphagus carolinus*)

STATUS: an uncommon migrant from March to late April and from mid-October to mid-December; it favors wet woodlands and shrubby swamps. It occasionally lingers to early January, very rare in midwinter. In winter it is most apt to be found along the coast.

Earliest spring arrival: Feb. 23, 1971; Feb. 25, 1943; Feb. 27, 1983.

Latest spring departure: May 22, 1955, May 12, 1967, May 11, 1971.

Earliest fall arrival: Sept. 20, 1956; Sept. 24, 1950; Sept. 25, 1975.

Latest fall departure: difficult to determine because of the number of early winter records.

COMMENTS: Several individuals were present at Union in mid-June, 1950, but nesting was not proved (WB 63:69).

HISTORICAL NOTES: In the 1860s this species was "rather rare" and "decidedly less numerous" than in the 1930s (Bagg and Eliot). In 1908, Job (1922) said the Rusty Blackbird was a "rather common migrant" in Litchfield. Small numbers were occasionally reported in winter along the coast before 1900 (Merriam). It became more regular in the winter season after 1946 (Bull 1964).

Boat-tailed Grackle (*Quiscalus major*)

STATUS: an accidental visitor from the south; it nests along the Atlantic coast north to Long Island, New York.

RECORDS: There are three records for the state: two individuals at New Haven on October 7, 1985 (J. Blair, R. English, CW 6:22, 7:50); two to six photographed at Stratford from October 30, 1985, to late February 1986 (C. Hills et al., CW 6:22, 39); and one at Madison on May 18, 1986 (D. Varza, CW 6:51). All of these reports were possibly related to the passage of Hurricane Gloria on September 30, 1985, which produced other New England records of this species.

COMMENTS: According to Linsley (1843a), Dr. Whelpley reported this species at New Haven. However, both C. Hart Merriam and E. Coues say this report was "probably a mistake" (E. Coues, *Birds of the Northwest,* 1874, p. 204).

HISTORICAL NOTES: After the mid-1950s the northern edge of its nesting range was in southern New Jersey (Bent 1958), and it has since expanded northward to Long Island (NYBBA), where its numbers have steadily increased.

Common Grackle (*Quiscalus quiscula*)

STATUS: a common migrant from late February to mid-May and from early September to late November; it is often abundant during peak migration days in mid-April and mid-October. In winter it is uncommon to common along the coast from Stratford east to Stonington and along the Connecticut River valley; it is usually rare or uncommon along the western coast and inland. It is a common and widespread nester throughout the state, favoring pines and spruces near water bodies and wetlands.

SUBSPECIES: The subspecies *Q. q. stonei* ("Purple" Grackle) and *Q. q. versicolor* ("Bronzed" Grackle) were once considered separate species.

The Purple Grackle occurs from late February to early December and occasionally may winter. It is at the northern edge of its nesting range in southern Connecticut. It is distinguished from the Bronzed Grackle by its plain dull purplish back. The Bronzed Grackle nests from northern Connecticut north, is a widespread migrant, and winters along the shore. It is most apt to be found from early March to late October and has a dull bronze back. Intergrade individuals ("Ridgway's Grackle") show characteristics of both forms, and on their backs they have broken iridescent bars that are visible in good light (Huntington 1952). A. Bagg reported that these intergrades were present in the Portland area (*Auk* 40:262).

HISTORICAL NOTES: This species was ubiquitous during early colonial times, so much so that local governments paid bounties for its destruction because of its fondness for grains. It was reportedly extirpated from New England by 1750 (Merriam 1877). From the early 1840s through 1913 it became reestablished and was a "common" summer resident (Linsley 1843a; Merriam; Sage et al. 1913). Its numbers generally increased after 1920, and it has subsequently been described as "abundant" (Howes; Bagg and Eliot; Bull 1964; Manter 1975).

Brown-headed Cowbird (*Molothrus ater*)

STATUS: a fairly common migrant from late February to mid-May and from early September to late November; it is often abundant during peak migration days in mid-April and particularly in mid-October. In winter it is uncommon to common along the coast from Stratford east to Stonington and along the Connecticut River valley, less numerous along the western shore and inland. It is a common breeder throughout the state.

HISTORICAL NOTES: A number of authorities feel that this species moved east from the Great Plains as the settlers cleared the land and introduced farm animals (Bent 1958). Linsley (1843a) said this species was "common," and Merriam (1877) called it an "abundant summer resident." Sage et al. (1913) said it was "common." A decline occurred around the New York City area, where both Griscom (1923) and Cruickshank (1942) said that it was decreasing (NYBBA). More recently, this species may be declining as agricultural land reverts to forest. Robbins et al. found that it decreased on Breeding Bird Survey routes in Connecticut from 1965 to 1979. Individuals of this species are known to have been killed in East Hartford and Meriden in the 1980s by organophosphate poisoning resulting from lawn treatments (Anderson and Glowa).

Brown-headed Cowbird remains numerous, possibly aided by the fragmentation of the forest, which enables easier penetration for finding host species (NYBBA).

Orchard Oriole (*Icterus spurius*)

STATUS: an uncommon migrant from early May to June and from mid-July to early August; it is infrequently observed in migration. An uncommon but increasing nester in open-grown trees in less-developed areas, often near streams and ponds. It nests mainly near the coast and along the larger river valleys; usually absent in the northernmost towns in the western and eastern corners of the state.

Earliest spring arrival: Apr. 23, 1976; Apr. 26, 1983; Apr. 28, 1938.
Latest fall departure: Aug. 16, 1947; Aug. 14, 1943; Aug. 12, 1986.

COMMENTS: Remarkable, if authentic, was a female that reportedly was present at a West Haven feeder from October 12, 1953, to February 9, 1954 (RNEB 8:232, 9:14, 9:34). The published accounts of this sighting do not indicate whether any knowledgeable observer verified this report.

HISTORICAL NOTES: Bull (1964) describes accounts of this species from the 1840s, when it was more numerous on Long Island than the Northern Oriole. In Connecticut, Merriam (1877) said it was "a common summer resident," the same description given for the Northern Oriole. Often favoring orchards, the Orchard Oriole was "common" from about 1880 to the very early 1900s and then decreased as its nesting range withdrew southward (Griscom and Snyder; Bull 1964). In 1913 Sage et al. noted that it was a "tolerably common" nester along the coast and inland north to New Milford and Portland. In 1933 it nested north to Canaan (PLSNY No. 42/43). Decreasing, in about 1950 it was uncommon, nesting mostly along the western coast (Griscom and Snyder; Mackenzie; Bull 1964) and, to a lesser degree, east to the Connecticut River and inland along the Connecticut River valley (Bent 1958). Since the 1960s it has steadily expanded its nesting range east and north.

Northern Oriole (*Icterus galbula*)

STATUS: a fairly common migrant from late April to late May and from mid-August to mid-October; migrations peak in early May and late August. It infrequently lingers to late December, very rarely through the winter, usually at feeders. It is a widespread nester throughout the state in large open-grown trees in residential and rural areas.

Earliest spring arrival: Apr. 1, 1986; Apr. 4, 1988; Apr. 7, 1985.

Winter: There are at least 25 published reports of this species in the winter months, from December through March. Most sightings are of immatures or females at feeding stations. It is likely that most reports in March and early April are of birds that wintered locally.

Northern Oriole

HISTORICAL NOTES: From the late 1800s to about 1920 this species was apparently an "abundant" nester (Merriam; Sage et al.; Howes 1928). Sage et al. (1913) indicated that it had decreased "near New Haven in recent years." Since then it has usually been called a "common" nester (Forbush 1927; Bagg and Eliot; Bull 1964; Manter 1975). After about 1920 winter sightings have increased (Bagg and Eliot; Bull 1964; Manter 1975), most notably since 1950 (Bent 1958).

COMMENTS: In the 1960s there was concern that the great decline of American elm trees, a favorite nesting location for these birds, would result in a decrease in the number of orioles. Apparently, however, the decline of elm trees has had little effect on oriole numbers.

SUBSPECIES: Bullock's Oriole (I. g. bullocki) is reported every few years, often in the fall, with at least one apparently overwintering (fall 1957 to late May 1958 at Greenwich; C. Roesler, AFN 12:266, 339).

Pine Grosbeak (*Pinicola enucleator*)

STATUS: a rare to uncommon but very irregular winter visitor from late October to early April; often several years pass with no sightings, but it is occasionally fairly common in flight years. It is most apt to be seen at inland areas; it is much less numerous along the coast.

Earliest fall arrival: Sept. 13, 1984; Sept. 22, 1986; Oct. 12, 1957.
Latest spring departure: Apr. 24, 1962; Apr. 13, 1956; Apr. 6, 1903.

HISTORICAL NOTES: Since 1900 large flights into the state occurred during the winters of 1903–1904, 1929–1930, 1951–1952, 1961–1962, and 1977–1978.

COMMENTS: Bent reported that this species attempted and then abandoned nesting at Wilton from May 28 to June 11, 1933 (*Auk* 50:442). This report was credited as a full breeding record by the 1957 AOU Check-list. The 1983 AOU Check-list does not include this report, implying that the AOU no longer accepts it. Bull (1964), noting that this species nests in spruce forests in Canada and northern New England, rejects the record as a case of misidentification. He also added that the account in *The Auk* was "completely vague."

Purple Finch (*Carpodacus purpureus*)

STATUS: a fairly common migrant from mid-March to late May and sometimes very common from late August to early December; fall migration peaks in early October. It is variable in winter but is usually uncommon to fairly common. It is a rare to uncommon nester throughout the state except near the coast and in the Connecticut River Valley, where it very rarely nests; it is most numerous in the northwest hills.

HISTORICAL NOTES: This species increased from the mid-1850s to about 1885 (Merriam; Bagg and Eliot; Bent et al. 1968) and then decreased as House Sparrows prospered (Bent et al. 1968). From the late 1930s nesting reports increased throughout the state, especially from the northern portions, partly as a result of the maturation of native and ornamental evergreens (Bagg and Eliot; Pink and Waterman 1965; Hill).

House Finch (*Carpodacus mexicanus*)

STATUS: introduced. This species is a fairly common to very common resident throughout the state. Increasing, it nests in a wide variety of settings, including evergreen trees, ivy growing on buildings, and even hanging outdoor flowerpots, wreaths, and other ornaments. In winter it often congregates in flocks exceeding 50 individuals.

HISTORICAL NOTES: The House Finch was first introduced in the eastern United States in 1940 at Long Island, New York, and it flourished in the eastern urban and suburban environment (*Auk* 70:31). It apparently first nested in Connecticut in 1951 at Greenwich (*Auk* 70:31), and in 1953 a colony at Stamford was "increasing in numbers and spreading in territory" (AFN 7:206). Nesting expanded east to Fairfield in 1957 (*Auk* 70:31). By the early 1960s, it was present throughout Fairfield County, had nested east along the coast to New London, and had been reported north in the higher elevations in Litchfield, Hartford, and Tolland counties (AmB 36:347; Pink and Waterman 1965; Manter 1975). In the late 1960s it nested in the Connecticut River valley north to Massachusetts (AmB 36:347). By the early 1970s it nested throughout the state, although locally in the northwest and northeast hills. It had become an established resident statewide by the mid-1970s.

Red Crossbill (*Loxia curvirostra*)

STATUS: a rare and irregular winter visitor from early November to April. Variable in numbers, in some years it is not present at all, whereas in flight years it may be common. There is a single breeding report: a nest with nestlings was found at Manchester, June 8–14, 1970, by Mr. and Mrs. G. Walker (AFN 24:665).

Earliest fall arrival: Sept. 13, 1984 (CW 5:23); Oct. 11, 1906; Oct. 20, 1967.

Latest spring departure: May 29, 1884 (spec.); May 22, 1970; May 21, 1965.

Summer: One was collected on Aug. 8, 1875, at New Haven (BCM No. B369). One was seen at Branford on Aug. 1, 1972 (D. Finch, MFCYM 72:10).

SUBSPECIES: Three subspecies are believed to occur in Connecticut, although separation in the field is difficult. "Newfoundland" Red Crossbills (*L. c. percna*) have large bills, and males are quite dark. The "Sitka" Red Crossbill (*L. c. minor*) are smaller, with stumpy bills, and males have a brick-red plumage. The "Eastern" Red Crossbill (*L. c. neogaea*) has an intermediate-size bill and is thought to be nearly extinct as a result of widespread removal of white pine (*Pinus strobus*) forests in New England. There is an excellent report on this subject by R. W. Dickerman (AmB 41:189).

HISTORICAL NOTES: According to Griscom and Snyder (1955), the Red Crossbill has greatly decreased since 1900. In Connecticut, Linsley (1843a) reported this species, and Merriam (1877) said it was an "irregular" visitor and more frequently seen than the White-winged Crossbill. In 1913 Sage et al. termed this species "rare and irregular."

White-winged Crossbill (*Loxia leucoptera*)

STATUS: a rare and very irregular winter visitor from early November to early April; it is occasionally fairly common in flight years. The only known nesting in the state was of a pair feeding three downy young at Voluntown in early June 1986 (J. Laffley, CW 7:11).

Generally, this species is reported less often than the Red Crossbill but occasionally outnumbers it in flight years.

Earliest fall arrival: Sept. 13, 1984 (CW 5:23); Oct. 11, 1906; Oct. 31, 1954.

Latest spring departure: May 12, 1900; May 11, 1955; Apr. 15, 1982.

HISTORICAL NOTES: Linsley (1843a) said this species "is more common than the [Red Crossbill]." Merriam (1877) noted that the White-winged Crossbill was "an irregular winter visitant" and was "not uncommon" during the winter months. Sage et al. (1913) simply called it "a rare straggler in winter." According to Griscom and Snyder (1955), the White-winged Crossbill has increased since the mid-1940s.

Common Redpoll (*Carduelis flammea*)

STATUS: an erratic winter visitor from November to April, absent or rare in most years and fairly common to infrequently abundant in other years; reported less often along the coast and more frequently from inland areas.

Earliest fall arrival: Oct. 20, 1971; Oct. 25, 1949; Oct. 29, 1906.
Latest spring departure: May 11, 1900; May 9, 1936; May 5, 1911.

HISTORICAL NOTES: The Common Redpoll apparently has not significantly changed in status in Connecticut in the last 100 years. Linsley (1843a) recorded this species at New Haven, and Merriam (1877) said it was "an irregular" visitor. Similarly, Sage et al. (1913) called it "irregular" but added that it was "formerly sometimes common." Presumably, the loss of open fields to development and the regrowth of forest in recent decades has reduced the amount of suitable habitat in the state.

Hoary Redpoll (*Carduelis hornemanni*)

STATUS: a casual winter visitor, most apt to be reported in mid-winter in flocks of Common Redpolls during flight years of that species. There are two specimen records: one was collected at East Haven on November 24, 1906, by L. Bishop (Sage et al. 1913), and one was taken at New Haven on December 17, 1977 (AmB 32:324, 511).

COMMENTS: There are at least 10 uncorroborated sight reports published that are not listed here because of the difficulty in separating this species from Common Redpoll. Some authorities consider this species merely a form of Common Redpoll (AmB 32:330).

Pine Siskin (*Carduelis pinus*)

STATUS: an uncommon to fairly common migrant from early March to late April and from late October to mid-December. It can be irregular in winter but is usually fairly common. In some years it is rare in spring, depending on whether a significant flight occurred during the preceding fall. Nonbreeders sometimes linger at feeders into June. It is a rare and irregular nester in the northwest hills south to Kent, Morris, and Harwington and east to Burlington, Canton, and Granby; it has also nested in West Hartford, Mansfield, and Waterford.

Earliest fall arrival: Sept. 23, 1983; Sept. 25, 1943; Sept. 26, 1916.
Latest spring departure: June 25, 1978; June 6, 1970; May 31, 1978.

COMMENTS: Maximum counts include 2,000 seen near New Haven on November 9, 1952, and 250–300 that same day at Westport (AFN 7:9). Like the Red Crossbill, it occasionally nests in the region following large flights the preceding fall (Bull 1964). This may explain the nesting at East Haddam in 1937 (Bent et al. 1968) and several more recent nestings.

American Goldfinch (*Carduelis tristis*)

STATUS: a fairly common migrant from mid-March to early May and from late September to November. Variable but usually uncommon in winter, depending on the availability of its food supply. It is a fairly common nester throughout the state in open areas with overgrown fields and thickets. This species nests later in the summer than most other passerines.

HISTORICAL NOTES: The American Goldfinch has historically been considered a common or abundant resident. This species was possibly more numerous in the early part of this century when fields and brushy areas were more numerous, and may have declined from the loss of habitat to urban and suburban sprawl and regrowth of forests.

Evening Grosbeak (*Coccothraustes vespertinus*)

STATUS: variable but usually a fairly common migrant from late February to mid-May and occasionally very common from mid-October to mid-December; it may appear as early as mid-September. Migrations peak in mid-April and early November. It is usually uncommon in winter but is sometimes fairly common; generally less numerous on the coastal plain. In some winters it may be largely absent. It is a very rare nester in the northeast hills: it nested at Chaplin in 1983 and at Ashford in 1986 (CW 7:12).
   Earliest fall arrival: Sept. 3, 1975; Sept. 14, 1951; Sept. 19, 1971.
   Latest spring departure: May 28, 1958; May 26, 1962; May 25, 1946.

HISTORICAL NOTES: This species has increased markedly in New England in historical times. It has extended its nesting range eastward from south-central Canada since the mid-1800s (Forbush 1929; Bagg and Eliot 1937). A large flight occurred during the winter of 1890–1891, which accounted for most of New England's first records. The first Connecticut specimen record was on March 10, 1890, at New Milford (E. Austin, *Auk* 7:211). There were several reports in the state in the winter of 1891–1892. It was reported in the winters of 1907 and 1909, and another large flight occurred in the winter of 1910–1911 (Sage et al., Forbush 1929). From 1911 to the mid-1940s it was more frequently observed (Bagg and Eliot 1937). In 1922 it was said to have been a "very rare visitant in the past" but became "more plentiful the past two or three years" (OO 39:93). It increased markedly thereafter, becoming an annual visitor in the 1950s (Bull 1964; Manter 1975).

In 1962 four nesting pairs were reported at Glastonbury and were observed feeding young (L. Whittles, AFN 16:463).

WEAVER FINCHES (FAMILY PASSERIDAE)

House Sparrow (*Passer domesticus*)

STATUS: introduced. This species is a fairly common to abundant resident throughout the state, most numerous in urban settings and near farms.

HISTORICAL NOTES: The House Sparrow was introduced at Brooklyn, New York, in 1853 to rid the city of injurious insects (Bent). It was also released, for the same reason, at Portland, Maine, in 1854; in Rhode Island in 1858; at Boston, Massachusetts, 1858 to 1860; again in New York from 1860 to 1866; and in New Haven in 1867 (Bent et al. 1968; Forbush 1929; Bagg and Eliot; Bull 1964). In the 1860s a few were reported breeding in the upper Connecticut River valley (Bagg and Eliot 1937). Its population increased dramatically; by the 1870s it was "an abundant resident in all the larger, and most of the smaller, towns throughout the state" (Merriam 1877). It outcompeted bluebirds, wrens, phoebes, and swallows (especially Purple Martins and Tree Swallows) for nesting cavities and was widely blamed for the decline of those species (*Auk* 26:129; Bent). According to W. Brewster, declines were also noted in numbers of Purple Finch, Song Sparrow, Indigo Bunting, and Least Flycatcher (BMAS 37(5): 187).

The House Sparrow population peaked between 1890 and 1915 (Griscom and Snyder 1955), and then it decreased as agriculture declined and as automobiles and tractors replaced grain-fed horses. Competition with the starling caused additional decreases (Bent et al. 1968; Bull 1964). Its numbers have continued to decrease as the decline in agriculture has continued and as newer urban architecture yielded fewer nesting sites than those formerly available (Bagg and Eliot; Griscom and Snyder; Hill). Also, this species has not adapted well to suburban settings, which have proliferated in the last 25 years.

List of Miscellaneous Reports

One of the most difficult tasks faced by any compiler of ornithological data is the evaluation and judgment of sight reports. Some species of birds are easily identified in the field, but some are nearly impossible to identify. When views are hampered by high winds, poor light conditions, or precipitation, easily identified species often cannot be recognized even by highly trained experts. Beginners should not start with an unrealistic expectation of identifying all that they see. In the past many incorrect sight reports have been accepted, and some have been published and perpetuated.

Of great importance is the continuing work of the Connecticut Rare Records Committee (CRRC) of the Connecticut Ornithological Association, which has taken on the task of regularly evaluating sight reports of rare species in the state. The CRRC also has assembled a checklist of the state's birds (CW 8:18). The authors fully support the work and objectives of the CRRC. Additions and changes to the state list as determined by the CRRC are published in the Connecticut Ornithological Association's *Connecticut Warbler*. The committee's work will ensure a better-quality record of the state's birds.

The authors' bias is to not grant full weight to sight reports of rarities by single or even pairs of observers. Listed in this section are published reports that for one or more of the following reasons did not meet the authors' criteria for inclusion in the main text:

1. The report is of a species not otherwise corroborated as present in the state by specimen or photographic evidence.
2. The identification was made by fewer than three sufficiently experienced observers.

3. The species was correctly identified, but the bird was in all likelihood an escapee from captivity or was otherwise assisted by humans in a manner that made its entry into the state possible.

Arctic Loon (*Gavia arctica*)

One was reported at Guilford January 15 and 22, 1967 (NHBC), but details of this sighting were not published. Another, reported on November 16, 1980, at Milford, was not accepted by the CRRC (CW 7:50).

White-tailed Tropicbird (*Phaethon lepturus*)

One was reportedly seen by two observers at Groton on September 1, 1954, after Hurricane Carol (AFN 9:317; RNEB). This sighting was not sufficiently corroborated. Details of this sighting were reviewed by the CRRC, and after deliberation the sighting was not accepted.

Brown Booby (*Sula leucogaster*)

This species was reportedly collected by Linsley (1843a) at Guilford sometime prior to 1843. Linsley's identification is questionable; although both Merriam (1877) and Sage et al. (1913) accept his account, the CRRC does not. The current location of the specimen is not known. It is possible that this species once ranged farther north than presently.

Anhinga (*Anhinga anhinga*)

One was reported by one observer on September 25, 1987. Details of this sighting were reviewed and accepted by the CRRC (No. 87-31).

Reddish Egret (*Egretta rufescens*)

One was reported at Madison on September 28, 1975 (AmB 30:30). Details of this sighting were reviewed by the CRRC and, after deliberation, were not accepted.

American Flamingo (*Phoenicopterus ruber*)

There are several sight reports of this species in the state. One was reported at Black Point (East Lyme) August 25–31, 1964 (AFN 19:19). What was certainly the same bird was at Niantic (East Lyme) September 1–14 (RNEB 20:9). One was seen at West Haven on May 4, 1965 (AFN

19:450) and is believed to be the same individual that escaped from Tuxedo Park, New York, several days earlier. All reports of this species in Connecticut are undoubtedly of escaped birds.

Scarlet Ibis (*Eudocimus ruber*)

One was sighted at Ridgefield September 5 and 6, 1937 (BL 39:468). This bird was undoubtedly an escapee.

Spot-billed Duck (*Anas poecilorhyncha*)

One was reported by S. Dillon Ripley "in his wildfowl preserve" at Litchfield from May 26 to June 5, 1955 (AFN 9:366). This species was undoubtedly an escapee.

Whooping Crane (*Grus americana*)

Bagg and Eliot (1937, p. 177) refer to an individual that was supposedly shot in "southwestern Connecticut" in 1908. The specimen now resides at the Boston Museum of Science (specimen No. X03.183). The label states that it was collected in April 1908 at "Congamuck Pond, Connecticut (or lower Massachusetts)." The specimen was taken by the unnamed collector to the American Museum of Natural History, where it was received "in the flesh" by W. Dewitt Miller. The label also states that there is no record of the specimen's sex and that there is "some question as to the locality" of its collection. In 1918 the specimen was traded to the Boston Society of Natural History for a Labrador Duck. The specimen was mounted at Harvard University sometime before 1918.

This interesting record is not included in the main text because of the uncertainty surrounding the location of its collection. There is no known "Congamuck Pond" in the state, but there is a Congamond Lake that straddles the state line at Granby and Southwick. Most of the lake is in Massachusetts. Also, there is a likelihood that the bird was an escapee from human captivity. The record was reviewed and not accepted by the CRRC.

Trumpeter Swan (*Cygnus buccinator*)

A hunter familiar with this species heard one at South Windsor in the 1860s and sometime thereafter saw and heard a flock near his farm (Merriam 1877). This report was not sufficiently corroborated to include in the main text. There is a possibility that this species was present in New England during early colonial times (Forbush 1916). This sighting was reviewed and rejected by the CRRC.

Cinnamon Teal (*Anas cyanoptera*)

One was reported at Wethersfield on October 14 or 21, 1944 (NHBC). This individual was probably an escapee, as it was and is a popular aviary species. There are several other reports of this species, and although it is possible that it might appear here naturally, virtually all reports are believed to be of escapes.

White-tailed Eagle (*Haliaeetus albicilla*)

One of this species was reportedly captured on March 29, 1934, when it flew into high-tension wires in Branford (Bergstrom, YPM records). The specimen was apparently lost (CW 7:50). There is considerable doubt that the specimen was ever examined by any knowledgeable person. This matter was reviewed and rejected by the CRRC.

Chukar (*Alectoris chukar*)

This species nested at Greenwich in 1975 (AmB 30:928). These introduced birds have not established any sustained population.

Sharp-tailed Grouse (*Tympanuchus phasianellus*)

One was shot in the fall of 1893 at East Windsor and was presumably one of the birds released at nearby Springfield, Massachusetts, in 1892 and 1893 (Bagg and Eliot 1937). The introduction of this species at Springfield was a complete failure (Morris 1901).

California Quail (*Callipepla californica*)

This species was introduced at Bridgeport in December, 1840 (Linsley 1843a) and, like many other introductions, was a complete failure.

Long-toed Stint (*Calidris subminuta*)

An individual reportedly of this species was photographed at New Haven on September 11, 1983 (CW 4:24). Inspection of the photos has revealed that the bird was an immature Least Sandpiper (CW 7:51). This sighting was reviewed by the CRRC and, after deliberation, was not accepted.

Rufous-necked Stint (*Calidris ruficollis*)

One was reportedly seen by a single observer at Guilford on August 25, 1975 (AmB 30:31; CW 7:51). Details of this sighting were reviewed by the CRRC and, after deliberation, not accepted.

Greenshank (*Tringa nebularia*)

This species was reported, without comment, by Linsley (1843a).

Pomarine Jaeger (*Stercorarius pomarinus*)

There are no known specimens or photographs of this species taken in Connecticut, and none of the sightings is published with satisfactory details or is by three or more competent observers. Published sight reports include August 31, 1939, at Fairfield (BNEBL 3:9); September 7, 1979, at Branford (AmB 34:140); August 6, 1985, at West Haven (CW 6:21); and one on the unusually late date of November 28, 1985 (CW 6:21).

South Polar Skua (*Catharacta maccormicki*)

One was reportedly seen by a single observer on August 19, 1983, off Bridgeport (CW 3:43). A photograph of this bird was inconclusive (CW 7:51). This sighting was reviewed by the CRRC and not accepted after deliberation.

Heermann's Gull (*Larus heermanni*)

This species was reportedly seen at New Haven harbor, but the published account does not include the observation date or any other details about the sighting (Proctor 1978).

Thayer's Gull (*Larus thayeri*)

One was reported by two observers on January 25, 1988, at Shelton (CW 8(3):65).

Ivory Gull (*Pagophila eburnea*)

One was reportedly sighted at Hartford on December 21, 1975 (AmB 30:244), and another at East Windsor on January 11, 1986 (CW 9:23). These reports lack sufficient corroboration. Details of these sightings were reviewed and not accepted by the CRRC.

Gull-billed Tern (*Gelochelidon nilotica*)

There is no specimen or photographic evidence to support the presence of this species in the state, and none of the published sightings is by three or more competent observers. Sight reports include August 7, 1936, at Westbrook (Bagg and Eliot 1937); August 27, 1937, at Madison (HAS); September 6, 1952 at Guilford (RNEB 8:188); June 23 through August 28, 1964, at Stratford (Hills 1978); August 1, 1973, at Stonington (YPM records); November 5, 1973, at Milford (AmB 28:30); September 10, 1979, at Branford (AmB 34:140); August 29, 1982, at Madison (CW 2:46); and October 6, 1985, at Madison (CW 6:21).

White-winged Tern (*Chlidonias leucopterus*)

One was reported by four observers on May 13, 1979, at New Milford, but the report was inconclusive (CW 7:51). Details of this sighting were reviewed and not accepted by the CRRC.

Bridled Tern (*Sterna anaethetus*)

One was reported inland by a single observer during Hurricane Gloria on September 27, 1985, at Guilford (CW 6:21, 7:51). Details of this sighting were reviewed and not accepted by the CRRC.

Monk Parakeet (*Myiopsitta monachus*)

There are many substantiated reports of this introduced species in the state. It is not included in the main text because it has not established a sustained population independent of human assistance. In August 1988 the authors viewed a congregation of 28 individuals of this species in Bridgeport. According to neighbors, these birds have been present in the area since about 1977 and depend on feeding stations to survive the winter. Apparently, the birds were not fed for one or two winters, and the population declined until feeding resumed (M. Bull, pers. comm.).

Ash-throated Flycatcher (*Myiarchus cinerascens*)

One was reportedly sighted by three observers on October 6, 1984, at Bethany (CW 5:22). This species is difficult to identify in the field, and its presence would be hard to prove without a specimen or photographic evidence. This report was reviewed by the CRRC and not accepted on the basis of lack of sufficient documentation (CW 7:50).

Chough (*Pyrrhocorax pyrrhocorax*)

One seen in November and December, 1988 at Newtown was undoubtedly an escapee (CW 8(3):66).

Black-billed Magpie (*Pica pica*)

One was reported on October 30, 1974, at Madison (AmB 28:31). Other sightings include one in the fall of 1950 (exact location not specified, AFN 8:9) and one on May 18, 1957, at Westbrook (AFN 11:329; RNEB 13:10). There is no way of ascertaining the origins of these birds—the likelihood of escape is strong.

Carolina Chickadee (*Parus carolinensis*)

One was reportedly seen on December 26, 1960, at New Haven (AFN 15:114), and another at Seymore on September 17, 1964, but both accounts were published without details.

Brown-headed Nuthatch (*Sitta pusilla*)

There are three sight reports in the state: one at Wethersfield on December 19, 1954; one at Darien on May 2, 1962; and one at Canton on February 13, 1966. All are unsupported by any corroborating evidence and were seen by single observers.

Bewick's Wren (*Thryomanes bewickii*)

One was reported at South Windsor in October 1932 (HAS; Bagg and Eliot, p. 428). This report lacks sufficient corroboration.

European Robin (*Erithacus rubecula*)

One was reported in late winter–early spring 1960 at West Cornwall. "A dozen of this species were imported, and were released in pairs, between New England and Washington, D.C. As far as is known no other of the released birds has been recognized. The point of discovery is far from any known point of release but the explanation seems reasonable" (AFN 14:294).

Sprague's Pipit (*Anthus spragueii*)

One was reportedly observed on April 17, 1962, at South Windsor "at close range from car" (HAS). This report is without any corroborating evidence.

Bell's Vireo (*Vireo bellii*)

One was reported at Redding on May 11, 1947, by three observers (*Auk* 65:613). This sighting is not supported by photographic or specimen evidence, and the written report is not conclusive. Details of this sighting were reviewed by the CRRC and not accepted.

Swainson's Warbler (*Limnothlypis swainsonii*)

One was reported by a single observer at Redding on May 11, 1975 (Hills 1978). This report lacks sufficient corroboration. Details of this sighting were reviewed by the CRRC and not accepted.

MacGillivray's Warbler (*Oporornis tolmiei*)

An adult male collected in May 1890 at New Haven was believed to be this species (AMNH No. 507395; *Bird-Banding* 38:187–194). Recent reexamination of the specimen by Dr. Jay Pitocchelli of the American Museum of Natural History has been inconclusive as to its taxonomic status.

Red-crested Cardinal (*Paroaria coronata*)

There are several reports of this South American species, also known as Brazilian Cardinal (AFN 21:117; HAS). It has reportedly bred in the state (Peterson 1980). All sightings are certainly of escaped cage birds.

Green-tailed Towhee (*Pipilo chlorurus*)

One was reported by a single observer at Orange on February 7, 1983 (CW 7:50). Unfortunately, this report was not supported by any photographic or specimen evidence.

Golden-crowned Sparrow (*Zonotrichia atricapilla*)

One was reportedly seen at Glastonbury on April 25, 1929 (Forbush 1929, p. 443). This report lacks sufficient corroboration. Also, one was reported at South Windsor on April 21, 1933 (Bagg and Eliot 1937) but was not verified by any active observer.

Western Meadowlark (*Sturnella neglecta*)

Male meadowlarks singing the songs typical of the Western Meadowlark have been reported at the University of Connecticut agricultural fields and other fields in Mansfield several times over the years: May 22, 1965; May 2–4, 1966; May 11–13, 1967; June 3, 1974; June 2–12, 1975 (Manter, AmB 29:750). In all probability, these were hybrids rather than pure Western Meadowlarks.

Brewer's Blackbird (*Euphagus cyanocephalus*)

One was reported by two observers at a Westport feeder on January 2, 1981, in a weakened condition (CW 7:50). Subsequent searches failed to locate the bird. Unfortunately, this sighting is not supported by a photograph or specimen. There are several Christmas Bird Count reports, but apparently none is supported by photographic or specimen evidence (AFN 21:117, 24:149, 24:154; AmB 36:465; CW 2:26).

European Goldfinch (*Carduelis carduelis*)

Individuals of this species are occasionally reported in the state (e.g., AFN 6:240). One was collected at New Haven on May 9, 1892 (*Auk* 9:301; YPM No. 14989). The species has been a common cage pet, and all sightings are probably of escapes.

Other published accounts. In addition to the species listed above, the following species have occurred in Connecticut as a result of introductions, escapes, or releases but have not survived in the wild: Black Swan, Egyptian Goose, Ruddy Shelduck, Common Shelduck, Kalij Pheasant, European Quail, Rose-ringed Parakeet, Blue-crowned Conure, Canary-winged Parakeet, Red-crowned Parrot, Yellow-billed Magpie, and Cuban Crow.

Birding Areas in Connecticut

Getting Started

Bird watching, usually called "birding," is easy to do. Birds are all around us virtually all hours of the day and every month of the year, and some species are quite conspicuous. The only prerequisite to becoming a birder is curiosity and interest in birds. A good eye, a keen ear, and a little patience are helpful. Some basic equipment is also needed and, once acquired, will provide many years of useful service.

A good pair of binoculars is essential. Seven-, eight-, and ten-power models with central focusing are popular. Become acquainted with the operation and focusing of your binoculars. The identification of fleeting birds will depend on your ability to focus quickly and to follow the bird through thickets and woods without losing sight through the glasses. A spotting scope and tripod can be valuable acquisitions, especially for identifying distant waterfowl, shorebirds, and hawks.

Second, information on bird distribution and identification is essential, and the best place to obtain such knowledge is in a field guide. Roger Tory Peterson's *A Field Guide to the Birds* (east of the Rockies) is undoubtedly still the best field guide for use by novice birders. More advanced birders may add to their library the more comprehensive National Geographic Society's *Field Guide to the Birds of North America*. The authors prefer these two guides over those that use photographs to describe different birds.

Field guides are full of helpful hints to aid in distinguishing one species from another. The guide will simplify the task of becoming familiar with a large number of different field marks and characteristics.

An hour spent studying the field guide before going out into the woods and fields is time well spent.

Most birders have one or two favorite birding areas, usually close to home. A small pond, a wooded ravine, a local park, an old orchard—in some ways these local haunts are the most productive and rewarding birding spots. Keep in mind that birds are wild creatures and have three critical needs: food, shelter, and water. Quietly approaching a berry-filled bush might yield a glimpse of a thrush, a close look at a dense thicket might reveal a flock of sparrows within; a careful hike along a lake's edge might flush a sandpiper or duck. Learning the habitat needs of different types of birds will make their observation easier.

There are a few hazards of birding. Some birders have a tendency, while driving, of keeping one eye on the road and one eye on the sky. This has more than once led to an unfriendly meeting with a roadside ditch or telephone pole. Occasionally, a birder might stumble upon a waist-high nest of bald-faced hornets or tread on a nest of yellow jacket wasps. Occasions like these test one's fleetness of foot. Most people are sensitive to poison ivy. Birders should learn to recognize this plant and avoid contact with it at all seasons. Lyme disease is carried by the pinhead-size deer tick. Birders are urged to take precautions to avoid tick bites and to familiarize themselves with the symptoms of this easily treated but dangerous disease.

One of the best ways to learn how to find and identify birds is to join a local bird club or Audubon Society. These groups regularly conduct trips to productive birding areas and are normally led by experienced birders. By listening and watching carefully, the new birder can learn helpful tips. A number of events are popular with active birders: The Christmas Bird Count, held at the national level since 1900, is perhaps the favorite of most birders; other activities, such as the Summer Bird Count, Big Day competitions, and hawk-watching, are increasing in popularity.

The Connecticut Ornithological Association (COA) is the only statewide organization exclusively devoted to Connecticut birds and birding. The COA publishes a quarterly journal, the *Connecticut Warbler*, sponsors the Rare Records Committee, co-supports the Rare Bird Alert, and regularly sponsors activities and events of interest. It is entirely worthwhile for the casual birder to join the COA; it is essential for serious bird students. Observers are encouraged to report their sightings to the COA for recording in its journal.

Once involved in the fascinating sport and science of birding, the birder can look forward to endless challenge, fun, and satisfaction.

Birding Areas

Every town in Connecticut has areas where birds are certain to be found. Any field, wooded area, thicket, swamp, or pond is home to one or another species. There are, however, several celebrated birding areas that, over the years, have proved to be productive and have yielded a fair share of rarities.

BARN ISLAND FISH AND WILDLIFE AREA: Located off Route 1 in Stonington, this area offers a wide variety of habitats and is nearly 1,000 acres in size. Barn Island contains several large freshwater marshes, large areas of tidal marshes, upland woods and thickets, and a saltwater embayment.

Barn Island is most productive in spring and fall migration, although a visit during the summer months also can be rewarding. The abundant thickets along the entrance road and along the path to the impoundments usually yield good numbers of passerines. A scan of each of the four impoundments often produces an assortment of herons, egrets, and shorebirds. Least Bitterns have nested in the second and third impoundments in past years. Willet, Osprey, and Sharp-tailed and Seaside Sparrow nest in the tidal marsh located along the south side of the main path. Willow Flycatcher and White-eyed Vireo are very common here in summer. Also, this is one of the few areas in the state where Northern Bobwhite can still be found. Shorebirds are common in the impoundments in May and from late July through September. A spotting scope is helpful when looking for these birds.

In winter a scan over Long Island Sound and Wequoteqouck Cove often produces fair numbers of seaducks, loons, and grebes. The thickets along the park's paths also contain numerous sparrows.

Over the years many rarities have been discovered here that were observed by numbers of birders, including American Avocet, Curlew Sandpiper, American Oystercatcher, White Ibis, Orange-crowned Warbler, and Yellow-breasted Chat.

HAMMONASSET BEACH STATE PARK: Located in the town of Madison, this 900-acre park ranks among the most popular birding areas in Connecticut. Like Milford Point, this park is worth visiting at any time of the year. Only 30 minutes from New Haven, the park is easily reached by taking Exit 62 from Interstate 95. During the summer months the park is visited by thousands of people who sunbathe along the mile-long sandy beach. As with other coastal parks, the hordes often make summertime birding difficult except, of course, when foul weather keeps people away. The authors suggest that when visiting this park in summer you should plan to bird from dawn to about 10 A.M., before the crowds arrive. A scan of the large tidal marsh along the north side of the park road often yields Willet, Osprey, and both Sharp-tailed and Seaside Sparrow. If there has been a recent rain, the pools formed in the unpaved parking areas often attract migrant shorebirds during high tides in May and from late July through September.

In fall the park is often action-packed, particularly after the passage of a cold front. Hawks can be common when the winds are from the northwest, and once a group of birders were fortunate enough to photograph a Swainson's Hawk migrating by. Peregrine Falcon, Merlin, American Kestrel, Sharp-shinned Hawk, and Osprey are nearly guaranteed during a visit in late September and early October. A good vantage point to observe migrant hawks is Meig's Point, located at the eastern end of the park.

Other fall visitors include good numbers of passerines. A visit to "Willard's Island," located north of the Nature Center, often produces many migrant sparrows, warblers, and flycatchers. The thickets around the old orchard provide abundant food and cover and should be carefully searched. Western Kingbird, Clay-colored Sparrow, and other rarities have been observed here. Once the authors were viewing a White-crowned Sparrow at this location only to have a Sharp-shinned Hawk swoop upon the sparrow before our eyes. The sparrow was lucky—that time.

In winter, a visit to Meig's Point normally produces fair numbers of ducks and gulls. A spotting scope is helpful to detect offshore grebes, loons, mergansers, and goldeneye. Stops along the beach are worthwhile for good views of seaducks and gulls. The cedars along the park entrance road and rotary should be checked for owls; at least five species have been found here over the year. Be sure not to disturb the roosting birds by making noise or creating commotion. Also, owls are adversely affected by camera flashes.

The birding at the park is also very good during the spring. The nesting birds are in full song, and careful approach to the marsh edge usually produces a Clapper Rail.

Over the years the park has yielded several rarities that lingered long enough to enable views by many birders. Such finds include Upland Sandpiper, Baird's Sandpiper, Buff-breasted Sandpiper, Mew Gull, Barn Owl, and Northern Wheatear.

NEW HAVEN HARBOR: Located immediately adjacent to Interstate 95 in downtown New Haven, the harbor is one of the best shorebird spots in the state, albeit one of the noisiest. The acres of mudflats exposed at low tide during May and from late July through September often produce numbers of shorebirds unmatched in the state. The sewage treatment plant at the west end of the mudflat attracts large numbers of gulls, particularly from November through March. A scan of the harbor often yields numbers of seaducks, cormorants, loons, and grebes.

Easily reached from exit 46 of Interstate 95, the harbor is readily birded by parking along Frontage Road in the designated areas. The authors do not recommend birding this area alone.

A trip to nearby Lighthouse Point Park is highly encouraged, particularly during the fall months. Located off exit 50 of Interstate 95, on Lighthouse Road, the park is one of the best hawk-watching locations in Connecticut. The spot is staffed daily (weather permitting) by volunteers, from August through October, and impressive numbers of hawks migrate directly overhead in close view. The weedy thickets located east of the main parking area are extremely productive during peak migration days in fall and, to a lesser degree, in spring.

Needless to say, New Haven harbor and Lighthouse Point have produced a large list of rarities over the years. The state's only record of Spotted Redshank was collected here, and a Franklin's Gull was photographed here for the only corroborated state record. Other rarities include Eared Grebe, Western Grebe, Gyrfalcon, Burrowing Owl, Barrow's Goldeneye, Marbled Godwit, Curlew Sandpiper, Little Gull, Common Black-headed Gull, and Black-legged Kittiwake.

MILFORD POINT: Perhaps the most popular birding spot in Connecticut, Milford Point contains a variety of habitats, ranging from upland thickets to sandy beach to tidal marsh. The Milford Point Sanctuary, recently leased to the Connecticut Audubon Society, is located at the end of Seaview Avenue in Milford. The grounds around the sanctuary buildings contain thickets and deciduous woods that often yield migrant passerines in spring and fall. A review of the book of sightings contained in the shelter will tell of current sightings and other birding information.

From May through September the beach area at Milford Point is the site of a Least Tern colony, and Piping Plovers also nest in the vicinity. The shoreline and mudflats are among the most productive in the state for migrant shorebirds in May and from late July through September. In winter the area is noted for its concentrations of wintering gulls and ducks, and the offshore sandbars occasionally sport a Snowy Owl or two.

The extreme western end of Milford Point, long slated for condominium development, was recently acquired by the federal government and is now part of the Stuart B. McKinney National Wildlife Refuge. In summer the view from the refuge across the large tidal marshes often yields numerous ducks, shorebirds, and terns. In winter the large marsh teems with bird activity and at least once supported the culinary needs of a Gyrfalcon for a period of weeks.

Over the years many rarities have been found at Milford Point. Those enjoyed by many observers include King and Common Eider, Lesser Golden Plover, American Oystercatcher, Whimbrel, Marbled Godwit, Curlew Sandpiper, Buff-breasted Sandpiper, Black Tern, Western Kingbird, and Loggerhead Shrike.

AUDUBON CENTER OF GREENWICH: Situated in the southwestern corner of the state, the Center contains a variety of upland and freshwater habitats. It is located in Greenwich at the intersection of John Street and Riversville Road and is easily reached by either the Merritt Parkway or Interstate 95. The Center is run by the National Audubon Society, and the sanctuary headquarters has a bookstore, an interpretive area, a showroom, and a bird-feeding station.

The birding at the Center can be rewarding at any time of year, but it is particularly spectacular during spring and fall migration, when large numbers of passerines rest in the thickets and woods. During the summer a number of nesting specialties can be found: Louisiana Waterthrush nests along the Byram River and Mead Lake; Worm-eating Warbler nests on steep hillsides; Eastern Bluebird nests in boxes in the western field; Broad-winged and Red-tailed Hawks nest in the dense deciduous woods; and Red-bellied Woodpeckers are common.

Of special interest here is the Quaker Ridge Hawk Watch site, staffed by the Greenwich Audubon Society from August through October. One of the best hawk-watch locations in the state, the Ridge is in the path of thousands of migrant hawks. On peak migration days in mid- and late September it is not unusual to see several thousand Broad-winged Hawks per day. Recently, more than 30,000 were seen on a single day! Several other species of hawks are regularly counted here, including Sharp-shinned Hawk, Cooper's Hawk, Osprey, American Kestrel, Northern Harrier, Red-tailed Hawk, and Turkey Vulture. Rarities include Peregrine Falcon, Merlin, both Bald and Golden Eagle, and Northern Goshawk.

A visit to the nearby Fairchild Wildflower Garden, also run by the National Audubon Society, is encouraged. Located about a half mile south of the Center on North Porchuck Road, its wet thickets and wooded hillsides are very productive during migration, and Worm-eating Warbler, American Redstart, and Black and White Warbler all nest during the summer. Unfortunately, much of the Wildflower Garden has reverted to deciduous growth and is less viable as a birding spot than in former years, when the area was open fields and open water marsh. The days of nesting Henslow's Sparrow and Yellow-breasted Chat are long gone from this location.

The Center and Wildflower Garden have produced some outstanding rarities over the years. Perhaps the cream of the crop was a Black-backed Woodpecker that frequented the apple orchard near the sanctuary headquarters for several weeks and the Yellow-throated Warbler that stayed for two days near Discovery Pond. Both birds, fortunately, were viewed and enjoyed by many birders. Other rarities include Prothonotary Warbler, Cerulean Warbler, Kentucky Warbler, Summer Tanager, Blue Grosbreak, and American Bittern.

WHITE MEMORIAL FOUNDATION: Located mainly in the town of Litchfield in the northwestern part of the state, this 4,000-acre preserve includes upland fields, pastures, orchards, and woodland, as well as numerous streams and wetlands. The entrance to the preserve is on Route 202 about 2 miles southwest of the Litchfield village green. A visit to the museum is worthwhile: interesting displays, maps, and interpretive information are available.

White Memorial Foundation is a favorite stop for birders. The preserve is very productive during spring and fall migration, and a number of specialties nest during the summer months. Following maps available at the Museum is advised. In May and June a search of Laurel Hill and Catlin Woods can produce at least 10 species of nesting warblers, including Black-throated Blue, Nashville, Blue-winged, Pine, Yellow, Blackburnian, Chestnut-sided, American Redstart, Common Yellowthroat, Black-throated Green, and Ovenbird. Catlin Woods usually yields a Barred Owl or two, even during daylight hours if in response to a loud "who-cooks-for-you-all." A stop at Little Pond during the nesting season can yield Virginia Rail, Swamp Sparrow, and Willow and Alder Flycatcher.

OTHER AREAS: There are many good birding spots in Connecticut despite the rampant loss of upland and wetland habitat throughout the state. The following list is far from complete but is at least an offering of what is available.

South Windsor: Station 43, on the east side of the Connecticut River on Vibert Road (west side of Main Street), contains large freshwater marshes and an assortment of nesting birds. Best birding is in May, June, September, and October.

Ashford: For Boston Hollow, take Center Turnpike east from Westford Village a half mile and bear left (north) onto a dirt road. Best birding is in May and June. Nesting species include Acadian and Least Flycatcher, Red-breasted Nuthatch, White-throated Sparrow, both waterthrushes, Hermit Thrush, and other "northern" species.

East Haddam: Devil's Hopyard State Park, off Route 82, has best birding during May and June. Nesting Cerulean Warbler, Black-throated Green Warbler, and Acadian Flycatcher are specialties of this area.

Norwalk: Norwalk Islands is part of the Stuart B. Mckinney National Wildlife Refuge. An appointment needed to enter upon the islands; call 203-579-5617 for reservations. The islands contain the state's largest heron rookery.

Greenwich: Greenwich Point Park, open to the public from about November 1 to April 1, is located at west end of Shore Road off exit 5 of Interstate 95. It is an excellent spot for wintering seaducks, loons, grebes, owls, and passerines. Check thickets for sparrows and finches.

New Haven: East Rock Park is off Whitney Avenue on East Rock Road; best birding in May and June for migrant passerines.

Westport: Sherwood Island State Park, off exit 18 of Interstate 95, offers excellent winter habitat for seaducks, loons, and grebes. Large pines often contain roosting owls. Rarities here include Sandhill Crane and Eared Grebe. Look over large gravel parking lot for longspurs and larks.

Stratford: For Long Beach, use exit 30 of Interstate 95, onto Lordship Blvd, east to Oak Bluff Avenue and south to parking lot. It has excellent views of the remaining portions of Great Meadows tidal marsh; best birding May, June, and August through December. Nesting Piping Plovers and Least Terns, migrant shorebirds, and wintering seaducks, loons, and grebes are major attractions.

Sharon: Miles Sanctuary, on West Cornwall Road, west from Route 7 about 2.5 miles, is a series of ponds and wetlands that support a variety of nesting species, including Turkey, Barred Owl, Golden-winged Warbler, and an occasional Hooded Merganser. The best birding is in May and June.

Checklist of Connecticut Birds

This checklist includes all species that have been verified in Connecticut by specimen or photographic evidence or have sufficient documentation to be included as a hypothetical species. Introduced species that have established stable and sustained populations are also included.

The following designations are used in this list:

Hypothetical (Hy)—no photo or specimen evidence is known but the species has been adequately documented in the historical literature or sightings are of individuals of questionable origin.

Extirpated or Extinct (Ex)—has been extirpated from the state or is extinct.

	STATE LIST		OTHER LISTS			
COMMON NAME	**Date**	**Location**	**Town**	**Yard**		
Red-throated Loon						
Common Loon						
Pied-billed Grebe						
Horned Grebe						
Red-necked Grebe						
Eared Grebe						
Western Grebe						

COMMON NAME	STATE LIST		OTHER LISTS			
	Date	Location	Town	Yard		
Northern Fulmar						
Black-capped Petrel						
Cory's Shearwater						
Greater Shearwater						
Manx Shearwater (Hy)						
Wilson's Storm-Petrel						
Leach's Storm-Petrel						
White-faced Storm-Petrel						
Northern Gannet						
American White Pelican						
Brown Pelican						
Great Cormorant						
Double-crested Cormorant						
Magnificent Frigatebird						
American Bittern						
Least Bittern						
Great Blue Heron						
Great Egret						
Snowy Egret						
Little Blue Heron						
Tricolored Heron						
Cattle Egret						
Green-backed Heron						

COMMON NAME	STATE LIST		OTHER LISTS			
	Date	Location	Town	Yard	_____	_____
Black-crowned Night-Heron	____	_____	_____	_____	_____	_____
Yellow-crowned Night-Heron	____	_____	_____	_____	_____	_____
Glossy Ibis	____	_____	_____	_____	_____	_____
White Ibis	____	_____	_____	_____	_____	_____
Wood Stork	____	_____	_____	_____	_____	_____
Fulvous Whistling-Duck	____	_____	_____	_____	_____	_____
Tundra Swan	____	_____	_____	_____	_____	_____
Mute Swan	____	_____	_____	_____	_____	_____
Greater White-fronted Goose	____	_____	_____	_____	_____	_____
Snow Goose	____	_____	_____	_____	_____	_____
Brant	____	_____	_____	_____	_____	_____
Barnacle Goose (Hy)	____	_____	_____	_____	_____	_____
Canada Goose	____	_____	_____	_____	_____	_____
Wood Duck	____	_____	_____	_____	_____	_____
Green-winged Teal	____	_____	_____	_____	_____	_____
American Black Duck	____	_____	_____	_____	_____	_____
Mallard	____	_____	_____	_____	_____	_____
Northern Pintail	____	_____	_____	_____	_____	_____
Blue-winged Teal	____	_____	_____	_____	_____	_____
Northern Shoveler	____	_____	_____	_____	_____	_____
Gadwall	____	_____	_____	_____	_____	_____
Eurasian Wigeon	____	_____	_____	_____	_____	_____
American Wigeon	____	_____	_____	_____	_____	_____

COMMON NAME	STATE LIST		OTHER LISTS			
	Date	Location	Town	Yard		
Canvasback	___	___	___	___	___	___
Redhead	___	___	___	___	___	___
Ring-necked Duck	___					___
Tufted Duck (Hy)	___	___	___	___	___	___
Greater Scaup	___	___	___	___	___	___
Lesser Scaup	___	___	___	___	___	___
Common Eider	___	___	___	___	___	___
King Eider	___	___	___	___	___	___
Labrador Duck (Ex)	___	___	___	___	___	___
Harlequin Duck	___	___	___	___	___	___
Oldsquaw	___	___	___	___	___	___
Black Scoter	___	___	___	___	___	___
Surf Scoter	___	___	___	___	___	___
White-winged Scoter	___	___	___	___	___	___
Common Goldeneye	___	___	___	___	___	___
Barrow's Goldeneye	___	___	___	___	___	___
Bufflehead	___	___	___	___	___	___
Hooded Merganser	___	___	___	___	___	___
Common Merganser	___	___	___	___	___	___
Red-breasted Merganser	___	___	___	___	___	___
Ruddy Duck	___	___	___	___	___	___
Black Vulture	___	___	___	___	___	___
Turkey Vulture	___	___	___	___	___	___
Osprey	___	___	___	___	___	___

COMMON NAME	STATE LIST		OTHER LISTS			
	Date	Location	Town	Yard		
American Swallow-tailed Kite						
Bald Eagle						
Northern Harrier						
Sharp-shinned Hawk						
Cooper's Hawk						
Northern Goshawk						
Red-shouldered Hawk						
Broad-winged Hawk						
Swainson's Hawk						
Red-tailed Hawk						
Rough-legged Hawk						
Golden Eagle						
American Kestrel						
Merlin						
Peregrine Falcon						
Gyrfalcon						
Gray Partridge (Ex)						
Ring-necked Pheasant						
Ruffed Grouse						
Greater Prairie Chicken (Heath Hen) (Ex)						
Wild Turkey						
Northern Bobwhite						
Yellow Rail						
Black Rail						

COMMON NAME	STATE LIST		OTHER LISTS			
	Date	Location	Town	Yard		
Corn Crake						
Clapper Rail						
King Rail						
Virginia Rail						
Sora						
Purple Gallinule						
Common Moorhen						
American Coot						
Sandhill Crane						
Black-bellied Plover						
Lesser Golden Plover						
Wilson's Plover						
Semipalmated Plover						
Piping Plover						
Killdeer						
American Oystercatcher						
Black-necked Stilt						
American Avocet						
Greater Yellowlegs						
Lesser Yellowlegs						
Spotted Redshank						
Solitary Sandpiper						
Willet						
Spotted Sandpiper						
Upland Sandpiper						

COMMON NAME	STATE LIST		OTHER LISTS			
	Date	Location	Town	Yard		
Eskimo Curlew						
Whimbrel						
Long-billed Curlew						
Hudsonian Godwit						
Marbled Godwit						
Ruddy Turnstone						
Red Knot						
Sanderling						
Semipalmated Sandpiper						
Western Sandpiper						
Least Sandpiper						
White-rumped Sandpiper						
Baird's Sandpiper						
Pectoral Sandpiper						
Sharp-tailed Sandpiper						
Purple Sandpiper						
Dunlin						
Curlew Sandpiper						
Stilt Sandpiper						
Buff-breasted Sandpiper						
Ruff						
Short-billed Dowitcher						
Long-billed Dowitcher						

COMMON NAME	STATE LIST		OTHER LISTS			
	Date	Location	Town	Yard		
Common Snipe						
American Woodcock						
Wilson's Phalarope						
Red-necked Phalarope						
Red Phalarope						
Parasitic Jaeger						
Long-tailed Jaeger						
Laughing Gull						
Franklin's Gull						
Little Gull						
Common Black-headed Gull						
Bonaparte's Gull						
Mew Gull (Hy)						
Ring-billed Gull						
Herring Gull						
Iceland Gull						
Lesser Black-backed Gull						
Glaucous Gull						
Great Black-backed Gull						
Black-legged Kittiwake						
Ross' Gull						
Caspian Tern						
Royal Tern						

COMMON NAME	STATE LIST		OTHER LISTS			
	Date	Location	Town	Yard		
Roseate Tern						
Common Tern						
Arctic Tern (Hy)						
Forster's Tern						
Least Tern						
Sooty Tern						
Black Tern						
Black Skimmer						
Dovekie						
Thick-billed Murre						
Razorbill (Hy)						
Black Guillemot						
Atlantic Puffin						
Rock Dove						
Band-tailed Pigeon (Hy)						
White-winged Dove (Hy)						
Mourning Dove						
Passenger Pigeon (Ex)						
Black-billed Cuckoo						
Yellow-billed Cuckoo						
Barn Owl						
Eastern Screech Owl						
Great Horned Owl						
Snowy Owl						

COMMON NAME	STATE LIST		OTHER LISTS			
	Date	Location	Town	Yard	_____	_____
Northern Hawk Owl	____	_____	____	____	____	____
Burrowing Owl	____	_____	____	____	____	____
Barred Owl	____	_____	____	____	____	____
Great Gray Owl	____	_____	____	____	____	____
Long-eared Owl	____	_____	____	____	____	____
Short-eared Owl	____	_____	____	____	____	____
Boreal Owl	____	_____	____	____	____	____
Northern Saw-whet Owl	____	_____	____	____	____	____
Common Nighthawk	____	_____	____	____	____	____
Chuck-will's-widow	____	_____	____	____	____	____
Whip-poor-will	____	_____	____	____	____	____
Chimney Swift	____	_____	____	____	____	____
Ruby-throated Hummingbird	____	_____	____	____	____	____
Belted Kingfisher	____	_____	____	____	____	____
Red-headed Woodpecker	____	_____	____	____	____	____
Red-bellied Woodpecker	____	_____	____	____	____	____
Yellow-bellied Sapsucker	____	_____	____	____	____	____
Downy Woodpecker	____	_____	____	____	____	____
Hairy Woodpecker	____	_____	____	____	____	____
Black-backed Woodpecker	____	_____	____	____	____	____
Northern Flicker	____	_____	____	____	____	____
Pileated Woodpecker	____	_____	____	____	____	____

COMMON NAME	STATE LIST		OTHER LISTS			
	Date	Location	Town	Yard		
Olive-sided Flycatcher						
Eastern Wood-Pewee						
Yellow-bellied Flycatcher						
Acadian Flycatcher						
Alder Flycatcher						
Willow Flycatcher						
Least Flycatcher						
Eastern Phoebe						
Say's Phoebe						
Great Crested Flycatcher						
Western Kingbird						
Eastern Kingbird						
Gray Kingbird						
Scissor-tailed Flycatcher						
Horned Lark						
Purple Martin						
Tree Swallow						
Northern Rough-winged Swallow						
Bank Swallow						
Cliff Swallow						
Barn Swallow						
Gray Jay (Hy)						
Blue Jay						

COMMON NAME	STATE LIST		OTHER LISTS			
	Date	Location	Town	Yard		
Eurasian Jackdaw	___	_____	_____	_____	_____	_____
American Crow	___	_____	_____	_____	_____	_____
Fish Crow				_____	__	
Common Raven	___	_____	_____	_____	_____	_____
Black-capped Chickadee	___	_____	_____	_____	_____	_____
Boreal Chickadee	___	_____	_____	_____	_____	_____
Tufted Titmouse	___	_____	_____	_____	_____	_____
Red-breasted Nuthatch	___	_____	_____	_____	_____	_____
White-breasted Nuthatch	___	_____	_____	_____	_____	_____
Brown Creeper	___	_____	_____	_____	_____	_____
Carolina Wren	___	_____	_____	_____	_____	_____
House Wren	___	_____	_____	_____	_____	_____
Winter Wren	___	_____	_____	_____	_____	_____
Sedge Wren	___	_____	_____	_____	_____	_____
Marsh Wren	___	_____	_____	_____	_____	_____
Golden-crowned Kinglet	___	_____	_____	_____	_____	_____
Ruby-crowned Kinglet	___	_____	_____	_____	_____	_____
Blue-gray Gnatcatcher	___	_____	_____	_____	_____	_____
Northern Wheatear	___	_____	_____	_____	_____	_____
Eastern Bluebird	___	_____	_____	_____	_____	_____
Townsend's Solitaire (Hy)	___	_____	_____	_____	_____	_____
Veery	___	_____	_____	_____	_____	_____

COMMON NAME	STATE LIST		OTHER LISTS			
	Date	Location	Town	Yard		
Gray-cheeked Thrush	___	___	___	___	___	___
Swainson's Thrush	___	___	___	___	___	___
Hermit Thrush	___	___	___	___	___	___
Wood Thrush	___	___	___	___	___	___
Fieldfare (Hy)	___	___	___	___	___	___
American Robin	___	___	___	___	___	___
Varied Thrush	___	___	___	___	___	___
Gray Catbird	___	___	___	___	___	___
Northern Mockingbird	___	___	___	___	___	___
Brown Thrasher	___	___	___	___	___	___
American Pipit	___	___	___	___	___	___
Bohemian Waxwing	___	___	___	___	___	___
Cedar Waxwing	___	___	___	___	___	___
Northern Shrike	___	___	___	___	___	___
Loggerhead Shrike	___	___	___	___	___	___
European Starling	___	___	___	___	___	___
White-eyed Vireo	___	___	___	___	___	___
Solitary Vireo	___	___	___	___	___	___
Yellow-throated Vireo	___	___	___	___	___	___
Warbling Vireo	___	___	___	___	___	___
Philadelphia Vireo	___	___	___	___	___	___
Red-eyed Vireo	___	___	___	___	___	___
Blue-winged Warbler	___	___	___	___	___	___
Golden-winged Warbler	___	___	___	___	___	___

COMMON NAME	STATE LIST		OTHER LISTS			
	Date	Location	Town	Yard		
Tennessee Warbler						
Orange-crowned Warbler						
Nashville Warbler						
Northern Parula						
Yellow Warbler						
Chestnut-sided Warbler						
Magnolia Warbler						
Cape May Warbler						
Black-throated Blue Warbler						
Yellow-rumped Warbler						
Black-throated Gray Warbler (Hy)						
Hermit Warbler (Hy)						
Black-throated Green Warbler						
Blackburnian Warbler						
Yellow-throated Warbler						
Pine Warbler						
Prairie Warbler						
Palm Warbler						
Bay-breasted Warbler						
Blackpoll Warbler						
Cerulean Warbler						

COMMON NAME	STATE LIST		OTHER LISTS			
	Date	Location	Town	Yard		
Black-and-White Warbler						
American Redstart						
Prothonotary Warbler						
Worm-eating Warbler						
Ovenbird						
Northern Waterthrush						
Louisiana Waterthrush						
Kentucky Warbler						
Connecticut Warbler						
Mourning Warbler						
Common Yellowthroat						
Hooded Warbler						
Wilson's Warbler						
Canada Warbler						
Yellow-breasted Chat						
Summer Tanager						
Scarlet Tanager						
Western Tanager						
Northern Cardinal						
Rose-breasted Grosbeak						
Black-headed Grosbeak						
Blue Grosbeak						
Indigo Bunting						

COMMON NAME	STATE LIST Date	Location	OTHER LISTS Town	Yard		
Painted Bunting						
Dickcissel						
Rufous-sided Towhee						
American Tree Sparrow						
Chipping Sparrow						
Clay-colored Sparrow						
Field Sparrow						
Vesper Sparrow						
Lark Sparrow						
Lark Bunting						
Savannah Sparrow						
Grasshopper Sparrow						
Henslow's Sparrow						
Le Conte's Sparrow						
Sharp-tailed Sparrow						
Seaside Sparrow						
Fox Sparrow						
Song Sparrow						
Lincoln's Sparrow						
Swamp Sparrow						
White-throated Sparrow						
White-crowned Sparrow						
Harris' Sparrow						

COMMON NAME	STATE LIST		OTHER LISTS			
	Date	Location	Town	Yard		
Dark-eyed Junco						
Lapland Longspur						
Smith's Longspur						
Chestnut-collared Longspur						
Snow Bunting						
Bobolink						
Red-winged Blackbird						
Eastern Meadowlark						
Yellow-headed Blackbird						
Rusty Blackbird						
Boat-tailed Grackle						
Common Grackle						
Brown-headed Cowbird						
Orchard Oriole						
Northern Oriole						
Pine Grosbeak						
Purple Finch						
House Finch						
Red Crossbill						
White-winged Crossbill						
Common Redpoll						
Hoary Redpoll						
Pine Siskin						

COMMON NAME	STATE LIST		OTHER LISTS			
	Date	Location	Town	Yard		
American Goldfinch	——	————	————	————	————	————
Evening Grosbeak	——	————	————	————	————	————
House Sparrow	——	————	————	————	————	————
———————	—	————	————	————	————	————
———————	—	————	————	————	————	————
———————	—	————	————	————	————	————
———————	—	————	————	————	————	————
———————	—	————	————	————	————	————
———————	—	————	————	————	————	————

Bibliography

This bibliography includes material through December 1988.

American Birds. Seasonal journal of the birds of the Americas (1970–1988). New York: National Audubon Society.

American Ornithologists' Union Check-list Committee. 1957. *Check-list of North American Birds.* (5th ed.) Lawrence, KS: American Ornithologists' Union.

——— 1983. *Check-list of North American Birds.* (6th ed.) Lawrence, KS: American Ornithologists' Union.

Anderson, J. F., and W. Glowa. 1985. Diazinon poisoning of Brown-headed Cowbirds. *Journal of Field Ornithology* 56:407–408.

Anderson, Ruth O. M. 1975. *From Yankees to Americans: Connecticut 1865–1914.* Chester, CT: Pequot Press.

Andrle, Robert F., and Janet H. Carroll. 1988. *The atlas of breeding birds in New York State.* Ithaca, NY: Cornell University Press.

Arbib, Robert S. 1963. The Common Loon in New York State. *Kingbird* 13:132–140.

Askins, R. A., M. J. Philbrick, and D. S. Sugeno. 1987. Relationship between regional abundance of forest and the composition of forest bird communities. *Biological Conservation* 39:129–152.

Audubon Field Notes. Journal of the birds of North America (1946–1970). New York: National Audubon Society.

Audubon, John J. 1870. *Birds of America.* 8 vols. New York: George Lockwood & Son.

Averill, C. K. Jr. 1892. *Birds found in the vicinity of Bridgeport, Connecticut.* Bridgeport, CT: Bridgeport Scientific Society.

Bagg, Aaron C., and Samuel A. Eliot. 1937. *The birds of the Connecticut River valley.* Northampton, MA: The Hampshire Bookshop.

Bailey, Wallace. 1955. *Birds in Massachusetts.* South Lancaster, MA: The College Press.

1968. *Birds of the Cape Cod National Seashore.* South Wellfleet, MA: Eastern National Park and Monument Association.

Barkman, Leon. c. 1986. *Checklist of Connecticut birds.* Newtown, CT: Author.

Barrows, Harlan. 1962. *Lectures on the Historical Geography of the United States.* Edited by William Koelsch. Chicago: University of Chicago, Department of Geography. Research Paper No. 77.

Beddall, B. G. 1963. Range expansion of the Cardinal and other birds in the northeastern states. *Wilson Bulletin* 75:140–156.

Bell, Michael. 1985. *The Face of Connecticut.* Hartford, CT: Geological and Natural History Survey of Connecticut.

Bellrose, F. C. 1976. *Ducks, geese and swans of North America.* Harrisburg, PA: Stackpole Books.

Bent, Arthur C. 1919. *Life histories of North American diving birds.* Washington, DC: U.S. National Museum Bulletin No. 107.

1921. *Life histories of North American gulls and terns.* Washington, DC: U.S. National Musuem Bulletin No. 113.

1922. *Life histories of North American petrels and pelicans and their allies.* Washington, DC: U.S. National Museum Bulletin No. 121.

1923. *Life histories of North American wildfowl.* Washington, DC: U.S. National Museum Bulletin No. 126, Part 1.

1925. *Life histories of North American wildfowl.* Washington, DC: U.S. National Museum Bulletin No. 130, Part 2.

1926. *Life histories of North American marsh birds.* Washington, DC: U.S. National Museum Bulletin No. 135.

1927. *Life histories of North American shore birds.* Washington, DC: U.S. National Museum Bulletin No. 142, Part 1.

1929. *Life histories of North American shore birds.* Washington, DC: U.S. National Museum Bulletin No. 146, Part 2.

1932. *Life histories of North American gallinaceous birds.* Washington, DC: U.S. National Museum Bulletin No. 162.

1937. *Life histories of North American birds of prey.* Washington, DC: U.S. National Museum Bulletin No. 167, Part 1.

1938. *Life histories of North American birds of prey.* Washington, DC: U.S. National Museum Bulletin No. 170, Part 2.

1939. *Life histories of North American woodpeckers.* Washington, DC: U.S. National Museum Bulletin No. 174.

1940. *Life histories of North American cuckoos, goatsuckers, hummingbirds, and their allies.* Washington, DC: U.S. National Museum Bulletin No. 176.

1942. *Life histories of North American flycatchers, larks, swallows, and their allies.* Washington, DC: U.S. National Museum Bulletin No. 179.

1946. *Life histories of North American jays, crows and titmice.* Washington, DC: U.S. National Museum Bulletin No. 191.

1948. *Life histories of North American nuthatches, wrens, thrashers, and their allies.* Washington, DC: U.S. National Museum Bulletin No. 195.

1949. *Life histories of North American thrushes, kinglets and their allies.* Washington, DC: U.S. National Museum Bulletin No. 196.

1950. *Life histories of North American wagtails, shrikes, vireos, and their allies.* Washington, DC: U.S. National Museum Bulletin No. 197.

1953. *Life histories of North American wood warblers.* Washington, DC: U.S. National Museum Bulletin No. 203.

1958. *Life histories of North American blackbirds, orioles, tanagers, and their allies.* Washington, DC: U.S. National Museum Bulletin No. 211.

Bent, Arthur C. et al. comps. 1968. *Life histories of North American cardinals, grosbeaks, buntings, towhees, finches, sparrows, and their allies.* Edited by O. L. Austin, Jr. Washington, DC: U.S. National Museum Bulletin No. 211.

Bergstrom, E. Alexander. c. 1960. Unpublished partial draft manuscript on Connecticut birds. Loons through Turkey Vulture. On file at Connecticut State Museum of Natural History, Storrs.

Bertin, R. I. 1977. Breeding habitats of the Wood Thrush and Veery. *Condor* 79:303–311.

Bevier, Louis, et al. In preparation. Breeding Bird Atlas of Connecticut.

Braun, E. Lucy. 1964. *Deciduous forest of eastern North America.* New York and London: Hafner.

Bromley, S. W. 1935. The original forest types of southern New England. *Ecology Monographs,* 5:61–89.

Brumbach, Joseph J. 1965. *The climate of Connecticut.* Hartford, CT: Connecticut Geological and Natural History Survey Bulletin No. 99.

Buckley, F. G., M. Gochfeld, and P. A. Buckley. 1978. Breeding Laughing Gulls return to Long Island. *Kingbird* 28:203.

Bull, John. 1964. *Birds of the New York area.* New York: Dover Publications.

1974. *Birds of New York State.* Reissued 1985, including 1976 supplement. Ithaca, NY: Cornell University Press.

Bulmer, Walter. 1970. First specimens of Chestnut-collared Longspur and Little Gull from Connecticut. *Wilson Bulletin,* 82:226–227.

Clark, George A., Jr. 1984. Centers of learning. *American Birds* 38:7.

1986. Highlights of Connecticut ornithology, 1780–1930. *Connecticut Warbler* 6:42–44.

Connecticut Board of Fisheries and Game. 1970. *Places to look for birds.* Hartford, CT: Connecticut Board of Fish and Game.

Connecticut Department of Environmental Protection. 1973 to present. *Connecticut environment: The citizens' bulletin of the Connecticut Department of Environmental Protection.* Hartford, CT: Author.

1977. *Long Island Sound: An atlas of natural resources.* Hartford, CT: Author.

Connecticut Natural Diversity Data Base. 1985. *Connecticut's species of special concern animal list.* Hartford, CT: Connecticut Geological and Natural History Survey, Department of Environmental Protection.

Connecticut Ornithological Association Records. 1981–1987. *A list of published and unpublished avian observations in Connecticut.* Fairfield, CT: COA.

Connecticut Warbler. 1981–1988. *A journal of Connecticut ornithology.* Fairfield, CT: The Connecticut Ornithological Association.

Connors, P. G. 1983. Taxonomy, distribution, and evolution of golden plovers (*Pluvialis dominica* and *P. fulva*). *Auk* 100:607–620.

Conover, M. R., and G. G. Chasko. 1985. Nuisance Canada Goose problems in the eastern United States. *Wildlife Society Bulletin* 13:228–233.

Converse, Kathryn A. 1985. A study of resident nuisance Canada Geese in Connecticut and New York. *Dissertation Abstracts International* 46(03):717.

Conway, Robert A. 1979. *Field checklist of Rhode Island birds.* Providence, RI: Rhode Island Ornithological Club and Audubon Society of Rhode Island.

Craig, Robert J. 1970. *The rare vertebrates of Connecticut.* Storrs, CT. USDA Soil Conservation Service.

1985. Comparative habitat use by Louisiana and Northern Waterthrushes. *Wilson Bulletin* 97:347–355.

Craig, Robert J., E. S. Mitchell, and J. E. Mitchell. 1988. Time and energy budgets of Bald Eagles wintering along the Connecticut River. *Journal of Field Ornithology* 59:22–32.

Cronon, William. 1983. *Changes in the land: Indians, colonists, and the ecology of New England.* New York: Hill and Wang.

Cruickshank, Allan D. 1942. Birds around New York City. New York: American Museum of Natural History.

Currie, Neil. 1971–1987. *New England Hawk Watch Annual Report.* Sharon, CT: Connecticut Audubon Council.

Dater, Carroll. 1968. *Status survey of rails and wading birds in Connecticut.* Harwington, CT: Connecticut Audubon Council.

Davis, Thomas H. 1982. The 1981 fall shorebird season at Jamaica Bay wildlife refuge. *Kingbird* 32:85–96.

DeGraaf, R. M., G. M. Witman, J. W. Lanier, B. J. Hill, and J. M. Keniston. 1980. *Forest habitat for birds of the Northeast.* Washington, DC: U.S. Dept. of Agriculture, Forest Service.

Dinsmore, James J., T. H. Kent, D. Koenig, P. C. Peterson, and D. M. Roosa. 1984. *Iowa birds.* Ames, IA: Iowa State University Press.

Destler, Chester M. 1973. *Connecticut the Provision State.* Chester, CT: Pequot Press.

Dowhan, Joseph J., and Robert J. Craig. 1976. *Rare and endangered species of Connecticut and their habitats.* Hartford, CT: State Geological and Natural History Survey of Connecticut, Department of Environmental Protection.

Egler, Frank E., and William A. Niering. 1965. *Connecticut natural areas: 1. Yale Nature Preserve, New Haven.* Hartford, CT: Connecticut Geographic and Natural History Survey.

1966. *Connecticut natural areas: 2. Audubon Center of Greenwich.* Hartford, CT: Connecticut Geographic and Natural History Survey.

1967. *Connecticut natural areas: 3. McLean Game Refuge, Granby.* Hartford, CT: Connecticut Geographic and Natural History Survey.

Ellison, W. G. 1985. House Wren. In *The atlas of breeding birds of Vermont,* edited by S. B. Laughlin and D. P. Kibbe. Hanover, NH: University Press of New England.

Ermer, E. M. 1984. *The status of beaver management in New York: Report to the Annual Meeting of the New York Chapter of the Wildlife Society.* Utica, NY: New York Dept. of Environmental Conservation.

Erskine, A. J. 1988. The changing pattern of Brant migration in eastern North America. *Journal of Field Ornithology* 59:110–119.

Faccia, S. P., and H. I. Russack. 1984. Status of a population of Bald Eagles wintering in western Connecticut. *Raptor Research,* 18:77–78.

Forbush, Edward H. 1916. *A history of gamebirds, wildfowl, and shore birds of Massachusetts and adjacent states* (2nd ed.). Boston: Massachusetts State Board of Agriculture.

1925. *Birds of Massachusetts and other New England states,* Vol. 1. Boston: Massachusetts Department of Agriculture.

1927. *Birds of Massachusetts and other New England states,* Vol. 2. Boston: Massachusetts Department of Agriculture.

1929. *Birds of Massachusetts and other New England states,* Vol. 3. Boston: Massachusetts Department of Agriculture.

Frederickson, L. H., J. M. Anderson, F. M. Kozlik, and R. A. Ryder. 1977. American Coot. In *Management of migratory shore and upland game birds in North America,* edited by G. C. Sanderson. Washington, DC: International Association of Fish and Wildlife Agencies.

Gill, F. B. 1980. Historical aspects of hybridization of the Blue-winged and Golden-winged Warblers. *Auk* 97:1–18.

Gorski, Leon J. 1970. Banding the two songforms of Traill's Flycatcher. *Bird-Banding* 41:204–206.

Griscom, Ludlow. 1923. *Birds of the New York City region.* New York: American Museum of Natural History.

Griscom, Ludlow, and Dorothy E. Snyder. 1955. *The birds of Massachusetts, an annotated and revised checklist.* Salem, MA: Peabody Museum.

Guillette, Mary E. 1979. *American Indians in Connecticut.* Hartford, CT: Connecticut Indian Affairs Council.

Harrison, Peter. 1983. *Seabirds: An identification guide.* Boston: Houghton Mifflin.

Hartford Audubon Society. 1964. *Check list and records of the birds seen in the vicinity of Hartford, Connecticut.* Hartford, CT: Author.

Hartford Audubon Society Records. Unpublished records of the Hartford Bird Study Club. Hartford, CT.

Hayman, Peter, John Marchant, and Tony Prater. 1986. *Shorebirds: An identification guide to the waders of the world.* Boston: Houghton Mifflin.

Henninger, W. F. 1917. The diary of a New England ornithologist. *Wilson Bulletin* 29:1–17.

Hill, Norman P. 1965. *The birds of Cape Cod, Massachusetts.* New York: William Morrow.

Hills, Charles F., III. c. 1978. *The birds of Fairfield County, Connecticut and vicinity.* Unpublished manuscript.

———. 1983. *Report on the status of Connecticut birds.* Unpublished manuscript.

Honeywill, Alfred W., Jr., F. F. Burr, P. L. Buttrick, D. B. Pangburn, A. A. Saunders, C. H. Pangburn. 1908. List of the birds of the New Haven region. *New Haven Bird Club Bulletin,* No. 1.

Howes, Paul G. 1928. Notes on the birds of Stamford, Connecticut and vicinity. *Oologist,* 45: 70–96.

Hughes, A. H., and M. S. Allen. 1976. *Connecticut place names.* Hartford, CT: Connecticut Historical Society.

Huntington, Charles E. 1952. Hybridization in the Purple Grackle, *Quiscalus quiscula. Systematic Zoology* 1:149–170.

Job, Herbert K. 1922. A list of birds observed in Litchfield County, Connecticut. Compiled through 1908 and contained in *The sport of bird study.* New York: Outing Publishing Co.

Jones, Clinton M. 1931. Field notes on Connecticut birds. *University of Iowa Studies in Natural History* 13(4).

Jorgensen, Neil. 1978. *Southern New England.* San Francisco: Sierra Club Books.

Josselyn, John. 1672. *New-Englands Rarities Discovered.* Reprinted 1972. Boston: Massachusetts Historical Society.

Kilham, L. 1983. Life history studies of Woodpeckers of eastern North America. Cambridge, MA: Nuttall Ornithological Club. No. 20.

Kortright, F. H. 1942. The ducks, geese and swans of North America. Harrisburg, PA: Stackpole Co./Wildlife Management Institute.

Kuerzi, John F., and Richard G. Kuerzi. 1934. Notes on the summer birds of western Litchfield County, Connecticut. *Proceedings of the Linnaean Society of New York* 43:1–13.

Kuslan, Louis I. 1978. Connecticut science, technology, and medicine in the era of the American revolution. Deep River, CT: The American Revolution Bicentennial Committee of Connecticut.

Linsley, Rev. James H. 1843a. A catalogue of the birds of Connecticut, arranged according to their natural families. *American Journal of Science and Arts,* 44:249–274.

———. 1843b. Additional notes on Connecticut birds. *American Journal of Science and Arts,* 46:51.

Loery, Gordon, and J. D. Nichols. 1985. Dynamics of a Black-capped Chickadee population, 1958–1983. *Ecology* 66:1195–1203.

Loery, Gordon, K. H. Pollack, J. D. Nichols, and J. E. Hinds. 1987. Age-specificity of Black-capped Chickadee survival rates: Analysis of capture-recapture data. *Ecology* 68:1038–1044.

Ludlum, David. 1976. *New England weather book.* Boston: Houghton Mifflin.

Lynch, P. J., and D. J. Smith. 1984. Census of Eastern Screech-Owls (*Otus asio*) in urban open space areas using tape-recorded song. *American Birds* 38:388–391.

Mackenzie, Locke. 1961. The birds of Guilford, Connecticut. New Haven, CT: Yale Peabody Museum of Natural History.

Main, Jackson T. 1977. Connecticut society in the era of the American revolution. Chester, CT: Pequot Press.

Manter, Jerauld A. 1975. The birds of Storrs, Connecticut and vicinity (2nd ed.). Storrs, CT: Parousia Press.

Massachusetts Audubon Society. 1916–present. *Bulletin of the Massachusetts Audubon Society.*

Mayr, Ernst, John Kuerzi, and Richard Kuerzi. 1937. Additional notes from Litchfield County, Conn. *Proceedings of the Linnaean Society of New York* 48:98.

Merk, Frederick. 1985. *History of the westward movement.* New York: Alfred A. Knopf.

Merriam, C. Hart. 1877. A review of the birds of Connecticut. *Transactions of the Connecticut Academy,* Vol. 4, 1877. New Haven, CT: The Connecticut Academy.

Mianus Field Notes. 1972–1987. A quarterly record of avian observations in the greater Greenwich–Stamford area. Thomas W. Burke, editor. Greenwich, CT: Greenwich Audubon Society.

Morris, Robert O. 1901. *The birds of Springfield (Massachusetts).* Springfield, MA: Henry R. Johnson.

Mulliken, E. 1938. Waterfowl, rail and shore birds commonly hunted for sport in Connecticut. Hartford, CT: Connecticut Fish and Game Department.

New Haven Bird Club. c. 1960–1970. *New Haven Bird Club Newsletter.*

Niering, William A. 1981. The role of fire management in altering ecosystems. *Proceedings of the Conference on Fire Regimes and Ecosystem Properties,* pp. 489–510. Honolulu, Hawaii.

Nuttall, Thomas. 1832. *A manual of ornithology of the United States and Canada.* Boston: Hilliard, Gray and Co.

The Oologist. c. 1883–1932. Birds, nests, eggs, taxidermy. Albion, NY.

Palmer, R. S. 1962. *Handbook of North American birds.* Vol. 1, *Loons through flamingos.* New Haven, CT: Yale University Press.

1976. *Handbook of North American birds.* Vol. 2, *Waterfowl* (pt. 1). New Haven, CT: Yale University Press.

Parkes, K. C. 1953. The Yellow-throated Warbler in New York. *Kingbird* 3:4–6.

Parker, Johnson. 1987. Changing paleoecological relationships during the late Pleistocene and Holocene in New England. *Bulletin of the Archaeology Society of Connecticut,* No. 50, 1987, pp. 1–16.

Pattee, O. H., M. R. Fuller, and T. E. Kaiser. 1985. Environmental contaminants in eastern Cooper's Hawk eggs. *Journal of Wildlife Management,* 49:1040–1044.

Peters, Harold S. 1965. Birds of the service-six area—southern Connecticut and northern Long Island. Bridgeport, CT: Author.

Peterson, Roger T. 1947. *A field guide to the birds: Eastern land and water birds.* New York: Houghton Mifflin.

1980. *A field guide to the birds: Eastern land and water birds.* New York: Houghton Mifflin.

Phillips, H. 1928. *Wild birds introduced or transplanted in North America.* Technical Bulletin No. 61. Washington, DC: U.S. Department of Agriculture.

Pink, E., and O. Waterman. 1965. *The birds of Dutchess County, 1933–1964.* Dutchess County, New York: Ralph T. Waterman Bird Club.

1980. *The birds of Dutchess County, 1964–1979.* Dutchess County, New York: Ralph T. Waterman Bird Club.

Poole, A., and Paul Spitzer. 1983. An Osprey revival. *Oceanus,* 26:49–54.

Poor, H. H. 1946. Breeding of the Herring Gull in Connecticut. *Proceedings of the Linnaean Society of New York,* 54–57:43–44.

Proctor, N. S. 1978. *25 birding areas in Connecticut.* Chester, CT: Pequot Press.

Record of New England Birds. 1945–1968. *The Bulletin of the Massachusetts Audubon Society.*

Reiger, John. 1975. *American sportsmen and the origins of conservation.* New York: Winchester Press.

Reynolds, R. 1985. *Report to the Atlantic Waterfowl Council: Technical Section Minutes.* Atlanta, GA: Atlantic Waterfowl Council.

Robbins, Chandler S., D. Bystrak, and P. H. Geissler. 1986. *The Breeding Bird Survey: Its first fifteen years, 1965–1979.* USFWS Resource Publication No. 157. Washington, DC: U.S. Fish and Wildlife Service.

Roth, David M., and Freeman Meyer. 1975. *Connecticut 1763–1818.* Chester, CT: Pequot Press.

Russell, Howard S. 1980. *Indian New England before the Mayflower.* Hanover, NH: University Press of New England.

1982. *A long deep furrow: Three centuries of farming in New England.* Hanover, NH: University Press of New England.

Sage, John H., Louis B. Bishop, and Walter P. Bliss. 1913. *The birds of Connecticut.* State Geological and Natural History Survey, Bulletin No. 20. Hartford, CT: State of Connecticut.

Samuels, Edward A. 1867. *Ornithology and oology of New England.* Boston: Nichols and Noyes.

———. 1883. *Northern and eastern birds.* New York: E. Worthington.

Saunders, Aretas A. 1950. Changes in status of Connecticut Birds. *Auk* 67:253–255.

———. 1959. Forty years of spring migration in southern Connecticut. *Wilson Bulletin* 71:208–217.

Schorger, A. W. 1955. *The passenger pigeon.* Madison, WI: University of Wisconsin Press.

Shipley, Donald. 1931. *Birds of Stamford, Connecticut.* Unpublished manuscript (through hawks), University of Connecticut.

Sibley, Fred. 1987. *Summary of Connecticut Bird Christmas Counts, 1977–1986.* Unpublished manuscript.

Siebenheller, N. 1981. *Breeding birds of Staten Island, 1881–1981.* New York: Institute of Arts and Sciences.

Smith, Dwight G., and Ray Gilbert. 1984. Eastern Screech-Owl home range and use of suburban habitats in southern Connecticut. *Journal of Field Ornithology,* 55:322–329.

Smith, Wilbur F. 1950. *Birds of Norwalk, Connecticut.* Unpublished annotated checklist with work journal, Bruce Museum, Greenwich, CT.

Stern, W. A. 1881. *New England bird life* (2nd ed.), Part 1. Boston: Lee and Shepard.

Stevens, George R., and Paul E. Waggoner. 1980. *A half century of natural transition in mixed hardwood forests.* Bulletin No. 783. New Haven, CT: Connecticut Agricultural Experiment Station.

Stone, W. B., and P. Gradoni. 1985. Recent poisonings of wild birds by diazinon and carbofuran. *Northeast Environmental Science* 4:160–164.

———. 1986. Poisoning of birds by cholinesterase inhibitor pesticides. In *Wildlife rehabilitation,* Vol. 5, edited by P. Beaver and D. J. Mackay, Coconut Creek, FL: D. J. Mackay.

Strohmeyer, D. L. 1977. Common Gallinule. In *Management of migratory shore and upland game birds in North America,* edited by G. C. Sanderson. Washington, DC: International Association of Fish and Wildlife Agencies.

Terres, John K. 1980. *The Audubon Society encyclopedia of North American birds.* New York: Alfred A. Knopf.

Thomson, Keith S., W. H. Weed III, A. G. Taruski, and D. E. Simanek. 1978. *Saltwater fishes of Connecticut.* Bulletin 105. Hartford, CT: Connecticut Department of Environmental Protection.

Trecker, Janice Law. 1975. *Preachers, rebels, and traders: Connecticut 1818 to 1865.* Chester, CT: Pequot Press.

Trowbridge, C. C. 1895. Hawk flights in Connecticut. *Auk* 12:259–270.

Van Camp, L. R., and C. J. Henny. 1975. *The Screech Owl: Its life history and population ecology in northern Ohio.* North American Fauna, No. 71. Washington, DC: USFWS.

Van Dusen, Albert E. 1961. *Connecticut.* New York, NY: Random House.

1975. *Puritans against the wilderness.* Chester, CT: Pequot Press.

Walsh, James P. 1978. Connecticut industry and the revolution. Chester, CT: Pequot Press.

Welch, B. 1987. *Hawks at my wingtip.* Thorndike, ME: North Country Press.

White Memorial Foundation. 1965. *A checklist of the birds of White Memorial Foundation.* Litchfield, CT: Author.

Wilson, Alexander. 1808–1814. *American ornithology or the natural history of the birds of the United States.* 9 vols. Philadelphia: Bradford and Inskeep.

1828. *American ornithology, or the natural history of the birds of the United States.* 3 vols. New York: Collins & Co.

Wood, William. 1634. *New England's prospect,* edited by Alden T. Vaughan, 1977. Amherst, MA: University of Massachusetts Press.

Wright, Mabel Osgood. 1897. *Birdcraft.* New York: Macmillan.

Wystrach, V. P. 1975a. Ashton Blackburne—early collector in Connecticut. *Connecticut Newsletter,* Connecticut Audubon Council 8(3):3.

1975b. Ashton Blackburne's place in American ornithology. *Auk* 92:607.

Yale Peabody Museum Records. A list of unpublished and published avian observations in Connecticut. Yale Peabody Museum, New Haven, CT.

Zeranski, Joseph. 1980. *Checklist of the birds of southwest Fairfield County and southwest Westchester County.* Greenwich, CT: Greenwich Audubon Society.

Zimmerman, J. L. 1977. *Virginia Rail* (Rallus limicola): *Management of migratory shore and upland game birds in North America,* edited by G. C. Sanderson. Washington, DC: International Association of Fish and Wildlife Agencies.

INDEX OF COMMON NAMES

INDEX OF SCIENTIFIC NAMES